ABOUT THE AUTHOR

JACK KORNFIELD is an internationally renowned meditation teacher and one of the leaders in introducing Buddhist practice and psychology to the West. After graduating in Asian studies from Dartmouth College, he joined the Peace Corps and later trained as a Buddhist monk in Thailand, Burma, and India. Kornfield is a co-founder of the Insight Meditation Society and he also holds a Ph.D. in clinical psychology. His books include *A Path with Heart; After the Ecstasy, the Laundry;* and *The Art of Forgiveness, Lovingkindness, and Peace.*

More Praise for Jack Kornfield and
The Wise Heart

"One of Western Buddhism's wise elders,
Jack Kornfield harvests a lifetime of
experiences to create a masterful, clear, and
moving picture of the human mind and heart,
a picture whose hopeful healing power I find
astounding. You will find *The Wise Heart* a joy
to read and live with."
—Norman Fischer, former abbot, San Francisco
Zen Center, author of *Sailing Home: Using the
Wisdom of Homer's Odyssey to Navigate Life's Perils
and Pitfalls*

"Through Jack Kornfield's clear teaching and
wonderful storytelling, *The Wise Heart* inspires
us to realize and embody the love, presence
and freedom that is our very essence."
—Tara Brach, author of *Radical Acceptance*

OTHER BOOKS BY JACK KORNFIELD

A PATH WITH HEART

AFTER THE ECSTASY, THE LAUNDRY

THE ART OF FORGIVENESS, LOVINGKINDNESS, AND PEACE

SEEKING THE HEART OF WISDOM (with Joseph Goldstein)

TEACHINGS OF THE BUDDHA

A STILL FOREST POOL (with Paul Breiter)

LIVING BUDDHIST MASTERS (Living Dharma)

STORIES OF THE SPIRIT, STORIES OF THE HEART/SOUL FOOD
(with Christina Feldman)

BUDDHA'S LITTLE INSTRUCTION BOOK

MEDITATION FOR BEGINNERS

THE
WISE
HEART

Buddhist Psychology
for the West

JACK KORNFIELD

RIDER

LONDON · SYDNEY · AUCKLAND · JOHANNESBURG

18

Published in 2008 by Rider, an imprint of Ebury Publishing
First published in the USA by Bantam Dell, a Division of Random House, Inc., in 2008

Ebury Publishing is a Random House Group company

Copyright © Jack Kornfield 2008

Jack Kornfield has asserted his right to be identified as the author of this Work in accordance
with the Copyright, Designs and Patents Act 1988.

The Random House Group Limited Reg. No. 954009

Addresses for companies within The Random House Group Limited
can be found at: www.randomhouse.co.uk/offices.htm

A CIP catalogue record for this book is available from the British Library

Penguin Random House is committed to a sustainable future for
our business, our readers and our planet. This book is made from
Forest Stewardship Council® certified paper.

Printed and bound in Great Britain by Clays Ltd, Elcograf S.p.A.

ISBN 9781846041259

Copies are available at special rates for bulk orders. Contact the sales development team on
020 7840 8487 or for more information.

To buy books by your favourite authors and register for offers, visit
www.randomhouse.co.uk

To

Aung San Suu Kyi

and the

monks and nuns of Burma

and

To all our children:

May they live with a wise heart

Contents

Introduction 1

PART I WHO ARE YOU REALLY?

1 Nobility: Our Original Goodness 11

2 Holding the World in Kindness: A Psychology of Compassion 22

3 Who Looks in the Mirror? The Nature of Consciousness 35

4 The Colorings of Consciousness 48

5 The Mysterious Illusion of Self 61

6 From the Universal to the Personal:
   A Psychology of Paradox 79

PART II MINDFULNESS: THE GREAT MEDICINE

7 The Liberating Power of Mindfulness 95

8 This Precious Human Body 110

9 The River of Feelings 124

10 The Storytelling Mind 137

11 The Ancient Unconscious 150

Contents

PART III   TRANSFORMING THE ROOTS OF SUFFERING

12   Buddhist Personality Types   167

13   The Transformation of Desire into Abundance   184

14   Beyond Hatred to a Non-Contentious Heart   205

15   From Delusion to Wisdom: Awakening from the Dream   222

PART IV   FINDING FREEDOM

16   Suffering and Letting Go   241

17   The Compass of the Heart: Intention and Karma   257

18   Sacred Vision: Imagination, Ritual, and Refuge   274

19   Behaviorism with Heart: Buddhist Cognitive Training   293

20   Concentration and the Mystical Dimensions of Mind   308

PART V   EMBODYING THE WISE HEART

21   A Psychology of Virtue, Redemption, and Forgiveness   331

22   The Bodhisattva: Tending the World   352

23   The Wisdom of the Middle Way   367

24   The Awakened Heart   382

Related Readings   403
Permissions   409
Acknowledgments   411
Index   413

Buddhist teachings are not a religion,
they are a science of mind.

—THE DALAI LAMA

THE
WISE
HEART

INTRODUCTION

L ast year I joined with Zen Master Thich Nhat Hanh to co-lead a conference on mindfulness and psychotherapy at UCLA. As I stood at the podium looking over a crowd of almost two thousand people, I wondered what had drawn so many to this three-day gathering. Was it the need to take a deep breath and find a wiser way to cope with the conflict, stress, fears, and exhaustion so common in modern life? Was it the longing for a psychology that included the spiritual dimension and the highest human potential in its vision of healing? Was it a hope to find simple ways to quiet the mind and open the heart?

I found that I had to speak personally and practically, as I do in this book. These conference participants wanted the same inspiration and support as the students who come to Spirit Rock Meditation Center near San Francisco. Those who enter our light-filled meditation hall are not running away from life, but seeking a wise path through it. They each bring their personal problems and their genuine search for happiness. Often they carry a burden of concern for the world, with its continuing warfare and ever-deepening environmental problems. They wonder what will be left for their children's generation. They have heard about meditation and hope to find the joy and inner freedom that Buddhist teachings promise, along with a wiser way to care for the world.

Forty years ago, I arrived at a forest monastery in Thailand in search of my own happiness. A confused, lonely young man with a painful family history, I had graduated from Dartmouth College in Asian studies and asked the Peace Corps to send me to a Buddhist country. Looking back, I can see that I was trying to escape not only my family pain but also the materialism and suffering—so evident in the Vietnam War—of our culture at large. Working on rural health and medical teams in the provinces along the Mekong River, I heard about a meditation master, Ajahn Chah, who welcomed Western students. I was full of ideas and hopes that Buddhist teachings would help me, maybe even lead me to become enlightened. After months of visits to Ajahn Chah's monastery, I took monk's vows. Over the next three years I was introduced to the practices of mindfulness, generosity, loving-kindness, and integrity, which are at the heart of Buddhist training. That was the beginning of a lifetime journey with Buddhist teachings.

Like Spirit Rock today, the forest monastery received a stream of visitors. Every day, Ajahn Chah would sit on a wooden bench at the edge of a clearing and greet them all: local rice farmers and devout pilgrims, seekers and soldiers, young people, government ministers from the capital, and Western students. All brought their spiritual questions and conflicts, their sorrows, fears, and aspirations. At one moment Ajahn Chah would be gently holding the head of a man whose young son had just died, at another laughing with a disillusioned shopkeeper at the arrogance of humanity. In the morning he might be teaching ethics to a semi-corrupt government official, in the afternoon offering a meditation on the nature of undying consciousness to a devout old nun.

Even among these total strangers, there was a remarkable atmosphere of safety and trust. All were held by the compassion of the master and the teachings that guided us together in the human journey of birth and death, joy and sorrow. We sat together as one human family.

Ajahn Chah and other Buddhist masters like him are practitioners of a living psychology: one of the oldest and most well-
developed systems of healing and understanding on the face of the
earth. This psychology makes no distinction between worldly and
spiritual problems. To Ajahn Chah, anxiety, trauma, financial problems, physical difficulties, struggles with meditation, ethical dilem-
mas, and community conflict were all forms of suffering to be
treated with the medicine of Buddhist teaching. He was able to respond to the wide range of human troubles and possibilities from
his own deep meditation, and also from the vast array of skillful
means passed down by his teachers. Sophisticated meditative disciplines, healing practices, cognitive and emotional trainings, conflict resolution techniques—he used them all to awaken his visitors
to their own qualities of integrity, equanimity, gratitude, and forgiveness.

The wisdom Ajahn Chah embodied as a healer also exists as an
ancient written tradition, first set down as a record of the Buddha's
teachings and then expanded by more than a hundred generations
of study, commentary, and practice. This written tradition is a great
storehouse of wisdom, a profound exploration of the human mind,
but it is not easily accessible to Westerners.

At this moment, a winter rainstorm is drenching my simple
writer's cabin in the woods above Spirit Rock. On my desk are classic texts from many of the major historic schools of Buddhism: the
Comprehensive Manual of Abhidhamma, the eight-thousand-verse
"large version" of the Heart Sutra, with its teachings on form and
emptiness, and a Tibetan text on consciousness by Longchenpa.
Over time, I have learned to treasure these texts and know that
they are filled with jewels of wisdom. Yet the Abhidhamma (or
Abhidharma in Sanskrit), considered the masterwork of the early
Theravada tradition and the ultimate compendium of Buddhist psychology, is also one of the most impenetrable books ever written.
What are we to make of passages such as, "The inseparable material phenomena constitute the pure octad; leading to the dodecad
of bodily intimation and the lightness triad; all as material groups
originating from consciousness"? And the Heart Sutra, revered as

a sacred text of Mahayana Buddhism in India, China, and Japan, can sound like a mixture of fantastical mythology and nearly indecipherable Zen puzzles. In the same way, for most readers, analyzing the biochemistry of a lifesaving drug might be as easy as deciphering some of Longchenpa's teachings on self-existent empty primal cognition.

What we are all seeking is the experience that underlies these texts, which is rich and deep and joyfully free. When Laura arrives at Spirit Rock with her cancer diagnosis, or Sharon, the judge, comes to learn about forgiveness, each wants the pith, the heart understanding that illuminates these words. But how to find it?

Like my teacher Ajahn Chah, I've tried to convey the essence of these texts as a living, immediate, and practical psychology. I have become part of a generation of Buddhist elders that includes Pema Chödrön, Sharon Salzberg, Joseph Goldstein, Thich Nhat Hanh, and others who have helped to introduce Buddhist teachings widely in the West. To do this while remaining true to our own roots, we have primarily focused on the core teachings, the essence of Buddhist wisdom that spans all traditions. Though this is a role different from that of more orthodox and scholarly Buddhists, it is central to bringing Buddhist teachings to a new culture. It has been a way of forging a non-sectarian and accessible approach to these remarkable teachings. This is what another of my teachers, Ajahn Buddhadasa, encouraged: not dividing the teachings into the schools of Theravada, Mahayana, or Vajrayana, but offering Buddhayana, the core living principles of awakening.

As a parallel to these essential Buddhist teachings, I also bring in important insights from our Western psychological tradition. My interest in Western psychology began after I returned from Asia and encountered problems that had not come up in the monastery. I had difficulties with my girlfriend, with my family, with money and livelihood, with making my way as a young man in the world. I discovered that I could not use silent meditation alone to transform my problems. There was no shortcut, no spiritual bypass that could spare me from the work of integration and day-to-day embodiment of the principles I had learned in meditation.

To complement my Buddhist practice, I entered graduate

school in psychology and sought out practice and training in a variety of therapeutic approaches: Reichian, analytic, Gestalt, psychodrama, Jungian. I became part of a growing dialogue between Eastern and Western psychology as I worked with innovative colleagues in the early years of Naropa Buddhist University and Esalen Institute and at meditation centers and professional conferences around the world. Gradually, this dialogue has become more fertile, more nuanced, more open-minded. Today there is widespread interest from clinicians of every school in a more positive, spiritual, and visionary approach to mental health. Many who work within the constraints of our insurance and medical system struggle with the limitations of our medical clinical approach. There is a palpable relief when I teach the perspective of nobility, of training in compassion, of non-religious ways to transform suffering and nurture our sacred connection to life.

The recent explosion of knowledge in neuropsychology has opened this dialogue still further. We can now peer into the brain to study the same central questions explored by the Buddha so many centuries ago. Neuroscientists are reporting remarkable data when studying meditation adepts, studies that corroborate the refined analysis of human potential described by Buddhist psychology. Because they are based on millennia of experimentation and observation, Buddhist principles and teachings are a good fit for the psychological science of the West. They are already contributing to our understanding of perception, stress, healing, emotion, psychotherapy, human potential, and consciousness itself.

I've learned through my own experience that the actual practice of psychology—both Eastern and Western—makes me more open, free, and strangely vulnerable to life. Instead of using the technical terms of the West, such as *countertransference* and *cathexis,* or the Eastern terms *adverting consciousness* and *mutable intimating phenomenon,* I find it helpful to speak of *longing, hurt, anger, loving, hope, rejection, letting go, feeling close, self-acceptance, independence,* and *inner freedom.* In place of the word *enlightenment,* which is laden with so many ideas and misunderstandings, I have used the terms *inner freedom* and *liberation* to clearly express the full range of awakenings available to us through Buddhist practice. I want the stories and awakenings of students and practitioners to help us trust our own profound capacity for kindness and wisdom. I want us to discover the power of the heart to hold all things—sorrow, loneliness, shame, desire, regret, frustration, happiness, and peace—and to find a deep trust that wherever we are and whatever we face, we can be free in their midst.

As a Western Buddhist teacher, I don't sit outside on a bench like Ajahn Chah, but I do meet with students and seekers often. I usually work with those who are attending classes or on residential retreats, where students come to meditate for periods of three days up to three months. These retreats offer daily teachings and meditation instruction, a schedule of group practice periods, and long hours of silence. Every other day, students meet individually with a teacher. These individual sessions, or interviews, are short— fifteen or twenty minutes.

When a student comes for an interview, we sit together quietly for a few moments. Then I ask them about their experience at the retreat and how they are working with it. From this, a deep conversation can unfold. Sometimes I simply try to witness their practice with compassion; at other times I offer advice. Often we enter into a present-time investigation of the student's own body and mind, as the Buddha regularly did with those who came to see him. In the course of these pages you will see more fully how I and other teachers do this work. And you will get a feeling for how we can actually apply this vast and compassionate psychology in our lives today.

If you are a clinician or mental health professional, Buddhist psychology will present you with provocative new understandings and possibilities. It may inform or transform the way you work. If you are new to Buddhist teachings and meditation has seemed foreign to you, you will learn that meditation is quite natural. Simply directing your attention in a careful, considered way is the beginning. You are doing a form of meditative contemplation as you read and consider this book. If you are someone more experienced in Buddhist practice, I hope to challenge you with entirely new ways of envisioning and practicing the path of awakening.

In approaching this dialogue, I'd like to underscore a point the

Dalai Lama has made repeatedly: "Buddhist teachings are not a religion, they are a science of mind." This does not deny the fact that
for many people around the world Buddhism has also come to function as a religion. Like most religions, it offers its followers a rich
tradition of devotional practices, communal rituals, and sacred stories. But this is not the origin of Buddhism or its core. The Buddha
was a human being, not a god, and what he offered his followers
were experiential teachings and practices, a revolutionary way to
understand and release suffering. From his own inner experiments,
he discovered a systematic and remarkable set of trainings to bring
about happiness and fulfill the highest levels of human development. Today, it is this path of practice and liberation that draws most
Western students to Buddhism.

The teachings in this book are a compelling challenge to much
of Western psychology and to the materialism, cynicism, and despair found in Western culture as well. From the first pages they
outline a radical and positive approach to psychology and to human
life. Starting with nobility and compassion, Part I explains the
Buddhist vision of mental health and consciousness. Part II details
healing and awakening through the practices of mindfulness. Part
III is devoted to the transformation of unhealthy emotions. Part IV
outlines a broad range of Buddhist psychological tools, from the
power of concentration and visualization to sophisticated cognitive
trainings and transformative social practices. Part V explores the
highest possibilities of development, extreme mental well-being,
and liberation.

At the end of most chapters, I have suggested specific Buddhist
practices for you to try. Think of these as experiments to explore
with an open mind. If you don't have time to undertake all of them,
trust your intuition and begin with the practices that you feel will
best serve your heart. If you give yourself to them for a period of
time, you will find that they transform your perspective and your
way of being in the world.

It is an urgent task for the psychology of our time to understand and foster the highest possibilities of human development.
The suffering and happiness in our world, both individual and col-

lective, depend on our consciousness. We have to find a wiser way to live. The good news is that it is eminently possible to do so. In this book I offer the visionary and universal perspectives of Buddhism for the healing of our hearts, the freeing of our minds, and the benefit of all beings.

I

WHO
ARE YOU
REALLY?

1

NOBILITY

OUR ORIGINAL GOODNESS

O Nobly Born, O you of glorious origins, remember your radiant true nature, the essence of mind. Trust it. Return to it. It is home.
—Tibetan Book of the Dead

Then it was as if I suddenly saw the secret beauty of their hearts, the depths of their hearts where neither sin nor desire nor self-knowledge can reach, the core of their reality, the person that each one is in the eyes of the Divine. If only they could all see themselves as they really are. If only we could see each other that way all the time. There would be no more war, no more hatred, no more cruelty, no more greed. . . . I suppose the big problem would be that we would fall down and worship each other.
—Thomas Merton

In a large temple north of Thailand's ancient capital, Sukotai, there once stood an enormous and ancient clay Buddha. Though not the most handsome or refined work of Thai Buddhist art, it had been cared for over a period of five hundred years and become revered for its sheer longevity. Violent storms, changes of government, and invading armies had come and gone, but the Buddha endured.

At one point, however, the monks who tended the temple noticed that the statue had begun to crack and would soon be in need of repair and repainting. After a stretch of particularly hot, dry weather, one of the cracks became so wide that a curious monk took his flashlight and peered inside. What shone back at him was a flash of brilliant gold! Inside this plain old statue, the temple residents discovered one of the largest and most luminous gold images of Buddha ever created in Southeast Asia. Now uncovered, the golden Buddha draws throngs of devoted pilgrims from all over Thailand.

The monks believe that this shining work of art had been covered in plaster and clay to protect it during times of conflict and unrest. In much the same way, each of us has encountered threatening situations that lead us to cover our innate nobility. Just as the people of Sukotai had forgotten about the golden Buddha, we too have forgotten our essential nature. Much of the time we operate from the protective layer. The primary aim of Buddhist psychology is to help us see beneath this armoring and bring out our original goodness, called our Buddha nature.

This is a first principle of Buddhist psychology:

---

1 See the inner nobility and beauty of all human beings.

Robert Johnson, the noted Jungian analyst, acknowledges how difficult it is for many of us to believe in our goodness. We more easily take our worst fears and thoughts to be who we are, the unacknowledged traits called our "shadow" by Jung. "Curiously," writes Johnson, "people resist the noble aspects of their shadow more strenuously than they hide the dark sides. . . . It is more disrupting to find that you have a profound nobility of character than to find out you are a bum."

Our belief in a limited and impoverished identity is such a strong habit that without it we are afraid we wouldn't know how to be. If we fully acknowledged our dignity, it could lead to radical life changes. It could ask something huge of us. And yet some part of us knows that the frightened and damaged self is not who we are. Each of us needs to find our way to be whole and free.

In my family, it was not easy to see my own goodness. My earliest memories are of a paranoid and unpredictably violent father, a bruised and frightened mother, and four boys who each wondered, "How did we get here?" We would all hold our breath when our father pulled the car into the driveway. On good days he could be attentive and humorous and we would feel relieved, but more often we had to hide or cower to avoid his hair-trigger anger and tirades. On family trips the pressure might lead him to smash my mother's head into the windshield or to punish his children for the erratic behavior of other drivers. I remember my father's grandmother pleading with my mother not to divorce him. "At least he can sometimes hold a job. He's not so crazy as those ones in the mental hospitals."

Yet I knew this unhappiness was not all there was to existence. I can remember running out of the house on painful days, at age six or seven, while my parents fought. Something in me felt I didn't belong in that house, as if I had been born into the wrong family. At times I imagined, as children do, that one day there would come a knock at the door and an elegant gentleman would ask for me by name. He would then announce that Jack and his brothers had been secretly placed in this home, but that now his real parents, the king and queen, wanted him to return to his rightful family. These childhood fantasies gave rise to one of the strongest currents of my life, a longing to be part of something worthy and true. I was seeking my real family of noble birth.

In these often cynical times, we might think of original goodness as merely an uplifting phrase, but through its lens we discover a radically different way of seeing and being: one whose aim is to transform our world. This does not mean that we ignore the enormousness of people's sorrows or that we make ourselves foolishly vulnerable to unstable and perhaps violent individuals. Indeed, to find the dignity in others, their suffering has to be acknowledged. Among the most central of all Buddhist psychological principles are the Four Noble Truths, which begin by acknowledging the inevitable suffering in human life. This truth, too, is hard to talk about in modern culture, where people are taught to avoid discomfort at any cost, where "the pursuit of happiness" has become "the right to happiness." And yet when we are suffering it is so refreshing and helpful to have the truth of suffering acknowledged.

Buddhist teachings help us to face our individual suffering, from shame and depression to anxiety and grief. They address the collective suffering of the world and help us to work with the source of this sorrow: the forces of greed, hatred, and delusion in the human psyche. While tending to our suffering is critical, this does not eclipse our fundamental nobility.

The word *nobility* does not refer to medieval knights and courts. It derives from the Greek *gno* (as in *gnosis*), meaning "wisdom" or "inner illumination." In English, nobility is defined as human excellence, as that which is illustrious, admirable, lofty, and distinguished, in values, conduct, and bearing. How might we intuitively connect with this quality in those around us? Just as no one can tell us how to feel love, each of us can find our own way to sense the underlying goodness in others. One way is to shift the frame of time, imagining the person before us as a small child, still young and innocent. Once after a particularly difficult day with my teenage daughter, I found myself sitting beside her as she slept. Just hours before, we had been struggling over her plans for the evening; now she lay sleeping with the innocence and beauty of her childhood. Such innocence is there in all people, if we are willing to see it.

Or, instead of moving back in time, we can move forward. We can visualize the person at the end of his life, lying on his deathbed, vulnerable, open, with nothing to hide. Or we can simply see him as a fellow wayfarer, struggling with his burdens, wanting happiness and dignity. Beneath the fears and needs, the aggression and pain, whoever we encounter is a being who, like us, has the tremendous potential for understanding and compassion, whose goodness is there to be touched.

We can perhaps most easily admire the human spirit when it shines in the world's great moral leaders. We see an unshakable compassion in the Nobel Peace Prize winner Aung San Suu Kyi, who remains steadfast and loving in spite of long years of house arrest in Burma. We remember how South African president Nelson Mandela walked out of prison with a gracious spirit of courage and dignity that was unbent by twenty-seven years of torture and hardship. But the same spirit also beams from healthy children everywhere. Their joy and natural beauty can reawaken us to our Buddha nature. They remind us that we are born with this shining spirit.

So why, in Western psychology, have we been so focused on the dark side of human nature? Even before Freud, Western psychology was based on a medical model, and it still focuses primarily on pathology. The psychiatric profession's *Diagnostic and Statistical Manual of Mental Disorders,* which orients the work of most therapists, clinics, and health care providers, is a comprehensive listing of hundreds of psychological problems and diseases. Categorizing problems helps us study them and then, it is hoped, cure them in the most scientific and economically efficient way. But often we give so much attention to our protective layers of fear, depression, confusion, and aggression that we forget who we really are.

As a teacher, I see this all the time. When a middle-aged man named Marty came to see me after a year of painful separation and divorce, he was caught in the repetitive cycles of unworthiness and shame that he had carried since childhood. He believed there was something terribly wrong with him. He had forgotten his original goodness. When a young woman, Jan, came to Buddhist practice after a long struggle with anxiety and depression, she had a hard time letting go of her self-image as a broken and damaged person. For years she had seen herself only through her diagnosis and the various medications that had failed to control it.

As psychology becomes more pharmacologically oriented, this medical model is reinforced. Today, most of the millions of adults seeking mental health support are quickly put on medication. Even more troubling, hundreds of thousands of children are being prescribed powerful psychiatric drugs for conditions ranging from ADHD to the newly popular diagnosis of childhood bipolar disorder. While these medications may be appropriate, even lifesaving, in some cases, laypeople and professionals increasingly look for a pill as the answer to human confusion and suffering. It need not be so.

INNER FREEDOM: LIBERATION OF THE HEART

If we do not focus on human limits and pathology, what is the alternative? It is the belief that human freedom is possible under any circumstances. Buddhist teachings put it this way: "Just as the great oceans have but one taste, the taste of salt, so do all of the teachings of Buddha have but one taste, the taste of liberation."

Psychologist Viktor Frankl was the sole member of his family to survive the Nazi death camps. Nevertheless, in spite of this suffering, he found a path to healing. Frankl wrote, "We who lived in concentration camps can remember the men who walked through the huts comforting others, giving away their last piece of bread. They may have been few in number, but they offer sufficient proof that everything can be taken from a man but one thing: the last of the human freedoms—to choose one's attitude in any given set of circumstances, to choose one's own way."

When we are lost in our worst crises and conflicts, in the deepest states of fear and confusion, our pain can seem endless. We can feel as if there is no exit, no hope. Yet some hidden wisdom longs for freedom. "If it were not possible to free the heart from entanglement in unhealthy states," says the Buddha, "I would not teach you to do so. But just because it is possible to free the heart from entanglement in unhealthy states do I offer these teachings."

Awakening this inner freedom of spirit is the purpose of the hundreds of Buddhist practices and trainings. Each of these practices helps us to recognize and let go of unhealthy patterns that create suffering and develop healthy patterns in their place. What is important about the Buddhist psychological approach is the emphasis on training and practice, as well as understanding. Instead of going into therapy to discuss your problems and be listened to once a week, there is a regimen of daily and ongoing trainings and disciplines to help you learn and practice healthy ways of being. These practices return us to our innate wisdom and compassion, and they direct us toward freedom.

SACRED PERCEPTION

The saints are what they are, not because their sanctity makes them admirable to others, but because the gift of sainthood makes it possible for them to admire everybody else.
—Thomas Merton

Each time we meet another human being and honor their dignity, we help those around us. Their hearts resonate with ours in exactly the same way the strings of an unplucked violin vibrate with the sounds of a violin played nearby. Western psychology has documented this phenomenon of "mood contagion" or limbic resonance. If a person filled with panic or hatred walks into a room, we feel it immediately, and unless we are very mindful, that person's negative state will begin to overtake our own. When a joyfully expressive person walks into a room, we can feel that state as well. And when we see the goodness of those before us, the dignity in them resonates with our admiration and respect.

This resonance can begin very simply. In India, when people greet one another they put their palms together and bow, saying *namaste,* "I honor the divine within you." It is a way of acknowledging your Buddha nature, who you really are. Some believe that the Western handshake evolved to demonstrate friendliness and safety, to show that we are not holding any weapon. But the greeting *namaste* goes a step further, from "I will not harm you" to "I see that which is holy in you." It creates the basis for sacred relationship.

When I began my training as a Buddhist monk, I found a taste of this sacred relationship. Around Ajahn Chah was an aura of straightforwardness, graciousness, and trust. It was the opposite of my early family life, and though it initially felt strange and unfamiliar, something in me loved it. Instead of a field of judgment, criticism, and unpredictable violence, here was a community dedicated to treating each person with respect and dignity. It was beautiful.

In the monastery, the walking paths were swept daily, the robes and bowls of the monks were tended with care. Our vows required us to cherish life in every form. We carefully avoided stepping on ants; we valued birds and insects, snakes and mammals. We learned to value ourselves and others equally. When conflict arose, we called on practices of patience, and in seeking forgiveness we were guided by councils of elders who demonstrated how to approach our failings with mindful respect.

Whether practiced in a forest monastery or in the West, Buddhist psychology begins by deliberately cultivating respect, starting with ourselves. When we learn to rest in our own goodness, we can see the goodness more clearly in others. As our sense of respect and care is developed, it serves us well under most ordinary circumstances. It becomes invaluable in extremity.

One Buddhist practitioner tells of being part of a group taken hostage in a bank in St. Louis. She describes the initial confusion and fear that spread through the hostages. She remembers trying to quiet her own racing heart. And then she tells how she made a decision not to panic. She used her meditation and her breath to quiet her mind. Over the hours, even as she helped others in her group, she addressed her captors respectfully and expressed a genuine concern for them. She saw their desperation and their underlying needs. When she and the other hostages were later released unharmed, she gratefully believed that the care and respect they showed to their captors had made their release possible.

When we bring respect and honor to those around us, we open a channel to their own goodness. I have seen this truth in working with prisoners and gang members. When they experience someone who respects and values them, it gives them the ability to admire themselves, to accept and acknowledge the good inside. When we see what is holy in another, whether we meet them in our family or our community, at a business meeting or in a therapy session, we transform their hearts.

The Dalai Lama embodies this sacred perception as he moves through the world, and it is one of the reasons so many people seek to be around him. Several years ago His Holiness visited San

Francisco and we invited him to offer teachings at Spirit Rock Meditation Center. The Dalai Lama is the head of the Tibetan government in exile, and the State Department had assigned dozens of Secret Service agents to protect him and his entourage. Accustomed to guarding foreign leaders, princes, and kings, the Secret Service agents were surprisingly moved by the Dalai Lama's respectful attitude and friendly heart. At the end, they asked for his blessing. Then they all wanted to have a photo taken with him. Several said, "We have had the privilege of protecting political leaders, princes, and prime ministers, yet there is something different about the Dalai Lama. He treats us as if we are special."

Later, during a series of public teachings, he stayed at a San Francisco hotel famous for hosting dignitaries. Just before he departed, the Dalai Lama told the hotel management that he would like to thank the staff in person, as many as wished to meet him. So on the last morning a long line of maids and dishwashers, cooks and maintenance men, secretaries and managers made their way to the circular driveway at the hotel entrance. And before the Dalai Lama's motorcade left, he walked down the line of employees, lovingly touching each hand, vibrating the strings of each heart.

Some years ago, I heard the story of a high school history teacher who knew this same secret. On one particularly fidgety and distracted afternoon she told her class to stop all their academic work. She let her students rest while she wrote on the blackboard a list of the names of everyone in the class. Then she asked them to copy the list. She instructed them to use the rest of the period to write beside each name one thing they liked or admired about that student. At the end of class she collected the papers.

Weeks later, on another difficult day just before winter break, the teacher again stopped the class. She handed each student a sheet with his or her name on top. On it she had pasted all twenty-six good things the other students had written about that person. They smiled and gasped in pleasure that so many beautiful qualities were noticed about them.

Three years later this teacher received a call from the mother of one of her former students. Robert had been a cut-up, but also one of her favorites. His mother sadly passed on the terrible news that Robert had been killed in the Gulf War. The teacher attended the funeral, where many of Robert's former friends and high school classmates spoke. Just as the service was ending, Robert's mother approached her. She took out a worn piece of paper, obviously folded and refolded many times, and said, "This was one of the few things in Robert's pocket when the military retrieved his body." It was the paper on which the teacher had so carefully pasted the twenty-six things his classmates had admired.

Seeing this, Robert's teacher's eyes filled with tears. As she dried her wet cheeks, another former student standing nearby opened her purse, pulled out her own carefully folded page, and confessed that she always kept it with her. A third ex-student said that his page was framed and hanging in his kitchen; another told how the page had become part of her wedding vows. The perception of goodness invited by this teacher had transformed the hearts of her students in ways she might only have dreamed about.

We can each remember a moment when someone saw this goodness in us and blessed us. On retreat, a middle-aged woman remembers the one person, a nun, who was kind to her when, as a frightened and lonely teenager, she gave birth out of wedlock. She's carried her name all these years. A young man I worked with in juvenile hall remembers the old gardener next door who loved and valued him. The gardener's respect stuck with him through all his troubles. This possibility is voiced by the Nobel laureate Nelson Mandela: "It never hurts to think too highly of a person; often they become ennobled and act better because of it."

To see with sacred perception does not mean we ignore the need for development and change in an individual. Sacred perception is one half of a paradox. Zen master Shunryu Suzuki remarked to a disciple, "You are perfect just the way you are. And . . . there is still room for improvement!" Buddhist psychology offers meditations, cognitive strategies, ethical trainings, a powerful set of practices that foster inner transformation. But it starts with a most radical vision, one that transforms everyone it touches: a recognition of the innate nobility and the freedom of heart that are available wherever we are.

PRACTICE: SEEING THE SECRET GOODNESS

Wait for a day when you awaken in a fine mood, when your heart is open to the world. If such days are rare, choose the best you have. Before you start for work, set the clear intention that during the morning you will look for the inner nobility of three people. Carry that intention in your heart as you speak or work with them. Notice how this perception affects your interaction with them, how it affects your own heart, how it affects your work. Then choose five more days of your best moods, and do this practice on each of these days.

After looking at three people a day in this way five times, set the clear intention to practice seeing the secret goodness for a whole day with as many people as you can. Of course, you will find certain people difficult. Save them for later, and practice first with those whose nobility and beauty is seen most easily. When you have done this as best you can for a day, choose one day a week to continue this practice for a month or two.

Finally, as you become more naturally able to see the secret goodness, expand your practice. Add more days. Try practicing on days that are more stressful. Gradually include strangers and difficult people, until your heart learns to silently acknowledge and bless all whom you meet. Aim to see as many beings as you can with a silent, loving respect. Go through the day as if you were the Dalai Lama undercover.

2

HOLDING THE WORLD IN KINDNESS
A PSYCHOLOGY OF COMPASSION

O Nobly Born, now there is born in you exceeding compassion for all those living creatures who have forgotten their true nature.
—Mahamudra text of Tibetan yogi Longchenpa

Overcome any bitterness because you were not up to the magnitude of the pain entrusted to you. . . . Like the mother of the world who carries the pain of the world in her heart, you are sharing in the totality of this pain and are called upon to meet it in compassion and joy instead of self-pity.
—Sufi master Pir Vilayat Khan

Alan Wallace, a leading Western teacher of Tibetan Buddhism, puts it like this: "Imagine walking along a sidewalk with your arms full of groceries, and someone roughly bumps into you so that you fall and your groceries are strewn over the ground. As you rise up from the puddle of broken eggs and tomato juice, you are ready to shout out, 'You idiot! What's wrong with you? Are you blind?' But just before you can catch your breath to speak, you see that the person who bumped into you is actually blind. He, too, is sprawled in the spilled groceries, and your anger vanishes in an instant, to be replaced by sympathetic concern: 'Are you hurt? Can I help you up?' Our situation is like that. When we clearly realize that the source of disharmony and misery in the world is ignorance, we can open the door of wisdom and compassion."

Each person who comes for spiritual teachings or psychotherapy carries his or her measure of confusion and sorrow. Buddhism teaches that we suffer not because we have sinned but because we are blind. Compassion is the natural response to this blindness; it arises whenever we see our human situation clearly. Buddhist texts describe compassion as the quivering of the heart in the face of pain, as the capacity to see our struggles with "kindly eyes." We need compassion, not anger, to help us be tender with our difficulties and not close off to them in fear. This is how healing takes place.

This is a second principle of Buddhist psychology:

---

2   Compassion is our deepest nature. It arises from our interconnection with all things.

When I first came to Buddhist practice as a monk, I wasn't conscious of how much pain I carried. I had managed to shut down the childhood memories of violence, the self-doubt and feelings of unworthiness, the struggle to be loved. In meditation and the monastery life they all came up: the stored history, the judgments and buried pains. At first, the demanding schedule and practices increased my sense of struggle and unworthiness. I tried to force myself to be disciplined, to be better. Eventually I discovered that unworthiness is not helped by striving. I learned that for real healing I needed compassion.

On one occasion I was sick with what was probably malaria, lying in my hut, feverish and wretched. I had received medicine from a monastery elder, but it was slow in taking effect. Ajahn Chah came to visit me. "Sick and feverish, huh?" he asked. "Yes," I replied weakly. "It's painful all over, isn't it?" I nodded. "Makes you feel sorry for yourself, doesn't it?" I smiled a bit. "Makes you want to go home to see your mother." He smiled, and then nodded. "Yes, it's suffering, alright. Almost all the forest monks have had it. At least now we have good medicine." He paused. "Here. This is where we have to practice. Not just sitting in the meditation hall. It's hard. All the body torment and mind states. You learn a lot." He waited for a while, then he looked at me with the warmth of a kind grand-father. "You can bear it, you know. You can do it." And I felt that he was fully there with me, that he knew my pain from his own hard struggles. It took another day for the medicine to kick in, but his simple kindness made the situation bearable. His compassion gave me courage and helped me find my own freedom in the midst of hardship.

Beneath the sophistication of Buddhist psychology lies the sim-plicity of compassion. We can touch into this compassion whenever the mind is quiet, whenever we allow the heart to open. Unfortunately, like the clay covering the golden Buddha, thick lay-ers of ignorance and trauma can obscure our compassion. On the global scale, ignorance manifests as injustice, racism, exploitation, and violence. On a personal scale, we see our own states of envy, anxiety, addiction, and aggression. When we take this blindness to be the end of the story, we limit the possibility of human develop-ment. Consider Freud, whose revolutionary work brought so much understanding of the psyche. But in *Civilization and Its Discontents*, he comes to a deeply pessimistic conclusion about the human heart. He states, "Civilization has to use its utmost efforts in order to set limits to man's aggressive instincts . . . the ideal's commandment to love one's neighbour as yourself . . . is really jus-tified by the fact that nothing else runs so strongly counter to orig-inal human nature as this." Yes, we must recognize this aggressive aspect of our human nature. But in this essay, Freud stops there, completely missing the opposite and more powerful fact that our individual lives and our whole society are built upon innumerable acts of kindness.

COMPASSION IS OUR NATURE

From the perspective of Buddhist psychology, compassion is natural. It derives from our interconnection, which Buddhism calls "interdependence." This can be readily seen in the physical world. In the womb, every child is interdependent with its mother's body. If either of them is sick, the other is affected. In the same way we are interdependent with the body of the earth. The minerals of the soil make up our wheat and our bones, the storm clouds become our drinks and our blood, the oxygen from the trees and forests is the air we breathe. The more consciously we realize this shared destiny, the more compassion arises for the earth itself.

The human community is equally interconnected. Nobel Peace Prize winner Desmond Tutu puts it simply: "In Africa when you ask someone 'How are you?' the reply you get is in the plural even when you are speaking to one person. A man would say, 'We are well' or 'We are not well.' He himself may be quite well, but his grandmother is not well and so he is not well either. . . . The solitary, isolated human being is really a contradiction in terms." Fortunately, we are becoming more and more aware of our global interconnection. Every meal we eat is intertwined with the sweat of farmers, migrant workers, and long-haul truckers. It depends on the global climate and the earthworms in our soil, centuries of experiments in crop rotation, and Gregor Mendel's scientific breakthroughs in seed selection. Its roots extend from the earliest agriculture in Mesopotamia and China to this morning's market rates at the Chicago mercantile exchange.

Just as we are interdependent with the earth and one another, we are also connected in consciousness. Western psychology does not yet acknowledge this, but it is true. Years ago when my wife and I were studying at an ashram in the mountains of India, my wife had a very clear but difficult vision of a death in her family. I tried to reassure her that images of death were simply a part of the meditative process. Sadly, I was wrong. Ten days later we received a telegram that began, "Your brother Paul has died." When we read further we discovered that the telegram was sent on the day of her vision, and that Paul had died on that day in exactly the manner she had seen. We have all heard stories like this. This is because we are connected in consciousness. This fact is the basis for compassion.

There is a neurological basis for compassion as well. In the 1980s, Italian scientist Giacomo Rizzolatti and his colleagues discovered a class of brain cells called "mirror neurons." Extensive research since that time has shown that through our mirror neurons, we actually feel the emotions, movements, and intentions of others. Researchers describe this natural empathy as part of the social brain, a neural circuitry that connects us intimately in every human encounter.

In Buddhist psychology, compassion is not a struggle or a sacrifice. Within our body, compassion is natural and intuitive. We don't think, "Oh, my poor toe or finger is hurt, maybe I should help it." As soon as it is injured, we instantly respond because it is a part of us. Through meditation we gradually open the boundaries of consciousness to compassion for all beings, as if they were part of our family. We learn that even when our compassion is lost through fear and trauma, it can be reawakened. Faced with a crying child in a burning house, a hardened criminal is as likely as anyone else to take the risk of rescuing her. We all have moments when the openness and beauty of our Buddha nature shines.

D. S. Barnett, writing in the magazine *The Sun,* shows how compassion can bloom even in the midst of a terrible childhood.

> *Mother always assured me that unspeakable punishments were bound to befall any child as naughty as I was. "If I were you," she'd say, "I'd be afraid to go to sleep at night, for fear God would strike me dead." She would speak these words softly, regretfully, as though saddened by her errant daughter's fate.*

After describing years of abuse and violation, Barnett goes on:

> *The most devastating words my mother ever spoke to me came when I asked her if she loved me. (I had just been escorted home by the police after one of my many attempts to run away, so it was bad timing on my part.)*
> *She answered, "How could anyone ever love you!"*

It took me almost fifty years to heal the damage from all her ugly remarks.

Then she relates a childhood ritual that helped her survive.

From the age of five or six until I was well into my teens, whenever I had trouble sleeping, I would slip out from under my covers and steal into the kitchen for a bit of bread or cheese, which I would carry back to bed with me. There, I'd pretend my hands belonged to someone else, a comforting, reassuring being without a name—an angel, perhaps. The right hand would feed me little bites of cheese or bread as the left hand stroked my cheeks and hair. My eyes closed, I would whisper softly to myself, "There, there. Go to sleep. You're safe now. Everything will be all right. I love you."

Describing the life-denying landscape of her childhood, Barnett shows how caring floods through us like an inner angel of mercy, like green shoots forcing their way through cracks in the sidewalk. We can see the natural hand of compassion in all the ways we try to keep ourselves from harm, in a thousand daily gestures of self-protection.

THE PROBLEM OF SELF-HATRED

In 1989, at one of the first international Buddhist teacher meetings, we Western teachers brought up the enormous problem of unworthiness and self-criticism, shame and self-hatred, and how frequently they arose in Western students' practice. The Dalai Lama and other Asian teachers were shocked. They could not quite comprehend the word *self-hatred*. It took the Dalai Lama ten minutes of conferring with Geshe Thupten Jinpa, his translator, even to understand it. Then he turned and asked how many of us experienced this problem in ourselves and our students. He saw us all nod affirmatively. He seemed genuinely surprised. "But that's a mistake," he said. "Every being is precious!"

Nevertheless, self-judgment and shame were there in many of those who came to Buddhist practice. I certainly knew it in myself.

In order to survive the periods of extreme conflict within my family, I covered over my pain. I became a peacemaker and a good boy. When my parents were battling I tried to calm them down—without much success. When I went to school, I tried to stay safe by pleasing the teachers. Secretly I envied the "bad boys"—the ones who skipped class, smoked behind the school, and got into fights. It looked like they were having more fun. Today, of course, I know that many of them were struggling too, acting cool to deal with their own fears.

While trying to be good, underneath I had a feeling of being unloved, of forever seeking acceptance. In meditation and body-oriented therapy, I got to know these feelings more fully, they came so often. I learned to put my hands on my belly and heart to hold the pain and emptiness. At times it felt like an insatiable hunger, and at times it left me feeling very young. I was a tiny infant whose parents were already fighting horribly, my mother tells me, while I cried and cried. My twin brother and I, and my next brother, born a year later, were all allies in survival for most of our childhood, while my parents were triply overwhelmed. For me, the bottle I got on a schedule, it seems, was not enough. So inside I felt the hole in my belly and heart and the sense of being unlovable. I would curl up in a ball, and in the image that came, I felt like a starving Ethiopian child I had seen on television. I named this boy Ethie. Yes, he wanted food, but most of all he wanted love. This was the food he was starved for, and through years of practice, I gradually learned to provide it. My sympathy for Ethie has strongly inspired me to support organizations that feed hungry children.

Each of us has our own measure of pain. Sometimes the pain we suffer is great and obvious; sometimes it is subtle. Our pain can reflect the coldness of our families, the trauma of our parents, the stultifying influence of much modern education and media, the difficulties of being a man or a woman. As a result, we often feel that we have been cast out. To survive we have to cover our heart, build up a layer of clay, and defend ourselves.

We lose the belief that we are worthy of love. The mystic Simone Weil tells us, "The danger is not that the soul should doubt whether there is any bread, but that, by a lie, it should persuade itself that it is not hungry." Compassion reminds us that we do belong, as surely as we have been lost. As you read this book, at times Buddhist psychology may appear dry, full of lists and practices. Always remember to put your trust in compassion. The experiences of practitioners whose stories are told here continually describe the reclaiming of compassion and self-love. From this comes a shift of identity, a release from the covering of clay, a return to our original goodness.

A divorced veteran of the first Gulf War, Andrew came to meditation to find relief. He had lost his heart in the desert. His patrol came upon a bunker with Iraqi soldiers. They shot and then threw in grenades. Afterward, they found it filled with the bodies of very young men, holding a white flag, unable to signal their surrender. Andrew carried the soul-numbing demand of having to kill at twenty years of age. He also carried the sorrow of his military friends who were still caught in the aftereffects of the war. Coming to retreat, Andrew didn't know what he wanted, but I felt in him an unexpressed longing for forgiveness, healing, and a reconnection with the world. In the simplest terms, he needed the healing waters of compassion.

In the beginning, much of Andrew's training was simply to breathe gently and make room for the waves of his grief. He had feared this opening because he believed that he would be overwhelmed by the tragic memories and the guilt. On retreat, with the support of the meditators around him, he slowly learned to hold his battered body with kindness. Gradually he extended his heart to the suffering of both the Iraqi people and the American people. When the painful images and guilt arose, he began to experience his innate compassion, the soul force he had felt was lost. This was the start of his return to life.

When we lose connection with this tenderness, we may not realize that it can be reawakened so simply and directly. Compassion is only a few breaths away. Rose, a Buddhist practitioner, came to a small group meeting with me on retreat. When it was her turn to talk she just wanted to sit quietly, settle into herself, be silent. She was naturally shy. "It is so much more difficult when I relate to people," Rose said. "I know part of this is just my nature, but part of it is the pain of my family history. I can't stand to have anyone's eyes on me." As we talked, she closed her eyes so she would feel safe. Speaking in the group was terrifying. When I inquired into how long she had been this way, it was as early as she could remember. "My parents were always watching me, annoyed, scowling, angry, filled with judgment. I have no memories of it ever being another way."

As Rose continued to be attentive to her experience, she wept. I asked if she could find any safe place in her body. There was none, she said. Could she remember from her childhood a single instant of well-being? It took her a while. Finally Rose opened her eyes, rubbed the palm of her right hand, and said, "Crayons." She smiled. She could remember being five years old and joyfully holding a box of crayons. I suggested that then she could draw with them. "No, no!" she answered. "Anything I draw, they'll criticize me. I'm only safe when I hold them."

The Buddha taught that we can develop loving-kindness by visualizing how a caring mother holds her beloved child. I had Rose close her eyes and imagine holding this little girl with the box of crayons. Then I asked, "If no one was looking, what would happen next?" With her eyes still closed, her face lit up, she threw out her arms, and she said, "I'd hold them and dance. Like a fairy princess. That's what I always wanted to be."

When the group was over, I went to the market and bought her a box of crayons. That day Rose went out into the woods and danced. Then she colored a picture, the first she had drawn since childhood. She showed it to me. When she went back to meditate her heart was filled with joy, her mind was open, well-being filled her sixty-four-year-old body.

Compassion for our own fear and shame opens us to others. After Rose had learned to color pictures and to practice compassion for herself, she began to include all the suffering girls like herself, near and far, who have been betrayed, lost, isolated. She could feel them as her sisters, and she knew that she was not alone. Now it was not just Rose's pain. She held the sorrows of the women of the world in her heart.

COMPASSION IS COURAGE

As children, many of us were taught courage in the form of the war-rior or the explorer, bravely facing danger. In the Buddhist under-standing, however, great courage is not demonstrated by aggression or ambition. Aggression and ambition are more often expressions of fear and delusion. The courageous heart is the one that is unafraid to open to the world. With compassion we come to trust our capacity to open to life without armoring. As the poet Rilke reminds us, "Ultimately it is on our vulnerability that we de-pend." This is not a poetic ideal but a living reality, demonstrated by our most beloved sages. Mahatma Gandhi had the courage to be jailed and beaten, to persevere through difficulties without giving in to bitterness and despair. His vulnerability became his strength.

We need this same courage to pass through a difficult divorce without lashing out and increasing the pain and anguish. We need it when our children are in trouble, when things go wrong at work. In all these situations we are vulnerable and everyone involved needs compassion.

Buddhist teachings often speak of compassion for all beings. But for most of us, compassion is developed one person and one difficult situation at a time. Novelist Ann Patchett, writing during the first Gulf War, put it this way: "When it gets down to one life, the mind achieves a vivid understanding. If I take the deaths in one at a time, I notice that marine lance corporal Michael E. Linderman, Jr., of Douglas, Oregon, was only 19, and I know what it was like to be 19. And I notice that there wasn't a standard mili-tary portrait taken of marine private, first class, Dion J. Stephenson of Bountiful, Utah, and so they used his prom picture and you can see the hook on the strap of his bow tie. . . . After you look at these pictures, the war becomes difficult to follow, because to be decent, you have to stop and love them and mourn their passing, and there are getting to be so many of them it's impossible not to fall behind."

Martin Luther King Jr. exhorted us, "Never succumb to the temptation of becoming bitter. As you press for justice, be sure to move with dignity and discipline, using only the instruments of love."At the worst times, such an attitude may seem impossible.Yet even though some of King's followers later rejected his precepts of non-violence, something in us knows that closing down is not the way.Yes, the world is full of pain, uncertainty, and injustice. But in this vulnerable human life, every loss is an opportunity either to shut out the world or to stand up with dignity and let the heart respond.

Israeli businessman Yitzhak Frankenthal faced this choice when his son was murdered by Palestinian gunmen. Only days later, Frankenthal stood before the Israeli prime minster's residence and said, "I am unwilling to delegate my ethics to soldiers and politicians. If the security forces were to strike back now and kill innocent Palestinians in retaliation, I would tell them they were no better than my son's killers. Even if they found that his killer was planning another murderous attack, if he were surrounded by innocent children and civilians I would say no. Do not seek revenge. Do all you can to avoid and prevent the violence, the death of all Israelis or Palestinians. But do not kill. In my son's name, please listen." He went on to found the Arik Institute, named for his son, which works for reconciliation and peace.

Living with compassion does not mean we have to give away all our possessions, take in every homeless person we meet, and fix every difficulty in our extended family and community. Compassion is not co-dependence. It does not mean we lose our self-respect or sacrifice ourself blindly for others. In the West we are confused about this point. We mistakenly fear that if we become too compassionate we will be overwhelmed by the suffering of others. But this happens only when our compassion is one-sided. In Buddhist psychology compassion is a circle that encompasses all beings, *including ourselves*. Compassion blossoms only when we remember ourself and others, when the two sides are in harmony.

Compassion is not foolish. It doesn't just go along with what others want so they don't feel bad. There is a yes in compassion, and there is also a no, said with the same courage of heart. No to abuse, no to racism, no to violence, both personal and worldwide. The no is said not out of hate but out of an unwavering care.

Buddhists call this the fierce sword of compassion. It is the power-ful no of leaving a destructive family, the agonizing no of allowing an addict to experience the consequences of his acts.

Wherever it is practiced, compassion brings us back to life. When a woman named Lavonne came to Buddhist practice three years after her husband's death, she was angry and depressed. She had closed herself off from the world as if her loss were an unfor-givable betrayal. She lived alone, out of contact with old friends and her sisters and their children, and she had abandoned the political work that once inspired her. Life felt cold, unforgiving, meaning-less. Her body grew stiff. She knew she needed help.

Over the two months of her meditation retreat, with a thou-sand soft breaths, she began to release the pains of her grieving body. She practiced loving-kindness and compassion for herself. Then her compassion grew to include all those who, like her, had lost their most beloved family members. Lavonne's heart began to ease. One morning she came to see me and pulled out of her pocket an egg, a hard-boiled egg she had kept from breakfast two days be-fore. She said it was her heart, round and smooth and warm, and she kept it in her hand all day as she walked and sat. It was her way of holding herself, of bringing the living warmth back to her own grieving heart. "Now," she said, "I am ready to go back and love the world again."

PRACTICE: A MEDITATION ON COMPASSION

To cultivate compassion, let yourself sit in a centered and quiet way. In this traditional form of practice you will combine a re-peated inner intention with visualization and the evocation of the feeling of compassion. As you first sit, breathe softly and feel your body, your heartbeat, the life within you. Feel how you treasure your own life, how you guard yourself in the face of your sorrows. After some time, bring to mind someone close to you whom you dearly love. Picture them and feel your natural caring for them. Notice how you hold them in your heart. Then let yourself be aware of their measure of sorrows, their suffering in life. Feel how your heart opens to wish them well, to extend comfort, to share in their pain and meet it with compassion. This is the natural response of the heart. Inwardly recite these phrases:

> *May you be held in compassion.*
> *May your pain and sorrow be eased.*
> *May you be at peace.*

Continue reciting all the while you are holding that person in your heart. You can modify these phrases in any way that makes them true to your heart's intention.

After a few minutes, turn your compassion toward yourself and the measure of sorrows you carry. Recite the same phrases:

> *May I be held in compassion.*
> *May my pain and sorrow be eased.*
> *May I be at peace.*

After a time, begin to extend compassion to others you know. Picture loved ones, one after another. Hold the image of each in your heart, be aware of that person's difficulties, and wish him or her well with the same phrases.

Then you can open your compassion further, a step at a time, to the suffering of your friends, to your neighbors, to your community, to all who suffer, to difficult people, to your enemies, and finally to the brotherhood and sisterhood of all beings. Sense your tenderhearted connection with all life and its creatures.

Work with compassion practice intuitively. At times it may feel difficult, as though you might be overwhelmed by the pain. Remember, you are not trying to "fix" the pain of the world, only to hold it with a compassionate heart. As you practice again and again, relax and be gentle. Breathe. Let your breath and heart rest naturally, as a center of compassion in the midst of the world.

3

WHO LOOKS IN THE MIRROR?
THE NATURE OF CONSCIOUSNESS

*In its true state consciousness is naked, immaculate, clear, vacuous, transparent,
timeless, beyond all conditions. O Nobly Born, remember the
pure open sky of your own true nature.*
—Tibetan Book of the Great Liberation

*Luminous is consciousness, brightly shining is its nature, but it becomes
clouded by the attachments that visit it.*
—Anguttara Nikaya

Dr. Rachel Remen, who trains physicians to attend to the heart
and mind as well as the body, tells this story:

> For the last ten years of his life, Tim's father had Alzheimer's dis-
> ease. Despite the devoted care of Tim's mother, he had slowly dete-
> riorated until he had become a sort of walking vegetable. He was
> unable to speak and was fed, clothed, and cared for as if he were
> a very young child. . . . One Sunday, while [Tim's mother] was
> out doing the shopping, [Tim and his brother], then fifteen and

seventeen, watched football as their father sat nearby in a chair. Suddenly, he slumped forward and fell to the floor. Both sons realized immediately that something was terribly wrong. His color was gray and his breath uneven and rasping. Frightened, Tim's older brother told him to call 911. Before he could respond, a voice he had not heard in ten years, a voice he could barely remember, interrupted. "Don't call 911, son. Tell your mother that I love her. Tell her that I am all right." And Tim's father died. . . .

Tim, now a cardiologist, goes on: "Because he died unexpectedly at home, the law required that we have an autopsy. My father's brain was almost entirely destroyed by his disease. For many years, I have asked myself, 'Who spoke? Who are we really?' I have never found the slightest help from any medical knowledge. Much of life cannot be explained, it can only be witnessed."

As a physician and scientist, Tim was confronted with the mystery of consciousness beyond the brain, beyond the body. Western science is just beginning to open to questions about the nature and origin of consciousness, even though Western philosophers have been concerned with such questions for centuries. Recent scientific studies of near-death and out-of-body experiences, along with experiments in remote viewing, allow us to glimpse other dimensions of consciousness. But what are we to make of them?

Buddhist psychology sends us directly into this mystery, to see for ourselves how consciousness works, independent of any object or content. It first describes consciousness as "that which knows," that which experiences. To understand this, we can deliberately turn our attention to examine consciousness.

We can start very simply by looking in the mirror. When we do so we are often startled to notice that our body looks older, even though we don't feel older. This is because the body exists in time, but the consciousness that perceives it is outside of time, never aging. We intuitively sense this. Instead of being caught up in the spilled groceries, it's as if we step back and see our experience with a timeless understanding.

Ordinarily we take consciousness for granted, ignoring it as a fish ignores water. And so we focus endlessly on the contents of experience: what is happening in our body, feelings, and thoughts. Yet each time we move, listen, think, or perceive, consciousness receives all that occurs. Unless we grasp the nature and function of consciousness, it is impossible to live wisely.

This is a third principle of Buddhist psychology:

---

3   When we shift attention from experience to the spacious consciousness that knows, wisdom arises.

The capacity to be mindful, to observe without being caught in our experience, is both remarkable and liberating. "Mindfulness is all helpful," taught the Buddha. As we shall see, the transforming power of mindfulness underlies all of Buddhist psychology. To those who seek self-understanding, the Buddha teaches, "With the mind, to observe the mind." The central tool for investigating consciousness is our own observation. With mindfulness, we can direct our attention to notice what is going on inside us, and study how our mind and experience operate.

What we ordinarily call the mind usually refers to the "thinking mind," the ceaseless fountain of ideas, images, creativity, evaluation, and problem solving that spontaneously streams through our mind. But when we look closely, we discover that the mind is not just its thoughts, not just the ever-changing stream of ideas and images. It also includes a wide range of mind states or qualities around and below the thought process: feelings, moods, intuition, instincts. Even more important, though usually unnoticed, is the sheer fact of conscious awareness. This central capacity to be conscious is the essence of mind.

Physicists since the time of Isaac Newton have studied the mysterious operation of gravity. They have described its laws and characteristics. Consciousness is like gravity, a central part of existence that can also be described, whose laws can be known, whose power, range, and function can be studied. But unfortunately, Western

psychology has almost completely neglected the study of consciousness. Perhaps this is because the Western tradition has so
emphasized pathology, or because there are no easy external ways
to measure consciousness. In his later years, Francis Crick, the
Nobel Prize–winning co-discoverer of the DNA double helix,
turned his attention to the central question of consciousness.
Consciousness, he believed, is as central to understanding biological life as gravity is to physics, and he rued the way the scientific
community had avoided this elephant in their midst: "For many
years consciousness was taboo in American psychology . . . and
even recently it has been ignored because it is too elusive to study."

Western materialistic science describes consciousness and its
contents as a product of the brain. Scientists can indeed show that
when different parts of the brain are stimulated or damaged, they
directly change the mood or content of our conscious experience.
But these experiments give us only a partial picture. What of awareness itself? Is it merely an evolutionary "product" of the neurons of
the brain? Or is our nervous system more like a television and
DVD, the receiver and recorder of events but not the actual source
of consciousness? Buddhist psychology posits that consciousness is
the condition for life, and that the physical body interacts with consciousness but is not its source.

If you sit quietly and try to turn your attention to your own
consciousness, it is hard to pinpoint or describe. You will experience that there is awareness, but it doesn't have a color or location.
At first this can feel frustrating and difficult to grasp. But the very
transparent, unfixed, yet alive quality of consciousness is its nature,
a bit like air around us. If you relax and allow this experience of
unfixed knowing, you will discover what Buddhist writers call the
clear open sky of awareness. It is empty like space, but unlike space
it is sentient; it knows experience. In its true state, consciousness
is simply this knowing—clear, open, awake, without color or
form, containing all things, yet not limited by them. This open quality of consciousness is described as unconditioned. As with the sky,
all kinds of clouds and weather conditions can appear in it, but they
have no effect on the sky itself. Storms may appear or disappear,

but the sky remains open, limitless, unaffected by all that arises. Consciousness is unaffected by experience, just like the sky.

Consciousness is also compared to a mirror. A mirror reflects all things, yet remains bright and shining, unchanged by whatever images, beautiful or terrible, may appear within it. A brief meditation can help you to understand. After you read the next three sentences, look up from the book. Sit quietly and try to *stop being aware.* Don't be conscious of any sounds, any sights, any sensations, or any thoughts. Try it. Immediately you will discover that you can't do it. Sights, sounds, feelings, and thoughts continue to be known by consciousness. Sense how you cannot stop this conscious awareness. Notice how consciousness knows the whole variety of experiences without closing off to one in favor of another. This is the mirror-like nature of consciousness: reflective, luminous, untarnished, and peaceful.

THE TWO DIMENSIONS OF CONSCIOUSNESS

But the mirror and the open sky represent only one aspect of consciousness. Through Buddhist analysis, consciousness, like light, is found to have two dimensions. Just as light can be described as both a wave and a particle, consciousness has an unbound wave or sky-like nature and it has particular particle-like aspects. In its sky-like function, consciousness is unchanging, like the sky or the mirror. In its particle-like function, consciousness is momentary. A single state of consciousness arises together with each moment of experience and is flavored by that experience. With precise mindfulness training, meditators can experience this particle-like nature of consciousness arising and passing away like bubbles or grains of sand.

When the momentary aspect of consciousness receives an experience, it is colored by the experience, carried by it. In one Buddhist text, the particle-like quality of consciousness is described with 121 different flavors or states. There are joyful states of consciousness, fearful states, expanded and contracted ones, regretful states and loving ones. These states come with stories, feelings, perceptions, with beliefs and intentions. Zen master Thich Nhat Hanh describes it this way: "The mind is like a television set with hundreds of channels. Which channel will you turn on?" Usually we are so focused on the dramatic story being told that we don't notice that there is always consciousness that receives it.

Through mindfulness, we can learn to acknowledge which channel is playing. We can learn to change the channels, the stories and states, by recognizing that all states are simply appearances in consciousness. Most importantly, we can begin to understand the underlying nature of consciousness itself.

Here is a description of the two fundamental aspects of consciousness:

CONSCIOUSNESS IN ITS SKY-LIKE NATURE	CONSCIOUSNESS IN ITS PARTICLE-LIKE NATURE
Open	Momentary
Transparent	Impersonal
Timeless	Registering a sense experience
Cognizant	Flavored by mental states
Pure	Conditioned
Wave-like, unbounded	Rapid
Unborn, undying	Ephemeral

AWAKENING TO PURE CONSCIOUSNESS: THE SKY

Develop a mind that is vast like space, where experiences both pleasant and unpleasant can appear and disappear without conflict, struggle, or harm.
—Majjhima Nikaya

While studying Buddhism in college, I tried a little meditation on my own. But I was unsuccessful because I didn't know what I was doing. It wasn't that I was afraid of silence or of some terrible darkness that I would find inside, though these are common misunderstandings of meditation. It was that my body would get uncomfortable and my mind would spin out in a million directions. When I heard Ajahn Chah's teaching, the practice became gradually clearer. He taught me to relax and feel my breath carefully, which helped focus and quiet my mind. Then he taught me just to mindfully notice the stream of thoughts and sensations without reacting to them as a problem. This took some practice.

Finally he taught the most important lesson, to rest in consciousness itself. As his own teacher Ajahn Mun explains, "We can notice the distinction between consciousness and all the transient states and experiences that arise and pass away within it. When we do not understand this point, we take each of the passing states to be real. But when changing conditions such as happiness and unhappiness are seen for what they are, we find the way to peace. If you can rest in the knowing, the pure consciousness, there's not much more to do."

Does resting in consciousness mean we are simply checking out of the world or withdrawing into navel gazing? Not at all. Resting in the knowing is not the same as detachment. When I look back at my own life I can see my own struggles to discover this truth. Because of the conflict and unpredictable violence in my family, there were many times I wanted to run away but couldn't. To cope with the trauma, at times I became depressed, angry, or cynical. But as a primary protection, I developed the capacity to detach myself from what was happening. Detachment came naturally to me. I used it to become peaceful within myself and to try to calm those around me. Of course, these patterns persist, and now I do it for a living.

So when I first tried to meditate, I confused it with my familiar strategy of detachment. Gradually I discovered how wrong I was. My detachment had been a withdrawal from the pain and conflict into a protective shell. It was more like indifference. In Buddhist psychology indifference is called the "near enemy" of true openness and equanimity, a misguided imitation. To rest in consciousness, I had to unlearn this defensive detachment and learn to feel everything. I had to allow myself to recognize and experience the feelings and thoughts, the conflicts, the unpredictability of life in order to learn that I could trust the openness of consciousness itself. To rest in consciousness is the opposite of contraction and fear. When we rest in consciousness we become unafraid of the changing conditions of life.

In the monastery Ajahn Chah would often notice when we were caught up in a state of worry, anger, doubt, or sorrow. He would smile with amusement and urge us to inquire, "Who is doubting? Who is angry? Can you rest in the consciousness that is aware of these states?" Sometimes he would instruct us to sit at the side of a person who was dying, to be particularly aware of the mysterious moment when consciousness leaves and a person full of life turns into a lifeless corpse. Sometimes he would say, "If you are lost in the forest, that is not really being lost. You are really lost if you forget who you are."

This knowing or pure consciousness is called by many names, all of which point to our timeless essence. Ajahn Chah and the forest monks of Thailand speak of it as the "Original Mind" or the "One Who Knows." In Tibetan Buddhism it is referred to as *rigpa,* silent and intelligent. In Zen it is called the "mind ground" or "mind essence." Hindu yogis speak of the "timeless witness." While these teachings may sound abstract, they are quite practical. To understand them we can simply notice the two distinct dimensions to our life: the ever-changing flow of experiences, and that which knows the experiences.

Perhaps we can better understand this through a story of a Palestinian named Salam, one of my good friends. I met Salam when I was doing some teaching for the hospices of the Bay Area. He was able to sit with the dying because he had no fear of death. In the late 1960s and 1970s Salam had lived in Jerusalem as an activist and a journalist. Because he was writing about creating a Palestinian capital in East Jerusalem and the establishment of a Palestinian state, he was regularly arrested. He spent nearly six years in Israeli prisons. He was frequently interrogated and periodically beaten and tortured. This happens on every side in war.

One afternoon after he had been badly beaten, his body was

lying on the floor of the prison and he was being kicked by a particularly cruel guard. Blood poured out of his mouth, and as the police report later stated, the authorities believed he had died.

He remembers the pain of being beaten. Then, as is often reported by accident and torture victims, he felt his consciousness leave his body and float up to the ceiling. At first it was peaceful and still, like in a silent movie, as he watched his own body lying below being kicked. It was so peaceful he didn't know what all the fuss was about. And then Salam described how, in a remarkable way, his consciousness expanded further. He knew it was his body lying below, but now he felt he was also the boot kicking the body. He was also the peeling green paint on the prison walls, the goat whose bleat could be heard outside, the dirt under the guard's fingernails—he was life, all of it and the eternal consciousness of it all, with no separation. Being everything, he could never die. All his fears vanished. He realized that death was an illusion. A well-being and joy beyond description opened in him. And then a spontaneous compassion arose for the astonishing folly of humans, believing we are separate, clinging to nations and making war.

Two days later, as Salam describes it, he came back to consciousness in a bruised and beaten body on the floor of a cell, without fear or remorse, just amazement. His experience changed his whole sense of life and death. He refused to continue to participate in any form of conflict. When he was released, he married a Jewish woman and had Palestinian-Jewish children. That, he said, was his answer to the misguided madness of the world.

TURNING TOWARD OUR ESSENCE

"Who are we, really?" the Zen koans demand. "Who is dragging this body around?" or "What was your original face before your parents were born?" These questions force us to look directly at the consciousness that inhabits our body. Ajahn Chah asked us to "be the Knowing." Tibetan teachers instruct their students to direct their gaze inside to see who or what is doing the looking. Ajahn Jumnian, a Thai forest master, tells his students to witness all experience as if from the "third eye" in the center of the forehead. In each of these practices we turn toward and rest in consciousness itself.

It is as if we were in a movie theater, completely lost in whatever film—romance, adventure, comedy, or tragedy—is currently starring ourselves. Then we are told to look behind us, to find the source. Turning our heads, we recognize for the first time that the entire drama arises from a series of changing images projected by a beam of light onto the screen. The light, clear and shining, is colored by the various forms on the film, yet its essential nature is pure and unchanging.

At some moments there are also gaps in the action; the show gets a bit slow, even boring. We might shift in our seats, notice the people eating popcorn around us, remember we're in a movie. In the same way we can notice that there are gaps between our thoughts, gaps in the whole sense of our self. Instead of being lost in ideas and the problems in front of us, creating the whole drama of ourself, there are moments when we sense the space around our experience, let go, and relax. "These gaps," says the meditation master Chögyam Trungpa, "are extremely good news." They remind us that we can always rest in awareness, that freedom is always possible.

We do not require special meditative circumstances or a near-death experience like Salam's to return to awareness. A boy in school suddenly notices a sunbeam illuminating the dust and he is no longer the earnest fifth grader struggling with math. He smiles as he senses the ever-present mystery and his whole building and schoolboy drama are held in a silent, free awareness. A woman walking down the street thinks of a distant friend and for a moment forgets her errands, feeling eternity and her own small life passing through it. In an argument we stop, laugh, let go, and become silent. Each of these moments offers a taste of freedom.

As we have seen, when we first turn to investigate who is being aware, we may feel confused, like a fish looking for water. We discover that there's nothing solid, no one who is perceiving. This is a wonderful discovery. Awareness has no shape or color. It is beyond presence or absence, coming or going. Instead there is only a clear space of knowing, of consciousness, which is empty and yet cognizant at the same time. As you hold this book, consciousness is reading the words and reflecting about the nature of consciousness. Turn and ask who is reading. Your first answer may be "I can't sense anything there, it's just empty." Stay with this knowing, this empty openness. Learn to trust it. It is consciousness without limitation, reflecting all that appears, yet untouched by it all.

As you work with this inquiry regularly, you can gradually develop the capacity to distinguish between the events and experiences of life and the consciousness that is knowing. You learn to rest in the knowing, unperturbed, to settle back in the midst of any circumstance, even those that are difficult or confusing.

This resting, settling, is quite different from the sort of pathological detachment that I learned as a child. Out of fear, I split my experience, protecting myself through the subtle distance of my role as witness. When we truly rest in awareness, our experience is spacious and intimate, without defenses. With it arises compassion; we feel our heart's natural connection with life.

One meditation practitioner, Maria, works as a nurse in the emergency room of a local hospital. She describes how she has learned to use the art of resting in awareness: "Sometimes it's not too busy and I can work on automatic, check on a patient or do the paperwork while my mind drifts off to think about a million other things. Then we might get a whole crowd of incoming patients: accidents, heart attacks, asthma emergencies. I do my part, but I'm also tuned in to the whole of what's going on. I've learned to open the awareness. It's as if my mind gets spacious and still, present, sensitive to what is needed and yet kind of detached at the same time. I guess it's like the flow state that athletes talk about. I'm in the middle, doing all the right things, yet some part of me is just watching it all, silent.

"It happens more these days, not just at work. When I do my meditation practice it gets stronger. I had a big fight with my son and in the middle of it I could feel my body tightening, how right I thought my view was. Just feeling that, I relaxed and shifted to the space of awareness, and things opened up. I was saying no, but I could also feel all the love underneath and how these were just our roles and we had to play them well and behind it, it was all spacious, all OK."

When we learn to rest in awareness, there's both caring and silence. There is listening for what's the next thing to do and awareness of all that's happening, a big space and a connected feeling of love. When there is enough space, our whole being can both apprehend the situation and be at ease. We see the dance of life, we dance beautifully, yet we're not caught in it. In any situation, we can open up, relax, and return to the sky-like nature of consciousness.

PRACTICE: THE RIVER OF SOUND

Sit comfortably and at ease. Close your eyes. Let your body be at rest and your breathing be natural. Begin to listen to the play of sounds around you. Notice those that are loud or soft, far and near. Notice how sounds arise and vanish on their own, leaving no trace. After you have listened for a few minutes, let yourself sense, feel, or imagine that your mind is not limited to your head. Sense that your mind is expanding to be open like the sky—clear, vast like space. Feel that your mind extends outward beyond the most distant sounds. Imagine there are no boundaries to your mind, no inside or outside. Let the awareness of your mind extend in every direction like the open sky.

Relax in this openness and just listen. Now every sound you hear—people, cars, wind, soft sounds—will arise and pass away like a cloud in the open space of your own mind. Let the sounds come and go, whether loud or soft, far or near, let them be clouds in the vast sky of your own awareness, appearing and disappearing without resistance. As you rest in this open awareness for a time, notice how thoughts and feelings also arise and vanish like sounds in the open space of mind. Let the thoughts and feelings come and go without struggle or resistance. Pleasant and unpleasant thoughts, pictures, words, joys, and sorrows—let them all come and go like clouds in the clear sky of mind.

Then, in this spacious awareness also notice how you experience the body. The mind is not in the body. The body sensations float and change in the open sky of mind. The breath breathes it-self; it moves like a breeze. If you observe carefully, the body is not solid. It reveals itself as areas of hardness and softness, pressure and tingling, warm and cool sensation, all floating in the space of aware-ness.

Relax. Rest in this openness. Let sensations float and change. Allow thoughts and images, feelings and sounds to come and go like clouds in the clear, open space of awareness. As you do, pay at-tention to the consciousness itself. Notice how the open space of awareness is clear, transparent, timeless, and without conflict—al-lowing for all things but not limited by them. This is your own true nature. Rest in it. Trust it. It is home.

4

THE COLORINGS OF CONSCIOUSNESS

Consciousness is colored by the states that visit it.
—Buddha

Speak or act with a deluded mind and sorrow will follow you
As the wheel follows the ox who draws the cart
Speak or act with a clear mind and happiness will follow you
As closely as your shadow, unshakable.
—Dhammapada

"Eh," Ajahn Chah would peer at me when I was having a hard time, "caught in some state again?" In the forest monastery we were constantly being directed both to look at consciousness itself and to precisely name the states that rose to fill it throughout the day: *frightened, bored, relaxed, confused, resentful, calm, frustrated,* and so forth.

Ajahn Chah would sometimes ask us out loud about our states so that we could acknowledge them more clearly. To a recently divorced monk from Bangkok he chided, "Is there sadness? Anger? Self-pity? Hey, these are natural. Look at them all." And to a confused English monk he laughed, "Can you see what is happening? There is distraction, confusion, being in a muddle. They're only mind states, you know. Come on. Do you believe your mind states? Are you trapped by them? You'll suffer for sure."

Once we became more skilled at noticing, he would up the ante. He would deliberately make things difficult and watch what happened. In the hottest season, he would send us out barefoot to collect alms food on a ten-mile round trip, and smile at us when we came back to see if we were frustrated or discouraged. He'd have us sit up all night long for endless teachings, without any break, and check in on us cheerfully at four in the morning. When we got annoyed, he'd ask, "Are you angry? Whose fault is that?"

In popular Western culture we are taught that the way to achieve happiness is to change our external environment to fit our wishes. But this strategy doesn't work. In every life, pleasure and pain, gain and loss, praise and blame keep showing up, no matter how hard we struggle to have only pleasure, gain, and praise. Buddhist psychology offers a different approach to happiness, teaching that states of consciousness are far more crucial than outer circumstances.

More than anything else, the way we experience life is created by the particular states of mind with which we meet it. If you are watching a high school soccer playoff and your daughter is the nervous goalie, your consciousness will be filled with worry, sympathy, and excitement at each turn of the game. If you are a hired driver waiting to pick up someone's kid, you will see the same sights, the players and ball, in a bored, disinterested way. If you are the referee, you will perceive the sights and sounds in yet another mode. It is the same way with hearing Beethoven, pulling weeds, watching a Woody Allen movie, or visiting Mexico City. Pure awareness becomes colored by our thoughts, emotions, and expectations.

"Just as when a lute is played upon," the Buddha says, "the sound arises due to the qualities of the wooden instrument, the strings, and the exertions of the musician, in the same way do moments of experience and consciousness appear and, having come into existence, pass away."

When consciousness is colored or conditioned, it acts like particles, arising and passing, taking on whatever qualities happen to arise with it. It can be felt as a succession of discrete moments, each arising from the present conditions of both mind and senses. As with light or sound, the way in which consciousness arises as discrete, particular moments can be observed. And, as Ajahn Chah tried to teach us, some of these moments can also be changed.

Here is a fourth principle of Buddhist psychology:

4   Recognize the mental states that fill consciousness. Shift from unhealthy states to healthy ones.

To explore this particle-like aspect of consciousness, we will need to look at some of the Buddha's lists, which are among the most detailed maps of human psychology ever developed. For Westerners, this is one of the more challenging aspects of Buddhist psychology. There are hundreds of lists and tables of states and relations. In certain monasteries of Burma and Thailand, especially those that study the refined psychological analysis of the Abhidharma, I have seen blackboards covered with complex diagrams of how subtle states of perception, responses, and consciousness interact at the microscopic level. It looks like a physics class at MIT, or a seminar on cybernetics and systems theory.

Simply put, the Buddha was a list maker. There are the Two Truths, the Three Characteristics, the Four Foundations of Mindfulness, the Five Hindrances, the Six Perfections, the Seven Factors of Enlightenment, and the Eightfold Path. There are lists of 52, 89, and 121 states of consciousness. In later schools of Buddhism the lists get bigger, with 80,000 verses of wisdom and 84,000 skillful means. Some engineering types, such as Robert Hover, an American who became a meditation teacher in Burma in

the 1960s, loved the lists. Alas, for many of us they bring up a sinking feeling, like memories of badly taught arithmetic or an old obsessive uncle. It's not our way to learn.

Nevertheless, these lists served a critical function. Buddhist
psychology was originally an oral tradition, recited for five hundred years before ever being written down. Numbered lists are a
traditional mnemonic device, a way to remember the teachings in
detail and depth without losing critical information. They were
part of the science of the times, ordered and repeated, used in inner
experiments of exquisite accuracy for centuries. Even though they
now exist as written texts, these lists are still recited from memory and regarded as a precious legacy. Indeed, this form of system-
atized knowledge was respected not just in India, but throughout
the educated cultures of the ancient world. It is recorded that Abdul
Kassem Ismael, grand vizier of Persia in the tenth century, couldn't
bear to part with his 117,000-volume library. When he traveled,
these books were carried by a caravan of four hundred camels,
trained to walk in a way that preserved the library's alphabetical
order.

To help us understand the momentary colorings of consciousness, Buddhist psychology places them in a three-part system.
Described as "the all," this system encompasses the whole of our
human experience. Part one includes all the impressions received
through our sense doors. This list is short because our sense experience comprises only six things: sights, sounds, tastes, smells,
touch/bodily perceptions, and thoughts/feelings. It's worth noticing that in the Buddhist system, the mind is considered to be the
sixth sense door, receiving thoughts and feelings and intuitions just
the way the eye receives sights and the ear receives sounds.

Part two is comprised of the discrete moments of consciousness that receive each sense experience. A fresh corpse also receives
sense input, sunlight or breeze on the skin, but there is no consciousness to register it. For us to experience something, there
must arise a moment of consciousness at the sense door. These six
basic particles of consciousness are individual moments of knowing called, respectively, eye, ear, tongue, nose, body, and mind consciousness.

With the six senses and their individual consciousnesses we construct our reality, just as an artist can paint the whole world using any combination of the colors red, orange, yellow, green, blue, and purple. The Buddha explains, "Monks, have you seen a masterwork of painting? That masterwork is designed by the mind together with the senses. Indeed, monks, the mind is more artistic and creative than any created masterpiece; it is the source of all human creativity."

Initially I thought these lists were archaic and at times arbitrary, but my teachers insisted they could help me understand my direct experience more insightfully. When I received meditation instruction from the Burmese master Mahasi Sayadaw, I was taught to slow down and note the arising and passing of each moment in precise detail. In the monastery dining hall, every second brought new sights, sounds, smells, and thoughts. When I sat down to eat rice and fish curry, I could feel the tug of my robes, hear the changing play of voices from the visitors, and feel and smell the sweat on my body; as I mindfully moved my arm to lift a mango and chew, I became aware of a background commentary of thoughts and feelings. At first these all blended together, but after months of training in mindfulness, my perception became microscopic. A few minutes contained thousands of moments of sound and ear consciousness, sight and eye consciousness, taste and tongue consciousness, all blended together like the spots of color in an impressionist painting or the dots of light on a television screen to create my experience of lunch.

Even now as you read, you can notice these six sense impressions and the six consciousnesses, rapidly arising and passing like frames of a movie, one after another. Take a moment, look up from the page, and notice how the book and the ideas it carries disappear from consciousness, replaced by the sights in front of you. Return to this page, and again, after you read this sentence, shift your attention to your bodily sensations: contact with the seat and floor, warmth and cool, tingling, tensions, vibrations. Notice how the book and its contents recede in consciousness as you do. Sense impressions and sense consciousnesses are the first two steps in constructing our world.

HEALTHY AND UNHEALTHY MENTAL STATES

To complete this picture of our world, let's go back to the woman watching her daughter play soccer. She sees the game and hears the sounds, each received by eye and ear consciousness. She is also excited, worried, proud, sympathetic. Her sense experiences are colored by many states of mind. These states of mind constitute the third aspect of human experience. These qualities of mind, called mental states, color consciousness. One common list has 52 qualities, while other lists have up to 121. Apparently, between the monasteries, the monks could never fully decide.

With every sense impression and the consciousness that receives it, there arise qualities of mind such as worry, pride, and excitement. They arise between the senses and consciousness, and add their color to experience. These mental qualities and what they bring to each experience are critical for our happiness.

A friend sent Dennis, a real estate broker, to practice at a Spirit Rock meditation class. An attractive man in his late thirties, Dennis had lists of his own, having just broken up with his seventeenth girlfriend. He was sad because none of them had been quite right. He'd gone through a number of spiritual teachers too. I was sure I was going to be the next disappointment on his list.

Initially Dennis hated meditation. "Can't I just find another girl?" he asked. I told him to forget the girl and to be mindful of his breath and body. During the following weeks I asked him to pay attention and mindfully notice not his external experiences but his mind states, the mental qualities that filled his day. Dennis was not prepared for what he saw. He thought of himself as a happy guy, but he discovered more moments of dissatisfaction than he could have imagined. Along with them were mind states of aversion, boredom, judgment, and anxiety. There were many moments of pleasure too, but he was surprised by the frequency of dissatisfaction and anxiety. Immediately Dennis began to judge himself: "What's the matter with me? Why can't I be more serene?" Now he was dissatisfied with his own mind. When he told me, I laughed and pointed out that he was simply caught in the mind state of being dissatisfied, and suffering from it, instead of noticing it as simply a thought.

THE ALL

SENSE EXPERIENCES	MENTAL STATES	SENSE CONSCIOUSNESSES
SIGHTS *colors, shapes, sizes*	COMMON MENTAL STATES such as memory, stability, feeling tone (pleasant or unpleasant), will, and life force	EYE CONSCIOUSNESS *seeing*
SOUNDS *tinkling, rattling, talking*	**plus either**	EAR CONSCIOUSNESS *hearing*
TASTES *sour, sweet, bitter*	UNHEALTHY STATES The 3 roots of: **grasping, aversion, and delusion** give rise to worry, envy, rigidity, agitation,	TONGUE CONSCIOUSNESS *tasting*
SMELLS *pungent, fragrant, delicate*	greed, self-centeredness, hate, avarice, shamelessness, dullness, closed-mindedness, confusion, misperception, recklessness, and others.	NOSE CONSCIOUSNESS *smelling*
BODILY PERCEPTIONS *soft, itchy, warm*	**or**	BODY CONSCIOUSNESS *sensing*
THOUGHTS, FEELINGS *Emotions, images, ideas*	HEALTHY STATES The 3 roots of: **wisdom, love, and generosity** give rise to mindfulness, confidence, graciousness, modesty, joy, insight, flexibility, clarity, equanimity, adaptability, kindness, and others.	MIND CONSCIOUSNESS *thinking, feeling, intuiting*

This was a turning point for Dennis, the moment he began to understand the nature of happiness. Finally Dennis was shifting his focus from outer problems to the inner states that were shaping his experience.

Buddhist psychology makes mental health simple for us to understand. The presence of healthy mental states creates a healthy mind; the presence of unhealthy states creates mental distress, unhappiness, and mental illness. This reflects a significant difference with much of Western psychology, which focuses primarily on the residual contents of consciousness, on *what* we think about. Although this focus has given rise to many creative therapeutic approaches, it often leaves us entangled in the never-ending production of thoughts and emotions. Here, Buddhist psychology takes a liberating turn, stepping back with mindfulness to investigate the play of the mental states themselves, teaching us to release those states that bring sorrow and foster those that create joy.

Let's go back to the list of mental factors. The mental factors are divided into three groups. First are thirteen common and universal qualities that everyone experiences in most moments. They include stability, life force, memory, feeling tone (pleasant or unpleasant), will, and recognition. These are the basic operating system of the mind. Seeing how these factors arise, we can understand how the mind receives and processes information in a rapid-fire way.

Next, and most importantly, we turn our attention to the mental factors that are subject to training. These are divided into healthy states and unhealthy ones. The unhealthy factors have three roots: grasping, aversion, and delusion. From these three roots arise states of envy, rigidity, anxiety, dullness, shamelessness, self-centeredness, doubt, agitation, and misperception. We all experience them at times. The stronger these states are, the more extensively we suffer. At their worst, they create psychopathology. Grasping and greed become addiction, worry becomes paranoia, shamelessness becomes sociopathy, aversion becomes hatred and rage. War, violence, racism, exploitation, and injustice are their fruits.

The healthy factors have three healthy roots: love, generosity, and mindfulness. From these three roots arise states of clarity, composure, insight, joy, adaptability, confidence, discretion, and balance. Each of these healthy mental states creates a happy and free mind. They grow from mindful attention, and like sunlight on fog, the presence of these healthy states dissolves the unhealthy ones. Almost all of the myriad Buddhist trainings and practices work to release unhealthy states and cultivate healthy ones.

The division of mental qualities into healthy and unhealthy states helps us see the causes of our happiness and our suffering clearly. It also describes an important psychological truth: healthy and unhealthy factors are mutually inhibiting. When healthy factors are present, unhealthy ones are not. So when we foster healthy states, unhealthy ones disappear.

To work with our mental states, we have to acknowledge how rapidly these states can change, often disappearing without our noticing. Because we are not aware of our inner states, we feel controlled by outside influences. The world will alternately please us or be at fault, and we will be caught in habitual grasping or frustration. There was an article in a San Francisco paper about angry drivers in the nearby town of Pleasanton. It seems the police had trouble with habitual speeders on the main highway. They asked their traffic engineers to create signals that can sense the speed of a car 350 feet before the intersections. Drivers who habitually speed find all the lights turning red in their path. There were a lot of mad drivers. "Instant karma," it was called in the press. A better way to travel is to look at our states of mind.

Training in mindfulness, we learn to be aware of our own mental states without being caught in them. This capacity for self-reflection is the key to Buddhist psychology. The Buddha asks, "How does a practitioner remain established in observation of states of mind in the mind?" He instructs, "The practitioner becomes aware when the mind is tense and when the mind is relaxed . . . the practitioner becomes aware when the mind contains hatred and when the mind contains love . . . the practitioner becomes aware when the mind contains worry and when the mind is composed."

When we look at our own mind, we can notice the mental

states that predominate, as if we were noticing the weather. Just as a storm can bring rain, wind, and cold, we can observe the clusters of unhealthy states that appear on our bad days. We may find resentment, fear, anger, worry, doubt, envy, or agitation. We can notice how often they arise and how attached we are to their point of view.

We can also notice the healthy states in our most free and open-hearted periods. We can notice how love, generosity, flexibility, ease, and simplicity are natural to us. These states are important to notice. They give us trust in our original goodness, our own Buddha nature.

June came to see me in the middle of a messy divorce. She was especially worried about her eleven-year-old daughter. We began by sitting together, not trying to fix anything, but holding the grief and hurt of the whole situation in compassion. Instead of treating her experience as an emergency and trying to change it, we took some deep breaths and settled into the experience of just being present in the moment. With this new spaciousness, I asked June to be mindful of her inner states, what she was feeling and thinking. Immediately she began to weep. She said her inner life ranged from extreme worry and agitation to self-recrimination, guilt, and anger. She couldn't sleep; she obsessed over an imagined future that had not yet happened. June's doctor had given her tranquilizers, which calmed her somewhat. But still her mind was easily overwhelmed.

I invited June to gently acknowledge out loud the states that became present. She began to identify the clusters of angry and fearful mind states as they arose. She could feel how sticky they were, how easy it was to believe the spell they cast. And yet, as we sat and her mindfulness grew stronger, she began to notice that they were not all there was to her life. She laughed a little and realized how long it had been since she'd felt any relief.

To support this newfound openness, I suggested to June a whole program including daily sitting meditations using both mindfulness and compassion practices. She also undertook a commitment to practice non-harming, even toward her soon-to-be-ex-husband. Each morning she recited a daily intention of com-

passion and peace for herself and all she encountered. She simpli-
fied her living situation and with some friends began to exercise
again. She spent a lot of time with her daughter. I met with June
periodically to support the changes that would foster her healthy
mind states and help her trust her inner strength and goodness.

June went through a long legal process and eventually ended
up with enough money and shared custody. Even with the meditations, she said, she suffered and agonized during the whole period.
However, because she was suffering so much, she was also moti-
vated to work with her mind. Through her dedication to mindfulness, June began to recognize more and more clearly the fearful
and jealous patterns as unhealthy mind states. She noticed how
much pain they brought to her body and mind. Because they were
toxic and destructive, and because she wanted to live in a more loving way, she slowly began to let them go.

RELEASING UNHEALTHY CONDITIONING

"To become your own psychologist," says Lama Yeshe, "you don't
have to learn some big philosophy. All you have to do is examine
your own mind every day. You already examine material things
every day—every morning you check out the food in your refrigerator. Why not check out the state of your own mind?
Investigating your own mind is much more important!"

When we learn to be mindful of mental states, we also begin
to see the ways that they are habitual, how conditioned they are.
Modern neuroscience tells us that our past reactions are engraved
onto the synapses that send messages from one neuron to another,
making them more likely to send the same message in the future.
Paying attention, we recognize how often a moment's experience
is followed by an immediate reaction. It can be shocking to realize
how impersonal and habitual our responses are. But gradually we
realize that mindfulness gives us the option to choose a healthier
response.

A meditation student, Jeremy, told me about a difficult
encounter with a former friend, Zach, who had betrayed him in a

business deal. Previously, whenever Jeremy encountered Zach, he experienced the sight of his friend together with the arising of affection, excitement, and happiness. Now seeing Zach, there arose the mental qualities of anger, sadness, worry, and unhappiness.

In these two scenarios, the sense experience of meeting Zach is the same. The critical difference is the mental qualities that arise with the experience. Because he lived nearby, Jeremy regularly encountered Zach. They had tried to talk to each other; they had even tried mediation. Still the feelings of anger and resentment persisted. At the sight of Zach there followed an automatic response conditioned by the betrayal. Jeremy could feel his mind and body contract in pain as the memory arose again.

With the next encounter, instead of replaying the story of how he had been wronged for the five hundredth time, Jeremy paused. Feeling the pain, he inquired deeper. Yes, there was hurt. But he had already done what was necessary to prevent further loss. Breathing gently, he could notice that there was no new problem, that his states of mind were the result of past conflict. He breathed again and let the anger and agitation be there, held in mindfulness, without feeding them. They began to subside, and a quiet relief arose. As his ex-friend walked by, Jeremy could acknowledge the betrayal, but he didn't have to dwell in the unhappy states. In this simple act of looking at his states, Jeremy had taken a step toward understanding and liberation.

As Ajahn Chah taught, "When you have wisdom, contact with experience is like standing at the bottom of a ripe mango tree. We get to choose between the good and rotten mangoes. It is all to your profit, because you know which fruits will make you sick and which are healthy." By training ourselves in mindfulness we begin to see clearly the healthy and unhealthy fruit. As we practice mindfulness with pleasant and unpleasant experiences, we discover the power of the mindfulness to allow a healthy response to whatever arises. Mindfulness is the king or queen of all the healthy states. It sees what experiences are present and creates the conditions for our natural integrity, love, generosity, and simplicity to arise.

With mindfulness of mental states, we can choose whether we

practice peace or go to war, whether we want to be imprisoned and stuck or to release the painful states and be healthy. We can let go of the clay and let the gold within us shine.

PRACTICE: RECOGNIZING MENTAL STATES

Choose a day when you are having difficulties to mindfully observe your mental states like an anthropologist, without judgment or resistance. Usually several difficult states will appear together. They may include worry, agitation, anger, confusion, grasping, restlessness, and misperception.

Determine that three times during this day you have deemed difficult, you will carefully notice and track the course of your mental states. Without any judgment, notice which states are present, their level of intensity, how long they last, and how much you are caught up in them. If it is helpful, make notes and write them down. Do this again on two more such days. After three days, sense what effect the mindful acknowledgment of difficult states has had. If it has been illuminating or released you from their grip, continue the practice.

Next, in the same way, look for a day that you feel to be most positive, and start to mindfully observe the healthy states that are present. You can review the healthy mental factors on page 54. You may notice states of balance, clarity, flexibility, graciousness, love, wisdom, confidence, or joy. Notice the predominant states, their level of intensity, how long they last, and whether there is grasping of them. Again, if helpful, make notes. Do this again on two more such days.

After three days, sense the effect this mindful acknowledgment of healthy states has had. Recognize that you can be aware of and support these healthy states with your attention. Now that you have learned to do so, continue this practice.

5

THE MYSTERIOUS ILLUSION OF SELF

To study the way is to study the self
To study the self is to forget the self
To forget the self is to be enlightened by all things.
—Zen master Dogen

We take things very personally. The more tightly we hold self, the more problem.
No self, well . . . [laughing] . . . no problem.
—Master Hina-Tyana Dhamma Loka

At the end of the Buddhist ordination ceremony, in the sacred grove deep in the forest monastery, the new monk is given the first meditation instruction. It is the inquiry "Who am I?", a practice of systematic self-investigation. Starting with the body, we ask, "Am I the skin, the hair, the muscles and bones, the organs or the blood? Am I this body?" Modern science tells us that the molecules of the body are completely replaced every seven years. If I am not the physical elements of this body, then what am I? Am I the stream of changing feelings? Am I the memories and perceptions? Am I the thoughts and concepts, the views and beliefs? Who am I?

This is not a theoretical question; it is the most practical question for us to ask in the midst of our problems and our sorrows. Who do I take myself to be: at work, in my family, in my community, in my own heart? The way we answer this question can lead to entanglement and struggle or—no matter where we are—to freedom and ease. It is absolutely crucial to understanding the human predicament.

According to the classic Buddhist understanding, two mental states create the sense of self. One is called "self-view," which takes some aspect of experience as *I, me,* or *mine*. The second is "compared view," which evaluates the created sense of self as better than, worse than, or equal to others. We create a sense of self whenever we identify with our body, our mind, our beliefs, our roles, our situation in life. This identification happens unconsciously, over and over, whenever we hold our feelings, thoughts, and perceptions as me or mine.

The sense of self can be created in healthy and unhealthy ways. A friend loses an election for a seat on the local school board, after some scurrilous things are said about her. She identifies with the blame. She takes it very personally. A man is told by his aging, controlling father that he probably won't be included in the will. Only his "good" sisters will get the money. He compares himself to them and becomes lost and identified with the role of the rejected son. A woman's daughter gets pregnant and becomes a mother at seventeen. The older woman identifies herself as a bad mother who let this happen to her daughter. The grandchild is born and she is beautiful. The woman lets go of all the judgment and becomes an excited, loving grandmother. Now this is her identity and redeems her life. But then her daughter moves away. She identifies herself as a person who is always abandoned or betrayed. Who is she really?

In Buddhist training, we inquire into the very notion of identity, asking who we are in the midst of all these roles. As we do, we find the layers of identity opening and dropping away or dissolving gradually through the systematic practice of mindfulness. We discover how our identification with a limited sense of self creates our suffering. Releasing ourselves from these limits can free us from a lifetime of struggle.

This is a fifth principle of Buddhist psychology:

---

5 Our ideas of self are created by identification. The less we cling to ideas of self, the freer and happier we will be.

Mitch, who came to a meditation retreat, had a long, painful history. At age four his gambler father abandoned the family and was replaced by a stepfather who physically and sexually abused all three children. By high school Mitch had begun a serious drug habit to numb his pain. His older sister had been in and out of the mental hospital. In twelve-step groups Mitch had found enough support to finish college and develop a career as a software engineer. Now Mitch was married and had two children of his own. Reading about Buddhism, Mitch found that the systematic approach to inner life appealed to his technical intelligence. Although the first few retreats he attended were difficult and he experienced a lot of restlessness, he persisted, and gradually discovered that he struggled less with his body pain and thought processes. Much relieved, he registered for another retreat.

At that retreat Mitch began to fall apart. All of the adult roles he had worked so hard to construct—his sense of himself as an engineer, a father, a husband—seemed like a false front. He began to reexperience the terrible state of fear and confusion he had lived in as a child. He was experiencing the regression that often happens on retreat. He looked hurt, frightened, and very young. Mitch was afraid that his pain would last forever. I encouraged him to trust that he could learn to tolerate it all. "I feel so terrible, so worthless. How do I work with this?" he asked. I invited him to take a few breaths and sense his body seated on the earth. When he was ready, he began to mindfully examine the state of his body. It felt small, tight, pained, contracted. Painful though it was, he gradually relaxed around it. I invited him to notice whatever feelings were present. There was shock, vulnerability, helplessness, fear, and anger. I inquired how old he felt. "Eight," he stated. Then I asked, "And what thoughts and stories arise with these feelings?" He told me, "I keep saying, 'I hate myself. I'm a terrible person. It feels like this will last forever.' " Gradually Mitch was able to step back and witness these thoughts with mindfulness.

Then I asked Mitch, "And these stories you have told for so long, are they true? Is this who you are?" I looked at him gently and directly. His sense of identity with the story began to become shaky, uncertain. I went on: "All the changing sensations of your body, the pain and tension, is that who you are?" "Not exactly." "And the difficult feelings, the fear and helplessness, are these your true self?" "Well, no." "And the judgmental thoughts and stories, are these who you are?" "No. I contain all these things, but no, they're not who I am." "And who is being aware of all of this? Look and see." "I can't exactly find anybody. There's awareness, but I'm not sure who's being aware." "How does it feel?" With a big laugh, Mitch said, "Much, much freer!" We sat for a time, resting in the awareness.

Gradually, Mitch was learning to open to each level of experience without resistance or identification. Like the Buddha witnessing the painful conditions of a past life, he practiced holding it all with great compassion. In doing so, some part of him learned that the injured self was not who he really is. Slowly, Mitch began to heal.

In dialogue with his followers, the Buddha regularly asked them to inquire into their true nature. "Monks, these things which are constantly changing, can we call them the self?" "No sir, they are not." "Are the changing sense experiences of the body the self?" "No sir," they replied. "Are the changing feelings and perceptions the self?" "No sir, they are not." "Are the changing thoughts and mental formations the self?" "No sir, they are not." "And are the

changing states of consciousness to be grasped as self?" "No, vener-
able sir." "In the ultimate sense," the Buddha went on, "all these are
found to be selfless."

What we take to be a self is tentative, fictitious, constructed by
clinging, a temporary identification with some parts of experience.
Self arises, solidifying itself, like ice floating in water. Ice is actually
made of the same substance as water. Identification and clinging
harden the water into ice. In a similar way, we sense ourself as separate.

THE PARADOX OF DEVELOPMENT

Both Western and Buddhist psychologies acknowledge the need for
a healthy development of self. Indeed, from a Western clinical perspective, not finding an identity is considered a crisis. Ordinarily,
the development of a healthy sense of self is a natural process. In
Western psychology, Freud and his followers described the stages
of the self's development, and how a child gradually separates her
identity from her mother, sensing herself as a separate being. As a
child discovers that her deepest needs and longings are not always
met by the mother, a powerful need arises to manage and control
the unpredictable world, and her sense of self grows stronger. Her
mind learns to sense itself as separate and to cope with the fears
and frustrations of life by developing comforting memories,
language skills, and problem-solving strategies. The successful
sense of self identifies with maturing physical and social capacities.
The functioning of this central capacity, called "ego" by Freud, is
one of the most important definitions of mental health in Western
psychology.

A similar development of self is described in such Buddhist psychological texts as the Visuddhimagga. They tell how the original
radiance of beings born on earth becomes changed as they shift
from the ambrosia of mother's milk to solid food. Liking and dis-
liking grow stronger, and frustrations form. The world where all
the food originally tastes of jasmine flowers becomes harder. The

new beings become aware of their need to urinate and defecate. They become conscious of maleness and femaleness and brood over one another. They set up boundaries of "I" and "mine" and hit one another, creating the need for self-protection. Then they learn to restrain their impulses and inner leadership grows. To help navigate the world, the tentative sense of self grows stronger through these various stages.

From the smallest organisms through complex life-forms to human beings, the creation of boundaries and the perception of separateness is universal. The gift of Buddhist psychology is to take us to the next step, the evolutionary capacity to see beyond the separate self. The functional self, even at its most healthy, is not who we are. And to the extent that we adults remain caught and identified with any of the earlier stages of development, our suffering is perpetuated. Unlike its Western counterpart, Buddhist psychology recognizes that the ordinary process of development does not end the story. From a functional self, it offers a path to the discovery of selflessness. It shows us how the sense of self is created moment by moment. Then it dissolves identification and shows the joyful openness which exists beyond the self.

When we compare the understanding of self in Buddhist and Western psychology, the language can be confusing. For example, there is a dual use of the psychological concept of ego. Technically, in Western psychology, ego describes a healthy organizing aspect of mind. But in common spiritual parlance, ego has a more negative connotation, as in egotistical, selfish. Similarly, in describing the self, we find a sometimes bewildering multiplicity of terms, all the way from the healthy sense of self to the Buddhist description of no-self. The following diagram offers some clarification:

WESTERN PSYCHOLOGY

EGO—Theoretical Use	*HEALTHY SENSE OF SELF*
Used to describe the necessary organizing function of the mind. Regulates energies from superego (conditioned beliefs) and id (unconscious drives). There can be a healthy ego or a fragile, needy ego.	Functional ability to direct life, deal with frustrations, marshal resources, cope with conflict, work, love, create, and care for self and others.

BUDDHIST PSYCHOLOGY

EGO—Common Spiritual Use	*MENTAL HEALTH*
Used to describe states of clinging and identification and the qualities of self-importance and self-centeredness that arise from the small sense of self. Derives from illusion of separation and the anxiety it creates.	Maturing of healthy mental qualities such as wisdom, confidence, composure, flexibility, love, integrity, insight, and generosity.

NON-SELF

Discovery that sense of self and separation is tentative, false, created by clinging and identification. Release from identification with self brings the highest mental health, freedom, compassion, and joy.

IDENTIFICATION

When we first hear them, the teachings of non-self can arouse confusion or even fear. We might fear that non-self means the loss of our self, as if we were going to die. But the psychology of non-self is quite different. In practice, we don't have to change or get rid of anything. We merely learn to see through the false ideas of our self. We discover that we can let go of the limited sense of self, that grasping and identification are optional.

To examine this process of identification, let yourself play with it as you read. Imagine you are this book. Identify with it. Pretend it is you. How do you feel as a book? *I am a new book. I have a nice cover. I am full of words and understanding. Some people are interested in me. I like to be read. Maybe I'll become a big seller, famous. Maybe not.* Now notice what happens when you close the book. Close it gently. *I like to be respected.* Open it again and slam it shut. Toss it under a cushion or hide it among other books. How does this feel? *I don't like to be slammed shut, I don't want to be put away and lost, I don't like being dropped or hidden.* Now stop identifying with the book. Now it is just a book. Open and close it again. Put it away or hide it. Notice how different this feels. The book is not you.

This process of identification happens all the time. The Indian guru with whom I studied, Sri Nisargadatta, used to laugh and say—"You identify with everything so easily—with your body, your thoughts, your opinions, your roles—and so you suffer. I have released all identification." He would explain by holding up his hand. "Look how my thumb and forefinger touch. When I identify with my forefinger I am the feeler and the thumb the object that I experience. Reverse the identification and I am the thumb, feeling this forefinger as an object. I find that somehow by shifting the focus of attention I become the very thing I look at . . . I call this capacity of entering other focal points of consciousness love. You may give it any name you like. Love says, 'I am everything.' Wisdom says, 'I am nothing.' Between these two my life flows."

The ability to shift identities does not belong only to Indian gurus. It is a human skill. Many tasks cultivate an ability to enter into other identities. The best animal trackers become the animal they are following. Skillful detectives get inside the identity of their quarry. Actors succeed by their abilities to convincingly enter other identities. A mother naturally and instinctively identifies with her baby and knows why she is crying. Lovers say their hearts beat as one.

This healthy release of identification is not the self-estrangement of a psychotic looking at his hand as a foreign object. That is a misguided disconnection, the result of delusion and pathology. Nor is the release of identification a denial of the marvelous singular and unique essence of every individual. Our uniqueness remains, but without self-centered grasping and fear. We discover that our identity is more tentative, fluid like a river, each moment born anew. Wisdom says we are nothing. Love says we are everything. Between these two our life flows.

IDENTIFICATION WITH ROLE AND IMAGE

We can study identification directly by examining the many roles life gives us to play. At times, for example, I can sense myself as a man, son, parent, worker, student, husband, father, teacher, taxpayer, healer, patient, citizen, rebel, and member of a particular tribe, ethnic group, and religion. All are roles. Each arises due to circumstances and conditions. When we are young we feel the role of son or daughter most strongly when we are with our parents. We try to fulfill it and behave accordingly. Yet when our parents are absent and we are playing with our friends, our role as son or daughter drops away—unless, of course, we have a mother who, because of her own shaky identity, insists that we think about her all the time.

For forty hours a week, many of us enact our role as worker or provider. Yet to the extent that we cling to any of these identities, we suffer. If I try to keep my role as Buddhist teacher when I come home, it is a disaster. If I offer my frazzled wife Buddhist teachings on patience or generosity, she will feel patronized and simply remind me that it's my turn to water the garden and do the dishes. My daughter does not want a teacher of meditation or a psychologist; she wants an ordinary father who will listen, understand her experiences, and be playful, supportive, and sympathetic. When I am a partner, husband, and father, the three of us learn from each other. If a policewoman can't relax and be just a human being when she's out with her friends, she is imprisoned by her identity. If a CEO can't let go of his work when it's time to care for his son, they both suffer. I think of a cartoon I saw of a family on a Martha's Vineyard beach. Everyone is in swimsuits except the father. He is wearing his three-piece business suit and holding his briefcase. His wife is laughing, "Just because you go to the office every day . . ." The cartoon is funny, but it has tragic undertones.

To be wise we need to be able to enter each role fully, with awareness and compassion, and to let it go when our part is done. When we marry we have to let go of being single. When our children become adults, we have to let go of our old role of helping manage their life. When we take a new job or leave one, retire, or change from employee to manager, we need to let one role go and take up another. We can be free only if underneath all these temporary roles we do not forget that they are not who we really are.

In the same way that we identify with a role, we can identify with a self-image. Do I look intelligent, attractive, strong? Usually we worry in this way because we also feel the opposite qualities in ourselves. So to compensate, we create a self-image. A colleague of mine found these compensatory thoughts so frequent in his meditation, he began to humorously name them each time they arose: "Looking good, looking good." In simply seeing the constant struggle to look good, he felt more compassion and ease.

As a public speaker, I have learned to pay particular attention to the times when I feel nervous. For me that is a sure sign that I'm identified, worried about how I will look. In this state, I'm not really open to others. At these moments I directly experience how these thoughts create suffering. I hold my worry with a kind attention. Then I remember that it is my job to teach meditation, not to teach Jack Kornfield. In a moment I relax. I become more fully present. As Pema Chödrön tells us, "Being preoccupied with self-image is like coming upon a tree of singing birds while wearing earplugs." When we release our grasping of self-image there is a huge relief, and the world opens itself to us again.

Another way we create identity is seeing ourself as a member of a particular ethnic group, religion, tribe, caste, and class. I can identify myself as a middle-class, university-educated American. I can identify with being a Buddhist. I can identify with my ethnic roots as a Jewish person with Russian and Turkish ancestors. Each identification is a description of a particular circumstance and social structure, but on a deeper level they too are tentative, an illusion. Sometimes tribe and ethnic descriptions are used in healthy ways: to honor our culture, to awaken dignity and respect, to value our deep connection with others like ourselves.

But these same distinctions can be used for racist and discriminatory purposes, creating enormous suffering. Ethnic, religious, and tribal identifications are repeatedly exploited for power and security, for separating "us" from "them." Modern demagogues have used this identification to stir up powerful hatred of "the other." Hate mongers so successfully inflamed the feelings of Bosnians, Serbs, and Croats that they created the recent cycle of horrendous wars and ethnic cleansings. Hindu fundamentalists fan tension between Hindus and Muslims in India, all to gain political power. Here in the United States, similar fears and identifications are exploited in the conflicts between established citizens and new immigrants. Working with gang members, I see this all the time. Young men from the same neighborhood are forced to identify as either Crips or Bloods. At times their very life depends on a secret sign or the color of a jacket. At the root, these identifications are not who we really are.

In one of the most revolutionary statements of all time, the Buddha urged every one of us to see through the blindness of identification with role and caste, with race and belief. He declared: "Since you are searching for understanding of self, don't ask about caste or class, riches or birth, but instead ask about heart and conduct. Look at the flames from a fire. Where does the brightness arise? From the nature of wood—and it doesn't matter what kind of wood. In the same way the bright heart of wisdom can shine from wood of every sort. It is through virtuous conduct, through loving-kindness and compassion, and through understanding of truth that one becomes noble."

As we examine our self-image, our tribe, our roles, we can acknowledge that they are tentative. We can learn to honor them without being completely identified and lost in them. When Shakespeare was writing his plays, the limitations were only his imagination and the wide range of theatrical possibilities. But sometimes he directed his own plays, and then, while he could make certain choices, he had to follow the common script used by all the actors. In this role his freedom was curtailed. At still other times, Shakespeare himself became an actor. Then his only freedom was to vary his interpretation and recitation of his lines. But in each of these roles Shakespeare knew who he was. Inwardly, he was not limited to the role and the script.

In each of our lives we will have periods when it seems that we are the author, with great freedom to choose a direction. And then there will be times when more limited roles must be fulfilled: parent, breadwinner, citizen, community member, contemplative. A mature life requires an ability to enter each of the roles given to us. Freedom arises when we hold them lightly, when we see them for what they are.

IDENTIFICATION WITH SELF

After more than a century of looking for it, brain researchers have long since concluded that there is no conceivable place for a self to be located in the physical brain, and that it simply does not exist.
—Time *magazine, 2002*

Now we have to wrestle with one of the deepest and most demanding aspects of Buddhist psychology, the experience of non-self. Ajahn Chah said, "You have to consider and contemplate this slowly; you can't just think about this or your head will explode." It turns out that it is not just our roles and self-images that are tentative, without solidity. Our very sense of self is at its base untrue, only a concept. Buddhist psychology calls this selflessness or no-self. Ordinarily we identify with our habitual ways of acting, perceiving, thinking. Our body, thoughts, feelings, and personality all seem to be us, ours. And yet, upon examination, all these are also tentative, subject to change. We might be sick one year and healthy the next. We might be anxious and depressed at one stage of our life and confident at another. Even though we are reclusive for years, we might change to become more social, but we continue to think of ourself as a shy person. We take each identity to be who we are, but in truth we are not fixed in this way or that.

An older man, a lifetime smoker, was hospitalized with emphysema after a series of small strokes. Sitting beside his bed, his daughter urged him, as she had often done, to give up smoking. He refused and asked her to buy him some more cigarettes. He told her, "I'm a smoker this life, and that's how it is." But several days later he had another small stroke, apparently in one of the memory areas of the brain. Then he stopped smoking for good—but not because he decided to. He simply woke up one morning and forgot that he was a smoker.

We do not have to wait for a stroke to learn to let go of our identification with body and mind. We can train ourselves to release clinging to the body. Otherwise, as our body changes weight, gets sick, or ages, we will suffer. We must care for our body, but if we grasp an image of it, it will be a problem for us. Joelle, a forty-seven-year-old Buddhist practitioner, developed multiple sclerosis, which progressed rapidly. In the first few years she lost her balance, then she couldn't walk well or carry things, and finally she needed a wheelchair. As she got weaker she felt more and more apart from the world. She felt ashamed, as if there were something intrinsically wrong with her.

Then she came to a retreat with the American spiritual teacher Ram Dass, whose books (starting with *Be Here Now*) and lectures have inspired a generation of meditators. After more than thirty years of teaching and service to the poor, Ram Dass had had a major stroke. He too was in a wheelchair, his speech was impaired, and yet he was bright and joyful and free. He said, "If I take my body to be who I am, I am in trouble. But I have learned this is not who I am." Joelle's life was transformed by this encounter.

I remember speaking with Ram Dass when he first returned to public teaching, two years after his stroke. At this point, his speech still came painfully slowly; his legendary wit and spiritual perspective were impeded by a struggle to find the simplest words. When I asked him how it was to start teaching again he replied that it was hard. "Because," he went on with a smile, "they want me to be Ram Dass, and I'm not him anymore."

When we inquire carefully into the question of identity, the creation of self is discovered to be a moment-to-moment process. Like the meticulous observation of lunch I described in Chapter 4, we can examine our experience and see how every moment is comprised of many microscopic events of bodily sense impressions, feelings, perceptions, and thoughts. These events arise and pass quite simply. And then we can also notice how the sense of self is added to them and "I" is created. We identify with some part of our experience, owning the feelings, the beliefs, the inner narrative and stories as "me" and "mine." As soon as this identification, this self-view, arises, it creates the illusion of separateness, of "I" and "other." But the self and sense of other are not solid, any more than Texas and Oklahoma are different when we are standing at the state border. Without adding this identification, each moment's experience is just what it is, "suchness," without anyone owning it.

One of Ajahn Chah's favorite ways of teaching this truth was to get his students to question their social identities. Sometimes he would start by simply exaggerating our roles, introducing us like stock characters in a play: "That monk is my full professor, our resident intellectual over there. He has two graduate degrees, thinks all the time. I don't know how it all fits in his head. And this monk we call 'Sleepy'—he sleeps all the time, even when he sits up. And that one, he's a tough guy. He loves to fight, he's in conflict with everything. And this is our depressed monk, never smiles. The world's really heavy and he carries it about in his monk's bag. And me, I'm the teacher. That's a good one." Then Ajahn Chah would laugh with a great sense of freedom and say, "It's simple—be the knower, not the owner." When the thinking mind is quiet and the attention careful, all of a sudden we "get it." We take a step and realize that no one took it—there are just the sensations of body movement along with sights, perception, impulses. Thoughts and opinions arise but they think themselves and disappear, "like bubbles on the Ganges," says the Buddha. When we do not cling to them, they lose their hold on us. In the light of awareness, the constructed self of our identification relaxes. And what is seen is just the process of life, not self nor other, but life unfolding as part of the whole.

It is critical to note here that selflessness does not deny or reject our experience in any way. We don't get rid of anything. The experiences are the same. All that's changed is that we have stopped identifying with them, stopped calling them "me" or "mine." Some people feel as though a huge weight has lifted—they sob with compassion for themselves, realizing the illusory burden they've been carrying. More often we simply relax and discover a natural ease as we let go of the limited sense of self.

As a Buddhist psychologist, I am aware that sometimes when people hear about the teaching of selflessness, they can become agitated or afraid. This is because focusing on selflessness is not always the right medicine. Speaking of selflessness when a person feels shaky, traumatized, and fragile can bring up feelings of disorientation and even terror. At such times, what is needed is safety and a feeling of balance. We can provide this balance through our reassuring presence, through the reminders of compassion and spacious awareness. But even those who are fragile can eventually benefit from the freedom beyond self-image, beyond the illusion of self.

I think of Katherine, who had gone through several years of depression. Now feeling better, she was attending a weeklong retreat. After an afternoon meditation, she came to see me, worried about selflessness, asking, "Who will I be if I lose myself? How will I operate in the world?" From the point of view of her limited self, it seemed threatening and impossible. I told her to relax and not to struggle to understand, just to stay present with compassion. A few days later she walked in to see me with a big grin on her face. She said, "I was practicing mindfulness and after a very quiet sitting, I was getting up to go into the garden. When the intention came to get up, the body rose and I realized that it all happens by itself. I felt so liberated, so light, so free. I just stood there and laughed out loud. The whole idea of believing in a self was like a wonderful joke. It's obvious now." She smiled, twirled in a circle, and danced her way laughing out of the room. Like Katherine, we fear the loss of ourself. But the reality turns out to be quite different and perfectly safe. We relax and discover we can let go of the false sense of self created by identification.

SELFLESSNESS GIVES BIRTH TO THE TENDER HEART

We have all had the experience of being with people who belong to life in an easy and flexible way. They don't take things personally. They are gracious, receptive, present, yet not rigid. There is not a lot of clinging to their point of view, not a strong attachment to the way things should be, not a rigid grasping of "me" or "mine."

Dipama Barua of Calcutta, one of my teachers and a revered Buddhist elder, exemplified this spirit for me. She was both a meditation master at the highest level and a loving grandmother. When I visited her apartment she would teach in a practical and modest way. Around her was a palpable sense of stillness and profound well-being. It was not the well-being of outer security—she lived in a tiny apartment in one of Calcutta's poor neighborhoods. Nor was it the well-being of rank and position—she was mostly uncelebrated and unknown. Though she was a remarkably skillful teacher, her selflessness bloomed in her smile, in her care for others, in her openness to whatever was needed. She was both empty and radiantly present.

Dipama's heart seemed to pervade her whole body, the whole room, all who came into her orbit. Her presence had a big impact on others. Those who lived nearby said the whole apartment block became harmonious after she moved in. One day a student complained that ordinarily his mind was filled with thoughts and plans, judgments and regrets. He wondered what it was like to live more selflessly. So he asked Dipama directly about the alternative: "What is in your mind?" She smiled and said, "In my mind are only three things: loving-kindness, concentration, and peace." These are the fruits of selflessness. With selflessness there is less of us and yet presence, connectedness, and freedom come alive.

Selflessness is not a pathologically detached state, disconnected from the world. Nor is it a state where we are caught in a new spiritual identity, "See how selfless I am." Selflessness is always here. In any moment we can let go and experience life without calling it "me" or "mine." As the beloved Tibetan master Kalu Rinpoche has said, "When you understand, you will see that you are nothing. And being nothing, you are everything." When identification with the small sense of self drops away, what remains is the spacious heart that is connected with all things.

PRACTICE: THE CREATION AND DISSOLUTION OF SELF

To say there is a self is not true. To say there is no self is not true.
Then what is true?
—Ajahn Chah

The creation of self is a process that can be observed moment to moment. It arises when we identify with some part of our experience and call it "me" or "mine": my body, my personality, my views, my things. We can become mindful of the creation and dissolution of the sense of self. We can see what it's like when the identification with self is strong, when it is weak, when it is absent.

Choose a day to study the sense of self. Every half hour check in and notice how strong the sense of self is. At which times of day is it strongest? In what roles/situations? How does it feel when self is strong? How does the body feel? How do others respond to this strong sense of self? What would happen in the same situation without a strong identification with the self?

Notice when the clinging to self is mild or absent. Is it reduced when you relax or when you prepare to sleep? How is it when you take your role lightly? Let yourself experiment with caring but not taking things so personally. Can you operate well when the sense of self is not strong or even absent? Play with the sense of self. Notice what ideas, sensations, emotions you hold most strongly and identify with. Which ones do you easily release and let go? How about if you reverse it, release the strong ones and identify with the weak ones?

Become mindful of the comparing mind. See how the sense of self arises when we compare ourself with others. How does this form of self feel when it is grasped? How is it when it is absent? Then notice what happens when you are criticized. If someone insults or disparages you, notice the strength of the sense of self. With strong identification you get anxious, angry, upset. Without much identification you can laugh.

Finally, try this. Pretend there is no self. Let all experience be like a movie or a dream, without grasping or taking it seriously. See how it lightens the heart. Instead of being the star of your own movie, pretend you are in the audience. Watch how all the players act, including "yourself." Relax without a sense of self and rest in awareness. See how your life plays out without grasping.

6

FROM THE UNIVERSAL TO THE PERSONAL
A PSYCHOLOGY OF PARADOX

Form is not different from emptiness
Emptiness is not different from form
Yet form is form and emptiness is emptiness.
—Heart Sutra

You should know both the universal and the personal, the realm of forms
and the freedom to not cling to them. The forms of the world have
their place, but in another way there is nothing there. To be free, we
need to respect both of these truths.
—Ajahn Chah

In the simplest language, we are spiritual beings incarnated into human form. We need to remember our zip code as well as our Buddha nature. Any psychology that denies our spiritual nature cannot help us fulfill our deepest potential. But, to be true and complete, a spiritual psychology must also honor our human incarnation in the body, in feelings, society, and the earth itself. We are creatures of this paradox, this interpretation of form and emptiness.

Buddhist psychology embraces this multilevel perspective. We have seen how consciousness, like light, functions on one level as particles and on another like waves. So too our existence has both a universal and a personal dimension. This psychological paradox is called the Two Truths. Sometimes these two dimensions, two truths, are mistranslated as the "absolute" and the "relative." This mistranslation makes it appear that the absolute or universal has higher value than the relative or personal, but they are actually two complementary aspects of reality. Ajahn Chah called an understanding of the universal and personal dimensions essential for awakening.

Here is a sixth principle of Buddhist psychology:

6   Our life has universal and personal nature. Both dimensions must be respected if we are to be happy and free.

THE UNIVERSAL DIMENSION

Experience this world as a bubble, a wave, an illusion, a dream.
—The Dhammapada

The universal dimension is the big picture. When we remember the selflessness of all things, our life falls into perspective. The universal dimension reminds us that all things on earth are transitory, tentative, appearing out of emptiness and then disappearing.

People who are about to die face this truth. When Michele, a Buddhist practitioner, was dying of cancer and her body was wasting away, I visited her and she said, "As I was meditating last week, it became clear to me that I am not my body. But then today I realized I was not all the ideas I have about myself either. Nobody is. We have so many ideas about each other, based on our age, our personalities, our history, yet they are so tentative, we are only acting that way for a little while. When Shakespeare wrote, 'All the world's a stage,' he saw it so clearly." Michele was opening to the wisdom of the universal perspective.

There is nobility in speaking this truth. "Praise and blame, gain and loss, pleasure and pain are always changing. Notice how nothing lasts. It will put your successes and failures into perspective." Ajahn Chah said this to encourage us. His perspective was not nihilistic—he wasn't saying that life doesn't matter—but very practical. When the food was scanty and bad at the monastery, when the monsoon rains seemed endless, when news of the world brought grief, when certain monks got into conflict, Ajahn Chah offered a more universal perspective.

"We are not here just to gain pleasure and avoid any pain," Ajahn Chah would say. "No one can do that for very long, right? We are here to grow in wisdom and compassion, to grow in the path of awakening. Just remember the universal truth, then everything gets easier."

From the universal perspective, all things that are born eventually die. Death comes to our best friends and family members, sometimes even to young children. When we grieve, we join in the universal grieving for all those who have died. This is not a tragedy; it is wisdom. From the universal perspective, life is all the more precious and beautiful because it is so fleeting.

One of my teachers, Maha Ghosananda, was known as the Gandhi of Cambodia. He worked with those who had survived the 1975–88 genocide in Cambodia, when the country was taken over by radical Khmer Rouge Communists who killed two million people, including almost everyone who was educated. Those left alive after this holocaust had witnessed their villages and temples burned and their families killed. Wherever he went, Ghosananda would teach the survivors practices of compassion and loving-kindness for their own loss and the sorrows of everyone else who had suffered as they had. Then he would get them to chant with him, "Everything that arises, passes away." He went on, "You have lost so much. Now you know how precious everything is in this world. You must love again and let new things grow." Ghosananda saw their secret beauty and resilient spirit. He encouraged them to rebuild their communities, re-create temples and schools, and find caring families for the orphaned children.

The same universal healing was needed for Carla, whose best friend died in the same car accident in which Carla was hurt. A tire blew out on the car just ahead. It was no one's fault. Death happens. Carla needed to grieve, to heal, to remake her life. Over the months, her meditations helped her to grieve. Through her Buddhist practice, Carla began to reflect on the universal nature of birth and death. She saw how death comes to everyone all around the world, whether expected or not. It helped her pass through the trauma and grief and begin again.

Without a big picture, the inevitable changes in life can overwhelm us. But when we lose a job or win a promotion, end a marriage, have a grandchild, get sick or get well, it is not just personal. It is the dance of life. This broad perspective is especially important in the most extreme crises.

Recently I shared an evening's teaching with Pema Chödrön in San Francisco. During the question period a woman asked about the suicide of her partner several weeks before. The rawness of her grief was agonizing. Pema began with the need for compassion. After that, I added ways to help her release guilt and find forgiveness. Then I asked how many others among the three thousand present in that auditorium had had a family member or close loved one die from suicide. Almost three hundred people stood up. I suggested that the bereaved questioner look around and feel the compassion and support they offered her. The room became silent. It was a powerful moment for everyone to share.

When I work with parents who have lost children, I send them to groups of other bereaved parents. They need to be with others who have survived such grievous loss, to learn that sometimes, no matter what we do in this life, children die. When I work with veterans or suicide survivors or anorexics, I recommend that they form a connection with others who share their experience. When we share our suffering we remember that it is no longer "me" or "them," but "us." Both Buddhist and Western psychology understand the healing power of a universal perspective.

THE SACREDNESS OF FORM

Teach us to care and not to care.
—T. S. Eliot

If you tell a Zen master everything is like a dream, she will take her stick and whack you over the head. Then she will ask, "Is that a dream?" Focusing on the big picture alone is not enough. Form must be honored. A mature psychology requires us to see life from multiple perspectives. Ajahn Chah demonstrated this when he held out his hand fully open, flat, and explained that you can rest things on an open hand, but its use is limited. Similarly, if you hold it fully closed, it can strike things, but its use is also very limited. It is only because we can open and close our hand in response to circumstances that our hand works for us.

Sometimes people make the mistake of clinging to the universal level. Like the always open hand, this is a problem. Buddhist texts say that form arises out of emptiness, yet the world of form must be met on its own terms. This is sometimes called *suchness*. Things are the way they are. From the universal level, we have to return to the world of form and particulars, without being caught in them.

Once a villager came to Ajahn Chah to ask for help with a woman who had lost her mind. In the West we might call her manic or delusional. For days she had been wildly spouting obscenities mixed with Buddhist teachings on emptiness, running around, up all night, disturbing everyone. Many of the villagers felt she was possessed by an evil spirit. Ajahn Chah said he would see her.

He told his monks to quickly dig a big hole next to where he sat. Other monks built a big fire. "Put a huge water pot on the fire," he said. Soon a group of men and women pulled the poor woman to him and asked him to rid her of the evil spirit.

Ajahn Chah tried to talk to her, but she continued shouting obscenities and talking about emptiness and meaninglessness. He told the monks to hurry up and make the fire hotter and dig the hole deeper. He said that the only way to get rid of such a spirit was to put the woman in the hole, pour boiling water on her, and bury her. That should do it, he said. As the water got hot, he said, "You can carry her there in a minute."

All of a sudden the woman became very quiet and docile. She sat up and talked a bit to him. He sent most of the people away and began to ask what had happened, listening with real compassion. He heard her whole story. Later he told the superstitious villagers that fear of boiling to death had released her from the evil spirit. What it had really done, he told us, was awaken her instinct for self-preservation. Then he could begin to listen to her and direct her to the help she needed.

This is not to suggest that such a radical intervention would be right in our circumstances. Within his cultural context, Ajahn Chah was a kind of shaman. He knew that something in this woman's life had to die. Because Ajahn Chah knew that form is empty, he could play within it in an intuitive and wise way. Yet he never forgot the importance of honoring the tangible realities of the world. On one level, everything is like a dream. On another, what we do matters immensely.

When I came back to the United States after my years in the monastery, which had included a yearlong silent retreat, I was lost in the universal side. My mind was silent and empty, and everything appeared quite dream-like. From this perspective, the Western world seemed speedy and driven. It was appallingly materialistic, filled with images of violence, obsessed with success; it seemed to have lost its spiritual understanding altogether.

I had no idea how to fit back in. In my book *A Path with Heart*, I told the story of going to meet my sister-in-law at Elizabeth Arden in New York. I was still in monk's robes, and when I went upstairs to wait at the spa, it was hard to tell who looked weirder—me, a barefoot, shaven-headed mendicant, or the women with avocado and mud on their faces and their hair in fishing-reel contraptions.

After five years in Thailand, it was hard to reenter the world of form. I had to get a job, find a place to live, open a bank account, make a thousand decisions. I struggled with all these details because they didn't seem to matter very much in the big picture. Later I heard a story about Taizan Maezumi Roshi, who asked a student carpenter whether the remodeling of the zendo would be done soon. "It's basically done," replied the student. "There are just some details to finish up." The Zen master stood shocked for a moment and then announced, "But details are all there are!"

It took me years of work and practice in the world to learn respect for the details of work and money and relationship. Since then, as a teacher I have seen many people like myself who have used spirituality as a way to avoid the world of form. There was Mark, an aging but charming Sufi practitioner, a house-sitter and gardener. Mark had fathered a child in Germany, but he never paid any attention to him, never had any money to share with him. To Mark it was all a part of God's dance, a dream-like play. But when he was honest, Mark actually wanted a home, a settled life, but didn't know how to do it. And there was Theresa, whose depression was reinforced by the Buddhist teachings of suffering and impermanence. Theresa didn't know how to make the changes that would have transformed her life, so she justified her stuckness with spiritual platitudes. "It's all just impermanent and empty," she would say to make herself feel better.

The problem was that Theresa and Mark were not happy in their choices. Their past wounds and trauma kept them stuck on the universal level, spiritualizing their problems. This is common in spiritual circles. Whether it's a Buddhist saying that "everything is a dream" or a Christian who believes that "it's all God's will," these truths can be misused to refuse personal responsibility. Even the most genuine inner spiritual experience won't help us if we place ourselves above the world of form. As Alan Jones, dean of Grace Cathedral in San Francisco, once commented, "Spiritual experience can actually lead to inflation. There's no one more insufferable than someone who thinks they're more enlightened than anybody else, without a certain sense of humor. I know people who on one level are deeply at peace and enlightened, and yet go crazy if they miss a bus. On one level we may still be five years old, and on another level be a saint. That's what keeps us humble. That's why religion is very funny."

One day a student came to see Ajahn Chah and urgently confided, "Ajahn, I have attained the first level of enlightenment!" And

Ajahn Chah replied, "Well, that's a little better than being a dog, I guess." This comparison is a terrible insult in Thailand, and not said lightly to anyone. Telling the story, Ajahn Chah smiled and said, "The student didn't like that, and he went away in a great huff. The 'enlightened one' was angry!"

We can't pretend we are too spiritual for any experience. If we are angry, Ajahn Chah said, we must admit it, look at its causes, know its particulars. If we are sad or frightened or ashamed or needy, this is our human condition, the perfect place to practice. Ajahn Chah insisted we could not find freedom and enlightenment somewhere else, only here and now. "It is here, in the world of form. Only in form can we develop integrity, patience, generosity, truthfulness, dedication, compassion, the great heart of a Buddha."

If we fear living the life we're in, Buddhist psychology insists we explore our resistance. If we are caught in fear of failure, in past trauma or insecurity, engaging the world can be difficult for us. We need to make conscious whatever keeps us from living fully.

Sharon, at age forty-eight, was a successful human resources director at a Silicon Valley firm. She was an experienced meditator, having done many silent mindfulness retreats and years of Tibetan Buddhist practice. On sabbatical, she came for our two-month spring retreat at Spirit Rock. Her first two weeks were filled with the usual ups and downs of body and memory release, the gradual settling down. When her mind became more silent, the boundaries of her sense of self began to evaporate. Her consciousness opened. She would look at an oak tree and feel her arms as the branches. She would breathe and the room breathed too. As she became ever more carefully attentive, an almost atomic level of perception was revealed to her. Each sound, each step, each sight broke apart like a pointillist painting. Over the weeks, her senses became a river of thousands of vibrating points of light. At first this was alarming, but with trust she let go into the changing river. One day both her self and the universe itself dissolved, dropping away into luminous emptiness. Later a tentative sense of self reappeared and she floated between form and emptiness for some days. She described it as "sitting like the Buddha," experiencing a joyful release, the sweet fruit of years of practice.

Several days later she came to see me, full of tears. From emptiness, she began to come back into her body. It was very hard. She
started weeping "for her life, which wasn't her life." Uncertain of
her meaning, I asked her to explain. She said that her father had always wanted a boy, so much so that (as her mother had told her)
when the hospital called him at home to say his wife had given birth
to a beautiful baby girl, he misheard them and thought they had said
a boy. He even called his friends to announce the birth of his son.

Sharon, an only child, was raised to be that son. And she succeeded, doing well in sports and school, tailoring her mannerisms
in tomboy fashion to gain her father's love. This had flavored her
whole life. Now she looked at me with innocent eyes. In the days
before, the emptiness of self had been apparent. Now she was being
reborn into the fullness of form. At this moment, she looked very
young, like a newborn. I told her this was how she appeared to me
and that I wanted to properly welcome her here on this earth as a
beautiful girl. I felt like an honored witness to her birth, as if I were
in the role of her father. Her eyes moistened, her face grew soft,
and then she told me that just before coming to speak with me she
had stepped out of the shower and spontaneously stood naked for
a time in front of the big mirror in the women's bathroom. For the
first time in her life, she was appreciating her feminine body. Then
she stood up and I too admired her and welcomed her, only wishing I had a pink blanket to wrap around her shoulders.

This was the beginning of a whole new life for Sharon. She
began playfully exploring her incarnation as a woman, outwardly
with a new wardrobe and hairstyle. More importantly, she felt the
inner flowering of her feminine nature in all she did.

BETWEEN THE UNIVERSAL AND THE PERSONAL: THE REALM OF CONCEPTS

Ajahn Chah used to say, "Use concepts, but do not be fooled by
them." The Buddha explained, "When I say Ananda is going to
the village for alms, I understand these five empty, evanescent
processes of body, feelings, perceptions, thought, and conscious-

ness are going to the village, but for convenience I use the term *Ananda.*"

When people spoke loosely with Ajahn Chah, generalizing about European people or Thai people, he would smile and ask, "The pious Thai farmer to your left or the well-known Thai gangster in the local prison?" If you talked about being sad or happy all the time, he might ask, "All the time?" Even in our deepest grief, there come moments when we are busy and forget we are grieving. Even in our greatest joy, some part of us wonders, "How long can this last? What comes next?"

Buddhist psychology believes that healing occurs as we learn to move from the realm of concepts to the world of direct experience. Our mental concepts and ideas about things, about people, objects, or feelings, are static and unchanging. But the reality of experience is an ever-changing river. Direct perception drops beneath the names of things to show us their ephemeral, mysterious nature. When we bring our attention to the direct perception of experience, we become more alive and free.

When we hold an apple in our hand, we can call it by its name, *apple.* Even if we specify that it is a Macintosh or Winesap or Rome Beauty, it remains for us basically an apple. *Apple* is the name, the concept. The concept doesn't change from day to day: an apple in our lunch is an apple, and even cut up, it's still pieces of an apple.

But in the reality of experience, there is no solid apple. The sight of an apple is actually a subtly changing visual pattern, colors of rose and crimson, red and gold, luminous hues that continually transform as the light changes or we move our head slightly. As we pick up the apple, the hard yet soft, fragrant and cool waxy skin is changing moment by moment. We then experience the wafting smell, the crunch of its flesh, the complex flavors that unfold in our mouth, cool and delicate, as the apple disappears into water and sweetness in our body. The concept of "apple" is static, an object in thought. But directly seeing, holding, eating an apple is a succession of minute, ever-changing, subtle colors, shapes, and perceptions that are never still for a moment. Everything is like this: on one level a fixed, seemingly solid world of concepts, but on another, the immediate reality, a stream of a thousand sense perceptions appearing and disappearing moment after moment. In direct perception there is no solid apple, and no solid one who perceives it.

Paradoxically, of course, we need to use concepts all the time. We need to honor nationality, ownership, time, and the concept of self, even though they do not describe the direct experience of life. With wisdom we can learn to use concepts without being fooled, lost in them. We have to remember our address and social security number even though on another level there is no separate, independent self. When we meet a person, we can see how the concepts of race, class, and gender are true, but they are only a limited part of the story. Beyond concepts we can see into the true nature of the person before us.

In the same way, wisdom reveals that "to possess" is provisional. We do not possess our house, our car, or our children. We are simply in relation to them. The more tightly we cling to the idea that we "own" or possess, the greater the unhappiness we reap. With this understanding we can live as stewards, caring for things yet not being trapped by the concepts of self and possession.

Or consider our common concept of money. Because of our collective agreement, we give immense value to these small, printed pieces of colored paper. But we could change our agreement to value candle wax or even cow patties, and if everyone held this view, they would be our money. "How many cow patties are you worth?" Ajahn Chah used to ask.

Even time is a concept. In reality we are always in the eternal present. The past is just a memory, the future just an image or thought. All our stories about past and future are only ideas, arising in the moment. Our modern culture is so tyrannized by goals, plans, and improvement schemes that we constantly live for the future. But as Aldous Huxley reminded us in his writings, "An idolatrous religion is one in which time is substituted for eternity . . . the idea of endless progress is the devil's work, even today demanding human sacrifice on an enormous scale."

At the start of a retreat, participants are often invited to remove their watches. In mindfulness practice, we train ourselves to live here and now. For this is where the heart becomes free. The abode of wisdom is now, the changing circumstances of this day are now. When we are not worried about time, we come alive in the present.

Living in the present became essential for Margot after her husband, Brian, was diagnosed with pancreatic cancer. It was an early diagnosis, and after his tumor was removed his doctors gave him a 50 percent chance of living for three years. Brian, an easygoing man with a history of meditation practice and a good support network that helped him, maintained an attitude of balanced acceptance. Margot was having more trouble than her husband. She couldn't sleep. She worried all the time. After several panic attacks, her distress alarmed her friends and grown children. She came to see me.

We began to work on both the universal and the personal level. Brian might well die. Death is natural. Many people have cancer and some will die this year. Some will live years longer and then die. So will she. This is our human lot. We sat with all her pain— her fears of death, loneliness, and abandonment, her regrets— breathing, holding it all with mindfulness and compassion.

At the same time I invited Margot to practice living in the present. Practicing mindfulness, she began to be able to feel her body and focus on its sensations. She could feel her tension, but she could also hear the screech of a scrub jay outside the window and see the slant of the morning light. Coming into her senses, she could see her worry and panic as the product of fearful, imagined stories, not as present truths. Margo also learned mindful walking to feel her steps, to touch the earth in the here and now. Through Brian's treatment and hospital visits, his long struggle with cancer, Margo worked diligently with mindfulness to stay in the present. She said it was her only relief.

So much of the profound dissatisfaction in modern life arises because we live in increasingly disconnected ways. It is time for us to regain our connection to life. Renowned astrophysicist Victor Weisskopf tells this story:

Several years ago I received an invitation to give a series of lectures at the University of Arizona at Tucson. I was delighted to accept because it would give me a chance to visit the Kitts Peak astronomical observatory, which had a very powerful telescope I had always wanted to look through. I asked my hosts to arrange an evening to visit the observatory so I could look directly at some interesting objects through the telescope. But I was told this would be impossible because the telescope was constantly in use for computer photography and other research activities. There was no time for simply looking at objects. "In that case," I replied, "I will not be able to come to deliver my talks." Within days I was informed that everything had been arranged according to my wishes. We drove up the mountain on a wonderfully clear night. The stars and the Milky Way glistened intensely and seemed almost close enough to touch. I entered the cupola and told the technicians who ran the computer-activated telescope that I wanted to see Saturn and a number of the galaxies. It was a great pleasure to observe with my own eyes and with the utmost clarity all the details I had only seen on photographs before. As I looked at all that, I realized that the room had begun to fill with people, and one by one they too peeked into the telescope. I was told that those were astronomers attached to the observatory, but they had never before had the opportunity of looking directly at the objects of their investigations.

When we remember who we really are, we bring together the universal with the personal. Instead of becoming more disembodied or rigidly spiritual, we have a sense of humor about the whole dance of life, and everything becomes easier and lighter. We can care for the hydrangeas in our garden, watch our cholesterol, speak out against injustice, and raise money for tsunami and earthquake survivors. And we can meet each person in his or her nobility and timeless beauty, beyond age, gender, and race. We can accept the ever-changing seasons of life and know their fleeting, ephemeral dance. Honoring the paradox of our true nature, we can laugh with wisdom and tenderly care for the precious days we are given.

PRACTICE: SEEING FROM THE UNIVERSAL PERSPECTIVE

Buddhist psychology is filled with practices that shift us to the universal perspective. In one practice, students contemplate the cycles of birth and death, imagining the possibility that they have been born many times. In this reflection you picture the circumstances of your current life as offering you a perfect chance to learn important and universal lessons. Then you sincerely ask yourself what these lessons might be.

Next, extend this universal perspective to a person close to you: a loved one, or a close friend. Sit quietly and picture them. Feel how you ordinarily relate to him or her. Now step back in your mind to consider the roles and identities that person inhabits: male or female, son or daughter, partner, friend, student, teacher, artist, athlete, employee, boss, successes and failures.

Step back further and contemplate the unfolding of the person's karma. See how they were born into a certain family; picture them as an infant, a child, a teenager, adult, an old person. Who are they really, underneath all the clay of their roles and life stages? What is their essence, their timeless spirit? What are they given an opportunity to learn? What is it like to relate to them outside of their roles, outside of time?

In the same way, you can bring a universal perspective to a problem, or to a situation where you are stuck in your life. Hold the difficult situation in your mind's eye as if in front of you. Now picture yourself near death at the end of your life, and reflect on how you see the problem. Then imagine how many other people have faced a similar problem. Look at it with the perspective of a hundred years from now. How does this difficulty appear? Finally, ask yourself how a universal perspective can bring a wise and heartfelt response to the difficulty you face.

MINDFULNESS: THE GREAT MEDICINE

II

7

THE LIBERATING POWER OF
MINDFULNESS

My friends, it is through the establishment of the lovely clarity of mindfulness
that you can let go of grasping after past and future, overcome
attachment and grief, abandon all clinging and anxiety, and awaken an
unshakable freedom of heart, here, now.
—Buddha

Establish a liberating clarity of mindfulness of the body, of the feelings,
of the mind and of the dharma.
—Digha Nikaya

In myths from around the world, men and women have searched for an elixir that will bring protection from suffering. Buddhist psychology's answer is mindfulness. How does mindfulness work? Let me illustrate with a story.

If you've ever seen the film *Gorillas in the Mist,* you know about Dian Fossey, the courageous field biologist who befriended a tribe of gorillas. Fossey had gone to Africa to continue the work of her mentor George Schaller, a renowned primatologist who had collected more intimate information about gorilla life than any scientist before him. When his colleagues asked how he was able to learn so much about these shy and elusive creatures, he attributed it to one simple thing: he didn't carry a gun.

Previous generations of biologists had entered the territory of these huge animals with the assumption that they were dangerous. So the scientists came with an aggressive spirit, large rifles in hand. The gorillas could sense the danger around these rifle-bearing men and kept a far distance. By contrast, Schaller—and later Fossey— entered their territory without weapons. They had to move slowly, gently, and above all respectfully toward these creatures. In time, sensing the benevolence of these humans, the gorillas allowed them to come among them and learn their ways. Sitting still, hour after hour, with careful, patient attention, Fossey finally understood what she saw: a whole new world of tribal and family relationships, unique personalities, habits, and communication. As the African American sage George Washington Carver explained, "Anything will give up its secrets if you love it enough."

Mindfulness is attention. It is a non-judging and respectful awareness. Unfortunately, much of the time we don't attend in this way. Instead, we continually react, judging whether we like, dislike, or can ignore what is happening. We evaluate ourselves and others with a stream of expectations, commentary, and criticism.

When people initially come to a meditation class to train in mindfulness, they hope to become calm and peaceful. Usually they are in for a big shock. The first hour of mindfulness meditation reveals its opposite, bringing an unseen stream of evaluation and judgment into stark relief. As the minutes pass, we may cycle between agitation and boredom. We hear a door slam and wish for quiet. Our knees hurt and we try to avoid the pain. We wish we had a better cushion. We can't feel our breath and we get frustrated. We notice our mind won't stop planning and we feel like a failure. Then we remember someone we're angry at and get upset, and if we notice how many judgments there are, we feel proud of ourself for noticing.

But like George Schaller, we can put aside these weapons of

judgment. We can become mindful. When we are mindful, it is as if we can bow to our experience without judgment or expectation. "Mindfulness," declared the Buddha, "is all helpful."

Here is a seventh principle of Buddhist psychology:

---

7   Mindful attention to any experience is liberating. Mindfulness brings perspective, balance, and freedom.

Paracelsus, the master healer of the Middle Ages, once declared: "The physician should speak of that which is invisible. What is visible should belong to his knowledge, and he should recognize illness, just as anyone who is not a physician can recognize illness from the symptoms. But this is far from what makes a physician. He becomes a physician only when he also knows that which is unnamed, invisible and immaterial, yet has its effects." So does mindfulness open us to that which is unseen in our experience.

Peter, a middle-aged computer designer, came to a meditation retreat looking for relief. He was coping with a recently failed business, a shaky marriage, and a sick mother. But meditation quickly became agony. The anger and disappointment that pervaded his current situation rose in the quiet room to fill his mind. His attempts to quiet himself by sensing his breath felt hopeless, and his attention repeatedly bounced away from his body like a tennis ball. Then it got worse. A restless woman seated nearby began to cough loudly and frequently. She began to fidget and move and cough more as the first day wore on.

Peter, who was struggling just to be with his own sorrow, became frustrated, angry, and, as she continued coughing, enraged. He sought my co-teacher Debra Chamberlin-Taylor and insisted that meditation was the wrong approach for him and he needed to leave. She asked Peter to close his eyes and mindfully notice the state of his body. It was filled with tension, hurting. With Debra's help he found he could hold the tension and hurt with a more accepting and kind attention. He breathed, relaxed a little, and recognized that the medicine he needed was nothing other than to understand his own pain.

The next instruction he was given was simple: to keep a gentle mindfulness on his body as he sat and to notice whatever happened. When he returned to the meditation hall, after only a few minutes his fidgety neighbor began a long coughing spell. With each cough Peter felt his own muscles clench and his breath stop. Now he became more curious, interested in how his body was reacting. He began to notice that hearing each cough produced an internal clenching and a wave of anger, which subsided as he practiced relaxing between the spells. Finally, at the end of the sitting period, he got up to walk down to the lunchroom. As he arrived, he noticed his tormentor, the cougher, in the line ahead of him. Immediately he noticed how, just seeing her, his stomach clenched and his breath stopped. Again, he relaxed. When he returned to the meditation hall after lunch he checked to see what time his name was listed for a private interview with his teacher. Farther down the same list he read the restless woman's name. Just seeing her name made his stomach clench and his breath tighten. Since he was still paying attention, he was able to relax again. He realized that his body had become a mirror, and that his mindfulness was showing him both the cause and the cure of his suffering, recognizing tension in the mind and consciously relaxing that tension.

As the retreat went on, his attention grew more precise. He noticed that his own anxious and angry thoughts about his family and business problems could trigger the same clenching and tightening as the woman's cough. He had always tried to have things under control. Now that his life had proved out of control, the habits of anger, blame, and judgment were tying him in knots. With each reaction, he could feel the knots arise. After each one he would pause mindfully and bring in a touch of ease. He began to trust mindfulness. By the close of the retreat, he was grateful to the restless woman near him. He wanted to thank her for her teaching.

With mindfulness Peter found relief. He also discovered the benefit of curiosity and openness, what Shunryu Suzuki famously called "beginner's mind." As he explains, "We pay attention with respect and interest, not in order to manipulate, but to understand what is true. And seeing what is true, the heart becomes free."

Mindfulness, which is to say patient, receptive, non-judging awareness, is important in Western psychotherapy as well. From the "even hovering attention" that Freud recommended to psychoanalysts to the "unconditional positive regard" of Carl Rogers and other humanistic psychologists to the "present centered awareness" of Gestalt, this open form of awareness is seen as a primary healing tool. Since 1980 nearly a thousand scientific papers have documented the effectiveness of mindfulness, often studying Western trainings that are based on a Buddhist approach. An important distinction to make, however, is that while Western psychology has focused primarily on the mindfulness of the therapist, Buddhist psychology asserts that the very foundation of well-being is a systematic training of mindfulness in the student. With mindfulness understanding unfolds naturally. As Buddhist teacher Sharon Salzberg quipped one day, "It's easy to teach. All you have to do is ask if they're being mindful."

MINDFULNESS AS FEARLESS PRESENCE

The art of living is neither careless drifting on the one hand nor fearful clinging on the other. It consists in being sensitive to each moment, in regarding it as utterly new and unique, in having the mind open and wholly receptive.
—Alan Watts

Sitting mindfully with our sorrows and fears, or with those of another, is an act of courage. It is not easy. Marge believed that confronting her rage might kill her. Jorgé's son's cystic fibrosis brought terrifying images of wheelchairs and early death. Perry was afraid to face his infidelities and sexual peculiarities. Jerry could hardly bear to think of the carnage he had seen during his work in Bosnia. For Angela, facing the recurrence of her cancer meant facing death.

With patience and courage, each of these people gradually learned how to sit firmly on the earth and sense the contraction and trembling of their body without running away. They learned how to feel the floods of emotions—fear, grief, and rage—and to allow them to slowly release with mindfulness. They learned to see the endless mental stories that repeat over and over, and, with the resources of mindfulness and compassion, to let them go and relax, to steady the mind and return to the present.

Sometimes we forget that the Buddha too had fears: "How would it be if in the dark of the month, with no moon, I were to enter the most strange and frightening places, near tombs and in the thick of the forest, that I might come to understand fear and terror. And doing so, a wild animal would approach or the wind rustle the leaves and I would think, 'Perhaps the fear and terror now comes.' And being resolved to dispel the hold of that fear and terror, I remained in whatever posture it arose, sitting or standing, walking or lying down. I did not change until I had faced that fear and terror in that very posture, until I was free of its hold upon me. . . . And having this thought, I did so. By facing the fear and terror I became free."

In the traditional training at Ajahn Chah's forest monastery, we were sent to sit alone in the forest at night practicing the meditations on death. Stories of monks who had encountered tigers and other wild animals helped keep us alert. There were many snakes, including cobras. At Ajahn Buddhadasa's forest monastery we were taught to tap our walking sticks on the paths at night so the snakes would "hear" us and move out of the way. At another monastery, I periodically sat all night at the charnel grounds. Every few weeks a body was brought for cremation. After the lighting of the funeral pyre and the chanting, most people would leave, with only monks remaining to tend the fire in the dark forest. Finally, one monk would be left alone to sit there until dawn, contemplating death. Not everyone did these practices. But I was a young man, looking for initiation, eager to prove myself, so I gravitated toward these difficulties.

As it turned out, sitting in the dark forest with its tigers and snakes was easier than sitting with my inner demons. My insecurity, loneliness, shame, and boredom came up, along with all my frustrations and hurts. Sitting with these took more courage than sitting at the charnel grounds. Little by little I learned to face them with mindfulness, to make a clearing within the dark woods of my own heart.

Mindfulness does not reject experience. It lets experience be the teacher. One Buddhist practitioner with severe asthma learned to bring a mindful attention to his breath. By becoming aware of the stress in his body and being patient as the muscles in his throat and chest relaxed, he was able to limit his attacks. Another man undergoing cancer treatment used mindfulness to quell his fear of pain and added loving-kindness for his body as a complement to his chemotherapy. Through mindfulness a local politician learned not to be discouraged by his attackers. A frazzled single mother of preschoolers used mindfulness to acknowledge her own tension and feeling of being overwhelmed, opening the space to become more respectful of herself and her boys. Each of these practitioners learned to trust mindfulness as they entered the difficulties in their lives. Like the Buddha in the thick of the forest, they found healing and freedom.

FOUR PRINCIPLES FOR MINDFUL TRANSFORMATION

Learning takes place only in a mind that is innocent and vulnerable.
—Krishnamurti

In many Western mindfulness retreats, the four principles for mindful transformation are taught with the acronym RAIN: recognition, acceptance, investigation, and non-identification. The Zen poets tell us that "the rain falls equally on all things," and like the nourishment of outer rain, the inner principles of RAIN can transform our difficulties.

THE TRANSFORMATIVE PRINCIPLES

1. Recognition	*3. Investigation (body, feelings,*
2. Acceptance	*mind, and dharma)*
	4. Non-identification

Recognition is the first principle of transformation. When we are stuck in our life, we must begin with a willingness to see what is so. It is as if someone were to ask us gently, "Hey, what is really happening now?" Do we reply brusquely, "Nothing"? Or do we pause and acknowledge the reality of our experience, here and now?

With recognition we step out of denial. Denial undermines our freedom. The diabetic who denies his body's illness is not free. Neither is the driven, stressed-out executive who denies the cost of her lifestyle or the self-critical would-be painter who denies his love of making art. The society that denies its poverty and injustice has lost a part of its freedom as well. If we deny our dissatisfaction, our anger, our pain, our ambition, we will suffer. If we deny our values, our beliefs, our longings, or our goodness, we will suffer.

There is a powerful opening that comes whenever we truly recognize what is so. "The emergence and blossoming of understanding, love, and intelligence has nothing to do with any outer tradition," observes Zen teacher Toni Packer. "It happens completely on its own when a human being questions, wonders, listens, and looks without getting stuck in fear. When self-concern is quiet, in abeyance, heaven and earth are open."

With recognition our awareness becomes like the dignified host. We name and inwardly bow to our experience: "Ah, sorrow; and now excitement; hmmm, yes, conflict, and yes, tension; oh, now pain, yes, and now, ah, the judging mind." Recognition moves us from delusion and ignorance toward freedom. "We can light a lamp in the darkness," says the Buddha. We can see what is so.

Acceptance is the next principle of transformation. Acceptance allows us to relax and open to the facts before us. It is necessary because with recognition, there can come a subtle aversion, a resistance, a wish it weren't so. Acceptance does not mean that we cannot work to improve things. But just now, this is what is so. Zen Buddhists say, "If you understand, things are just as they are. And if you don't understand, things are still just as they are."

Acceptance is not passivity. It is a courageous step in the process of transformation. "Trouble? Life is trouble. Only death is nice," Zorba the Greek declares. "To live is to roll up your sleeves and embrace trouble." Acceptance is a willing movement of the heart, to include whatever is before it: "This too." As individuals, we have to start with the reality of our own suffering. As a society, we have to start with the reality of collective suffering, of injustice, racism, greed, and hate. We can only transform the world as we learn to transform ourselves. As Carl Jung once remarked, "Perhaps I my-self am the enemy who must be loved."

With acceptance and respect, problems that seem intractable often become workable. A man began to give large doses of cod-liver oil to his Doberman because he had been told that the stuff was good for dogs. Each day he would hold the head of the protest-ing dog between his knees, force its jaws open, and pour the liquid down its throat. One day the dog broke loose and spilled the fish oil on the floor. Then, to the man's great surprise, it returned to lick the puddle. That is when he discovered that what the dog had been fighting was not the oil but the forceful way that it was being administered. With acceptance and respect, surprising transforma-tions can occur.

Investigation, the third principle, follows from recognition and acceptance. Zen master Thich Nhat Hanh calls this "seeing deeply." In recognition and acceptance we recognize our dilemma and ac-cept the truth of the whole situation. Then we must investigate more fully. Whenever we are stuck, it is because we have not looked deeply enough into the nature of the experience.

As we undertake investigation, we focus on the four critical areas of experience: body, feelings, mind, and dharma. These are called the Four Foundations of Mindfulness, and in the next four chapters we will examine them in detail. For now, here is a simple overview:

THE FOUR FOUNDATIONS OF MINDFULNESS	
1. Body	3. Mind
2. Feelings	4. Dharma

When we're investigating a difficulty and something's "cooking" in-side, we want first to become aware of what's happening in our body. Can we locate where our difficulties are held? Sometimes we find heat, contraction, hardness, or vibration. Sometimes we notice throbbing, numbness, a certain shape and color. Are we meeting this area with resistance or with mindfulness? What happens if we hold these sensations with mindfulness? Do they open? Are there other layers? Is there a center? Do they intensify, move, expand, change, repeat, dissolve, or transform?

Next we need to investigate what feelings are part of this difficulty. Is the primary feeling tone pleasant, unpleasant, or neutral? Are we meeting this feeling with mindfulness? And what are the secondary feelings associated with it? Often we discover a constellation of feelings. A man remembering his divorce may feel sadness, anger, jealousy, loss, fear, and loneliness. A woman who was unable to help her addicted nephew can feel longing, aversion, guilt, desire, emptiness, and unworthiness. With mindfulness, each feeling is recognized and accepted. We investigate whether it is pleasant or painful, contracted or relaxed, tense or sad. We notice where we feel the emotion in our body and what happens to it as it is held in awareness.

Looking next into the mind, we ask what thoughts and images are associated with this difficulty. We become aware of all the stories, judgments, and beliefs we are holding. When we look more closely, we often discover that some of them are one-sided, fixed points of view, or outmoded, habitual perspectives. We see that they are only stories. With mindfulness we loosen their hold on us. We cling less to them.

The fourth foundation of mindfulness is the dharma. *Dharma* is an important and multifaceted word. It can mean the teachings and the path of Buddhism. It can mean the Truth, and in this case it can also mean the elements and patterns that make up experience. Investigating the dharma, we look into the principles and laws that are operating. Is the experience actually as solid as it appears? Is it unchanging, or is it impermanent, moving, shifting, re-creating itself? Does the difficulty expand or contract the space in our mind? Is it under our control or does it seem to have a life of its own? We notice if it is self-constructed. We investigate whether we are clinging to it, resisting it, or simply letting it be. We see whether our relationship to it is a source of suffering or happiness. And finally, we notice how much we identify with it. This leads us back to RAIN, and to the principle of non-identification.

Non-identification means that we stop taking the experience as "me" or "mine." We see how our identification creates dependence, anxiety, and inauthenticity. In practicing non-identification, we inquire of every state, experience, and story, "Is this who I really am?" We see the tentativeness of this identity. Then we are free to let go and rest in awareness itself. This is the culmination of releasing difficulty through RAIN.

One Buddhist practitioner, Duane, identified himself as a failure. His life had many disappointments, and after a few years of Buddhist practice, he was disappointed by his meditation too. Yes, he had become somewhat calmer, but he was still plagued by unrelenting critical thoughts and self-judgments, leftovers from a harsh and painful past. He identified with these thoughts and his wounded history. Even the practice of compassion for himself brought little relief.

Then, during a ten-day mindfulness retreat, he was inspired by the teachings on non-identification. He was especially touched by the account of the Buddha, who on the night of his enlightenment faced his own demons in the form of the armies and temptations of Mara. Duane decided to stay up all night and directly face his own demons. For many hours, he tried to be mindful of his breath and body. In between sittings, he took periods of walking meditation. At each sitting, he was washed over by familiar waves of sleepiness, bodily pains, and critical thoughts. Then he began to notice that each changing experience was met by one common element: awareness itself.

Late one night, he had an "aha" moment. He realized that awareness was not affected by any of these experiences, that it was open and untouched, like space itself. All his struggles, all the painful feelings and thoughts, came and went without the slightest disturbance to awareness itself. Awareness became his refuge.

Duane decided to test his realization. The meditation hall was empty, so he rolled on the floor. Awareness just noticed. He stood up, shouted, laughed, made funny animal noises. Awareness just noticed. He ran around the room, lay down quietly, went outside to the edge of the forest, picked up a stone and threw it, jumped up and down, laughed, came back, and sat. Awareness just noticed it all. Finding this, he felt free. He watched the sun rise softly over the hills. Then he went back to sleep for a time. And when he reawakened, his day was full of joy. Even when his doubts came back, awareness just noticed. Like the rain, his awareness allowed all things equally.

It would be too rosy to end this story here. Later in the retreat Duane again fell into periods of doubt, self-judgment, and depression. But now, even in the middle of it, he could recognize that it was just doubt, just judgment, just depression. He could not take it fully as his identity anymore. Awareness noticed this too and was silent, free.

THE FRUITS OF NON-IDENTIFICATION

Buddhist psychology calls non-identification the abode of awakening, the end of clinging, true peace, nirvana. Without identification, we can respectfully care for ourselves and others, yet we are no longer bound by the fears and illusions of the small sense of self.

Does non-identification really work in the toughest situations? Maha Ghosananda embodied it for fifteen years as he walked through Cambodia's battle zones, teaching peace. In the same spirit, here is a story by a police officer that I found in Ram Dass' and Paul Gorman's book *How Can I Help?*

> Now there are two theories about crime and how to deal with it. Anticrime guys say, "You have to think like a criminal." And some police learn that so well they get a kind of criminal mentality themselves.
>
> How I'm working with it is really pretty different. I'm a peace officer. I see that man is essentially pure and innocent and of one good nature. . . .
>
> Now it's interesting how this works.
>
> I had arrested a very angry man who singled me out for real

animosity. When I had to take him to a paddy wagon, he spit in my face—that was something—and he went after me with a chair. We handcuffed him and put him in the truck. Well, on the way, I just had to get past this picture of things, and again I affirmed to my- self, "This guy and I are brothers in love." When I got to the sta- tion, I was moved spontaneously to say, "Look, if I've done anything to offend you, I apologize." The paddy wagon driver looked at me as if I was totally nuts.

The next day I had to take him from where he'd been housed overnight to criminal court. When I picked him up, I thought, "Well, if you trust this vision, you're not going to have to handcuff him." And I didn't. We got to a spot in the middle of the corridor, which was the place where he'd have jumped me if he had that intention. And he stopped suddenly. So did I. Then he said, "You know, I thought about what you said yesterday, and I want to apologize." I just felt this deep appreciation.

Turned out on his rap sheet he'd done a lot of time in a couple of bad prisons and had trouble with some harsh guards. I symbol- ized something. And I saw that turn around, saw a kind of heal- ing, I believe.

Mindfulness and fearless presence bring true protection. When we meet the world with recognition, acceptance, investigation, and non-identification, we discover that wherever we are, freedom is possible, just as the rain falls on and nurtures all things equally.

PRACTICE: ESTABLISHING A DAILY MEDITATION

First select a suitable place for your regular meditation. Put a med- itation cushion or chair there for your use, and add any books or images that help make it feel like a sacred and peaceful space.

Select a regular time for practice that suits your schedule and temperament. If you are a morning person, experiment with a sit- ting before breakfast. If evening fits your temperament or schedule better, try that first. Begin with sitting ten or twenty minutes at a time. Later you can sit longer or more frequently. Daily meditation can become like bathing or toothbrushing. It can bring a regular cleansing and calming to your heart and mind.

Whether you are on a chair or cushion, sit erect without being rigid. Let your body be firmly planted on the earth, your hands resting easily, your heart soft, your eyes closed gently. Sense your body and soften any obvious tension. Let go of any habitual thoughts or plans. Now, bring your attention to feel the sensations of your breathing. Take a few deep breaths to sense where you can feel the breath most easily—as coolness or tingling in the nostrils or throat, or as movement of the chest, or as rise and fall of the belly. Now let your breath be natural. Feel the sensations of each breath very carefully, relaxing into each breath as you feel it, noticing how the soft sensations of breathing come and go without effort.

After a few breaths your attention will probably wander. No matter how long or short a time you have been away, gently come back again to the breath. Before you return, you can mindfully acknowledge where you have gone with a soft word in the back of your mind, such as *thinking, wandering, hearing, itching.* After silently naming where your attention has been, relax and gently return to feel the next breath. As your meditation develops, you can become more fully mindful of the places where your attention wanders. When strong feelings, emotions, sensations, or thoughts carry you away from the breath, receive them with the same mindful noticing you give to the breath. Acknowledge them and name them gently. When they pass, return to the breath. Or if you are just beginning or want to become steadier, one word of acknowledgment and a return to breath is fine. As you sit with the breath, let the breathing rhythms change naturally, allow them to be short, long, fast, slow, rough, or easy. Steady yourself by relaxing into the breath. When your breath becomes soft, let your attention become gentle and careful, as soft as the breath itself.

As if you were training a puppy, you will gently bring yourself back a thousand times. Over weeks and months of this practice you will gradually calm and focus yourself using the breath. There will be many cycles in this process, stormy days alternating with clear days. Just stay with it. As you do, you will find awareness of the breath helping to steady and quiet your whole body and mind. From this initial mindfulness you can meet the other experiences that arise with balance. You will be centered amidst your ever-changing life.

8

THIS PRECIOUS HUMAN BODY

Within this fathom-long body and mind is found all of the teachings.
—Buddha

In your investigation of the world, never allow the mind to desert the body.
Examine its nature, see the elements that comprise it. When its true nature is seen
fully and lucidly by the heart, the wonders of the world will become clear.
—Ajahn Mun

One of the magical experiences in Buddhist training is our growing ability to quiet the mind and sense the body and the world anew. Zen poets celebrate the crunch of snow on the winter path, spring blossoms covering their robes, wind among the pines, walking wet in the autumn mist, listening to the laughter of children. In the forest monasteries of Asia and on retreat in America, practitioners eat unhurriedly in silence. With mindfulness we truly taste the pear, the cheddar, the orange, and the warm bread. We learn to walk unhurriedly again and notice the touch of breeze on our skin, the sound of birds, the rhythmic swinging of our gait, the ground beneath our feet. Like the solitary prisoner who after long months of aloneness has learned to savor the presence of a visiting ant, the smallest details of life appear vibrant and delightful.

Both Buddhist psychology and Western psychology have championed the need to include the body as part of a wise psychology. Freud and his followers such as Jung and Reich engaged in a hard-won battle to help us reinhabit our body as the conduit of life energy. Through their work we have learned the value of our instincts, the eloquence of our sexuality, the need to respect the root motivations and drives of physical life. This reclaiming of bodily life is part of a long and continuing struggle. The repressive Victorian society that Freud found so entrenched and unhealthy was built on centuries of denial. The Western heritage of neo-Platonism and medieval Christianity had devalued the physical and the instinctive in favor of the spiritual and the rational. For centuries, certain fearful and ascetic fathers of Christianity had celebrated mortification of the flesh as essential to avoiding sin.

And now, in its own way, we can see how technological society ignores the wisdom of the body. In modern life the body becomes a machine for living, the subject of managed care, of steroids and plastic surgery. Our flesh is mortified in new forms as we sit in traffic jams, work in cramped cubicles and at school desks under artificial light, and distract ourselves with fast food and video games. Too many of our children are raised by TV instead of by the communal holding and storytelling that was our human heritage for thousands of years. We have lost our connection to our own natural, instinctive life. Unfortunately, when we ignore the body, it makes itself known through the medium of various symptoms. Without a healthy physical connection we experience loss of vitality, chronic pain, and stress-related diseases. We suffer from ulcers and colitis, high blood pressure and strokes. We experience anorexia and obesity, depression and anxiety, road rage and addiction. Too many of us are lost like James Joyce's character Mr. Duffy, who "lived a short distance from his body." In New York, the Associated Press reported that the well-dressed body of a forty-one-year-old man who had died during the morning commute had ridden the crowded subways for a whole day before anyone noticed.

Unlike the unobservant subway riders, at Ajahn Chah's monastery we monks deliberately sat with corpses. We did so to see the fleeting nature of the body. But even more, we did so to fully value the gift of the body while it is alive.

In the Buddhist way of understanding, our human body is considered exceedingly precious because it provides the necessary conditions to realize freedom and true happiness. We begin with a systematic training of mindfulness of the body. In sitting and walking, in eating and moving, we cultivate mindfulness. We develop the ability to come into the life of the body. We notice suffering or well-being arising in our body. We discover how our body responds when our mind is clear or confused, when our heart is open or closed. We learn to hold the mystery of bodily life with respect.

Here is an eighth principle of Buddhist psychology:

8 Mindfulness of the body allows us to live fully. It brings healing, wisdom, and freedom.

When James came to Buddhist practice he suffered from high blood pressure and heart palpitations. A harried business owner and father of two middle-school children, he shared custody and parenting responsibility with his ex-wife. He hoped that meditation might help to reduce his level of stress. Beyond this he was interested in enlightenment because his readings in Zen told him that this would solve his problems. He envisioned enlightenment as a blissful state that, once attained, would allow him transcend the mundane difficulties of his life.

To his surprise, his Buddhist training began with detailed attention to the breath and body. He was disappointed that the focus was not on gaining enlightenment. It was on the here and now. As he practiced in this simple way, James saw how much he thought about the future, how tightly he held his body, how driven his life was. His family history was one of achievement in school, sports, and work. His ambitious parents and strict coaches had all forced him to keep striving. Now he drove himself and pushed his children.

Once James began to acknowledge his level of tension and restlessness, he was instructed to pay careful attention to the moments when he did not feel driven. With mindfulness, he began to notice these gaps, to acquaint himself with the experience of non-striving. An unfamiliar state arose, an uncomfortable, empty feeling that he had always avoided. Encouraged to pay even clearer attention, James discovered that the unfamiliar emptiness contained contentment. For the first time in years he felt moments of being at ease, at home in his own body. He was beginning to taste enlightenment.

In my own case, it was in the forest monastery of Ajahn Chah that I began to taste the beauty of embodied life. I remember how vividly mindfulness practice awakened my senses. I grew up in a suburban intellectual family, and the outdoors meant the backyard, and maybe the camping store in the mall. Even in college my outdoor experiences consisted mostly of moving between the library and the student center. But in the monastery, the temple buildings were in a central clearing, surrounded by towering teak trees and tropical vines, by thick woods filled with wild birds and cobras. Our small huts were scattered throughout this forest.

In this forest I learned to feel the turning of the seasons, the sweaty robes and loud singing of the cicadas on hot summer nights, the muddy feet and endless dampness of the monsoon rains, the dry winds of the cool season when I would wrap my towel under my robe for an extra layer of warmth. This was the first time I could actually watch the slowly changing phases of the moon and the appearance of morning and evening planets at dawn and dusk.

Every day we drew water from wells to wash and drink and bathe. I learned to share my hut with a menagerie of insects, to be mindful of not stepping on the trails of exquisitely painful fire ants, to see the tiny chicks of wild forest game hens.

I began to discover the organic rhythms of my own body. I would stay up late into the night to meditate and then rest in the late morning. At first I ate too much because I was afraid of being hungry after our one meal of the day. Later I learned not to follow my fears and eat just what my body needed.

When my physical pains grew strong I learned to work with them. The Thai villagers were accustomed to sitting for hours cross-legged, with no cushion, on the dirt and stone floors of the temple. But I was a stiff American used to a chair. My back and bottom and knees ached. Some of the meditation periods were like slow torture. I learned the art of softening, relaxing around the pain, inviting my body to accommodate strong sensations. Ajahn Chah repeatedly highlighted the difference between the pains that inevitably come in life and the suffering we create around the pain.

It is really helpful to learn how to work with pain because at certain times we will all experience it. Last year, Malik, a man with a progressive form of rheumatoid arthritis, came to a practice at a retreat. He had done all he could medically for himself, but he was still frustrated and angry. We worked together as he learned to soften the anger and aversion around the pain, to breathe and hold his body, even the contractions, with kind attention. He used the traditional image of a parent holding and protecting a crying child. Equally important, Malik had to learn to relax his judgments, his frustration and anger and self-pity. He learned compassion practice for himself and extended it to all those whose bodies are in pain.

Gradually Malik's physical pain and frustration became more workable. He discovered how to honor his crippled body with a tender attention. He recognized the lesson Anne Morrow Lindbergh discovered during the birth of her child. "Go *with* the pain, let it take you . . . open your palms and your body to the pain. It comes in waves like a tide, and you must be open as a vessel lying on the beach, letting it fill you up and then, retreating, leaving you empty and clear. . . . With a deep breath—it has to be as deep as the pain—one reaches a kind of inner freedom from pain, as though the pain were not yours but your body's. The spirit lays the body on the altar."

GUIDING THE HEART BACK TO THE BODY

*There is no reality except the one contained within us. That is why so many
people live such an unreal life. They take the images outside them for reality and
never allow the world within the body and mind to reveal itself.*
—Herman Hesse

For Katie, a young woman who had been abducted and raped, mindfulness of the body was a delicate and painful journey. She came to a monthlong meditation retreat to heal her trauma and find some inner peace. At first, the intensity of her painful memories kept her completely out of her body. Then, with a tenderhearted attention, Katie found that she could feel her feet when she walked. But sitting was too stressful for her. She had been tied up and the immobility was too similar to her abduction. So, instead of sitting practice, she walked and walked, learning to fully feel her feet on the earth, her legs, and her movement. Next she used her breath as she walked to breathe compassion into the rigidity and terror, into the tension in her shoulders, arms, and torso. Periodically waves of fear, rage, and grief washed over her and she had to rest. Sometimes she would reestablish a sense of well-being by holding on to a tree or feeling her feet touching the earth.

When Katie felt stronger she began to sit—"immobilized," as she called it—and little by little allow the memories of ropes and panic to arise. To support this practice, we sat together often, establishing a trusting field of compassion that could allow for her healing. Guiding her attention with kindness, she began to feel all the sensations she had avoided for so long. Her body wept and shook. Then she slowly opened to the feelings and images. By taking it a little at a time, she was gradually able to tolerate and release more and more of the memory. After several weeks of practice she relaxed her grip on the story. Her experience became just sensation, just feelings, just a memory. She realized with relief that her abduction was not present anymore. All that was present was sensations, thoughts, feeling, and spacious release. Katie began to feel free.

When we struggle with confusion, fear, ambition, depression, or loss, Buddhist psychology asks us to sense how we experience this in our body. A man whose marriage ended badly became aware of the boulder of grief that weighed upon his heart. A woman who was in remission from breast cancer found the fear of death in her tight chest and constricted breathing. Another man who had worked for years to build a business and family faced a huge hole of emptiness in his abdomen when his business was sold and his children left for college.

Like Katie's, sometimes our suffering and psychic disturbance are so great that we cannot sit to meditate or hold the body still. Then trainings in movement such as walking meditation and yoga, or mindful practices of sweeping the floor and preparing food, are used to settle the mind. On retreat we may suggest that a troubled student spend time working in the meditation center garden. Many people have come back to life through patiently tending the plants and digging in the earth. Such practices help to ground the fragmented mind in the body. For an extreme case, I remember an old Tibetan lama in India who asked a profoundly disturbed student to offer a hundred thousand full prostrations to the Buddha as a way to settle his fractured psyche. It took the student a whole year, and it helped. Then the lama had him do it twice again, adding a compassion practice as well. After three years the man's inner well-being was remarkably restored.

One of the first jobs I had when I returned to America from Ajahn Chah's monastery was as an aide on the acute ward of a large mental hospital. I enthusiastically told my co-workers about Buddhist mindfulness meditation, and they wondered if it could be helpful to the patients. But after a short while it became apparent to me that closing their eyes to meditate was not what most of these patients needed. They were already lost in their minds. The practices they needed required embodiment: walking meditation, yoga, tai chi, gardening. They needed to ground themselves back on the earth.

Then I realized that there was indeed a large population in the hospital that was desperately in need of meditation: the stressed-out psychologists, social workers, nurses, psychiatrists, and aides.

For them mindfulness could offer both personal well-being and greater effectiveness in their work. I volunteered to teach a class in mindfulness meditation for the hospital staff. A number of them came and told me that learning a systematic way to calm their minds and tend to their tired bodies was enormously helpful. I'm sure it helped the patients too.

Because our human body is considered precious in Buddhist psychology, no matter what the phase of our life, we are instructed to value and care for it. When physical illness arises, it often diminishes our sense of dignity. With this can also come shame and self-hatred. We can take the illness personally, as if it is our fault. But sickness and health are a part of every human life. When our hearts open with understanding we will treat this very body and mind with kindness no matter what the circumstances. I watched a renowned Burmese master, Taungpulu Sayadaw, guide a very sick student on one of our annual three-month retreats. Don was a forty-one-year-old man with metastatic brain cancer whose doctor had given up after treating him without success. The swelling of his head from the tumors was visible and it appeared that he had only a short while to live. I took him for a special interview with Taungpulu Sayadaw, expecting the master to give him the practices for conscious death that Buddhist tradition believes to be important. But that was not his response at all.

Taungpulu listened to Don's history and then placed his hands on the tumors to offer direct healing. He stated that human birth is precious and that Don must do everything he could to heal himself. The master chanted for a time to create special healing water for Don to drink and then gave him sacred prayers to recite and extensive healing visualizations. "You must try to heal yourself and live as long as possible because this human body is the most valuable source of spiritual learning of all forms of birth. Drink this water and practice these meditations and heal with your whole heart. And then only if this fails and you know you are dying is it time to switch to the death practices. Don't die yet." And although Don did not heal completely, with Taungpulu's encouragement he lived for years longer than the doctors had predicted.

THROUGH THE BODY TO THE DEATHLESS

Just as consciousness mysteriously mirrors the dual wave and particle nature of light, our own body is a realm of contradiction. Carl Jung reminds us to respect "the original animal nature of our body." But then he continues, the body is also "connected with the highest forms of the spirit." He insists that we can bloom only when spirit and instinct are in harmony. "Too much animal disfigures the civilized human being. Too much culture makes for a sick animal." For wisdom and nobility to flower, there has to be a balance that includes both embodied life and the universal perspective.

Because modern American culture fosters an intense identification with the outer appearance of the body, going beyond it is not easy. We devote enormous amounts of time to how we look, to dressing, adorning, and strengthening the body. Yet no matter how we cling, as we age the body betrays us. If we limit ourselves to the fulfillment of bodily desires and believe that the body is who we are, when we face age, sickness, difficulties, and death we will be lost and frightened.

Ajahn Chah explains, "We only rent this house. If it belonged to us, we could tell it not to get sick, not to grow old. But it takes no notice of these wishes. With wisdom, if you live, that's good. And when you have to die, that's fine too. If the doctors told me I had cancer and was going to die in a few months, I'd remind the doctors, 'Watch out, because death is coming to get you too. It's just a question of who goes first.' "

Buddhist psychology offers dozens of trainings to see our body from the universal perspective. There are meditations that allow us to sense our body as a vibrating energy field, or as a network of chakras and energy centers. There are practices for sensing the body as an anatomical system of flesh and bone, fluids and solids. Using these practices in one monastery, we would focus on sensing our own skeleton. When we were instructed to take our bones for a walk, we also looked at the skeletons of others walking by. This immediately snapped us out of our stories and melodramas and shifted our whole identity.

In another important training, we can learn to experience the body as four primary elements and twenty-four other derived elementary properties. Buddhist psychology describes our physical existence with the basic elements of earth, air, fire, and water. This is much like traditional systems of psychology and medicine in the ancient Greek, Chinese, African, or Native American societies. Modern readers can mistakenly believe this to be a primitive version of the periodic table of the elements. But actually, these four elements are a description of how we directly experience the body.

If you close your eyes and feel carefully, you won't feel a "body." *Body* is only a word, the idea or concept level. What you will actually feel are areas of hardness and softness, of pressure, heaviness, and textures such as rough and smooth. This is the earth element. You will also feel areas of warmth and coolness. This is the fire or temperature element. You will feel areas of vibrations and stillness. This is the air or vibratory element. And you will feel cohesion and fluidity. This is the water element: you only need to blink your eyes or swallow to sense it.

We know our body most directly this way. We also know it through the secondary elements of color, sound (air element at the ear), odor, and taste. A direct investigation of these bodily elements can free us from deep layers of identification and entanglement. This can happen simply as it did for Mike, a student who was obsessed by clearly irrational thoughts of jealousy. As Mike spoke to me, his rational mind knew that his tormenting thoughts had no basis in the reality of his relationship. He had tried to let them go, but he kept getting caught in their story. Sitting with him, I asked Mike to allow the jealous thoughts to be present, and to notice where he sensed them in his body. He became aware of strong sensations of heat and contraction in his chest, and then of aversion and fear as he felt the sensations directly. He noticed how his obsessive thoughts quieted when he felt the strong sensations and emotions under them. But Mike said that he couldn't understand the connection between the jealousy and the sensations in his chest.

So I invited Mike to notice each of the elements carefully. I asked about the earth element: did this area of his chest feel hard or soft, dense, smooth, heavy or light? What about the fire element: did it feel warm, cool, or neutral? The air element of motion: was the area vibrating or was it still? And the secondary elements of color and scent: if this area of his chest had a color or a scent, what would be present? He discovered the sensations in his chest were hard and rough-textured, pulsating, somewhat hot, and black in color.

Then I asked Mike to notice whatever feelings and images associated with these elemental sensations were present. He noticed fear arising and feelings of abandonment. Then came a rush of memories of his parents' divorce when he was seven. He remembered the worst part, the day when his mother moved out. He told the whole story and wept. As he sat, holding these experiences with mindfulness, Mike was gradually learning to tolerate the loss, the emptiness, the abandonment that he had carried unconsciously in his body and mind.

Mike worked with the feelings of grief, anger, loss, and fear for a long time. He began to recognize the repeated patterns of abandonment in his life. Now as he remembered himself as a lost seven-year-old boy, he felt a wave of kindness arise. After some time I invited him to broaden this compassion, to open to the pain of every child of divorce, of every abandoned human being. In this way he came to know both the personal and the universal nature of his suffering. His experience gradually became more impersonal. He was not just this injured being. He was the adult who was in meditation, he was the whole stream of his history, he was the consciousness witnessing it all.

THE ELEMENTAL LIFE OF THE BODY

The elements of our body can become a gateway to the hidden stories and unconscious patterns we carry. As we move through this gate we can sense the play of incarnation in a larger, more universal context. We can feel the elements of life moving in us. Our experiences of being shaken, rigid, trembling, weighted down, floating, flexible, grounded, clouded, or clear are all the play of the elements. Our stubborn stance and lighthearted dancings are the earth moving in our body. Our griefs are the water element, the ocean of tears. Our yawn and our songs are the octaves of the air. "At one time you were a mountain, you were a cloud," writes Thich Nhat Hanh. "This is not poetry, this is science."

Meditating on the elements is also used to understand death. This is among the most life-changing contemplations. In the West, we resist reflecting on aging and death because dying is held as failure and it frightens us. In the Buddhist approach, we deliberately turn to face death so that it can bring wisdom, perspective, and a motivation to live each day fully and well. Tibetan master Kalu Rinpoche gave this powerful description of how the elements dissolve as we die. He recommended we contemplate this carefully so that we can shift our identity from the body to the consciousness that is our true nature. As you read these graphic words about the process of dying, notice how the sense of yourself changes.

As we near death, the earth element begins to dissolve. We lose our strength, we cannot sit or hold anything up. Our cheeks become sunken. We can no longer support our head. It becomes hard to open and close our eyes. Pallor sets in. We feel heavy and uncomfortable in any position; we ask to be pulled up. Some texts say we feel as though we are falling or sinking underground, or being crushed by a great weight, even as if a mountain were pressing down on our body. The earth element is returning to earth.

The water element is next. We begin to lose control of our bodily fluids. Our nose begins to run, and we dribble. There can be a discharge from the eyes, and maybe we become incontinent. We cannot move our tongue. Our eyes start to feel dry in their sockets. Our lips are drawn and bloodless, our mouth and throat sticky and clogged. The nostrils cave in, and we become very thirsty. We tremble and twitch. Some texts say that we feel as if we were drowning in an ocean or being swept away by a huge river. The water element is returning to water.

The fire element is next. Our mouth and nose dry up completely. All the warmth of our body begins to seep away, usually from the feet and hands toward the heart. Perhaps a steamy heat rises from the crown of our head. Our breath is cold as it passes through our mouth and nose. We no longer have the warmth to digest anything. It becomes more and more difficult to perceive anything outside of us. The inner experience is of being consumed in a flame or a roaring blaze, or of the world being consumed in a holocaust of fire. The fire element is returning to fire.

The air element follows. It becomes harder and harder to breathe. The in-breaths become shallow and the out-breaths longer. We begin to rasp and pant. Our breaths become short and labored. Our body twitches and then becomes still. Our vision fades in and out, blurry and unclear. The inner experience is of a great wind sweeping away the world, a maelstrom of wind consuming the whole universe. The air element is returning to air.

As we visualize the dissolution of the elements, death becomes vivid. We are shaken awake and brought to feel the tentativeness of this incarnation. We are drawn to live more wisely. At the same time, the dissolution of the elements at death makes it clear that this body is not our true nature. Attention to this human body brings healing and regeneration. Then the universal practices shift consciousness to a spaciousness witnessing beyond the body. Through awareness of the body we remember who we really are.

PRACTICE: WALKING MEDITATION

One of the most useful and grounding ways of attending to our body is the practice of walking meditation. Walking meditation is a simple and universal practice for developing calm, connectedness, and embodied awareness. It can be practiced regularly, before or after sitting meditation or any time on its own, such as after a busy day at work or on a lazy Sunday morning.

To practice, select a quiet place where you can walk comfortably back and forth, indoors or out, about ten to thirty paces in length. Begin by standing at one end of this "walking path," with your feet firmly planted on the ground. Let your hands rest easily, wherever they are comfortable. Take a few deep breaths and then open your senses to see and feel the whole surroundings. After a minute, bring your attention back to focus on the body. Center yourself and feel how your body is standing on the earth. Feel the pressure on the bottoms of your feet and the other natural sensations of standing. Let yourself be present and alert.

Begin to walk a bit more slowly than usual. Let yourself walk with a sense of ease and dignity. Relax and let your walking be gracious and natural, as if you were a king or queen out for a royal stroll. Pay attention to your body. With each step feel the sensations of lifting your foot and leg off the earth. Then mindfully place your foot back down. Feel each step fully as you walk. When you reach the end of your path, pause for a moment. Center yourself, carefully turn around, and pause again so that you can be aware of the first step as you walk back. You can experiment with the speed, walking at whatever pace keeps you most present.

Continue to walk back and forth with mindfulness for ten or twenty minutes or longer. As with the breath in sitting, your attention will wander away many times. As soon as you notice this, acknowledge softly where it went: *wandering, thinking, hearing, planning.* Then return to feel the next step. As with training a puppy, you will come back a thousand times. Whether you have been away for one second or for ten minutes, no matter. Simply acknowledge where you have been, relax, and come back to being alive here and now with the next step you take.

Use this walking meditation to calm and collect yourself and to live more wakefully in your body. Practice at home first. You can then extend your mindful walking in an informal way when you go shopping, when you walk down the street or walk to or from your car. You can learn to enjoy walking for its own sake instead of being lost in planning and thinking. In this simple way, you can be truly present, bringing your body, heart, and mind together as you move through your life.

9

THE RIVER OF FEELINGS

When a pleasant feeling arises, know this is the experience of pleasant feeling.
When a painful experience arises, know this is the experience of painful feeling.
When a neutral feeling arises, know this is the experience of neutral feeling.
—The Great Discourse on Mindfulness

At the Supreme Court level where we work, 90 percent of any
decision is emotional. The rational part of us supplies the reasons
for supporting our predilections.
—Justice William O. Douglas

When my father was sixty-five years old, he had a serious heart attack. He was put in intensive care, a potential candidate for open heart surgery, but only if his failing kidneys and other body functions returned to adequate levels. My mother, three brothers, and I had gathered at the hospital. His prognosis was poor and the doctors were dubious about whether he would make it. We were very worried.

The ICU let us in one at a time for fifteen-minute stretches. I was sad and in the state of semi-shock, between worlds and without much sleep, that is common in an emergency. I thought about how my father had been such a complicated and difficult man, a brilliant scientist, yes, but a tyrant and a wife batterer as well. I remembered that however bad it was for us boys, it was worse for my mother. She took to hiding glass bottles behind the curtains in the house, so that she could grab one in self-defense. Not that it always worked. She wore long sleeves in the summer to cover the black-and-blue marks. But by this point, through forgiveness meditation and therapy, I had released much of my pain and anger.

On the third day in the ICU, it was clear he was losing strength. I went in to see him, aware that this could be my last visit with my father. He was hooked up to oxygen and a variety of beeping machines, and his arms and body were ensconced in a spiderweb of tubes and electronic monitoring wires. I sat by his bedside and asked him how he was doing. He grunted and made a pained and unhappy expression. I talked about him and our family and then fell silent for a few minutes.

Finally, I looked at my father: weak, vulnerable, maybe dying. I said, "I love you." His eyes got bigger. Struggling, he raised one arm, patched with tape and needles and tubes, up to his face. He pinched his nose as if to ward off a bad smell, frowned with disdain, and rolled his head from side to side, as if to say. *Not in our family. You don't acknowledge your feelings. It is too sentimental, too weak.*

For me it took years of training—as a monk, in meditation, in Western psychotherapy, and in the give-and-take of relationships—to reclaim my capacity to feel. But if we want to live wisely as human beings, we have to understand what we feel and how to work with these feelings.

THE PRIMARY FEELINGS

Buddhist psychology helps us distinguish two critical aspects of feeling. The first and most essential quality is called the primary feeling. According to this perspective, every moment of our sense experience has a feeling tone. Like valence in chemistry, each sight, sound, taste, touch, smell, or thought will have either a pleasant, painful, or neutral quality. Modern neuroscience confirms that everything that registers in the brain is assigned some negative or positive valence. The primary feeling tone comes first. Then, born out of this simple feeling tone, there arises a whole array of secondary feelings, all the emotions we are familiar with, from joy and anger to fear and delight.

"Working with the primary feelings is a direct route to enlightenment," explained one of my Burmese teachers. The stream of primary feelings is always with us, but we often have the mistaken notion that life is not supposed to be this way. We secretly believe that if we can act just right, then our stream of feelings will always be pleasant and there will be no pain, no loss.

So when a painful experience arises we often try to get rid of it, and when a pleasant experience arises we try to grasp it. When a neutral experience arises we tend to ignore it. We're always wanting the right (pleasant) feelings and trying to avoid the wrong (painful) ones. And when they are unpleasant we react endlessly, struggling to get it right.

As we become wiser we realize that fixing the flow of feelings doesn't work. Primary feelings are simply feelings, and every day consists of thousands of pleasant, painful, and neutral moments, for you, Condoleezza Rice, the Dalai Lama, Mick Jagger, and the Buddha alike. These feelings are not wrong or bad. They are the stream of life. Sylvia Boorstein, my colleague, writes, "What a relief it was for me to go to my first meditation retreat and hear people who seemed quite happy speak the truth so clearly—the First Noble Truth that life is difficult and painful, just by its nature, not because we're doing it wrong."

Our painful experience does not represent failure. Meditation masters have sickness and pain like the rest of us. Shunryu Suzuki, Ramana Maharshi, and the sixteenth Karmapa Lama died of cancer. Ajahn Chah suffered a brain hemorrhage that left him in a coma for years, and Lama Yeshe writes of the incredible difficulty of long periods of hospitalization from heart failure. "After 41 days of intensive care, my body was like the lord of a cemetery, my mind like an anti-god and my speech like the barking of an old, mad dog." And yet they were masters. Their practice was to accept pleasure, pain, and neutral experience in a gracious way.

This is a ninth principle of Buddhist psychology:

9   Wisdom knows what feelings are present without being lost in them.

In the forest monastery of Ajahn Buddhadasa, we were instructed to be mindful of the feeling tone of each sound and of each activity. As we walked the forest paths in the morning, we noticed the neutral tone of our steps, the pleasant way our body swayed. By the afternoon we felt the unpleasant, hot, sticky sweat of tropical midday bearing down on our body. Each time we slowed down to rest or sit or read, we tried to sense the feeling tone—pleasant, neutral, or unpleasant—and then to notice if there was a reaction to it. Now, as a meditation teacher, I frequently use mindfulness of primary feeling as a way to help students who are caught in automatic reactions.

Jamilla, a young artist, was easily overwhelmed by anxious thoughts. Instead of having her focus on the content of those thoughts, I asked her to notice the primary feelings in her body and mind preceding and during the anxiety. She noticed they were all unpleasant. She felt a painful tightness in her chest, nausea in her stomach, an uncomfortable sense of emptiness. It was as if the anxious thoughts were a habitual form of escape from the overall unpleasantness. She had spent a lot of time living in the repetitive stories her mind would tell. Now, shifting her attention to the primary feeling began to disengage her from the worrisome thoughts. She learned she could actually become mindful of the unpleasant sensations in her body. They were difficult to stand, but with some practice she learned to stay with them and accept them. As she did so, the anxious thoughts became less bothersome.

Frederick, another practitioner, had a body spasm, like a tic, that had distressed him for years. When I asked him to notice the feeling tone carefully, he discovered that just before the spasm, his body felt pleasure and then the movement erupted. When he allowed the pleasant sensation to become conscious, the spasm stopped.

A third student, Jacob, had lived for several years with a charismatic Tibetan lama. Then he married, had three children, and worked at the local newspaper. He still meditated every day, and when I first worked with him he told me how calm it made him feel. But I was struck by his drooping posture and how flat and dull he seemed. I wondered if he'd used his spiritual practice to justify a mild depression and to cover his fears.

Jacob wanted to go deeper in his practice, and he agreed to study his primary feelings. At first he reported lots of neutral feelings that led to a dull, stupefying state. He also had moments of pleasure, but they scared him. He was afraid of their intensity and he was anxious about what he would uncover if he allowed himself to feel more fully. I suggested he write a letter to himself about the things he was hiding from his own awareness.

Jacob wrote that if he were more alive, he'd probably be greedy all the time for more pleasure. When he felt angry, he'd probably mow people down with rage. Jacob continued noticing the primary feelings, the pleasant, neutral, and painful qualities of his day, and added the strong secondary feelings of desire, anger, and fear. Gradually he became able to identify and tolerate his feelings and his reactions to them.

As Jacob became more open and mindful of his feelings, I asked him to connect them with his body. I invited him to sit and stand upright, and to take the risk of being more alive. He was both interested and reluctant. I reminded Jacob of the Buddha's teachings of nobility and invited him to hold himself as if he were a prince. I asked him to acknowledge that he deserved to be fully alive. Jacob found this work very hard but gratifying. He later reported, "Once the initial terror subsided, the practice of walking like a prince, as though I have a right to be on this earth, has given me so much ease and happiness and energy in my body. I'm amazed. I feel so much freer. I hope it lasts." I told him that, like all states, it wouldn't last. But Jacob had touched nobility and freedom. He could always return.

Like Jacob, many people who come to spiritual practice are frightened by their feelings. They hope meditation will help them to transcend the messiness of the world and leave them invulnerable to difficult feelings. But this is a false transcendence, a denial of life. It is fear masquerading as wisdom.

WORKING WITH EMOTIONS

It's very helpful to realize that the emotions we have, the negativity and the positivity, are exactly what we need to be fully human, fully awake, fully alive.
—Pema Chödrön

In modern English, the words *feeling* and *emotion* are often used synonymously. However, Buddhist psychology distinguishes the primary feelings from the range of emotions that follow them. Each of the three primary feeling tones gives rise to secondary emotions, which include many of the mental states, both healthy and unhealthy, that we learned about in Chapter 4. We can see how a pleasant primary feeling can give rise either to unhealthy secondary emotions such as grasping, jealousy, and clinging or to healthy states of joy, ease, and happiness. Neutral feeling tone can give rise to unhealthy secondary emotions such as boredom, lethargy, and being spaced out or to healthy states of peace, ease, and contentment. Painful experiences can give rise to unhealthy states of aversion, judgment, rigidity, and fear or to healthy states of clarity, steadfastness, and wisdom. These secondary emotions are all mental states that flavor consciousness.

How do we work with our emotions from the perspective of Buddhist psychology? The mindfulness training of RAIN—recognition, acceptance, investigation, and non-identification—provides the basic alphabet of working with emotion. As we have seen, we have to first recognize what is present. How do our emotions manifest in our body? What do they feel like in the mind? When we feel caught by our experience, recognition of emotion is a critical first step. Are we confused, sad, angry, fearful, attached, or hopeful? Emotions can cluster together, so careful recognition may notice several at once. Often grief is present with our anger. There can be relief and happiness that come with letting go. Recognition requires a systematic and careful attention.

Emotional understanding is hard for those of us who, out of trauma and loss, have disconnected from our feelings. Growing up, I learned to be afraid of feelings. In our house strong feelings were either repressed or volatile. These patterns can be passed on for generations. I remember visiting my father's mother and grandmother. One was a miser, the other a glamorous spender. They lived across the street from each other and hated each other. I remember the same feelings of repression and volatility there. Now as a teacher, I frequently encounter a similar confusion and loss of connection to feelings in meditation students.

Mindfulness of feeling does not require great sophistication. It can start simply. I received the following letter from an eighth-grade student whose middle school had come to Spirit Rock for an afternoon of meditation. She wrote, "At first I did not take the meditating seriously, until I started to get in big fights with my parents. So I took the little knowledge I had about meditating one night after a big fight with my mom and went out on the roof to do it. When I opened my eyes and went back in my house, I was not as mad. Now I do it and it helps me with my anger. Thank you for showing us how to do it."

For many Western practitioners, it is important to spend a period actively reclaiming their feelings. Because this reclaiming is not easily done, we may need help. Practitioners and teachers can sit and inquire together. What feelings are present? Can they be recognized and accepted fully here and now? To release our resistance, we can begin to allow the state to intensify, to open and expand, to get bigger or change or dissolve as it will.

We learn to trust our capacity to experience difficult states in a fearless way. The poet Hafiz writes,

Don't surrender your loneliness
So quickly.
Let it cut more deep.
Let it ferment and season you
As few human
Or even divine ingredients can.

The space of mindfulness opens greater ease and humor. A meditation student who was often angered and judgmental reported, "One day on the highway a driver abruptly swerved and pulled out in front of me. In that moment I felt annoyance and fear, but then I smiled and thought, 'You stupid jerk . . . I'm not going to judge you.' "

On intensive meditation retreat, we can go through periods of strong emotions. Initially they overpower us, until we find a mindful middle where we neither suppress them nor are completely lost in them. And then, to our surprise, as we mindfully allow them, they can become more alive in themselves. We experience the intense, pure feelings of joy and sorrow in their own right. It's as though we can let ourselves be carried by the river of feelings, because we know how to swim.

When we have accepted the feelings that arise, we can investigate them. We can notice the way they feel in the body; the color, density, size, and energy of the mood; the stories our mind creates when they are present. We can also begin to recognize how automatic they can be, arising unbidden from past conditioning.

This was the case with Jacob, whose dull state had been transformed by attention to his feelings and by the practice of walking like a prince. "I find I can't sustain it," he complained. "I get busy and overwhelmed and my body slumps back down and the feelings change back to dullness and depression." "This is natural," I told him. I suggested he study his cycle of feelings further, like an anthropologist. When do they come out, in the daytime or at night? How long do they last? What precedes them and what follows them? Do you control them or do they have a life of their own?

Over the weeks Jacob saw how a sense of princely well-being

arose from being outdoors, inspiring reading, and certain friends, and how dullness and delusion arose after eating lunch and, if unnoticed, remained until bedtime. Then he connected this afternoon depression with his childhood: his parents' frequent anger had led him to hide in his room after school to avoid the tension. Most importantly, he noticed how rapidly his feelings changed. One moment he felt like a prince, another like a frightened child, another like a lonely or a needy person, then like a happy, strong, or sad adult. Each feeling is associated with a different point of view, a different way of seeing the world.

"It's so impersonal," Jacob finally declared. "All these feelings keep changing, and so does their point of view. Now I can feel them. What am I supposed to do next? Maybe just stop believing in each one?" Through mindfulness Jacob's intuitive wisdom grew. He saw that some of the quickly changing feelings were old habitual reactions that could be felt and released. Others held important messages and needed to be honored. Gradually his inner intelligence about feelings was growing. He could experience more fully the play of feelings and yet hold them with a more spacious perspective.

Like Jacob, as we develop recognition, acceptance, and investigation of feelings, we can also recognize their impersonal and empty nature. We can notice how a feeling arises, how long it lasts, and what happens afterward. Usually we think that feelings and emotions last for a long time. We speak of a morning of anxiety, a day of irritability, a week of infatuation, a month of depression. But as we investigate closely, we discover that most feelings last no longer than fifteen or thirty seconds.

Suppose we feel a state of anger or longing. If we sense it carefully in body and mind, it will inevitably begin to change, to expand or intensify, dissolve or shift from one feeling to another. Anger may change to rage and then to hurt and then cycle back to anger. Or perhaps longing will transform into love or sadness and then to contraction and then back to longing, and then the thought will come, "What are we having for dinner?" All of this in one or two minutes.

Feelings arise like a series of waves in consciousness; each feel-

ing can bring the sense of being young or old, spacious or contracted. As we learn to track our feelings, our emotional intelligence
grows. With mindfulness, a natural intuition and discrimination
begin to tell us which feelings call for action and which, if acted
upon, will lead to unnecessary suffering. Some feelings hold important messages, and we need to respond and address the conditions
from which they arise. Equally often, feeling states are simply present, the atmosphere in which we live. Even when they are strong,
we don't need to suppress them, nor grasp and identify with them.
Through all these permutations, we don't have to worry: no emotion is final.

When Aleesha came to Buddhist training, she said she had been
depressed since her divorce four years earlier. She was estranged
from her daughter and her two grandchildren. She was not sleeping well. For a time she had used antidepressants and sleep medication, but now she had stopped. I told her that I respect the value
of medication at certain times. For some people it can be important as they grapple with sustained depression, and it is even more
so for those dealing with bipolar disorder and with other, more severe mental illness. Many students undertake Buddhist training
while on medication and find that they are still able to practice relatively well.

But Aleesha had a sense that it was time to stop her medication
and work more directly with the fear and anger and grief that had
overwhelmed her. First I encouraged her to continually ground
herself in her body, so she wouldn't be overtaken by the waves of
emotion that frightened her. She saw how much she hated her feelings. As she opened to the resistance that usually kept her stuck,
she was surprised. When she gently named and acknowledged her
resistance (as *aversion, hating, judgment*) and allowed it space, it did
not stay long. After ten or twenty seconds there was a softening, a
relaxation that signaled an inner opening. As the resistance
dissolved, she was face-to-face with the emotions she had found so
difficult. The grief, anger, and fear were right there.

Aleesha named each emotion that presented itself. She felt it in
her body and allowed it space to expand, intensify, or dissolve as it
would. Again, to her surprise, none of the emotions lasted. The

anger became heat and contraction that intensified, igniting a rage that spread like fire and then softened. Then her heart began to pound and grief arose and grew stronger, until tears flowed and a tremendous pain spread from her heart to her throat. This was followed by a wave of resistance and then fear, followed by a contraction and a cry, then coldness and silent emptiness. On and on the feelings flowed, and Aleesha could see how the river of emotions and sensations changed, each morphing into the next. It all became quite impersonal, like watching the changing shapes of clouds in the sky.

Over the weeks, as Aleesha continued to open to the waves of emotion, they became accompanied by images and stories. She felt the grief of separation from her estranged daughter, the hurt they'd inflicted on each other. Aleesha's own history of childhood abuse arose, and with it waves of sorrow and shame. As Aleesha's understanding grew, she became neither frightened of these feelings nor lost in them. She saw how confused she and her daughter had been. She began to let go and accept her life with more respect. She felt a longing for it to be different, and she accepted this longing too as one more state to make peace with. Her wisdom grew. "She will never be exactly the daughter I imagined and I will never be exactly the mother she wanted. I feel a growing compassion for us all. I do not want grief and estrangement to be the legacy for my daughter and grandchildren."

As Aleesha learned to tolerate her own painful states, she also became more receptive to life's small pleasures. She noticed a hummingbird drinking from a hanging fuchsia, a beetle crossing her porch, a colorful plate of salad with spring vegetables. Her senses were bringing her back to life.

It takes courage to experience the full measure of our feelings and emotions without reacting to them or cutting them off. Yet here is where our freedom lies. As Albert Camus tells us, "We all carry within us our places of exile; our crimes, our ravages. Our task is not to unleash them on the world; it is to transform them in ourselves and others."

With mindfulness we can learn that even powerful feelings and emotions are not to be feared. They are simply energy. When they are recognized, acknowledged, investigated, we are liberated from our clinging. And then we can choose. We can act on those that need a response and let others become freed as the energy of life.

PRACTICE: A MEDITATION ON GRIEF

Among the most helpful meditations on feelings is mindfulness of grief. Because modern culture so often wants us to move on with our life, we have forgotton the importance of honoring our tears. Grief is one of the heart's natural responses to loss. When we grieve we allow ourselves to feel the truth of our pain, the measure of betrayal or tragedy in our life. By our willingness to mourn, we slowly acknowledge, integrate, and accept the truth of our losses. Often the best way to let go and move on is first to grieve fully.

To meditate on grief, let yourself sit, alone or with a comforting friend. Take the time to create an atmosphere of support. When you are ready, begin by sensing your breath. Feel your breathing in the area of your chest. This can help you become present to what is within you. Take one hand and hold it gently on your heart as if you were holding a vulnerable human being. You are.

As you continue to breathe, bring to mind the loss or pain you are grieving. Let the story, the images, the feelings come naturally. Hold them gently. Take your time. Let the feelings come layer by layer, a little at a time.

Keep breathing softly, compassionately. Let whatever feelings are there—pain and tears, anger and love, fear and sorrow—come as they will. Touch them gently. Let them unravel out of your body and mind. Make space for any images that arise. Allow the whole story to unwind. Breathe and hold it all with tenderness and compassion. Kindness for it all, for you and for others.

The grief we carry is part of the grief of the world. Hold it gently. Let it be honored. You do not have to keep it in anymore. You can let go into the heart of compassion; you can weep.

Releasing the grief we carry is a long, tear-filled process. Yet it follows the natural intelligence of the body and heart. Trust it, trust the unfolding. Along with meditation, some of your grief will want to be written, to be cried out, to be sung, to be danced. Let the timeless wisdom within you carry you through grief to an open heart.

10

THE STORYTELLING MIND

Who is your enemy? Mind is your enemy.
Who is your friend? Mind is your friend.
Learn the ways of the mind. Tend the mind with care.
—Buddha

How does the modern world look to a meditation master?
Lost in thought.
—Ajahn Buddhadasa

When I first took robes and entered the monastic community of Ajahn Chah, I had already been practicing meditation on my own for two years. Now, sitting and walking mindfully for hours in a little hut in the forest clearing, my mind became more open and sensitive. One day as I was scanning my attention through my body, I noticed with curiosity that there were some areas where I could hardly feel anything and my skin felt numb. With further awareness, this perception grew even clearer. Then I had the thought that

patches of numbness on the limbs are one of the first signs of leprosy. I was not usually prone to hypochondria, but during part of
my time in the Peace Corps, I had worked with lepers in a rural
health program. Now my mind got worried. I was afraid that the
numbness meant I'd contracted leprosy. What would I do? Do they
throw leprous monks out of the temple? My fear grew rapidly.
Thoughts proliferated. I pictured my whole life unfolding as a
leper, an outcast and then a beggar. Already isolated in my forest
hut, now I felt really alone. Then I imagined having to tell my
mother, "Your son is a leper and he can never come home." Self-
pity was added to the alarm. My thoughts went crazy. What was I
to do? I was too ashamed to say anything about it. What if it wasn't
true? What if it was? I waited and practiced while this whole movie
played for several days.

Then I noticed how the areas of numbness shifted and changed.
I got the courage to ask a senior monk about sensations, though not
about leprosy. He explained how bodily perceptions change in
meditation—sometimes you feel many new sensations, and sometimes parts of the body seem to dissolve or disappear. It could happen on the skin or inside the body. "You just notice it all with
mindfulness," he laughed, as if to ease my nervousness. For three
days I had lived as a leper. Now all these thoughts vanished like a
dream. What would my mind make up next?

How do we work with the storytelling mind? The poet Muriel
Rukeyser writes, "The universe is made of stories, not atoms."
Buddhist psychology emphasizes that we must understand the
power of the stories we tell, and differentiate them from the direct
experience of life. In this way we can use thoughts without being
trapped by them. As one of my teachers put it, "Thoughts make a
good servant, but a poor master."

The first step for us in working with the storytelling mind is to
notice the endless stream of thoughts and commentary that plays
along with our experience. Almost everyone who sits down to
meditate is startled by this process. Even though we try to focus
our attention on our breath or body or a prayer, we are interrupted
by a torrent of ideas, memories, plans. This is a key insight called

"seeing the waterfall." One Buddhist meditation teacher says that the average person has seventeen thousand thoughts a day.

Just as the salivary glands secrete saliva, the mind secretes thoughts. The thoughts think themselves. This thought production is not bad; it's simply what minds do. A cartoon I once saw depicts a car on a long western desert highway. A roadside sign warns, "Your own tedious thoughts next 200 miles." Buddhist psychology directs us to investigate both the content of those thoughts and the process of thinking itself.

Here is a tenth principle of Buddhist psychology:

---

10   Thoughts are often one-sided and untrue. Learn to be mindful of thought instead of being lost in it.

When we look at the constant and repetitive process of our own thinking, we see how habitually it creates a sense of self and other. As Don Juan, a Yaqui Indian shaman, explained to his disciple Carlos Castaneda, "You talk to yourself too much. You're not unique in that. Every one of us does. We maintain our world with our inner dialogue. A man (or woman) of knowledge is aware that the world will change completely as soon as they stop talking to themselves."

When mindfulness is focused on the process of thinking, an entirely different dimension of existence becomes visible. We see how our ridiculous, repetitive thought stream continually constructs our limited sense of self, with judgments, defenses, ambitions, and compensations. When they are unexamined, we believe them. But if someone were to follow us close by and repeatedly whisper to us our own thoughts, we would quickly become bored with their words. If they continued, we would be dismayed by their constant criticisms and fears, then angry that they wouldn't ever shut up. Finally we might simply conclude that they were crazy. Yet we do this to ourselves!

And usually, if we are honest, we find that our judgments are untrue. As Ajahn Chah says, "It's simple. When somebody calls you a dirty dog, all you have to do is look at your butt. If you don't see a tail there, then that settles it." This holds true when we judge ourselves as well.

Try an experiment. At the end of this paragraph, put this book down, close your eyes, and try to count your thoughts for one or two minutes. Sit quietly and wait for them, like a cat at a mouse hole. Number each one. See what happens.

As you do you will notice a few interesting facts. Some of us have primarily word thoughts, others have picture thoughts. Some of us have both. Some thoughts even take the subtle form of body-based or intuitive knowings. At first, the thoughts tend to slow down because you're not so lost and identified with them. Then in a minute or two there may be five or twelve or twenty word thoughts, or a similar number of picture thoughts. Some thoughts may sneak up from behind: "There haven't been many thoughts yet, have there?" Some may try to capture your identity: "Am I doing this right?" If you sense carefully, you can also become aware of the gaps between thoughts, the space of awareness within which thoughts arise. It's as if you become the witness of all things, silent, open, alive. And if you look further, you find you are not even the witness, for if you look for the self, there is only witnessing, awareness itself with no one doing it.

By developing mindfulness of thought, we can see how our beliefs and fears blind us. On retreat, Aaron, a sixty-five-year-old clinical psychologist, confronted his thoughts about God. Born in Poland during World War II, he and his family experienced bombings, deprivation, and refugee camps. Two of his siblings died. The rest of his childhood was only marginally better.

After years of education, healing, and inner work, Aaron had pretty much come to terms with his past. But when he came to pursue meditation, he found it hard to trust either himself or his teachers. It was as if he were allergic to anything spiritual or religious. And yet he was also drawn to it. When we talked, I suggested he be mindful whenever he felt the upwelling of doubts and lack of trust. I encouraged him to notice his feelings and stories without reacting to them. As Aaron did so, the doubt and fear got stronger, scarier. He felt small. I reminded him to allow the space of mindfulness to hold it all.

Then Aaron remembered being a young boy whose image of religion and spirituality was a simple one, right out of the Bible. God was a powerful bearded man in the sky judging who was righteous and who was not. But it was this same God who had allowed the war, the killing, the devastation and loss. Aaron had long ago concluded that God himself was untrustworthy. And in spite of his doctoral degree and years of psychotherapy, this belief remained submerged in his mind, as powerful as ever.

Aaron laughed as he recognized these unconscious fears of religion. The old image of God began to dissolve even as he acknowledged it. But what would happen without this thought? I encouraged him to stay open. The next day he came in with arms outspread, saying, "Now I understand. This is God! The whole world of earth, plants, animals, and humans—everything is holy, and I am in its midst." He had found the sacred in life, here, now.

EXAMINING THOUGHTS

Buddhist psychology helps us work with thoughts in two important ways. First, it teaches us how to acknowledge the content of our thoughts. Second, we learn the ability to disentangle from them.

When we examine our thought stream with mindfulness, we encounter the inner sound track. As it plays, we can become the hero, the victim, the princess, or the leper. There is a whole drama department in our head, and the casting director is indiscriminately handing out the roles of inner dictators and judges, adventurers and prodigal sons, inner entitlement and inner impoverishment. Sitting in a meditation class, we are forced to acknowledge them all. As Anne Lamott writes, "My mind is like a bad neighborhood. I try not to go there alone."

When we see how compulsively these thoughts repeat themselves, we begin to understand the psychological truth of *samsara,* the Sanskrit word for circular, repetitive existence. In Buddhist teaching, samsara most commonly refers to the wheel of life. On this wheel, beings are reborn and subject to suffering until they develop understanding and find liberation. Samsara also describes the unhealthy repetitions in our daily life. On a moment-to-moment level, we can see our samsaric thought patterns re-arise, in unconscious and limited ways. For example, we see how frequently our thoughts include fear, judgment, or grasping. Our thoughts try to justify our point of view. As an Indian saying points out: "He who cannot dance claims the floor is uneven."

When we first pay attention, we discover that unhealthy thoughts are sticky, hard to step out of, like treacle. As Ajahn Buddhadasa observed, most of the time we are "lost in thought." Fortunately, with training, we can become mindful of the patterns of thought that condition our perception. We can cut through the sticky patterns of fear or competition, jealousy, judgment, or ambition.

To start, it helps to acknowledge the most repetitious thoughts, the "top ten tunes," by naming them. They might be repeated thoughts about money, or conflict, or anxious planning. The judging mind is another common tune, representing all the critical, disappointed voices from our childhood. If we fight it—"I shouldn't be judging. I'm too harsh"—we only add more judging. When the judging mind appears, we can simply acknowledge it with an inward bow and say, "Ah, yes, the judging mind." As soon as we do, the judging thought loses its power over us. We can even say, "Thank you for your opinion."

Like a sculptor who has many tools, there are a variety of skillful means to cut through the thicket of thoughts. If we are swept away, we may initially quiet the mind by concentrating on the breath or use a visualization or the simple repetition of a mantra. We can step outside our thoughts through mindfulness of the body or contemplative walking. We can release our thoughts by reflecting on death, on love, on emptiness. We can begin to look for moments of stillness whenever they arise.

Sometimes a teacher can help the whole community find a way to stillness. There was a silence around Ajahn Chah when he sat with us that supported our own steadiness. Zen master Thich Nhat Hanh carries this stillness even as he moves. Periodically, he has come to offer teachings to several thousand students gathered outdoors at Spirit Rock Meditation Center. Each time, as he walked up the road to begin teaching, the slow, beautifully careful placement of his steps on the earth was visible to all. A stillness fell over the crowd. The power of Thich Nhat Hanh's mindfulness brought everyone into the present. His presence inspired a profound attention.

This kind of attention is possible for us all. We do not have to sit with Thich Nhat Hanh or walk at the edge of the Grand Canyon. There is a vast silence around us always. Wherever we are, we can take a deep breath, feel our body, open our senses, and step outside the endless stories of the mind. We can stop. We can rest our awareness in a spacious and compassionate heart. Then we can see thought streams, worries, and images as only one part of a much larger story.

DISENTANGLING FROM THE STORY

It is a great relief to discover that our stories do not fully define who we are or what is happening to us. One practitioner was on a summer retreat at a camp in the redwoods. She awoke in the middle of the night startled, heart pounding, because she heard a loud growl just outside. She was sure it was a bear close by, perhaps dangerous. Turning on a small flashlight, she looked around and waited fearfully for the unknown growler to make another noise. At first it was quiet. Then after a minute had passed, her stomach let out a loud growl. She realized that the bean soup from dinner was having its way with her digestive tract! The loud growl was herself.

With mindfulness we can step out of the story we tell and simply notice the telling of it. We become the witnessing, the space of awareness. When we do this we rest in what Ajahn Chah calls the One Who Knows. With a quiet mind, the One Who Knows sees how we construct our world through repeating our stories. And, like the growling bear, we discover the stories are mostly untrue.

When people tell me that their meditations are filled with thoughts, I ask, "What do you commonly think about?" They describe stories of their longings and resentments, success and failure. They tell stories of their families, their work, their bodies, their spiritual and political worlds. Then we inquire together whether they are lost inside the story. I might ask, "Are there any moments, like right now, when you can simply acknowledge the story and its attendant feelings without identification, with a kind attention?" They usually take a breath and often report feeling more at ease. If it's a difficult or fearful tale, we will sit together in the presence of the story, absorbing its atmosphere for a long time, until the whole constellation of thoughts and emotions has been seen. Then we inquire into whether it is true. What are the beliefs about ourself constructed by the story? What is its worldview? Is it really true?

One woman, Paula, came to meditate after a wrenching divorce. Her husband had left her and their six-year-old son. Her grief was great, as were her fear and anger. She worked to become mindful of her feelings over many weeks. Beneath Paula's fears, a voice kept telling her a story about how unlovable she was and how she would always be left, abandoned. I inquired how long she had sensed herself this way. Paula replied that this was the story of her life. When she was three years old her own father had walked out and abandoned both Paula and her mother, and died several years later. Growing up, she felt that somehow his leaving was her fault. Paula believed that she was the problem, that she was flawed and unlovable.

For weeks I listened to Paula becoming more mindful of her divorce, with all the attendant grief and anger and fear. She practiced holding her body and her painful history in compassion. Finally Paula was ready to go back to the most painful scene of all. I asked her to close her eyes and remember the night her father left. She was three years old, wearing a light blue cotton dress, standing at the top of the stairs listening to her parents fight. Then she saw her father grab his suitcase and, without looking up at her, storm out of the door and out of her life. It was agonizing. "He didn't even look at me. He didn't say anything to me." When I asked what this little girl was thinking, she said, "I did something wrong; there's something wrong with me. Otherwise he would have stayed."

After Paula held this grief-stricken three-year-old child in compassion for a time, I asked her to imagine that she could enter the experience of her father standing at the door. "When you become him, how does your body feel?" I asked. "Awful. Tight, rigid, like I could explode. I'm terrified. I'm stuck in a terrible marriage that I didn't want, in a dead-end job. We fight all the time and I'm losing my life. I have to escape. I have to run away, to save my life." "And now as you pick up your suitcase to go out the door, do you know that your daughter Paula is standing there at the top of the stairs?" "I do, but I can't look at her. I can't. If I see the look on her face, I could never leave. I love her so much, but if I don't leave I'll die. I have to get out." Paula began to weep for her father and for his fear, for everyone's pain.

As we sat quietly, I asked Paula about the story that she had told since this day, that she had done something wrong, that she was unlovable. "Who made up this story?" I asked. After a pause, she replied sheepishly, "I did." "Is it true?" "Not really," she said, and half smiled at me. "Are you sure?" I asked. She laughed. We talked about whether she wanted to keep repeating the story and pattern of unlovability. "Who are you if not this story?" I asked. We looked at each other in the stillness of the heart, outside of her fears, outside of time. We sat together in the sacred beauty of the present that contains all stories and yet so much more. Paula began to feel free.

THE REALITY BELOW THOUGHTS

As we observe our thoughts and question our beliefs, we come to understand that while thinking, planning, and remembering are vital to our lives, they are more tentative than we believe. Our thoughts are always more provisional and one-sided than we admit. Ordinarily we believe them. But questioning our thoughts is at the heart of Buddhist practice. Is what we believe real, solid, certain? As writer Richard Haight observed, "Chief Roman Nose of the Cheyenne, and his people, believed he was immortal, and he, and they, were right every day of his life except one."

Ajahn Chah said, "You have so many views and opinions, what's good and bad, right and wrong, about how things should be. You cling to your views and suffer so much. They are only views, you know." When we believe our own thoughts and opinions we become fundamentalists. There can be fundamentalist Buddhists, fundamentalist scientists, fundamentalist psychologists. But no matter how strongly we believe our perspective, there are always other points of view. In our personal relationships this is really obvious. A relationship matures when each partner grants the possibility that the other may be right (even though we may not always believe it).

Most of our mental suffering comes from how tightly we hold our beliefs. In the monastery Ajahn Chah used to smile and ask, "Is it true?" He wanted us to learn to hold our thoughts lightly. In Buddhist training, our thoughts are deconstructed, the entire structure dismantled plank by plank.

There is a famous Sufi story about the holy fool Mullah Nasrudin. A king, disenchanted with his subjects' dishonesty, decided to force them to tell the truth. When the city gates were opened one morning, gallows had been erected in front of them. A royal guard announced, "Whoever will enter the city must first answer a question that will be put to them by the captain of the guard." Mullah Nasrudin stepped forward first. The captain spoke: "Where are you going? Tell the truth . . . the alternative is death by hanging." "I am going," said Nasrudin, "to be hanged on those gallows." "I don't believe you!" replied the guard. Nasrudin calmly replied, "Very well then. If I have told a lie, hang me!" "But that would make it the truth!" said the confused guard. "Exactly," said Nasrudin, "your truth."

Within the stillness of meditation we see the insubstantial nature of thought. We learn to observe how words and images arise and then vanish, leaving no trace. The succession of images and associations—often called mental proliferations—builds thought castles. But these castles and plans float for a time and then disappear, like bubbles in a glass of soda. We can become so silent that we actually feel the subtle thought energy appear and vanish again.

But if thoughts are empty, what can we rely upon? Where is our refuge? Here is how the Indian sage Nisargadatta answered this question: "The mind creates the abyss, the heart crosses it." The thinking mind constructs views of right and wrong, good and bad, self and other. These are the abyss. When we let thoughts come and go without clinging, we can use thought, but we rest in the heart. There is an innocence to the heart. We are the child of the spirit. And there is an innate wisdom. We are the ancient one. Resting in the heart, we live in harmony with our breath, our body. Resting in the heart, we become trusting and courageous, and our patience grows. We do not have to think it all through. Life is unfolding around us. As the Indian master Charon Singh put it, "In time, even grass becomes milk."

Of course, stories have value. As a teacher and storyteller, I have come to respect their evocative power, and in this book, I tell many stories. But even these stories are like fingers pointing to the moon. At best, they replace a deluded cultural narrative or a misleading fantasy with a tale of compassion.

In my individual meditation interviews, I try to help people drop below the level of their story and see the beauty that shines all around them. Psychologist Len Bergantino writes about a series of frustrating therapy sessions with a patient who was either disconnected and detached or excessively aiming to please. "The feeling I had on this particular day was I just didn't want to say one more word to him about anything. So, to his surprise, I took out my mandolin and in the most loving mellow beautiful way I could, I played 'Come Back to Sorrento.' He broke down in tears and cried for the last forty minutes of the session, saying only, 'Bergantino, you sure earned your money today!' I replied, 'And to think, I wasted all these years talking to people.'" When we drop below our stories, we are led back to the mystery of here and now.

THE BABY, THE BATHWATER, AND SKILLFUL THINKING

The point of mindfulness is not to get rid of thought but to learn to see thought skillfully. The Buddhist tradition trains the thinking mind and intellect to think clearly and well. We need to plan, think, organize, imagine, and create. Considered thoughts are a great gift. Our thoughts can set a direction, bring us understanding, analyze and discern, and put us in tune with the life around us. When we rest in the heart, then we can use thought wisely, we can plan and imagine in benevolent ways.

A professor of mathematics and topography who had come to meditation was worried because his work involved hours of thought. He asked how he could practice meditation while thinking through these complex math problems. Should he try to step back and always be deliberately aware of his thinking? This made him feel self-conscious. It was confusing. I responded with a simple instruction: "First, check your motivation. Approach the math in a positive and creative way. Then, when thinking about math, just think about math. If you get competitive and worry about publishing your solution before another colleague, that's not math. If you find yourself dreaming about winning the Nobel Prize or the Field Medal, that's not math. Find a skillful motivation. Then do the math and enjoy the creativity of the mind."

The key to wise thought is to sense the energy state behind the thought. If we pay attention, we will notice that certain thoughts are produced by fear and the small sense of self. With them will be clinging, rigidity, unworthiness, defensiveness, aggression, or anxiety. We can sense their effect on the heart and the body. When we notice this suffering we can relax, breathe, loosen the identification. With this awareness the mind will become more open and malleable. With this pause we return to our Buddha nature. Now we can think, imagine, and plan, but from a state of ease and benevolence. It's that simple.

PRACTICE: ONE-SIDED THOUGHTS

Choose an important area of your life where you have difficulty or conflict. Bring to mind the key beliefs, the thoughts you hold about the situation, the people, the institution, the circumstance: "They are . . . ," "I am . . . ," "It is . . . ," and so on. After you have brought the beliefs to mind, question them. Are they completely true? Are they one-sided? Who made up this story? What if some of the opposite was also true? What is your experience if you let these thoughts and beliefs go? Try letting them go, and rest in not knowing, or rest in loving-kindness. How does this affect your body and mind? How does this affect the situation? How is it to live not so caught up in your thoughts?

11

THE ANCIENT UNCONSCIOUS

Consciousness receives and preserves all our sense experience and perceptions.
These become storehouse consciousness, unmanifested and unconscious, until the
conditions for manifestation again become present.
—Fifty Verses on the Nature of Consciousness

Some years ago I was enjoying a walk with my mother in Golden Gate Park. Suddenly a black Labrador retriever began to run toward us. For both of us there was a moment of pure seeing and then the recognition *This is a dog*. Almost immediately there arose our patterns of response. For me it was warm feelings and a love of big sloppy dogs. For my mother, it was fear.

When she was four years old, my mother had stayed with a strict uncle. He periodically threatened that if she misbehaved she would be put down in the dark basement where his big Rottweiler lived. On seeing a dog running toward her, her unconscious memories, beliefs, emotions, and bodily holdings all became activated. She saw this friendly black Lab with the unconscious perception of a traumatized four-year-old. For some years my mother did not know why she feared dogs. Now, because she understands the genesis of her fears, she is somewhat less afraid. But in many ways she is still unconscious of her identification with her fear. The story and conditioning still operates as if she were a child.

Two thousand years before Freud and Jung probed the unconscious, Buddhist psychology taught about the unconscious foundation of human behavior. It described this foundation as having two different levels: first, the individual unconscious, and second, the universal unconscious, called storehouse consciousness. Though these levels are not ordinarily available to conscious awareness, they rule our lives. And with mindfulness they can gradually be made conscious and transformed.

THE INDIVIDUAL UNCONSCIOUS

Like my mother's fear of dogs, the individual unconscious contains memories, images, and beliefs about the nature of the world and ourselves. It also contains impulses such as fears, aggression, desires, insecurities, protectiveness, altruism, love, courage, and wisdom.

The patterns of perception held by the individual unconscious are called *sankharas*. These stored patterns are like seeds, the results of our past actions and perceptions. Every experience we have leaves an imprint, and this impression is stored as a seed, until proper conditions arise for it to reemerge. These seeds hold the potential for the future. The more often we repeat a pattern, the stronger the seed. Even if we seem to forget an incident, its seeds and impressions remain in the unconscious and can reemerge to affect the present and shape future perceptions and events. My mother's fear of dogs is a childhood seed that still arises strongly.

These stored patterns of perception have memories and beliefs, associated emotions, and even a physical dimension of patterns in the body. Mindfulness practice uncovers these patterns held in the individual unconscious. These become revealed through our body, our emotions, our images, our dreams. Sankharas that are unconscious can become conscious.

Gene had been trying devotedly for some years to meditate on his breath. But, he told me, every time he brought his attention to his breathing, it would bounce off like water on a hot skillet, or in two breaths he would find himself wafting into a dreamy state, like a swoon.

I considered changing his meditation subject from his breath to his whole body, or recommending that he listen to sounds to help his mind to settle. But first I suggested he become more curious. I suggested he focus on his breathing and notice carefully what happened. Instantly he became frustrated; it was almost impossible to do. I asked him to become mindful of what the frustration felt like in his body, and as he did so the agitation increased. He described his throat and neck as tight and hot, and fear began to arise. His breathing almost stopped. He wanted to scream. I asked him to sense the whole physical and emotional process mindfully, allowing space for whatever wanted to unfold.

The fear grew stronger, Gene's body shook, and his face changed, looking frightened and younger. I asked him to be mindful of any images that were arising along with the fear. Tears rolled down his cheeks. Moments later he opened his eyes with a look of understanding and said, "I was six years old in 1938. My father was the community dentist and we lived just on the edge of town—an Ohio farming community. Our cat had a big litter of kittens and no one would take them. The local farmers would drown puppies and kittens they couldn't find homes for. I watched my father take a cloth soaked in ether and hold it over their noses until they stopped breathing. Then we buried them.

"Three weeks later I was told I needed to have my tonsils out. My father took me over to the office of a friend, a doctor who practiced nearby. They prepared me and then, just as he had for the kittens, my father took out a bottle of ether for the anesthesia. I became panicked, terrified. I resisted, and then succumbed in a swoon and my tonsils were removed. I haven't thought about this in years. Now I understand what makes it so hard to feel my breath. It's as though I've held my breath since then."

I asked Gene to close his eyes again and notice what was happening. The tightness and burning in his throat was dissipating. His breath was easier. The fear was melting. Quite excited, he said he could feel five breaths in a row. We sat together, checking in every few minutes, and he meditated in a new way. Months later Gene told me his breath was still easy, and his inner life and body sense were freer than ever before.

Gene's story shows how relief can come from bringing unconscious patterns into awareness. Yet this process does not always yield simple, rapid healing. Certain traumas and unconscious patterns can take years to unravel. Buddhist teacher and psychiatrist Robert Hall tells how at age forty, while receiving a session of healing body work, a powerful series of images arose as the therapist pressed into his legs. He saw images of ropes and felt intense fear as if he were tied up, but he had no memory of what this could be. It was deeply disturbing. He wondered whether it came from a dream or from a movie he'd seen.

Sometime later he mentioned this to his mother. She told him that when he was three years old he had been abducted for several days. Search teams eventually found him tied up on the floor of a shack in the fields. She still had the newspaper clippings about it. She told Robert that after he was rescued, the family decided that the best way to handle it was never to talk about it again. Bringing this traumatic memory to light explained many of Robert's fears and confusions and gave him some relief. But these new understandings were just the beginning of his coming to terms with this trauma. For many years after, Robert struggled to heal the fear and suffering that was so deep in his past. In doing so Robert gradually released the hold of these memories and became increasingly compassionate and free.

STOREHOUSE CONSCIOUSNESS

Storehouse consciousness is a term used in Buddhist psychology to describe the oceanic dimension of the unconscious where all memory, history, and potential are contained. Storehouse consciousness has both individual and universal dimensions. In the individual dimension, storehouse consciousness holds the patterns, the sankharas, of each person's past. In the universal dimension, it is a shared reservoir of collective memories, images, and desires. Carl Jung explored some aspects of storehouse consciousness, using the term *collective unconscious*. More recently, neuroscientist Karl Pribram and physicist David Bohm compared consciousness to a hologram where the smallest part contains the information of the whole. The holographic record is the interpenetration of the individual and universal aspects of storehouse consciousness. Yogis, mystics, and shamans of all cultures have explored and described this dimension of human experience.

In ancient times, a Buddhist master of the Hua Yen school tried to demonstrate the interpenetrating nature of consciousness to the emperor of China. He built a special twelve-sided pavilion and covered the walls, floor, and ceiling with mirrors. When he led the emperor inside, he lit a candle that hung in the center of the room. The emperor could see how the single candle flame appeared in hundreds of images in the mirrors reflecting one another. "This," said the master, "is a demonstration of the one becoming many." Then the master hung a multifaceted crystal beneath the candle. Looking closely, the emperor could see how the smallest facet of the crystal reflected the hundreds of candle images around it. "This," said the master, "is a demonstration of the many in the one."

In the course of Buddhist training, a practitioner will encounter both the individual and collective dimensions of the unconscious. A woman named Evelyn had an experience of this kind during a retreat at Spirit Rock. Evelyn's English ancestors had settled in Missouri in the 1840s, and she had heard family stories of covered wagons and of battles with Indians. Later, she learned that she was one-sixteenth Indian. In the middle of the meditation retreat the images of this family history, of struggles and battles, flooded her mind. They were mixed with the history she had learned in school and memories of her domineering father. Some of what Evelyn saw reflected her personal childhood. But the images also pointed to something greater. Since grade school she had been sensitive to workers' rights and to the plight of people being pushed off their land, from the Mayans in Guatemala to the Palestinians in Israel. In sitting, she could feel her Native American blood and the experience of being oppressed. She could also feel her English blood and sense the oppressor in herself. Evelyn was ashamed of her family. But she also realized that the killing of indigenous people was not just her own family karma. Everyone who lives in North America participates in this history. Then she realized this is true everywhere in the world. We have been the oppressor and the oppressed; it has happened to us all.

A wave of compassion swept over her. She saw how we all contain the source of suffering and the potential for good. We cannot simply blame others, for we are a part of the whole. As Aleksandr Solzhenitsyn puts it, "If only it were all so simple! If only there were evil people somewhere insidiously committing evil deeds, and it were necessary only to separate them from the rest of us and destroy them. But the line dividing good and evil cuts through the heart of every human being. And who among us is willing to destroy a piece of their own heart?"

In meditation, students experience this interplay of individual and universal unconscious. Practitioners may initially notice the spontaneous emergence of old memories, forgotten scenes from childhood, previously unrecognized impulses and feelings. Often meditators will first enter a hypnogogic, half-asleep state and experience dream-like images filled with jumbled scenes with unknown people, foreign objects, and strange places. Sometimes these coalesce into long, dream-like story lines that unfold in whole dramas.

As meditation deepens, unconscious patterns held in the body and mind can arise. We can become aware of past history, of beliefs and images that were previously unconscious. Then we can find ourselves confronted with powerful feelings of greed, rage, fear, or grief far beyond anything we have ever known or acknowledged.

Sometimes they are connected with our personal history, and sometimes they arise as the more universal dimension of storehouse consciousness. When storehouse consciousness opens, we can spontaneously experience what Buddhist psychology calls the many planes of existence. These range from heavenly realms to animal realms to painful realms of woe. In the consciousness of the heavenly realms we may experience spontaneous uprising of sacred and religious imagery from any tradition, or encounter a dozen forms of celestial pleasures. There are temples, saints, angels, devas, and the sounds of choirs. I have spent joyful hours listening to what seemed like celestial music sung by luminous beings, and seen a hundred forms of sacred groves and temples. At other times when the realm of animals arose, I actually felt myself as a salmon, a crow, or an ant.

At still other times I experienced the universal dimension of suffering, where the imagery is of loss and destruction. I sat for days on retreat as a hundred spontaneous images of death arose. I saw my body killed and stabbed and trampled in war, or lying helpless on a hundred sickbeds with diseases, or dying from an accident, a fall, a drowning, a blow. I could feel my flesh decay and fall off my bones, leaving only my skeleton. Sometimes these images were personal and individual, as if they were my own memories. Sometimes they felt more archetypal, as if the nature of life and death was displaying itself to me. At this point in my training I had developed a strong base of mindfulness and equanimity to meet these images wisely. My teacher encouraged me to steady my attention and rely on the space of awareness—he called this a training for equanimity at death.

Here is an eleventh principle of Buddhist psychology:

11   There is a personal and a universal unconscious. Turning awareness to the unconscious brings understanding and freedom.

PAST-LIFE UNCONSCIOUS

When my concentrated mind was thus purified, steady, and attained to
imperturbability, I directed my mind to the knowledge of recollection of past life.
I recollected my manifold past life, that is to say, one birth, five births, ten,
twenty, fifty births, a thousand births, a hundred thousand births.
—The Buddha in the Majjhima Nikaya

Now we enter a dimension of Buddhist psychology that can pose
real questions for the Western mind—the teachings about past and
future lives. This multiple-life perspective is rooted in formal cosmology as well as in popular culture, where it serves to explain
both individual and social circumstances.

When I came to the forest monastery I was a scientifically
minded young man who was quite dubious about rebirth. Ajahn
Chah laughed and told me not to worry, that I could find freedom
without believing in reincarnation. Then he described a famous dialogue where the Buddha was asked by a wanderer what happens
after death. In response the Buddha posed a series of questions.
First he asked, "If there is a future life, how would you live?" The
questioner answered, "If there are future lives, I would want to be
mindful in order to sow seeds for future wisdom. And I would want
to live with generosity and compassion, because they bring happiness now and because they sow the seeds for abundance in the future." "Just so," said the Buddha. Then he went on: "And if there are
no future lives, how would you live?" The questioner reflected and
then answered in the same way: "If this were my only life, I would
also want to live with mindfulness, so as not to miss anything. And
I would want to live with generosity and compassion because they
bring happiness here and now and because I will not be able to keep
anything in the end." "Just so," acknowledged the Buddha. Eliciting
the same answers to those two questions, the Buddha demonstrated that living wisely does not depend on belief in an afterlife.

Nevertheless, the Buddha did teach about past lives on many
occasions. This teaching serves two important psychological functions. When the circumstances of suffering and pleasure in our life

are attributed to our past lives and past deeds, anxiety about a capricious, chaotic fate is eased. This perspective can bring acceptance, ease, detachment, and grace in facing life's difficulties. The second function of teachings about rebirth is to bring about greater care. We become careful with our actions out of concern for the results they may produce in future rebirths.

While belief in rebirth can bring a sense of order and understanding to life, it can also be misused. In some eras rebirth has been used to blame the victims of suffering or to justify complacency in the face of injustice. Any cosmology can be used in healthy or unhealthy ways. In the West, our religious cosmologies of heavens and hells and our mechanistic scientific cosmologies have been used in both helpful and destructive ways. In Buddhist cultures, belief in past and future births is primarily a positive, steadying influence for those encountering depressive and difficult circumstances. For example, Buddhist practitioners who experienced great loss or suffering in Cambodia believe the pain they experienced was the result of their own past deeds or karma, and this belief led them to accept their suffering with equanimity and dignity. It enabled them not to add more hatred, as a way to prevent future pain.

Buddhist cosmology is also experiential. It describes how previous-birth memories can arise out of storehouse consciousness in meditation and inner exploration. Past-life memories can be accessed through deliberate training, such as that outlined in meditation texts such as the Path of Purification, or they can emerge spontaneously. Of course there is almost no way to prove the reality of past-life memories, although a few intriguing studies have attempted to validate the facts of such claims. For example, Dr. Ian Stephenson of the University of Virginia has published many accounts of young children who have guided researchers back to places they have never been and recalled details about their past lives, people, and circumstances that they couldn't possibly have known about in this life. But psychologically there is no certain way to distinguish a past-life memory from a fantasy or a dream.

Nevertheless, circumstances that feel like past-life memories do arise. In the second year of my stay at the forest monastery, I remembered being in a medieval Chinese monastery. I could feel details of the life there: the tasteless gruel we ate, the cold meditation hall, the hours of discipline. It also seemed that I didn't want to be there, and that because of my resistance I missed the point. So here I was mysteriously drawn back to live shaven-headed in a Buddhist monastery in Thailand, a life that felt oddly familiar. Only now it was voluntary, and these past-life memories had a strong effect, motivating me to do it right this time.

I have also worked with a number of students who seemed to experience past-life memories. When Shelley came to Buddhist practice, she was seeking to center herself. Her life was a busy one, generally happy. But she lived with a substrate of anxiety, especially about her children, a son and daughter ages seven and ten. When Shelley sat in meditation on her first retreat and her anxiety arose, her breath would become shallow and her body rigid; she felt tightness especially around her shoulders and arms. Gradually she learned to become mindful of the bodily tension and the fluttering waves of anxiety as they moved through her. She was pleased that she could acknowledge the anxious states without being so easily caught and identified with them.

A few days later she came in to report that her lifelong fear of water had arisen in meditation. She had learned to swim at a community pool at age eight but never felt comfortable around water. It was almost summer now and her children would be swimming at the local pool and in their friends' pools. This terrified her too. "Ever since my own childhood, I've been really afraid of drowning. I asked my mother, but there is nothing she knows of that would have caused this. . . . I was afraid of water from my first infant baths."

Shelley worked with this fear, and with the stories and the sensations it generated, using both mindfulness and compassion. Then in one deep, silent meditation her body began to tremble, and there came a vision of a peasant woman in her late twenties with two children, running from a torrent of water that was engulfing their village. She became that woman, struggling to hold on, being caught by the flood, having the children ripped away from her, drowning as the water sucked her under. Her fear and grief were tremendous.

As she told me all of this, I too could feel the strong emotions, the panic, the drownings, the loss. Even more interesting, the whole state had an unusual feel to me, not as a story or dream, but more like a genuine memory. This feeling of a past-life memory will come once or twice in a hundred sessions with meditation students, and it has a different quality from the usual archetypal images of the storehouse unconscious.

I had Shelley close her eyes and return to the scene. As her tears fell, she felt a wave of sympathy for herself. Then it spread to encompass all parents who had lost children, tears of universal compassion.

I asked Shelley to see these images with the eyes of a sage. Now she sat as if at a distance from this memory. Was it real? she wondered. And even if it was real, where was it now? Her own identity began to dissolve: was she the peasant woman, was she Shelley? She sat quietly acknowledging the mysterious web of creation and emptiness.

Her anxiety diminished for a time, but it didn't go away completely. It took Shelley a few years to learn to hold her bouts of anxiety with grace. But the understanding she gained from what seemed to be a past-life memory was a key. She became wiser, more relaxed, and freer through it all.

DREAMS AND THE UNCONSCIOUS

Shortly before the Buddha's birth, as the old tales recount, his royal mother had a dream of a white elephant. When the court wise men were called to interpret it, they predicted the birth of a world-turning monarch or a great sage. From the start, Buddhist psychology, like many ancient traditions, has recognized the symbolic and predictive value of dreams and the way dreams can reflect our desires, conflicts, and drives. In some schools dream interpretation is common. The teachings invite practitioners who remember their dreams to meditate upon waking. The dream images and strong feelings are investigated with mindfulness until an ease and freedom with them are established.

Two thousand years later, Freud, Jung, and their followers proclaimed dreams "the royal road to the unconscious." They found that dreams can reveal unconscious conflicts, desires, identities, and patterns and show us the unrecognized forces that operate in our daily lives. The wisdom of dreams is brought forth through interpretation, symbolism, active imagination, and dozens of forms of modern Western dream work. As in Buddhist mindfulness practice, most dream work begins through remembering our last dreams and dream fragments upon waking, and then investigating them.

But Buddhist psychology goes further, through the practices of dream yoga. These practices teach us not only to remember our dreams but also to be aware while we are dreaming. In dream yoga we can even direct our dreams to some extent, deliberately exploring the dimensions of consciousness that dreams represent. This ability, called lucid dreaming, was for a long time dismissed by Western science. Then twenty years ago at Stanford University sleep lab researchers led by Stephen LaBerge confirmed the possibility of conscious dreaming and intentionally directing our dreams.

In Buddhist training, lucid dreaming is systematically developed through concentration and repeated intention over many days. But even without deliberate training, lucid dreaming can arise spontaneously on extended retreats. I have had this experience many times when I reached a state of deep concentration. At this stage, I would carefully lie down to sleep, continuing to meditate as I began to relax. My body would become quite still and my breath very soft, my mind would sink into sleep, and initial dreams would appear. But the mindfulness that I had been practicing over days and weeks continued, and I could consciously notice myself falling asleep and see the dreams as they arose. I continued to be mindful of it, as if I were sitting in meditation, until the dream ended and dreamless sleep appeared.

These spontaneous episodes of lucid dreaming began to

happen to Kevin, a practitioner on a two-month spring retreat. One day he talked about watching himself dream: a familiar dream of standing at the edge of a cliff, terrified of falling. It was easy to find symbolic associations. He worried that his career as a writer was falling apart. And several weeks before the retreat began he had met a woman that he was "falling for."

I suggested that if this lucid dream recurred, he bring mindfulness to it as if he were sitting in meditation. Then he could just allow things to unfold. Several days later, the dream reappeared. Kevin let go and felt himself fall over the cliff. After a moment of panic he began to float. Then he found himself walking down a rural road in a very green countryside he'd never seen. Over the weeks after this dream, Kevin's meditation deepened. He had other lucid dreams. And he reported a new sense of trust that lasted his whole retreat.

In the final stage of Buddhist dream training, we are instructed to sustain meditative awareness until the waking state can be observed alternating with the dream state and with dreamless sleep, each appearing in consciousness for a time, each equally empty. From this perspective, dream content, so richly valued in the West, is seen as secondary in Buddhist practice. It is finding equanimity within the play of consciousness, an unshakable ease with every state of sleeping and waking, that is the purpose of meditation.

THE UNCONSCIOUS ROOTS OF SUFFERING

Buddhist psychology insists we come to terms with the power of our unconscious drives and instincts and the enormous suffering they can cause. The three unhealthy roots—grasping, aversion, and delusion—must be clearly understood and transformed. This is a difficult process, as we will see in the chapters ahead. These three roots are the primary unconscious drives, which generate all the difficult mental states. Grasping, aversion, and delusion give rise to anger, pride, fear, sloth, and overindulgence. They produce misperception, doubt, restlessness, clinging to subtle pleasure, and the comparing mind. These unconscious forces can lie dormant, and when conditions are right they are activated.

With mindfulness we can become aware of the impulses of greed or pride or anger and release some of their powerful effects. But we soon discover that even if we let go of our entanglement in them for a moment, they will return. This is because their unconscious roots remain untouched. Buddhist psychology describes how deep and powerful these roots can be. As Freud and his Western colleagues have done, it endeavors to bring them into conscious awareness. But then, Buddhist teaching shows how human development can take a significant step beyond the awareness and accommodation of drives that is the fruit of most Western clinical practices. It teaches that these deepest roots can be transformed in a way that brings a degree of freedom unknown to the West.

These deep drives, unconscious fears, graspings, and confusions are called the latent roots. Through profound insight and deep meditation, these latent roots can be released, bringing successive degrees of freedom, called stages of enlightenment. In the first enlightenment stage the confusions about the way, doubts about freedom, and misunderstandings about the self are released. In the next two enlightenment stages the instinctual roots of greed and aggression are weakened and then released. In the final stage the last unconscious clinging to refined states of consciousness and attachments to any sense of self are dissolved.

In this process, Buddhist practice directs awareness to penetrate to the very bottom of the individual psyche. In the forest monasteries, advanced meditators are instructed to deliberately investigate these unconscious forces and thus release themselves from their power. Meditators who have trained their mind to be concentrated, steady, clear, and transparent will examine the heart, search for the latent roots of suffering there, and release them. They will systematically bring up images of what they most deeply fear or hate or crave. In this practice, we can take any area of suffering in our life. We bring it to mind, then we carefully examine the unconscious roots of this suffering. Where is this suffering felt most strongly in our body? What are the underlying emotions, images, and beliefs that hold it in place? These difficult images, feelings, and bodily contractions are faced and examined repeatedly. With profound attention we discover these instincts and drives to be empty, the stuff of illusion, and we are released from them and become free.

Release from the unconscious tendencies is the work of a lifetime. In the next chapters we will see how transforming the latent tendencies that bind us is the key to our own liberation. Again and again we can discover that they are not who we really are.

III

TRANSFORMING
THE ROOTS OF
SUFFERING

12

BUDDHIST PERSONALITY TYPES

See how those whose nature inclines toward discipline are studying with Upali, master of discipline, and those of intuitive temperament are gathered with the master of psychic powers, Maha Mogallana, and those with a wisdom temperament are together with Sariputra, my wisest disciple.
—Buddha describing the temperaments of his senior disciples

When you see a straight piece of wood, you don't want to make it into a wheel, nor do you try to make a rafter of a crooked piece. You don't want to pervert its inborn quality, but rather see that it finds its proper place.
—Chuang Tzu

Any mother who has several children can attest to the distinctly individual style of each child, evident from the day of their birth. I am a fraternal twin, but my brother and I are quite different. Growing up, he was the more outgoing, social type. Bigger and more adventurous, he played football and took the lead in school plays, while I played oboe in the orchestra. I was a skinny nerd, more intellectual and insecure. When we turned sixty, my mother remarked, "Now I know what's alike about them. They're both losing their hair."

When people first begin to be mindful of their personality they are frequently dissatisfied by what they find: they often want to become like someone else. In Buddhist communities, students may try to overcome their dissatisfaction by unconsciously imitating the manner and personality of their teacher. I have seen the followers of one famous lama eat the same kinds of noodles, make the same hand gestures, and speak with a Tibetan accent. Students of a Western Zen teacher I know dress in similar hats and shoes and have become obsessed with her favorite TV game shows. When we are looking for ways to deal with our own confusion, anger, and fear, we try imitation. We hope to get rid of our own personality and become more like the Dalai Lama or some other admired person.

Ajahn Chah noticed this pervasive self-dissatisfaction when he helped lead a retreat at the Insight Meditation Society in Barre, Massachusetts, in 1979. He was struck by how hard Western students are on themselves and how much they struggle to change themselves. One afternoon during walking meditation, I took Ajahn Chah outside and we wandered among the dozens of students who were walking slowly up and down the grassy lawn. Ajahn Chah remarked to me that the meditation center was kind of like a hospital. As we passed by the students, he would smile and say to them with amusement, "I hope you get well soon."

What does it mean to transform ourselves? How much can and should human beings change? When we look at the state of our own mind these become urgent questions. Any comprehensive psychology must address them. Buddhist psychology offers radical change, but it differentiates between the gold of our natural personality and the unhealthy states that cover it up like the clay of the old Buddha. As we shall see in the chapters ahead, we can transform the unhealthy roots of suffering, but this must be done within the framework of our own personality and temperament, not by getting rid of them.

Ajahn Jumnian, one of my teachers from southern Thailand, liked to exaggerate personality and temperament in order to transform them. For example, he spoke of Somchai, a builder and contractor, who had come to his monastery to live for a year as a monk.

In Thai society, taking monastic ordination is considered a selfless act. But even as a monk, Somchai was quite full of himself. He repeatedly boasted of his beautiful homes and his business successes. Hearing this, Ajahn Jumnian praised him too. Then he told Somchai that the monastery needed a large and elegant receiving hall for the hundreds of daily visitors. He wasn't sure if Somchai was up to the task. Somchai took the bait and went to work. Later Ajahn Jumnian explained that if Somchai succeeded, by collaborating with people at the temple, he would learn to be more respectful and less boastful. Or else Somchai would fail, and that would be a good lesson for him as well. In the end, after a year of hard work, the monastery had a new hall, and Somchai had learned to work in concert with others.

The next year, Nak, a local boxer and tough guy, arrived at the monastery. His mother had died and he became a monk as a way to honor her memory. Ajahn Jumnian knew Nak by reputation, and after observing him for a while, he asked Nak to be his bodyguard. In fact, Ajahn Jumnian did not need a bodyguard. He was a famous peacemaker who had worked for fifteen years to end the war against the Communist rebels in his province. It was his practice to deliberately walk into the conflict and speak to both the Communist and the government sides openly and unguarded, trusting the dharma. But the role of bodyguard gave Nak a way to transform his aggression into dignity. It also kept him close to Ajahn Jumnian, where he could learn the compassion he needed to open his heart.

Another new monk, Prasert, was a likable villager but also an alcoholic. His charm and generous temperament quickly brought him many friendships within the monastery. Sometime after his arrival, however, the story reached Ajahn Jumnian that Prasert had been seen climbing over the monastery wall at night to drink with old friends on the outside. When confronted, Prasert confessed and vowed to change. But alcoholism needs more than vows. After Prasert was seen returning from another nighttime bout of drinking, Ajahn Jumnian called a meeting. He asked all of Prasert's good friends in and out of the monastery to come. He extolled Prasert's caring heart and acknowledged that many people loved him.

Unfortunately, he went on, the traditional monastic rules would require him to expel Prasert if he got drunk again. "Because you are all his friends," Ajahn Jumnian went on, "I must put him in your charge." And from that day Prasert's friends kept him out of trouble.

Ajahn Jumnian recognized the basic goodness in the temperaments of each of his students. Then he focused on transforming the grasping of Somchai, the aversion of Nak, and the delusion of Prasert.

Grasping, aversion, and delusion: we have met this trio before. These are the classic "three roots" of all unhealthy states, and they also create three unhealthy personality types, three styles of approaching the world. The first, like Somchai, is ruled by wanting. The second, like Nak, is ruled by rejecting. The third, like Prasert, is governed by confusion. With mindfulness, each of these unhealthy temperaments can be changed into healthy patterns. Then we can see that the personality is not a permanent essence. Like the body, it is a temporary condition. It is not who we really are.

Sometimes people read about Zen or hear Buddhist teachings about selflessness or non-attachment and mistakenly believe Buddhism is not interested in personality. New students can even be afraid that meditation will cause them to end up without one. But our temperament is to be understood, not eliminated. Knowing our temperament, we can use this understanding to bring compassion to ourselves and others. We can work with our personality to transform the aspects that are unhealthy. And then we can recognize our true nature that is beyond the limitations of any personality.

Here is a twelfth principle of Buddhist psychology:

12 The unhealthy patterns of our personality can be recognized and transformed into a healthy expression of our natural temperament.

Psychology East and West acknowledges that children come into this world with distinct temperaments and styles. Buddhism describes these as karmic tendencies. Western psychology might call this our genetic inheritance. But this is only one part of our personality. Later, our innate temperaments are shaped by conditioning from parents and environment. Through the interaction of inheritance and conditioning, nature and nurture, our personality is formed.

The West has produced dozens of descriptions of personality. Freud, Reich, Jung, Fromm, Erikson, and others offer a wide range of theories to account for personality development, temperament, and congnitive style. Each theory highlights different aspects of the personality: patterns of desire, relations to power and authority, degrees of autonomy, or modes of thinking. Each theory sheds light on human development and offers another channel for therapeutic intervention.

Within Buddhism, personality systems have also flourished. The list makers of the past have expanded the three basic personality types to include fourteen subtypes, eighty-four more subtle types, and a Tibetan system that divides these personalities into five major families. Fortunately, all these are rooted in the three types. They are all we need to illuminate the whole process of transformation. Here is how you can begin to understand the three basic types:

FINDING YOUR TYPE

Imagine you have been asked by a good friend to visit her recently purchased and newly furnished house for the first time. She greets you at the door and you enter.

Do you tend to see first what you like about the house—the stone fireplace, the Mexican tile, the paintings, the wall colors— and dwell on those features? In this spirit, do you linger, finding the things that you enjoy, imagining how you might build on them, fix the glitches and make each room even better?

Or perhaps as you look around you more naturally notice the

obvious problems: the too-small kitchen, the closeness of the neighbors, the cheap aluminum windows, the lack of an open view. You might move through quickly and wonder critically about how your friend will fare in this new house.

Or you may arrive a bit late, feeling somewhat overwhelmed, glad to see your friend, but not so focused on the house at all. You look around and congratulate your friend, but you're not sure what else to say. The truth is you're a bit distracted and thinking of other things.

Which of these scenarios most fits your style, the first, second, or third?

Next, suppose that during your visit, your friend tells you about a disrespectful remark made by a third friend, criticizing the work of the nonprofit organization at which you are employed. How do you most naturally respond? Do you try to soften it and cast it in a more sympathetic light? Do you see how wrong it is and get charged up about your conflict with their position? Or do you mostly try to ignore it and move on to whatever is next?

Finally, suppose your friend tells you enthusiastically about a new spiritual teaching she just attended. She repeats the inspiring words and perspective as if they were the best thing on earth. As you listen, do you too get inspired by her enthusiasm and enjoy the nuggets of truth in her words? Or do you feel somewhat skeptical of your friend's enthusiasm and view the teachings a bit critically, thinking they're a repackaging of the same old stuff, and not very well thought out at that? Or do you find her account confusing, because you're not sure how this new perspective fits with your own spiritual life, or how it relates to other things your friend believes? Which is your most likely response?

These three scenarios illustrate the common patterns of the three root temperaments. The first responses are those of the grasping temperament, the second are those of the aversive temperament, and the third are of the deluded temperament. Naturally, we all contain a measure of each temperament, as the traditional texts acknowledge. But often one pattern predominates as we move through the world.

Now let's look at them in greater depth.

THE GRASPING TEMPERAMENT BEFORE
TRANSFORMATION

The grasping or greed temperament is constructed around desire. It is experienced as a sense of seeking, of wanting more, and of addiction. It grasps after comfort and avoids disharmony in all situations. It desires fulfillment through pleasures, finding what it likes in the world of the senses. From liking, it can move quickly to craving, passion, and sensuality. Out of the roots of grasping there arise associated states of vanity, willfulness, pride, self-centeredness, jealousy, avarice, deceit, and addiction. The grasping temperament is associated with an even balance of the elements of earth, air, fire, and water.

Each temperament also has a distinctive physical style. The traditional teachings declare that those with a grasping temperament walk graciously, with an elegant and springy step; their stance is confident and composed. They like to sleep comfortably, wake up slowly, stretch, and relax, and take food unhurriedly, choosing rich, sweet food to savor. In modern life, the person with such a temperament drives a car with a relaxed, easy attention and moves gracefully in traffic.

When individuals with a grasping temperament enter a room, they see whatever is pleasing and linger upon it. They leave most pleasant circumstances slowly and with regret. When meeting new people, they seize on trivial virtues and discount genuine faults, and in conversation they avoid conflict and seek harmony, even by dishonesty.

THE AVERSIVE TEMPERAMENT BEFORE
TRANSFORMATION

The aversive temperament is constructed around judgment and rejection of experience. It has a disaffected quality that easily sees faults, and for this temperament, problems are apparent everywhere. It is critical, quickly displeased, quarrelsome, and disparaging of many things. Its quality of aversion can give rise to states of anger, vindictiveness, haughtiness, hatred, cruelty, aggression, and the struggle to control. There is a tight-fisted and rigid quality to this temperament. It is associated with the elements of fire and wind.

Traditionally, the aversive temperament is associated with one who walks quickly, with hard steps. The stance is rigid; such characters move stiffly and unevenly, with tension and tightness. The aversive temperament is described as one who lies down hastily, sleeps with a scowl, wakes up quickly as if annoyed, and takes food sometimes sour and rough, eating it hurriedly without savoring it. Yet they are displeased and aggrieved when their food is not right. Today, the person with such a temperament would drive hurriedly, gripping the wheel tightly, and move in traffic jerkily, easily annoyed by other drivers.

When people with an aversive temperament enter a room, they notice what is wrong, focusing on the difficulties, seizing upon any slightly unpleasant object, picking out trivial faults and discounting real virtues. Or they pay scanty attention, avoid real connection as if tired or bored, and leave quickly as if anxious to go.

THE DELUDED TEMPERAMENT BEFORE TRANSFORMATION

The deluded or confused temperament is constructed around uncertainty and confusion. People with this temperament experience not quite knowing what to do or how to relate to the world. They seek to establish ease by ignoring what is happening or through dullness or inaction. The deluded temperament gives rise to perplexity and worry, doubt, negligence, scattered thoughts, anxiety, and agitation. The deluded type can also seem easily intoxicated. It is associated with the heaviness of earth and the movement of water.

Traditionally deluded characters are those whose stance is muddled, who walk hesitantly with a perplexed gait, who shuffle along, and who act in an indecisive and uneven manner. They are described as those who sleep with limbs sprawling or facedown and wake with a "huh?" They take food casually, not knowing what they want, and eat messily, dropping bits with mind astray. In modern life, they are inattentive drivers, drifting over the road, mixed up and meandering in traffic.

When people with the deluded nature enter a room they feel confused, not knowing what to do or how they should act. They are not related to their own body and do not know themselves. In conversation they copy what others are doing: if everyone is praising, they praise, while if everyone is critical, they join in. In general, they are inconsistent and a bit lost.

ACCEPTING ONE'S QUIRKY PERSONALITY

No matter how old a mother is, she watches her middle-aged children
for signs of improvement.
—Florida Scott-Maxwell

Initially, none of these personality types sounds very appealing. Looking closely at personality and temperament is like looking closely at the body. The human body looks best when viewed from an intermediate distance, in soft light. When we look more closely, we see the pores, the teeth, the body hair, the shape, the blemishes. Even the youngest and most beautiful bodies can seem terribly flawed to their inhabitants. Observing the personality is even more distressing.

When students first sit with themselves on a silent meditation retreat, their personality patterns are magnified. Halfway through one retreat, a student's hand-lettered note appeared on the bulletin board with these words: "Self-knowledge is bad news." Aversive types become aware of hundreds of judgments—of themselves, of the other students, of the teacher, the room, and on and on. Grasping types discover their perennial hunger for what they are missing. They want the best seat, the coziest room, the big piece of dessert. Their addictive nature intensifies. If they are a confused type, their doubts become huge. They wonder what they are doing here and why. They doubt the teachers, they question the value of sitting quietly, they doubt themselves—*Am I worth all this attention?*

One student confessed that in trying to compensate for his personality, he spent five years of practice simply trying to look different. Another said what she hoped for was a total personality transformation. But it doesn't happen that way. We have to work with what we've got.

In the forest monastery, I quickly discovered that I am a classic greed type. Give me a run-down hovel or a forest hut and I will sweep it clean and look for a flower to put in the window. Some say the greed temperament is the easiest to work with. But in my experience, greed prevents me from seeing the world as clearly as the aversive types, and I get much more attached than deluded types. Without mindfulness, I am always looking for what I want, or for ways to make things better. There is an addictive quality to my relationship to food, contact, sensuality. And a deeper unfulfilled loneliness. Unconsciously, I'm always trying to please people. From this state, everything tilts toward the future. Get busy, get more, get things done, fix it all, do even better, bigger. When my grasping is strong, temptations, possibilities, arrogance, and pride grow. I can ignore conflicts and get lost in a goal. I want it all to work out, to be OK.

The good news is that I am not my personality. None of us is. At times, I think of the personality as a stubborn and demanding pet. We can train it to have better manners, but for the rest of its life, it will require a certain amount of affection, water, and kibble. It helps to have some humor in tending this pet, whatever its quirks are. In truth, the community of Buddhist, Hindu, and other spiritual teachers is as eccentric and weird a group of personalities as you will find anywhere, myself included.

One Zen teacher, a friend, describes herself as a total aversion type. When she travels, she's always dissatisfied with the food or the climate, how hot or cold or bumpy or tedious it is, or with how her body feels or what her friends are doing. But she has become so humorous about it that she's really rather fun when she describes her aversion attacks. She'll say, "I'm having an attack. I hate that stupid airport and the totally dumb way we had to check in at the gate. I'll never travel again." Then she'll pause. "Of course you know what I'm saying isn't true and we'll be traveling again next month and I'll complain just as much." Then she'll laugh in a way that's really quite endearing.

Another Buddhist teacher is a greed type who describes himself as a holdover from the Roman Empire. He loves food, sensuality, comfort, pleasure, and satisfaction. He's simply honest about it. He is self-effacing, warm, generous, charitable; he wants others to accept themselves. And around him they do: people love to spend time with him. His love of life translates as a palpable generosity to others.

A third spiritual teacher I know would call himself a deluded type, a bit confused, messy, not quite unkempt—not very together on the physical plane. As he travels he can be a space case on details, and he gets mixed up working with others, confused about what he's involved with, feeling like he doesn't know what he is doing. But he is greatly loved for his kind heart, deep compassion, and honest vulnerability, and his absentminded professor qualities are charming to those around him.

To make the three Buddhist types visible at one of our study retreats, we gathered groups of similar temperament together. We let the five or six people of the same type describe how they moved through the world. The greed types were harmonious and polite, giving lots of interesting examples of how they minimized problems and tried to manipulate circumstances to get the best outcome. As the aversive types told stories of judgments and problems, they got into conflict with each other and with some of the people who were watching. The deluded types were simply unfocused and confusing. And when we put different types together, the aversives said, "I never quite understood what was wrong with my deluded friends. Now I see it's a whole way of being."

Once we recognize the patterns of personality, we can see them for what they are: simply different patterns of energy. This perspective is so helpful to see in a marriage, a partnership, a community. Our personalities are not *wrong,* they are simply different. When we accept this fact, we can hold them with spacious consciousness.

The sage Krishnamurti sees this acceptance as the ground of awakening. "As long as you are trying to be something other than what you actually are, your mind wears itself out. But if you say, 'This is what I am, it is a fact that I am going to investigate and understand,' then you can go beyond."

Like Ajahn Jumnian and Ajahn Chah, when I work with people I am interested in the initial patterns of temperament they display. Critical and argumentative, gregarious or shy, confused or chaotic, each holds tremendous potential. Sara, a student who came to work with me, carried a lot of shame and insecurity from her family. She was shy and easily confused. It was hard to tell whether her confusion and inability to speak out were primarily the result of trauma or whether this had been her temperament from the start. It turned out to be both. She loved meditation and initially it helped release her from her family pain. As her mind quieted, her clarity grew. But Sara was still very shy in groups, and this made her very self-critical. She practiced seeing her self-judgments as impersonal, as past conditioned patterns, not true. Sara was an herbalist and gardener who loved spending time alone. She had trouble with too much people contact. Others judged her for being a loner, and she judged herself.

I asked her if she knew that she was quite introverted. She nodded. I acknowledged what a hard time introverts can have in our gregarious American culture. Like Sara, many introverts come to our meditation retreats. They describe how almost no one understands or appreciates them. This is not so in every culture. I told Sara of a friend who hitchhiked all through Finland and Lapland. He said that he rode for hundreds of miles with people who were comfortable not talking. Sara loved hearing about this. She told me she got disconnected from herself if she didn't get enough solitude, but she had always felt it was wrong. When we were done with our conversation she gave me a beautiful, timid smile. The gold of her original goodness was shining through.

Another student, Jeff, was a melancholy fellow who usually saw the glass as half empty. By temperament he was an aversive type; he easily judged himself and others. But he also had a creative wit and a clear vision. I liked talking to him. Even though somewhat depressive, he was smart, well educated, and funny. I once heard him sing the blues, with a few jokes added for relief. It was a perfect fit for Jeff, both suffering and humor. As Jeff worked with Buddhist practice, his humor began to include himself. He could see his personality patterns with more acceptance. The stream of judgments softened. With gratitude practice, his melancholy lifted somewhat. Then he quit working at a small business and became a high school science teacher. His self-revealing honesty and sharp wit endeared him to his students. Over the years, his temperament, though fundamentally the same, was transformed. His clarity, now carried with more dignity and nobility, became evident to all.

Another practitioner, Joseph, worked as a physical therapist. Joseph was an aversive type with an anxious and fearful temperament. Whenever there was a small glitch or problem, his imagination turned toward the most alarming possibilities. A missed call from his wife meant she was in the hospital. Storms in the weather forecast meant that his son's plane might crash when it landed. He had a tough family history. The Ku Klux Klan had burned his grandmother's house. His father had been hospitalized for depression. As a child he was hypersensitive and easily frightened and confused. This hypersensitivity now served him well in his work as a physical therapist, but it made his personal life difficult. With breath practice Joseph learned to relax the stress in his body and disidentify from his fretful and catastrophic thoughts. He remained thoughtful and caring, and as he better managed his own stress and anxiety, his sensitivity made him a brilliant healer. And even though he can still become anxious, he doesn't believe his anxieties. He became more fearless in spite of himself.

THE ALCHEMY OF TRANSFORMATION

The founder of modern chemistry, Antoine Lavoisier, said, "Nothing is lost, everything is transformed." He could have been speaking of the heart and mind as easily as of chemical reactions. Transformation is possible. It is not the exception, it is the rule.

This transformation is ritually portrayed whenever a statue of

the Buddha is cast for a temple. Before the casting, participants
gather at the temple. There is a special collection of gold for casting the flame of enlightenment that rises from the Buddha's head.
Precious jewelry, sacred amulets, even old wedding rings are offered into a crucible and melted to form the flame of wisdom.
Symbolically, the base metals of vanity, materialism, superstition,
and broken hearts are transformed into the gold of liberation.

In the same way, we can learn to transform the unhealthy states
of our personality. They are not who we really are and yet, like gold,
they are not lost. While our problems don't stop when we recognize and do not identify with them, we are no longer reactive and
stuck. Their liberated energy brings us more fully alive.

The grasping temperament, when transformed, gives rise to
beauty and abundance. Just as Somchai built an exquisite meditation hall for Ajahn Jumnian, we take whatever situation we find
ourselves in and bring beauty to it. We highlight the goodness and
generosity of the people around us and we make our home and
community places of harmony. As a greed type at Spirit Rock, I pay
attention to the aesthetics of stone walls, cushions, and artwork to
make it a beautiful place for practice. I also work to mentor and admire the people around me. I trust the benefits of a gracious work-
place. I think of a fellow greed type, a physician who tells me how
his whole surgical team performs better when he plays beautiful
music in the operating room. In this way, our habitual tendencies
can become gifts to those around us.

The aversive temperament, when transformed, gives rise to
discriminating wisdom, non-contentiousness, and loving-kindness.
Anger can be transformed into strength and clarity that unite the
opposites. Some of the most important ideas at Spirit Rock come
from the caring dissatisfaction of our aversive types. They don't want
to put up with mediocrity or lack of integrity, so they speak the
truth about our problems and catalyze the group energy. They are
not afraid of difficulties; they know the value of working creatively
with conflicts. As poet and businessman James Autry explains, "If
you think managing conflict and diversity are problematic, then you
haven't thought through the problems of managing sameness. I'd far

rather be faced with trying to achieve harmony and goodwill among people who are at one another's throats than try to squeeze an ounce of innovation or creativity or risk out of a group full of photocopies of each other."

When transformed, the deluded temperament gives rise to spaciousness, equanimity, and understanding, called the wisdom of great questioning. At Spirit Rock the confused types contribute an innocence and beginner's mind. They ask, "How does it feel to come here when you don't know anything about meditation? Will you understand what's going on? Will you feel safe? Why are we doing what we do—is it just from habit?" A Sufi story tells us, "A man who had studied much in the schools of wisdom finally died in the fullness of time and found himself at the Gates of Eternity. An angel of light approached him and said, 'Go no further, O mortal, until you have proven to me your worthiness to enter into Paradise!' But the man answered, 'Just a minute now—first of all, can you prove to me this is the real Heaven and not just the wishful fantasy of my disordered mind undergoing death?' Before the angel could reply, a voice from inside the gates shouted, 'Let him in—he is one of us!' "

Finally, beyond transformation, we can learn to release our identification with the personality altogether. Harrison Hoblitzelle, a Buddhist teacher and friend, demonstrated this transformation when he became sick. In his sixties Hob was diagnosed with Alzheimer's disease. Alzheimer's and other forms of dementia are terrifying to most people. And indeed, Hob's decline was a long, difficult ordeal for his family. Nevertheless, when he was first diagnosed, he was determined to use his disease as a place of practice. He had been a generous, gentlemanly figure, dedicated to his students and to the practice of loving-kindness. He continued to offer to the world a kind heart, even as his memory and identity failed.

During the first several years of his decline, Hob would still occasionally teach and speak about his experience. One evening, however, he found himself standing before a meditation group having forgotten who he was and why he was there. So he simply began to mindfully acknowledge out loud his experiences: "blank mind, nervousness, fear, body tense, embarrassment, coolness, curiosity, nervousness, calming, relaxing, blank mind, loving feelings, warmer, less trembling, still uncertainty," and so on for several minutes. It was all he could do. He stopped, rested quietly, and bowed to the audience. They stood up and applauded in honor of his presence and his courage. It was, as several said, "among the finest teachings I have ever received." For a moment, Hob had transformed even Alzheimer's into freedom.

PRACTICE: ACKNOWLEDGING YOUR PERSONALITY TYPE

Go back to the quiz that starts on page 171. Reflect on these three scenarios, and try to place your most predominant experience in one of the three basic temperaments. Once you choose the closest temperament, become mindful of it.

- Observe how your temperament functions for a whole day with people, circumstances, pleasures, difficulties.
- Notice how temperament is an impersonal pattern that operates rather automatically.
- Notice if there is any judgment of your personality, and see what happens if you let the judgment go.
- Notice what is most valuable about your temperament, such as appreciation, clarity, or an easygoing nature.
- See what happens if you focus on these positive aspects.

Now think of a good friend or any person close to you who has a very different temperament. Envision him or her in the three scenarios. Place this person into one of the three basic temperaments. Once you acknowledge their temperament, become mindful of it.

- Observe how their temperament functions with people, circumstances, pleasures, difficulties.
- Notice how this personality style is an impersonal pattern

that operates rather automatically.

- Notice if you hold any judgment about it, and see what happens if you let the judgment go.
- Notice what is most valuable about their temperament, such as appreciation, clarity, or an easygoing nature.
- See what happens if you focus on these positive aspects.

13

THE TRANSFORMATION OF DESIRE INTO ABUNDANCE

*Most people fail to see reality because of wanting. They are attached; they
cling to material objects, to pleasures, to the things of this world.
This very clinging is the source of suffering.*
—Majjhima Nikaya

*You, the richest person in the world, have been laboring and struggling endlessly,
not understanding that you already possess all that you seek.*
—The Lotus Sutra

When I was eight years old, after days in a highly fevered state,
I was taken to the hospital, mostly paralyzed from what was likely
polio. I remember lying there in this strange ward, wondering if I
was going to die. It was a particularly hot summer in St. Louis, and
even at night the hospital seemed to creak and groan and bake,
awash in strange smells. An enormous horse needle was used without anesthetic for spinal taps, the worst pain I ever imagined. It was
a Catholic hospital, and I was also scared of the black-robed priests

and nuns. They asked me questions about prayer and confession that were strange and disturbing.

All I wanted was to get out of there and run around with my brothers like a boy again. When I hoisted myself up I could see a patch of grass outside the window. One day I heard kids playing out there. How I longed for that single patch of grass. It was amazingly beautiful to me. My greatest desire was to walk on that grass, to move again. And then, one day, I could. After a time, my paralysis spontaneously receded and I was spared a lifetime in a wheelchair. When I was finally taken home, the first thing I did was get a balsa wood airplane and go straight to the park on the corner. It had a grassy lawn like the one I'd seen from the hospital window, and I rolled my whole body on the grass, tumbling over and over in my joy.

Our world runs on desire. We would not have been born without sexual desire. Without continuing desire we would die. There is desire for love, connection, understanding, growth. When people lose their desire to live, they jump off a bridge or swallow pills. We need desire. And yet desire is also a great challenge for us. Mistakenly, many people think that Buddhism condemns all desire. But there is no getting rid of desire. Instead, Buddhist psychology differentiates between healthy and unhealthy desire. Then it leads us to a freedom that is larger than the desire realm, where we can transform desire into true abundance.

Of course, such transformation isn't easy. As a young man headed to the forest monastery, I was conflicted about desire. I was swept up in the anti-materialistic feelings of the 1960s. With my peers I scorned America's plastic consumer culture, the world of endless acquisition, relentless workdays, and mind-numbing advertising. We thought we were the first to discover the loss of soul in our culture—but already in 1823, Alexis de Tocqueville had made this diagnosis: "I have seen the freest and best educated of men in the happiest circumstances the world can afford; yet it seemed to me that a cloud hung on their brow and they appeared serious and almost sad even when they were enjoying themselves . . . because they never stopped thinking of the good things they have not yet got."

Yet even as there was much that I repudiated, I knew that desire was not all bad. I wanted the pleasures of free love and good music and travel and adventure. The counterculture had rejected the puritanical view that worldly desires are sinful and base. Modern psychology had helped to liberate desire from the crushing weight of "civilized" repression. So here I was. I wanted some of my desires, but not all of them, and I saw many people around me conflicted in the same way.

It was in this swirl of confusion that I entered Ajahn Chah's monastery, which was known for its strict asceticism. If I was going to do monasticism, then as a greed type, I would do it right. I took on the demanding practices of the monastery, and then I intensified them. I lived with extreme simplicity. I used old robes and took one meal a day with no extra food. I learned to watch vast processions of desires come and go without acting on them. It felt purifying and freeing to live this way. Instead of being caught up in desires, I removed them all. But gradually I realized that even though I had learned a great deal from my experiment, it was an overcompensation.

This became glaringly clear to me when I returned to America. Initially I found work as a cab driver and got an apartment in Boston. I also got involved with a woman who was a teaching fellow at Harvard. Our first weeks were openhearted, romantic, and delightful. But she became more and more frustrated with me because I would never say what I wanted. If she asked whether I wanted to go to an Italian or Chinese or Indian restaurant, I replied that they all sounded good. When we were trying to decide on a movie, I said they were all fine. After a while, this drove her crazy. In the monastery I had learned to take the robes that were offered and eat whatever food was put in my bowl. Through this I learned acceptance and equanimity, but I also lost touch with my own desires. My preferences were so deeply buried, I was not aware of them. In desperation, my girlfriend got me a pocket notebook. She told me to write down five things I liked and five that I disliked every day until I could figure out how to live in the world again.

As I drove around Boston those first months at home, writing down my likes and dislikes in my little notebook, I realized I had misunderstood the Buddhist teachings. The idea is not to be without desire, but to have a wise relationship with desire. I think now of Ajahn Jumnian, who, as a meditation master and shaman, has collected thousands of sacred amulets and healing objects. And of Zen master Kapleau, who toward the very end of his life gave a bar of dark Swiss chocolate to a despondent friend and told her, "Eat it!" As the poet William Blake declared, "Those who enter the gates of heaven are not beings who have no passions or who have curbed the passions, but those who have cultivated an understanding of them."

Here is a thirteenth principle of Buddhist psychology:

---

13 There are both healthy desires and unhealthy desires. Know the difference. Then find freedom in their midst.

How do we practice this principle? Buddhists connect the root of desire with the neutral mental factor called the will to do. It is part of the energy of life. When the will to do is directed in healthy ways, it brings about healthy desires. When the will to do is directed in unhealthy ways, it brings about unhealthy desires. The traditional description of unhealthy desires include greed, addiction, overwhelming ambition, gambling, womanizing, and avarice. Unhealthy desire gives rise to possessiveness, self-centeredness, dissatisfaction, compulsion, unworthiness, insatiability, and similar forms of suffering.

Healthy desires allow us to feed and clothe and care for ourselves, to tend our body and our children, to develop our work and our community. Healthy desires are associated with caring, appreciation, and loving-kindness. This is evident in the healthy, caring bond between parents and children in Buddhist countries. Thai, Tibetan, and Sri Lankan children are held in every lap, with beaming faces, uninhibited playfulness, full of love of life. For all of us, these same healthy desires give rise to dedication, steadiness, stewardship, graciousness, generosity, and flexibility. They are the source of happiness.

Beyond healthy desire, Buddhist psychology describes a freedom that is outside our culture's understanding, yet we all know it. This is the place of inner freedom where the stickiness and clinging of desire is gone, where we can act, and yet not be caught up in desire. It's as if we were desperately hoping to buy a house and we lost it because someone else put in a higher bid. We let it go and then, two weeks later, the realtor calls and tells us the other bid fell through and we can have the house. Now, without the compulsion, we get to reconsider. Do we really want the house? Will it serve the needs of our family? Finally, we may choose to buy the house and furnish it. But we do so more freely, without worry and grasping. It feels so much better. This is the ability to enter the world of desire without clinging, playfully and freely.

This simple diagram may help to clarify the Buddhist understanding of desire:

THE WILL TO DO
A neutral mental state, an expression of life energy
that arises with all activity

UNHEALTHY DESIRE
Creates suffering
Based on greed and ignorance
Gives rise to possessiveness,
fear, avarice, clinging

HEALTHY DESIRE
Creates happiness
Based on wisdom and
compassion
Gives rise to care,
stewardship, generosity,
integrity, spiritual growth

FREEDOM AND ABUNDANCE BEYOND DESIRE
Brings playfulness
and ease into the world of desire

THE COST OF GRASPING OUR DESIRES

Although gold dust is precious, when it gets in your eyes, it obstructs your vision.
—Hsi Tang

Buddhist psychology wants us to release unhealthy desires and hold healthy desires lightly. To transform desire, we first have to feel how it works in the intimate experience of body and mind. Desire can lead us from sublime pleasure to raging addiction, from bodily survival to spiritual longings. Desire drives mushroom hunting and investment banking, Sufi dancing and rock and roll.

But these are the contents of desire. What does desire itself actually feel like when it is present? What is its effect? What happens when we grasp our desires most strongly? There is a tension in the body, an emotional contraction, a stickiness of mind, a focus on the future. There is a driven quality. Anxiety, jealousy, rigidity, and insecurity all become stronger.

Desire casts a spell and we pay a price. When we are lost in desire, the heart closes. In India they describe it this way: "When a pickpocket meets a saint, all he sees are the saint's pockets." When we meet someone and are full of our own desire, we become calculating, measuring what we say by what it will get us. It's the same when we are hungry. If we walk down the street with an empty stomach, we see only the restaurants; we miss the trees lining the sidewalk, the glow of the late-afternoon sunlight, and the faces of the passersby. A well-traveled friend confided, "I've seen entire European cities through the lens of 'Where's the restroom?' " In Zen it is said, "The secret waits for eyes unclouded by longing."

At its extreme, grasping and desire become addiction. Buddhist psychology describes the state of addiction as becoming a hungry ghost. No matter how much the ghost tries to eat, satisfaction is impossible. This is the state of consciousness where desire becomes insatiable, thirst becomes unquenchable. For the hungry ghost, like an addict, a few moments of relief come with the drink or the high or the binge, followed by a pause and craving for more.

The suffering of desire is apparent in addiction, but ordinary desire has its suffering too. We want to be thinner, more charming, admired, successful, secure. We use our desires to distract ourselves from discomfort. When an unconscious feeling of insecurity, boredom, or emptiness arises, desire follows. We open the refrigerator, turn on the TV, lose ourselves in distraction or busyness or addiction. We want another piece of chocolate cake to inspire us, a drink or a tidbit of gossip to make us feel better. Desires act like temporary painkillers—while they are harmless at first, we can become habituated. The more lonely and separate we feel, the more we turn to desires to compensate. We go through our day yanked by the chain of one desire after another until we finally lose touch with who we really are. Though the world may reward us for our drivenness, internally we are diminished. Virginia Woolf describes it this way: "If people are highly successful in their professions they lose their senses. . . . Sight goes. They have no time to look at pictures. Sound goes. They have no time to listen to music. Speech goes. They have no time for conversation. They lose their sense of proportion. . . . Humanity goes."

In modern life, compulsive desire is visible on a global scale: in the greed for oil, the clearing of rain forests, the privatization of rivers and lakes, and the patenting of such human staples as beans and corn. "The world," said Ajahn Chah, "is in a feverish state." Buddhist activist Helena Norberg-Hodge describes how modern desire has affected the Tibetan communities in Ladakh, India. For a thousand years, they believed they were blessed. They lived simply, with rainfall enough to grow their crops and time to tend their temples and follow the sacred rhythm of their year. When Ladakh first opened to the West in the 1970s, the Ladakhis told their visitors how abundant and rich they felt their lives were. Now, thirty years later, after exposure to television and wristwatches and music and fashion from India and America, the same Ladakhis and their children complain to visitors about how poor they are. It is all in comparison. Now feeling poor, many Ladakhis have left their villages to live in crowded, impoverished quarters in the city, seeking the happiness promised by the modern world. There are blessings in modernization, and we can understand the villagers' desire for running water and electric lights. But we can also recognize the costs of materialism when desire becomes out of balance.

To recover our innate freedom and balance, we have to study desire and be willing to work with it. How? It depends on our conditioning—on whether we are prone to indulgence or to suppression of desire. For those of us who easily indulge their desire, seeking to fulfill one desire after another, the wisest approach will require a powerful discipline of letting go. But for those of us who are afraid of desires, who have been conditioned to ignore, suppress, and fear them, another remedy is needed.

John, a successful real estate lawyer who had a background of indulgence in casual sex, cocaine, drinking, and seeking a "good time," required practices of limits and letting go. Feeling the suffering in his repeated indulgence, he began to follow the Buddhist disciplines of virtue. He lived near a small American forest monastery, and with the encouragement of his teacher and community, he took vows of non-harming and non-intoxication. His vows and his community helped him get sober. This renunciation led him to discover the first real moments of inner freedom that he had known in years. Then his meditations led him deeper, opening him to some of the painful sources of his desires, to the abandonment and betrayals in his history. Finally John began to discover the emptiness of desire itself, to relish the silence and well-being he had sought for so long.

For another student, Trudi, practicing with desire required the opposite approach. She was the successful owner of a greeting card store who worked long hours, saved carefully, and almost never indulged herself in any way. Her wardrobe was old, fitting for work but not much else. Her life was routine and limited. She felt she had never lived. She dreamed of leisure, travel, romance, and music. She needed to open her heart and appreciate desires that for too long had been shut down and closed off, dismissed as indulgent. Encouraged, she began to study her aversion to desire. She began to see how quickly she condemned them all. Gradually, she learned to discern which desires were healthy, which frightening, which confusing. She took a class in ballroom dance, then in tango.

She ate out once or twice a week with friends. She took a cruise. She met a man and let herself have an affair. It didn't work out. But as she dressed better and cared for herself more, she had more of an open heart to give others and to the world. Like John, though in a different way, Trudi began to find a new freedom in relation to desire.

WE ARE NOT OUR DESIRES

Beginning meditators are shocked by the number of desires that can arise in one sitting. There are desires for a quiet mind, for our back pain to go away, for the bell that ends the sitting to ring. In between these desires are hundreds of other desires: hoping for a tasty lunch, for a phone call to our loved one, for a nap, for the rain to stop so we can go for a walk, for the sun's warmth, for success when we go back to work.

With mindfulness we can witness the arising and passing of desire. We can allow the body sensations, the feeling states, and the stories of desire to be graciously received without judgment. When desire is met mindfully, the energy of desire will often intensify for a time and try to overcome us. If we don't rush to fulfill the desire, but simply stay present, the discomfort will eventually pass. Then we can notice what follows: usually a sense of ease, a peacefulness in body and mind, until desire arises once more a short time later. We can see this when we feel restless or uncomfortable toward the end of a sitting meditation. We feel the desire to move, accompanied by bodily tension and frustration. Fervently we hope the bell will ring. Then, as soon as it does, without our making a single movement, a dramatic change comes over us. The body relaxes and the tension disappears. The state of struggle is replaced by ease. Why is this so, since we have not done anything different? It's simple: with the ringing of the bell, the desire has ended, and without desire, the mind and heart are at peace.

In my years as a monk at Ajahn Chah's forest monastery, our life was extremely simple. I would have thought that this simplicity would have eliminated desires. We did not have to decide what clothes to wear; there was no menu to sort through, no cable TV, no wine list. We had almost no possessions, just a robe and a bowl and a few books. But desire has a force of its own. As a new monk, I had an old iron alms bowl, clunky and slightly discolored from rust. The senior monks had shapely stainless-steel bowls. I was shocked by my strong desire for a new bowl. I was like a middle school boy wanting cool clothes to wear. When I was finally given a stainless-steel bowl, I set it up in my hut and spent days admiring it. So much for the humble mendicant.

Since my vows included celibacy, I had to wrestle with much stronger desires, especially powerful sexual fantasies. I was a young man, and I tried to notice these natural desires mindfully. But they kept returning with great energy. Because they were so strong, my teacher had me pay close attention to the states that came with the fantasy. He especially wanted me to notice how they arose. To my surprise, I discovered that preceding most of these fantasies were feelings of loneliness. I have always had difficulty with loneliness. I am a twin and I suspect that I didn't even want to be alone in the womb. Accepting the loneliness was hard, but my teacher insisted I stay with it. As I explored the loneliness, I found insecurity and a needy kind of emptiness. I remembered these feelings from my early childhood. Much of my sexual desire was an unconscious attempt to fill the emptiness and loneliness. When I held these feelings with compassion, the loneliness began to subside. Gradually I became able to see the fantasies come and go with more mindfulness. In place of only longing, I started to rest in mindfulness, to belong to myself and to the world.

To the extent that our childhood was marked by deficiency, trauma, or lack of love, a deficient sense of self becomes very strong. I saw the workings of this in Arthur, a forty-three-year-old divorced man who came to speak with me at his first meditation retreat. Arthur was filled with desires. He was longing for a woman he had recently met. He was also about to sell the small business he had built. He was obsessed with the idea of making a pile of money, to free his life for travel. I suggested that instead of struggling against his desires, Arthur study desire mindfully, looking at the process as it arose in his body.

He started with the business deal. It was hard for him to stay in his body, but he began to notice that the desire came with tension and trembling and, below the surface, a sense of fear and insecurity. His mind swung between happy stories of success and frightening stories of failure. He felt stuck in the play of feelings and stories, trapped in an obsessive cycle of fantasies.

As we meditated together, I suggested that Arthur let the desire grow, giving it space to become as strong as it would. His body filled with more energy and tension; the pictures and stories of a successful sale filled his mind; the feelings of want and hope grew. "Where do you feel it most strongly in your body?" I asked. There was an aching in his chest and a contraction in his belly. Paying closer attention, he could see empty, needy, deficient feelings arise. They were familiar. He remembered when his father had lost his job. Though Arthur was only ten years old, he wanted to help his father get money and save the family. Continuing to meditate, Arthur felt younger still and sensed the sadness that accompanied his parents' rocky marriage and financial difficulties. Underneath the sadness he came to feel a poignant desire, an ache to be loved, until finally the bodily feelings of desire swelled to become a big inner emptiness.

I suggested that he let the feeling of emptiness grow bigger until it filled the room, filled the world. Slowly it did so. As it expanded and his resistance diminished, the suffering of his inner emptiness became less like a wound or a deficiency. It became more like space itself, open, still. His body relaxed and the emptiness became surprisingly pleasurable, filled with well-being and contentment. He felt how this contentment arose from not wanting anything. And then he smiled. There came to him images of the things he loved: his dog, walks in the woods, home and neighborhood, friends. And he saw that he could love them without wanting, because in this openness he was naturally connected to them, to everything. He sensed that this was the connection he had longed for all his life.

While he was in this state, I asked Arthur to remember obsessing about the sale of his business. How did it look from this perspective? He laughed. "Foolish. That contracted, fearful state is not me at all. I feel myself as a whole man now." This was an important step for Arthur. When the longing for a new partner arose, he could also see it in a more impersonal way. He felt the pull, the wanting, the inner emptiness. Then he smiled. He understood the desire for the fantasy it was. He knew he could choose to follow it or not. He was starting the long process of working with his desire. But now he also knew, "This desire is not who I am." He realized there could be tenderness without the squeeze of grasping. He began to experience that whatever choice he made could be more healthy and free.

HEALTHY DESIRE

Buddhist psychology teaches us to distinguish between the painful desire of addiction and driven ambition and the healthy energies of dedication and commitment. A dream or powerful goal, whether to write a successful novel, to compete in the Olympics, or to create a thriving business, can be pursued in different ways. If the goal exists to prove that we are worthy, to cover our insecurity, or to conquer others, it will ultimately prove unfulfilling and come to an unhappy end. And yet the very same activity can be done in a healthy way with dedication, commitment, and love.

The Tibetan monks who work tirelessly and delightedly for days on an exquisite and complex sand mandala know that after the ceremony it will blow away. Gardeners enthusiastically plant annuals knowing the same flowers will need to be planted again the next year. We all know this experience, giving ourselves to life out of dedication and care. Healthy desire leads to freedom. A skilled basketball player learns about letting go and "being in the zone." A dedicated commodities trader learns to blend dispassion, rhythm, and good intuition. The best lovemaking is not about a goal.

The Buddha praised healthy desire. He enjoined parents "to care for, morally instruct, educate, support, and nurture" their children. He taught partners to "honor, respect, be faithful to one another, care for, and work for the benefit of one another." He told employers to offer "suitable work and suitable wages, to offer sup-

port in times of sickness and appropriate rest," and urged employees to be "dedicated, honest, hardworking, and supportive."

As we can hear, all this sounds quite different from the stereo-
type of the Buddhist who is completely impassive, detached, wanting nothing, as I found out living with my exasperated girlfriend.
To live in this world wisely, we have to go beyond the extremes of
being numb to desire and being lost in desire. We need to release
unhealthy desire and learn to hold healthy desire lightly.

FROM GRASPING TO ABUNDANCE

Through the practice of mindfulness and compassion, desire can be
transformed. First we can release grasping, greed, our deficient
sense of self. Then, naturally, through the psychological principle
of reciprocity, there arise their opposites: states of generosity,
abundance, dedication, and love of beauty. We discover that our
natural state is one of wholeness and fulfillment beyond desire.

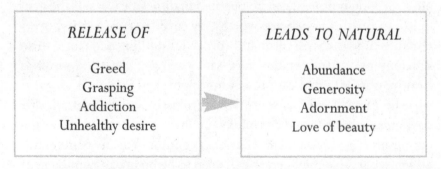

RELEASE OF	*LEADS TO NATURAL*
Greed	Abundance
Grasping	Generosity
Addiction	Adornment
Unhealthy desire	Love of beauty

Abundance beyond desire is not well understood in the West.
The Western psychoanalytic approach has been to liberate us from
the repression of desire. Western behaviorists have focused on re-
wards and reinforcements. Even in motivational psychology, little
has been studied about the absence of desire, except to acknowledge anhedonia, the painful lack of desire in depression. To study
liberation from desire is a radical act. Imagine if the *Diagnostic and
Statistical Manual of Mental Disorders* listed greed and driving ambition as human disorders. But we do not even recognize there is a
problem here. We have come to the point where commerce has co-

opted most of what we do. As novelist Rita Mae Brown declares, "In America the word *revolution* is used to sell pantyhose!"

It is revolutionary to step out of the thrall of desire. We lose touch with the joy and simplicity that letting go of desires can bring. A majority of the people I know say they would like to simplify their life. And it does indeed seem that happiness and simplicity go hand in hand. My good friend and colleague Joseph Goldstein tells the story of the winter Evie, his mother, came to visit him in India. Joseph had been practicing in Asia for seven years. He found his time there so inspiring that he persuaded his mother to join him. He wanted her to learn about the meditation practices guided by his wise and kindly teacher, Anagarika Munindra.

After a long, hard journey—twenty-four hours of airports and airplanes, followed by a slow, crowded Indian train, a ramshackle taxi, and finally a horse cart—Evie arrived at the Burmese temple in Bodh Gaya, India. Used to comfortable American furnishings and modern conveniences, Evie was shocked when she entered her room, which was the best in the temple. It was a small hut in the back with a concrete floor, a metal bed and mattress, and a wooden chair. The primitive latrine was a short walk away. With a make-do spirit, Evie set about joining Joseph for the teachings, and after some initial sightseeing she undertook a disciplined training of mindfulness for a month. She lived a meditative life. Then she returned to the United States, to her well-stocked kitchen and study, to her comfortable bed and bathroom, to piles of mail and visits with friends, to working and shopping. Afterward she said, quite simply, "Living in that concrete hut in India was the happiest month of my life."

Outer simplicity had allowed Evie to return to her inner abundance. But we do not have to go to a temple in India. We can live in the world without being lost in grasping and desire. A good example of how to do so is Ajahn Jumnian, the teacher from southern Thailand who visits Spirit Rock Meditation Center every year. Ajahn Jumnian is a joyful monk who embodies desirelessness and aliveness. He doesn't want anything. Instead, he is appreciative of whatever comes. "If someone puts food in my bowl, I am grateful. It gives me strength to teach. But if no one offers me food, this is good too—I get to go on a diet, which I could use! If students ask me to lead classes, I am happy to go anywhere. And if they take me sightseeing, I love to learn new things to help my teachings. But if no one invites me out, then I get to sit quietly and meditate. This makes me happy too. Whatever happens, I enjoy it."

"Well, he's a monk," we might protest, "living far from the pressures of the world. It's fine for him to be free from desire. He doesn't have to wake up every morning and find the motivation to put in another day at the office so he can pay the mortgage and his kids' tuition." But the story of Ajahn Jumnian is more interesting and pertinent to our life than it first appears. In the forests of southern Thailand, Ajahn Jumnian has created a huge temple and a thriving community with schools and a pilgrimage center for thousands of visitors. As abbot, he is responsible for the welfare of this large community, overseeing the scholastic and meditative training and development of myriad novices, monks, and nuns. As we learned, he has also been an extraordinarily successful political activist. During the bloody Communist insurgency period, for fifteen years he was one of the most effective peace brokers for all the warring factions in southern Thailand. Now, at seventy, he teaches worldwide.

How can this be done without grasping and desire? When asked, Ajahn Jumnian explained, "I relax and let my motivation be one of compassion and loving-kindness." The absence of greed and wanting does not bring about a withdrawal from the world. Instead, we awaken to the abundance of the world.

ABUNDANCE AND FULFILLMENT

The Indian sage Nisargatta, another of my teachers, challenged his students, saying, "The problem with you is not that you have desires, but that you desire so little. Why not desire it all? Why not want complete fulfillment, joy, and freedom?" Nisargadatta did not mean boundless greed. He spoke from the state of consciousness that knows it is not separate from the world. Kabir, the Indian mystic poet, put it this way: "I laugh when I hear the fish in the sea are thirsty."

We already contain all that we desire. With this realization, we can undertake all things with a sense of abundance. Our inner abundance radiates a sense of worth, value, and ease, of having something to give to the world and enjoying doing so. Without abundance, we can be in the midst of riches and feel like a hungry ghost. Wise parents and teachers bring out abundance in their children by helping them feel that each has much to give, and providing them the opportunity to do so. For each of us, whether raising a child, building a business, planting a garden, or serving our community, a heartfelt dedication is required. Wise dedication springs from our own sense of inner abundance.

For me, letting go of wanting and opening to the rhythms of the rain showers and the cries of the wildfowl during my time in the forest monastery helped me learn to experience abundance. Students of mindfulness experience the same openness when they leave a meditation retreat. They enter the supermarkets we usually take for granted, and stand there smiling at the wildest abundance of food ever presented to an ancient emperor. When we open to abundance, we can enjoy the fog lifting from this morning's melting snow, and the steam rising from the hot bowl of tomato rice soup on our lunch table. We can appreciate the half smile of the tired waitress and celebrate the fact that we are here, breathing and alive, on this marvelous earth.

This fulfillment is far beyond the "prosperity consciousness" that is promulgated in books and workshops that urge us to visualize fancy cars, sprawling mansions, and burgeoning bank accounts. This prosperity seeking, however "spiritual" the trappings, is a reflection of limitation, of a sense of insufficiency. The truly abundant heart is already whole. It embraces our world with all its joy and fear, gain and loss, nobility and selfishness. It even embraces death. When Zen master Shunryu Suzuki was dying of cancer he told his students, "If when I die, if I suffer, that is all right, you know. No confusion in it . . . this is just suffering Buddha." He showed them how to include everything right up to the end. In the last stages of grave pain he hauled himself out of bed, put on his finest robe, and completed the long transmission ceremony for the next abbot of the temple. Then, with the same gracious presence, he lay down and a few days later he died.

The state of abundance is connected with a deep sense of gratitude. In Japan there is a form of Buddhist therapy called *naikan* that emphasizes gratitude as a way to heal depression, anxiety, and neurosis. In this approach we are asked to slowly and systematically review our whole life and offer gratitude for each thing that was given to us. A similar approach worked for Bob, a practitioner who had been homeless for a year and was now living at a nearby mountain Zen center. Because of his memory of sleeping in the park, lying half awake every night in fear that someone would try to rob him or stab him, Bob was afraid to sleep. He had a history of family trauma: he had left his addicted father and stepmother for the streets at age fifteen and had used drugs himself. In his life he had been a carpenter and a mechanic.

When Bob went to the Buddhist center, he was trying to put his life together. The Zen teacher could feel his anxiety and mistrust. To help soften this state, the teacher instructed him in a simple practice of gratitude. Bob began offering thanks for whatever food, clothing, and shelter he had for the moment, living, as they say in AA, one day at a time. He was taught to stop and surreptitiously bow in gratitude ten times a day, wherever he found himself. Bob took to bowing. He bowed to his kitchen mates and to their shared breakfast. He bowed to his morning depression and to his feelings of unworthiness. He bowed to the carpentry tools he used in the shop, to his anxiety, to the afternoon sun, and to the noisy tractor in the nearby field.

A second instruction was given to Bob as well: to look beyond his suffering. Bob slowly began to notice moments of well-being, surprising breaks in his inner struggles, small periods of blessing. He loved being in the temple garden. He walked among the live oaks and mulch piles by the garden path, framed by sturdy redwood posts and delicate forget-me-nots and orange daisies. Bob described how his mind became quiet for the first time in years. The suffering he carried was still like a weight, but the vast silence was bigger. One day the temple bell rang for dinner and his heart was pierced. His pain and longing were swept over by a sublime wave of gratitude for just being alive. Bob was returning to life.

NATURAL GENEROSITY

As desire abates, generosity is born. When we are present and connected, what else is there to do but give? An African proverb puts
it this way: "It is the heart that gives, the fingers just let go." When
someone in our family is hungry or in difficulty, we naturally want
to help. When the heart is freed from grasping, our family grows.
The people we meet are all our uncles and aunties, our grandparents and our cousins. The animal brothers and sisters are our siblings. We sense our interdependence with all beings.

In the abundant heart, our sense of welfare expands. The Iowa
corn farmer whose corn always took first prize at the state fair had
the habit of sharing the best seed corn with all the farmers in the
neighborhood. When asked why, he said, "It's really a matter of self-
interest. The wind picks up the pollen and carries it from field to
field. So if my neighbors grow inferior corn, the cross-pollination
brings down the quality of my own corn. That is why I am concerned that they plant only the very best."

To reawaken our sense of abundance, Buddhist psychology offers deliberate trainings and practices to cultivate generosity as a
joyful way of being. There are daily practices of giving, vows of dedication to service, visualizations of our devotion to the welfare of
all. These are repeated until in the end there is no notion of separation, neither giver nor receiver. We are all the Buddha feeding
ourselves.

Paul was a retired banker at loose ends whose Buddhist teachers suggested that he develop the path of service. Paul began to help
at the temple, on committees, and at the community hospice. His
life had been dedicated to success and self-importance, but as he
began to serve others his self-interest faded, his unconscious fears
passed. His work at the hospice taught him that what mattered was
love. People who at first had been put off by his brusqueness and
arrogance began to enjoy his presence. As he devoted himself to
service, his heart mellowed like a good wine.

These generosity practices are not a way to become "good," but
a way to become happy. We do not have to work at a hospice or an

emergency room to serve. Sometimes our generosity is the giving of a smile, silence, listening, warm touch. Sometimes it involves action, time, money, our commitment to justice, our vision for a better world. Every form of giving is a blessing. Helping to run several large Buddhist centers, I have had to learn to become comfortable with money. There is so often shame and fear, judgments and expectations around money, whether it's having too much or too little. We have gotten the erroneous belief that money is not compatible with a genuine spiritual life. But money is a neutral energy that can used in either unskillful or skillful ways. Gained skillfully and used generously, material abundance is honored by the Buddha. When money is wisely used, says the Buddha, it benefits our welfare and that of our family, and its generosity extends to our community, our spiritual life, and the common good.

As countless travelers from the West have observed, in Buddhist cultures generosity is especially visible. This was certainly true in Thailand. At Ajahn Chah's, every morning at dawn I walked on the small dikes between the rice paddies to nearby villages to collect alms food. At the remote branch monasteries, the villages were poor and the food was scarce. Yet every morning villagers would kneel in the dirt, lovingly offering food to the monks. I, a relatively rich Westerner, wondered if I should feel guilty about taking their food. But the villagers offered it with such generosity. It was as if they were saying, "We so value the teachings of the Buddha and the blessings of the monastery that we joyfully give of the very little we have to support you." Because alms rounds are done in silence, I couldn't say thank you for the fish curry and dried mango. All I could do was accept their food as a blessing and an obligation, and practice with as much integrity and compassion as I could.

DESIRE BECOMES ADORNMENT

Several years ago I read about a study done in an impoverished neighborhood of London. Two parallel streets were selected, a mile apart, each with similar poverty and concomitant problems, including a high level of crime. Unbeknownst to the residents, one of these streets was secretly selected to be cleaned every day for a year. All the trash was picked up, graffiti removed, curbside flowers replanted and watered, and broken lamps and signs repaired, repainted, and cared for. Nothing was said publicly about this extra cleaning and beautification. After a year, however, the streets were compared. The statistics showed a nearly 50 percent reduction in crime on the cleaned and beautified street.

As we release grasping and desire, the play of the world becomes like adornment for our wise heart. We appreciate and embody a natural love of beauty. The Buddha said, "When we find the way, we find the beautiful here and now, we know what beauty truly is."

In one Buddhist monastery, we were trained to notice what was beautiful and to abandon the unbeautiful. We went through the day deliberately observing whether our thoughts, words, and deeds were beautiful or unbeautiful. We could sense the pleasure in beautiful thoughts and words and deeds. We could sense the suffering in the unbeautiful ones. We began to incline toward appreciating the beauty. We consciously enjoyed our good moods. We found ourselves savoring a cup of tea as if in a tea ceremony. Our walks became more flowing and harmonious. Even when conflict arose between community members we entered the difficulties with more graciousness and dignity. All that arose became used as adornments for the way.

Benedictine brother David Steindl-Rast explains it this way: "What is truly a part of our spiritual path is that which brings us alive. If gardening brings us alive, that is part of our path, if it is music, if it is conversation . . . we must follow what brings us alive." When our heart is released from grasping, generosity and beauty flower.

PRACTICE: GENEROSITY

Life is giving to life every moment of the day. Take several days to pay attention to this movement of endless generosity.

As you go about your daily rounds, first notice the gifts of the natural world. Notice the way the gift of sunlight streams behind everything. It feeds the plants we eat and gives us the oil from ancient forests that fuels our cars and lights our lamps at night. Notice too the rainfall and the rivers, the water that gives itself to the blood in your veins, to the neighborhood insects and trees, to the interdependent collaborative in which we swim. Now notice how generously you are held and supported by the earth under your home and your feet, by the air you breathe, by the warmth of the day and the coolness of the evening.

Now look at the unending care and generosity in humans around you: parents with children, teachers with students, healers and businesspeople, all serving one another. People stop at red lights so you are safe to go. They line up in the market, they share the parks, they cooperate in a thousand ways at the office. The shopkeeper and the mechanic, the bank teller and the cook, the healer and the engineer give themselves to their work, supporting others with countless hours of unspoken generosity and love. Of course there are also times of resentment and being overwhelmed, when people are disgruntled and disaffected. But most of the time, the people around you are giving: in conversation, in action, adding the generosity of their life energy to the flow of the whole. Spend a day or a week just noticing, naming, bowing to this stream of generosity everywhere.

Now you can deliberately choose to add to this stream of generosity, not as an obligation but as a way to be happy. Like all human beings, you already give in a myriad of ways. Delight in whatever you do. And discover you can let it grow. Try this practice: whenever a thought of giving enters your mind, do it. Whether it is a gift of money, time, helping care, or offering a possession, if you even think of a generous act, follow it. Sometimes we worry that we will regret our generous acts, we second-guess ourselves, and a bit of doubt comes in. Don't believe the doubts. Instead, look for any spontaneous thoughts of generosity and follow them. You will find that they inevitably make you happy. Try it.

14

BEYOND HATRED TO A
NON-CONTENTIOUS HEART

There is pleasure and pain, gain and loss, slander and honor, praise and blame.
The Awakened Ones are not controlled by these external things. They will cease as
quickly as they arise. If others speak against you, do not be angry, for that will
prevent your own inner freedom. Learn to bear their harsh words patiently
until they cease. Similarly if they praise you. Find out what is false
or true and acknowledge the facts.
—Digha Nikaya and the Dhammapada

Those who have hate will experience the pain and grief born of hate. Anger and
revenge, domineering and scolding, obstinacy and contempt are not
the way. Train yourself to abandon them all.
—Majjhima Nikaya

When I began Buddhist practice, it was terribly important for me to understand the roots of anger and fear. Because of the unpredictable violence I grew up with, I was careful, wary, never knowing what to expect. In the outside world, my father was a respected scientist who worked for the military in space medicine, taught in medical schools, and designed artificial hearts. At home, it was a different story. While he could be loving at times, he was also a controlling, paranoid man, always worried about who might be watching him. He was anxious about people on the street and about FBI investigations of the secret documents he kept for his military contracts. He even hated to have anyone drive behind him. When he came home, we never knew if it would be one of his bad days. He raged at my brothers and me, but the worst abuse he saved for my mother. He might throw her down the stairs or threaten to put her head through a window.

To learn about anger and how it gives rise to hatred and aggression, Ajahn Chah encouraged us to look unflinchingly at our own experience whenever it arose. The instructions were to start small. He wanted us to notice the initial movement of aversion, the sense of dissatisfaction, resentment, and judgment as we went through the day. "How does it arise?" he would ask. "Is it caused by outer things or by habit, bodily instincts, a story in the mind?"

One day I found myself getting quite angry at being treated unfairly by a senior monk. Ajahn Chah just laughed. "Good," he said, "you can see how anger works." He instructed me to go back to my little hut in the forest, close the door and window, put on all my robes, and sit and be angry. It was the middle of the hot season, and it was like sitting in a fire, hot outside, hotter inside. I could feel my anger at the situation, the seething bodily states, the aggression coming in waves. I noticed the fear that came too: fear of the other person, fear of what I might do, fear of repeating the past, fear of my shame.

My study of anger and fear continued for months. I saw how fear is never about what is actually here in the moment. When pain and hurt are present, they are just pain and hurt. It is fear that adds insecurity about what will come later. It comes as a scary story that takes over the body and mind. Fear would tell its story a hundred times, and until I could just notice it and ask "Is that you, fear?" I would be caught each time.

Along with anger and fear, I learned the ways of the inner critic, the judging mind. I could hear myself repeating the critical words of my parents, of teachers, and of spiritual authorities. I had so many judgments that one of my teachers had me count them. I judged my pain, my wandering mind, the noises I heard, the bugs, the monastery, the world! There were a hundred judgments in an hour. I saw how quickly my anger could turn into blame of others and, when turned on myself, into embarrassment and shame. It was like Jules Feiffer's cartoon of the man who says, "I grew up to have my father's looks, my father's speech patterns, my father's posture, my father's opinions, and my mother's contempt for my father." It was all in there.

I became familiar with every level of aversion, from the tiny contraction around a mosquito bite to the way anger can grow into hatred and finally to full-blown rage. I discovered that we all have within us the inner judge and jury, the Iron Curtain and the police. We have our inner Taliban and our places of exile. At times I felt like the Buddha under the bodhi tree, when he faced his own inner demons in the form of Mara. As the story is told, on the night of the Buddha's enlightenment, he took a seat under the bodhi tree in northern India. He resolved to sit there, unshakably, and not to rise from his seat until he had achieved complete freedom. After a short time, Mara, the Indian god of delusion and evil, appeared, intent on stopping the Buddha from this goal. To do so, Mara sent his daughters, the most beautiful temptresses imaginable. But the Buddha was unmoved and simply said, "I see you, Mara." When desire failed to work, Mara got angry and sent in his vast armies. There were fierce demons with frightening faces and war cries, hurling cudgels, flaming arrows, and deadly spears. Again, the Buddha sat unmoved, saying simply, "I see you, Mara." Then the Buddha raised his hand to touch the armies of Mara with compassion and all the spears and arrows fell as flower petals at his feet. Finally Mara attacked the Buddha with doubt: "Who do you think you are? What right do you have to sit here to become enlightened?" At this, the Buddha placed a hand on the ground and said, "The earth is my witness." And with this gesture, the earth goddess arose and bore witness to the lifetimes of patience, dedication, truthfulness, compassion, generosity, and wisdom that had prepared the Buddha for this night. Out of her hair came a flood of water and the armies of Mara were washed away.

In the same spirit, when I sat in the forest monastery and the states of anger and aversion, irritation, and judgment arose, I learned to say with compassion, "Is that you again, Mara?" Wherever we are, Mara will appear with his armies and we will have to find a way to hold our ground and remain unmoved.

THE NATURE OF HATE

Aversion, anger, and hatred are states of mind that strike against experience, pushing it away, rejecting what is presented in the moment. They do not come from without. This insight is a reversal of the ordinary way we perceive life. "Usually," says Ajahn Chah, "we believe outer problems attack us." Things are wrong and people misbehave, causing our hatred and suffering to arise. But however painful our experiences may be, they are just painful experiences until we add the response of aversion or hatred. Only then does suffering arise. If we react with hatred and aversion, these qualities become habitual. Like a distorted autoimmune response, our misguided reaction of hatred does not protect us; rather, it becomes the cause of our continued unhappiness.

This is a fourteenth principle of Buddhist psychology:

14   If we cling to anger or hatred, we will suffer.
It is possible to respond strongly, wisely, and compassionately, without hatred.

The Buddha declares, "Enraged with hate, with mind ensnared, humans aim at their own ruin and at the ruin of others." How do we break this tragic legacy—both in our own lives and in every blood-soaked corner of the globe? Only through a deep understanding of anger, hatred, and aggression. They are universal energies, archetypal forces that cause immense suffering in the world. Their source must be traced in the depths of our human hearts. And then we will discover an amazing truth: that with compassion, with courage and dedicated effort, we, like the Buddha, can meet the aggressive forces of Mara and these energies can be transformed.

As we have seen, Freud and his followers believed the aggressive instincts to be primary. Culture's "commandment to love one's neighbour as oneself . . . is really justified by the fact that nothing else runs so strongly counter to original human nature as this." Later, in the aftermath of World War II, sociobiologists such as Konrad Lorenz and Robert Ardrey hypothesized that our species, like our predecessor apes and many other animals, had necessary and inevitable instincts of territoriality and aggression. Today, evolutionary biology and neuroscience are carefully charting the genetic function and neural mechanisms of aggression.

But the fact that aggression, anger, and aversion are built into our universal heritage is only the starting point in Buddhist psychology. After we learn how to face them directly, to see how they arise and function in our life, we must take a revolutionary step. Through the profound practice of insight, through nonidentification and compassion, we reach below the very synapses and cells and free ourselves from the grasp of these instinctive forces. With dedication, we discover it is possible to do so.

Aversion and anger almost always arise as a direct reaction to a threatening or painful situation. If they are not understood they grow into hatred. As we have seen, pain and loss are undeniable parts of human life. Buddhist texts speak of a mountain of pain. They tell us our tears of grief could fill all four great oceans. When our experience is one of pain, hurt, loss, or frustration, our usual habit is to draw back in aversion or strike out in anger, to blame or run away.

Like pain, fear is the other common predecessor to anger and hate—fear of loss, of hurt, of embarrassment, of shame, of weakness, of not knowing. When fear arises, anger and aversion function as strategies to help us feel safe, to declare our strength and security. In fact, we actually feel insecure and vulnerable, but we cover this fear and vulnerability with anger and aggression. We do this at work, in marriage, on the road, in politics. A fearful situation turns to anger when we can't admit we are afraid. As the poet

Hafiz writes, "Fear is the cheapest room in the house. I'd rather see you in better living conditions." Without insight, we are doomed to live our lives in this cheap room.

Fortunately, we can train ourselves to live with mindfulness, to meet fear and pain with wisdom instead of with the habits of aversion and anger. When a painful or threatening event arises, we can open our eyes to it. When we learn to bear our own pain and face our own fears, we will no longer blame and inflict it on others, neither family members nor other tribes. With mindfulness, instead of reacting, we can respond with spacious clarity, purpose, firmness, and compassion. A wise response includes whatever action, fierce at times, is the most caring toward life, our own and others'.

Imagine a healthy mind as one that is free from entanglement in any level of hatred. At first this might seem impossible, an idealistic attempt to impose decorum on our innately aggressive human nature. But freedom from hatred is not spiritual repression, it is wisdom in the face of pain and fear. This diagram shows how such freedom arises:

PAINFUL OR THREATENING EXPERIENCE

UNHEALTHY REACTION

HEALTHY RESPONSE

AVERSION: all forms of resisting experience	NON-CONTENTION: freedom and clarity with experience
Anger	Mindfulness
Hatred	Connectedness
Aggression	Compassion
Fear	Concern
Judgment	Strength
Blame	Fearlessness

DEVELOPING A HEALTHY RESPONSE

In a healthy response to pain and fear, we establish awareness before it becomes anger. We can train ourselves to notice the gap between the moments of sense experience and the subsequent response. Because of the particle-like nature of consciousness, we can enter the space between instinct and action, between impulse and reaction. To do so we must learn to tolerate our pain and fear. This is not easy. As James Baldwin put it, "Most people discover that when hate is gone, they will be forced to deal with their own pain." That's why we start by paying attention to small things, small pains and disappointments. When I start to get into an argument with my wife, if I pay attention I notice that I usually feel hurt or afraid. If I speak to her angrily, she will become defensive and the argument will grow. But if I'm mindful, I can talk about the hurt or fears instead of being lost in anger and blame. Then my wife becomes interested and concerned. Out of this a different and more honest conversation occurs.

This is the first step. But to work honorably with anger, we must acknowledge the depth of the Buddha's First Noble Truth—the truth of suffering. There is pain in our lives, in the world—disappointments, injustice, betrayal, racism, loneliness, loss. As blues masters Buddy Guy and Junior Wells say, "The blues is the truth." No strategy can keep us exempt from loss and sorrow, sickness and death. This is human life. Even if we try to avoid this truth, it is still true. A Zen saying reminds us, "If you understand—things are just as they are. If you do not understand—things are just as they are."

When I first came to Ajahn Chah's monastery, I didn't think of myself as an angry person. My response to the violence in my family had been to try to become the family peacemaker. As the eldest son, I had tried to make myself calm, and now in the monastery, at age twenty-three, I believed I was the antithesis of my father. It shocked me to discover that my anger at being slightly mistreated in the monastery was enormous, far beyond what the situation called for. Meditation opened the door to the accumulated rage in me that had been too dangerous to feel as a child. When I let myself open to these energies, I found a volcano of anger and grief, images of nuclear explosions, a vast universe of hurt and rage. Inwardly, I was not different from my father.

Fortunately, as William Blake said, "The tigers of wrath are wiser than the horses of instruction." I learned a lot observing my frustration and judgment, sitting with my anger, feeling the force of my rage. I began to notice how any painful or frightening experience in the monastery could tap into the stored anger of my past, and my reaction would be all out of proportion. I began to notice how much self-judgment I carried, how hard it was to simply feel the hurt and vulnerability. Little by little I made my peace with the pain and frustration; I could bear them better. And little by little felt like a very big step indeed.

Yet I still had a long way to go. When I left the monastery and returned to America, I entered graduate school in psychology. There in Boston, I became involved in a tempestuous relationship. In a short while, my old family pain was triggered. Insecurity, anger, and my long history of dependence all came up. Being mindful, I could clearly recognize what I was thinking and feeling. But I was still afraid of expressing strong emotion. As a child I had so feared the explosive anger and sorrow in my home, I'd learned to suppress my own intense feelings, to stuff them inside, to maintain control. Now, studying the interface of Eastern and Western psychology, I entered therapy with Myron Sharaf, a psychologist at Harvard Medical School. Myron had worked directly with the controversial and brilliant body-centered psychiatrist Wilhelm Reich.

Myron tried to help me move and express my energy. Because I was so good at being aware of what was going on inside while staying calm outside, Myron called this "the monk's defense." After a frustrating period where not much happened, Myron asked what time of day was the most difficult for me. I said early morning. I don't function well at that time and I like to sleep late. Myron laughed and scheduled our sessions for 6:30 A.M., when my ego defenses would be weak. At 6:30 he would have me lie down and do powerful breathing practices to energize my whole system. Then he'd have me tell stories of my past. Sometimes he'd put on arias from great operas and while I listened, charged up from the breathing and filled with my stories, he'd push and manipulate my body to help free the energy. He worked so vigorously, one morning he accidentally cracked two of my ribs.

It worked. Little by little, I became able to rage and weep and shake with fear and excitement. I became more aware of my feelings and less afraid to express them, freer to choose my response. Anger and aversion were no longer terrifying forces to be bottled up; rather, they became an energy of aliveness to feel, to surrender, or to use consciously, deliberately, without causing harm.

In the thirty years since leaving the monastery and working with Myron, I have learned to be much more at ease with strong feeling states, letting them be or, when called for, expressing them. Grief and tears, anger and strength, joy and sorrow move through me now in a more open and playful way.

Some years ago, when my wife and I were remodeling our house, we had a problem with our contractor. I really liked him. He had been an excellent workman and a thoughtful collaborator on the project. But he was getting way behind the schedule we had agreed to in the contract. His crews were working three other jobs and no matter that I repeatedly pressed him to speed up, he continued at the same pace. Maybe my calm demeanor made him think it didn't really matter. But my family and I were soon to travel to Europe and we needed the job done. So I got mad. I shouted and swore (quite satisfyingly) for a while and said that he better get it done and if he didn't goddamn finish on schedule I was going to haul his ass into court.

He looked at me, eyes wide. "Hey, you really want it done, huh?" And the next morning, sure enough, there was a big crew at the house, all working away. Later I realized that I had been speaking "contractorese," and that angry shouting was just a way of talking in his business. I had used the right language, a code that worked.

What is the medicine that Buddhist psychology prescribes for the suffering of aversion? First we become aware of this force within ourselves. We recognize in our bodies the rigidity of aggression, the pain of rage, the contraction of fear. We become intimate with our frustration, anger, and blame.

Second, we learn the difference between reaction and response. When we're in a hurry and the toast burns, we can react by fuming or hitting the counter, or we can feel our frustration and put in another piece of bread. When someone cuts us off in traffic, we can angrily retaliate by racing up to them shouting, trying to get back at them, or we can breathe and let it go. When we are criticized, when we lose a sale, when we are betrayed, we don't have to reinforce the pain of the situation by adding to the pain by our reaction.

It's like two arrows, the Buddha said. The first arrow is the initial event itself, the painful experience. It has happened; we cannot avoid it. The second arrow is the one we shoot into ourselves. This arrow is optional. We can add to the initial pain a contracted, angry, rigid, frightened state of mind. Or we can learn to experience the same painful event with less identification and aversion, with a more relaxed and compassionate heart.

Does this mean that we cannot respond strongly? No. Sometimes we need to get up, shout out the truth, march, protest, do whatever is necessary to protect our life and the lives of others. The great exemplars of non-violence such as Gandhi and Martin Luther King Jr. were strategic and skilled in this way. They rallied people, used the courts, broke the law, blocked the way, negotiated, moved forward and back, found allies, and used money, power, shame, speeches, and politics all to stand up for what was right. But they did not act out of hate and violence. This is a powerful example. When self-righteous anger arises, we can let it go. Retaining our own fierce clarity, we too can seek justice, yet do so with a loving heart.

The Buddha urges us to let go of our anger even after extreme difficulties. Here are famous verses from the Dhammapada, the sayings of the Buddha: " 'He abused me and beat me, he threw me down and robbed me.' Repeat these thoughts and you live in hate. 'He abused me and beat me, he threw me down and robbed me.' Abandon these thoughts and live in love. In this world, hatred never ceases by hatred, but by love alone is healed. This is the ancient and eternal law."

I learned this lesson firsthand when I worked with Maha Ghosananda in the Cambodian refugee camps. A small, orange-robed man who was a great scholar, with missing teeth and an unshakable, innocent smile, Maha Ghosananda led unarmed peace marches through the war zones of the country to help refugees return to their villages. Year after year, like Gandhi, he offered his life for the healing of Cambodia. Though most of his family had been killed, he would not succumb to bitterness. When Maha Ghosananda met with thousands of refugees in the camps, those whose villages had been burned and loved ones killed, he would sit with them and chant, "Hatred never ceases by hatred, but by love alone is healed," over and over. He wanted to inspire them with a truth even bigger than their sorrows, to give them courage to start to live without hate again. The citizens of the world must all find a way to learn this truth. Their future happiness and liberation depend on it.

There are wars in our personal life too. Gretchen came to a meditation retreat at the end of a terrible custody battle and acrimonious divorce. She was a successful businesswoman, her husband was a lawyer, and a great deal of money was involved. They had both had affairs, although Gretchen claimed her brief affair was a reaction, a way to retaliate against her husband's earlier affair, his coldness and mistreatment. She also claimed that because he was a tough-minded lawyer he had been able to manipulate the court into declaring her unfit as a mother. She lost primary custody of her children, who were six and eight at the time. Gretchen had stood up for herself as powerfully as she could, but she had lost. The bitterness and pain were enormous.

During the retreat, Gretchen worked with mindfulness to gradually return to her body with a kind attention. She sat with the exhaustion, the contraction, the outrage, the fear. She watched all the stories her racing mind was telling of blame and self-recrimination, of angry revenge and alarm for the lives of her children.

Gradually she let herself touch the vulnerability underneath it all. She was raw and tender. She wept with grief for all her failures, for her children, for her marriage, for the injustices of this earth. She was encouraged to allow it all, to acknowledge each loss and pain, to see the contractions and stories. After six or seven days Gretchen could begin to see them as impersonal forces rising and passing like waves.

She was instructed to look for moments of rest between the waves of tears and anger and to rest in the awareness. From the teachings she began to question. Were bitterness and conflict the legacy she wanted to leave her children? Gretchen did a compassion meditation for herself, for her children—even a tiny bit for her ex-husband. One day, she walked into her interview with great dignity and said, "I can accept the pain and loss, but I will not live a life of bitterness and fear." It has been more than ten years since that retreat and she has stayed true to her word. Gretchen practiced compassion and cared for her children as much as she was allowed. Now that they have come of age, she has remade a strong and caring relationship with both of them.

When we examine anger and aversion with awareness, there is a radical shift of identity. These states are not who we really are. They are conditioned and impersonal, and they do not belong to us. For Gretchen it was initially scary to step out of her negative reactions. They seemed such necessary protections. It is scary to us and to those with whom we are locked in conflict when we release our blame. Sometimes our partners are confused when we step out of the dance of anger. They too will be required to change. In letting go of contention we return to our true strength and nobility.

When Nobel Peace Prize laureate Aung San Suu Kyi spoke about her many years of house arrest under a cloud of violence and the brutal repression of the Burmese dictatorship, she said, "It is from hardship rather than ease that we gather wisdom. We need to develop the capacity to draw strength from our hardships . . . to ignite the thunder flame of our own heart and let it illuminate the stormy night." In our hardships, we discover the courage not to succumb, not to retreat, not to strike out in fear and anger. And by resting in a non-contentious heart we become a lamp, a medicine, a strong presence; we become the healing the world so dearly needs.

HONESTY AND A NON-CONTENTIOUS HEART

"There is gain and loss, slander and honor, praise and blame, pleasure and pain; the awakened ones are not controlled by these external things; they will cease as quickly as they arise. If others speak against you, do not be angry, for that will prevent your own inner freedom. Learn to bear their harsh words patiently until they cease." When the Buddha spoke these words, his monks were being falsely blamed by jealous local priests. Their struggle was no less real than ours, and the Buddha's advice is just as relevant today. Yet like all teachings, we must use it wisely. We should not deliberately subject ourself to harsh words, nor think that we cannot respond strongly or leave when that is the best course.

Shannon, whose life work was environmental justice, came to Buddhist practice for help with her stress. She had fought to stop the pollution of some of the poorest neighborhoods of America and in the poorest corners of the world. She hated the people in power who abused the poor in this way. But at thirty-six, Shannon was exhausted. She had always tried to be strong. As she told me her story, I found out that Shannon was also in contention with her family, fighting with her father and brother over the family money. Even in yoga she chose a demanding Iyengar teacher whose poses pushed her to her limits.

In her first meditations, Shannon had to simply feel the stress, the drivenness and guilt. Gradually, she acknowledged the weight of her family history, the legacy of her grandparents who died in the Holocaust, and the struggles of her immigrant father, who'd made a lot of money. Slowly she allowed her own feelings to be present. She learned to bow to them and to deliberately breathe in and around them, to make space. As Shannon paid attention, the tension in her body gave way to anger, grief, and tears. She saw a succession of images of conflict and trauma starting with her early life and ending with the culture's betrayal of the environment. By adding compassion practice, her reactions to these conflicts and traumas gradually released. The tension in her body became experienced more as aliveness than as a problem. Her mindfulness brought a new sense of space and ease. But her fears grew too. Shannon had been a strong activist, and now she felt vulnerable, weak. The vulnerability was frightening to her.

I asked Shannon to close her eyes and to allow the fear and vulnerability to be held with kindness. The feelings shifted to an unpleasant emptiness that Shannon called an absence, a lack of holding or ground. The solidity of her world was dissolving. "Don't fight it," I suggested, "but let it open even more." As she allowed this groundlessness, she noted that her body began to change. Then a surprised look came over her. "I feel that my body has expanded. It feels as if I'm huge." I urged her to simply stay mindful of the inner unfolding. She described how her body was no longer sitting on the earth. She had become the earth. As the earth, she was solid, powerful, strong, unshakable. She felt full with a deep satisfaction. Her mind and body were quiet now, spacious but not weak. She was steady and strong. I encouraged her to stay with this realization.

From this perspective Shannon looked back over the years of struggle in both the personal and political spheres of her life and laughed. "I was trying to be strong in the wrong way. I kept trying to fight to be strong. I didn't realize that strength is a part of me, of life." She could sense how differently she would approach her conflicts and difficulties now. She could be strong not by struggling but with an unshakable steadiness firmly grounded on the earth.

TRUE STRENGTH AND THE SWORD OF WISDOM

Ajahn Chah called the practice of non-contentiousness "Stopping the War." He pointed out how we are constantly in battle with the world, fighting against what is wrong, against what is too long or short, too fast or too slow, courageously carrying on the battle. "Why not step out of the battle?" he would say, inviting us to rest in the non-contentious heart.

The opposite of aggression is not passivity, it is true strength.

When we have lost a sense of our innate nobility, we mistakenly be-lieve in our fear and weakness. We try to be strong through hate and aggression. When we release aggression, we discover true strength, a natural fearlessness, the courage to face our griefs and fears, and to respond without hate. Martin Luther King Jr. called this unshakable strength "soul force." In ancient Greece, anger was described as a noble emotion. It stood up for what was right; it spoke out against injustice. Non-contention carries this courage with a loving heart. Mahatma Gandhi acknowledged, "Non-violence requires more courage than violence."

True strength meets the vulnerability of life with caring and courage. True strength knows that there are two great powers in this world. The first is those who are unafraid to kill. The other is those who are unafraid to love. Even in situations of great dan-ger, true strength chooses love. Martin Luther King Jr. demon-strated the strength of this love in the darkest hours, saying, "We will meet suffering with soul force." True strength is what the Irish Catholics and Protestants, and the Palestinians and Israelis, will need to end their cycles of violence. It will take courage for them to truly feel the weight of each other's suffering, courage to honor the other side's fears of annihilation and loss of land, culture, and dignity. Yet until their pain and fear are held in a wise way, the cy-cles of hatred will continue.

True strength also brings clarity, like a sword that cuts through illusion. It is called discriminating wisdom. When we are not locked in blame or struggle, we can see things as they are. "We can," says William Butler Yeats, "make our minds so like still water that beings gather around us that they may see . . . their own images, and so live for a moment with a clearer, perhaps even with a fiercer life because of our quiet." When needed, we can be fierce and strong, wielding the sword of clarity. Liberated from anger, we can speak the truth fearlessly. At the same time we are free of ill will, so our actions care for the welfare of all.

As students we loved to watch Ajahn Chah pull out the sword of wisdom. He would sit with visitors and teach them in a compas-sionate way. But because he didn't need anything from them, he was also free to tell the truth. Once a rich and boastful merchant asked Ajahn Chah whether he should give some of his money to the forest monastery or just continue his high-profile giving to hospitals and public charities. Ajahn Chah laughed and said that the best thing a person like him could do would be to throw all his money off the Mun River bridge. Another time, soldiers came for blessings and protection. Ajahn Chah was sympathetic, but he told them their only real protection was not to kill. During the visits of government officials he "accidentally" lectured on virtue and the heavy karma of corruption. And when an old woman was brought by her family for healing he said, "They don't want to tell you, but you're headed for death. Relax," he went on, "it's only the body that dies," and then gave her teachings on the deathless.

Of course Ajahn Chah did not save his sword just for visitors. He pointed out our follies to us, his monks and nuns, individually and collectively—our clingings and fears, our pettiness and blame. It made the monastery a community of both honesty and compassion, the best environment in which to grow.

Erroneously, we have come to believe that anger and hate are inevitable. Buddhist psychology shows us another way. We can live in this world with a non-contentious heart. We can discover the courage not to succumb, not to retreat, not to strike out in fear and anger. With the transformation of anger and hatred, we can speak the truth and stand up for justice. And by resting in the wise heart, we can be a lamp, a medicine, a liberating presence for all.

PRACTICE: DISCOVERING THE PAIN AND FEAR BEHIND ANGER

Begin to notice mindfully how often states of anger arise in your life. Notice how anger can come in many forms: the critic, the self-righteous victim, the reactive controller, the judge, the know-it-all. Sense how anger affects the various parts of your body. Take your time and really feel it. Then notice the waves of other emotions such as aggression, vindictiveness, anxiety, and excitement, that come along with anger. Stay mindful. Next become aware of all the stories it tells, the self-justifying beliefs and views that support it. Notice how easy it is to be attached, to identify with all of these experiences.

Now you are ready to notice what is behind this anger. Sense the movement to strike out, to blame. And then ask yourself what is the hurt or fear that might be giving rise to this anger. Look honestly at how you feel hurt and pained, what you are afraid might happen. Acknowledge this deep level of vulnerability as a part of the whole situation. Now imagine how you might communicate about your fear and hurt rather than blame. Let your heart teach you. You can speak and respond to the problem in a way that respects yourself and others. Let this become a regular practice as you work with anger.

15

FROM DELUSION TO WISDOM
AWAKENING FROM THE DREAM

Delusion has the characteristic of blindness, of not penetrating reality,
of covering the true nature of experience, of fostering unwise
attention, of causing deluded action.
—Visuddhimagga

Hey there. You've been asleep for a long time. Isn't it time to awaken?
—Sign on the entry path to Ajahn Chah's monastery

The goal of Buddhist psychology is to help us see clearly. When we are lost in delusion, it's hard to see even the most obvious truths. Ajahn Chah said, "It's like we're riding a horse and asking, 'Where's the horse?'"

One of the most stunning revelations of modern psychology is how very wrong our habitual perception can be. In a study done at Harvard University, Daniel Simons showed a three-minute basketball video and asked the observers to count how many times a basketball was passed between the black team and the white team.

After a minute, a person in a gorilla suit walks slowly to the very middle of the court, faces the camera, beats his chest, and then walks away. At the end of three minutes, 50 percent of those watching the video missed the gorilla altogether. They were so busy counting, the basketball was all they saw. Even when asked if anything unusual had happened, they firmly said no. When the video was played back to them, their mouths dropped open in amazement. The gorilla is so obvious, yet they never saw a thing.

Of course, sometimes it is helpful to ignore distractions, even a video gorilla, so that we can focus on certain tasks to the exclusion of others. In fact, meditation can help us with that. But we also need to realize how one-sided our view of things can be, how much of reality we may be missing. Often we see only what we want to believe. We can be famously deluded about love, and equally so about our bodies, our plans, our finances, our past, and our future. Whole nations can be deluded about their domestic or foreign policy.

"You live in illusion and the appearance of things," says Tibetan lama Kalu Rinpoche. "There is a reality but you do not know this." Without seeing clearly, we take the surface illusion of things to be reality. Delusion underlies all the other unhealthy states. Grasping and clinging arise from the delusion of scarcity, an inability to sense our wholeness and life's abundance. Aversion and hatred arise from a misguided search for security, from the mistaken belief that hatred can make us safer. And at the root of delusion itself is the illusion of a separate, limited sense of self.

Freedom from delusion is so important that the first words of the Buddha after his enlightenment were a poem describing this liberation. "O housebuilder, thou art seen at last," he proclaims. "The ridgepole is broken, the rafters are shattered. No more shall you build this house of sorrow." Delusion is the ridgepole that holds up the rafters of clinging, anger, fear, and sorrow. Seeing through delusion, the Buddha liberated himself from the house of human suffering and walked away free.

When we awaken from delusion, our life is transformed. This is not easy, because the ridgepole of delusion is hard to see. When conflict and dissension arose among the monks at Ajahn Chah's monastery, he would stop them and say, "See this clearly. This is ignorance. This is delusion."

Delusion has a seductive power, and it can appear anywhere. Buddhist texts tell of the famous quarrel at Kosambi, when the Buddha's own monks wouldn't listen to him in their conflict. Zen master Dogen warns us how quickly delusion can appear: "One enlightened thought and you're a Buddha. One ordinary thought and you're again a deluded person." As a meditation teacher, I've seen delusion even at the top of the Buddhist world. There are certain masters and their disciples who arrogantly denigrate the practices of other masters or abuse their students, believing that it is for the students' own good. When I'm honest, I see that I too can be arrogant and insensitive; I too can get caught by my own delusions.

Delusion is different from lack of information. It is different from not knowing how a gasoline engine works or the facts of Middle Eastern history. Delusion can lead us to ignore the facts and cling to our views and opinions; it creates a loss of connection with reality. At its extreme, delusion becomes outright psychosis. Our ordinary delusion can take us from the reality of the present into the unreality of our thoughts and confused misperceptions. With delusion we can get lost in a dreamy and unconscious life. Even reading this chapter about delusion may put you to sleep. Notice how it works. Through awareness we can release the spell of delusion and the suffering it creates.

This is a fifteenth principle of Buddhist psychology:

15   Delusion misunderstands the world and forgets who we are. Delusion gives rise to all unhealthy states. Free yourself from delusion and see with wisdom.

INATTENTION: THE FIRST LEVEL OF DELUSION

Buddhist psychology describes three levels of delusion in our lives. The first is a lack of attention. Without attention, it is as if the Wicked Witch of the West has sown our hometown with poppies and we don't notice where we are. We could call this level forgetful delusion. Forgetful delusion arises when we don't notice what is happening, when we are lost in thought, half asleep. It is like the experience of driving to a destination, parking, and realizing that we have no memory of the whole drive. Or as a friend said once in a restaurant, after demolishing a plate of food, "I have no idea who just ate that!"

With delusion we live our lives on automatic pilot. We walk down the street and return home without registering where we are and what is happening. On a stormy day we miss the scudding clouds, the splash of rain at our feet, and the glow of windows at twilight. We miss the sparkle in the air on a sunny spring morning. We even miss the faces of our loved ones when we arrive home.

Whole periods of our lives disappear in the trance of delusion. We live in a culture of chronic inattention fed by the frenzied pace of modern life. Our schools and workplaces push us to multitask, and our fragmented attention becomes cursory, shallow. Surrounded by stimulation, we become bored and restless, prone to addictions of all kinds. As author Anne Wilson Schaef points out, "It is in the interests of consumer society to promote these things that take the edge off, keep us busy with our fixes, and keep us slightly numbed out and zombie-like." Unfortunately, what is commonly accepted by Western psychology as "normal" can actually mean we are functioning at a significant level of delusion. This delusion can happen even when we outwardly appear successful, possessing everything that money can buy, while experiencing an utter lack of inner peace.

Mindfulness training wakes us up from the trance of delusion. Mindfulness shifts us out of fantasy into seeing clearly. Without mindfulness, the deluded mind habitually grasps pleasant experiences and rejects unpleasant ones. Harder to see, delusion ignores neutral experience. When things are neutral, we get bored and spaced out because we are so culturally conditioned to seek high levels of stimulation. So we miss the aliveness behind the neutral experiences that make up much of our day. And yet when our attention grows, what seems neutral or dull becomes full with an unseen richness.

Instead of trying to dispel delusion, first we can simply notice the times it arises, when we go on automatic. We can take an interest in lack of awareness. To do this we can look for the areas of our life that are most unconscious. We will notice how delusion comes hand in hand with distractedness, speed, and addiction. It is a challenge to our habits to pay attention to delusion. As we do so we begin to wake up.

Sleepiness and dullness are also symptoms of the first level of delusion. On a biological level, sleepiness comes when we are tired and need renewal. When people first come on retreats, they often fall into grateful, exhausted sleep as soon as they start to meditate. At the least opportunity for calm, their body expresses its needs. This healthy sleepiness is a natural response and has to be respected. In certain monasteries this sleep is called "the poor man's nirvana." But at other times sleepiness and dullness are simply delusion. Like the opium den of the mind, they bring a seductive forgetfulness that just doesn't want to see.

On one retreat I worked with Kyle, a businessman who reported that at every sitting period he would become sleepy. He had been on retreat for several days and was well rested, so it wasn't exhaustion. And his energy level seemed strong enough to balance his growing stillness. I began to wonder if his sleepiness was functioning to hide his experience. When we sat together, I asked Kyle to close his eyes and investigate. He sat quietly for a time, paying attention. Then, as his sleepiness began, I asked him, "What might you feel if you weren't so sleepy?" Moments later, his eyes filled with tears. This sleepy state had covered over a well of sorrows— the suicide of his lover years before, his struggles and loneliness. Kyle's sad memories all flooded out in layers. His attention to delusion opened a level of grief and pain that he had avoided for years. Because he had not let himself feel the grief and pain he carried,

Kyle said he experienced life as if he were half alive, like living on hold. The dullness that blocked access to his suffering left him unable to feel fully, to act creatively, and to love again.

With mindfulness, we can awaken from delusion. Even the United States army is using mindfulness training based on the stress reduction programs of Jon Kabat-Zinn, which have had great success in hospitals and businesses. One young army officer who had a hot temper and a history of anger- and stress-related problems was ordered by his colonel to attend an eight-week mindfulness training class to help reduce his level of stress. One day, after attending the class for some weeks, he stopped for groceries on his way home. He was in a hurry and a bit irritated as usual. When he took his cart to check out, there were long lines. He noticed the woman in front of him had only one item but wasn't in the express line. She was carrying a baby and talking to the cashier. He became irritated. She was in the wrong line, talking, holding everyone up. Then she passed the baby to the cashier and the cashier spent a moment cooing over the child. He could feel his habitual anger rising. But because he'd been practicing mindfulness, he started to become aware of the heat and tightness in his body. He could feel the pain. He breathed and relaxed. When he looked up again he saw the little boy smiling. As he reached the cashier he said, "That was a cute little boy." "Oh, did you like him?" she responded. "That's my baby. His father was in the air force, but he was killed last winter. Now I have to work full time. My mom tries to bring my boy in once or twice a day so I can see him."

When we live in delusion, we are quick to judge others. We miss their inner beauty. We also miss their pain, and cannot respond to them with compassion. With inattention, we miss the meal in front of us, the parade of passersby, the ever-changing scenery, the openhearted connection with the world.

THE DELUSION OF DENIAL

Deeper than inattention, we find a second form of delusion: denial. Denial arises when we don't believe what is actually in front of our eyes. On a personal level, we can deny problems at work, difficulties in our marriage, depression, or addiction, as if denial will make them go away. With denial, we can start a love affair and actually believe that the romantic intoxication will last forever. We can think that the stock market will only go up and never go down.

Many of us learned denial early. We were taught to ignore family secrets. My mother made excuses for her bruises and tried to keep visitors from our house so no one would see how crazy my father could be. In denial, we become frightened to tell the truth to one another. I knew of a twelve-year-old girl, dying of cancer, whose parents bought her new skis for Christmas. It wasn't that they were trying to give her hope. They just couldn't face the fact that, after years of family ski vacations, she would never ski again. So often those who work with sick children say the children know they are dying, but they try to protect their parents from this knowledge. This can be a lonely task. When I have been with dying children, I am often amazed at their wisdom and fearlessness. They are the teachers for the brokenhearted adults who live in denial around them.

Denial can also function collectively. Buddhist psychology describes how whole societies can be manipulated into violent upheaval by ignorance, racism, and fear mongering. The consumer advertising and television propaganda around us can deliberately foster anxiety and reinforce our political and economic delusions. Collective delusions can operate for years before we awaken to the cost, asking ourselves why thousands of people lost their lives or billions of dollars were spent in the name of nonexistent "weapons of mass destruction."

An extraordinary lifting of denial occurred when the Soviet empire began to unravel under Mikhail Gorbachev in the 1980s. Previously the Russian Communist dictatorships had denied all wrongdoing. Their history books pretended that the tens of millions killed in Stalin's purges, the horrific Siberian political prisons, and the massive collective agricultural failures never happened. Even photographs were doctored to remove all traces of those officials who had been "eliminated." Then in 1988, at the peak of the new openness fostered by Gorbachev, *Izvestia,* the official government newspaper of the Soviet Union, reported on the front page that the Soviet government had decided to cancel the final history exams for fifty-three million students because the history text-books taught lies that "deluded one generation after another, poisoning their minds and souls." It went on, "Today we are reaping the bitter fruits of our own moral laxity. We are paying for succumbing to conformity and thus to giving silent approval of everything that now brings the blush of shame to our faces and about which we do not know how to answer our children honestly."

The cost of the Soviet Union's denial was obvious to us. Unfortunately, we too continue to deny our environmental crises, the continuing rise of racism and false nationalism, and our participation in the enormous global weapons industry. In looking for security, we somehow ignore the fact that 10 percent of the world's military budget would feed every hungry person on earth.

Sometimes we can cling to delusions even in the face of obvious danger. I like the story about a man who is driving down the highway when he hears a safety alert on the radio: "Anyone driving north on Interstate 187 should use great caution! There is a car driving on the wrong side of the divided highway." The man glares through his windshield and mutters, "There's not just one car driving the wrong way. There are hundreds of them."

Like the training in mindfulness, Western psychology has focused on helping us see through this middle level of delusion. In analysis and many other forms of therapy, we repeatedly confront our denial. We are probed and questioned and interpreted and forced to face and feel what we have ignored. I can remember sitting with one of my first therapists, talking on and on about a significant challenge in my relationship and my impending move to another city. Suddenly he stopped me cold. "You're sad, aren't you? Sad and angry." All at once my mind stopped dead. I was stunned by the simplicity of it. I began to weep and tremble and face the hard truth. I had needed to stop my story and step out of denial.

In the same way, Ajahn Chah helped his students by pointing out denial. To me he'd say, "Hey. You're not paying attention today, are you?" To John, "Hey there, you think you're meditating, but we can hear you snore." And to Prasert, "You're afraid of the ghosts near your hut. The closest thing I've seen to ghosts are these big white Western monks." Ajahn Chah kept the practices very simple for his most deluded monks. It was as if he wanted to cut through their confusion with simple words in big, obvious lettering. He gave them simple rituals: "Meditate four times a day and focus on your body." Or "Keep your robes neat." He offered simple instructions for the mind as well: "Don't believe your doubt. Just say 'This is doubt.' " Ajahn Chah said, "Anger is easy to see, and greed is more subtle, but delusion is the hardest. All the accompanying states get cloudy, confusing." He went on, "Look for moments of clarity. Keep to your experience, not your confusing thoughts. Learn the difference." Through our training, we were taught to step out of the confused mind.

MISPERCEPTION OF REALITY

The deepest level of delusion is called "misperception of reality." This level is the hardest to face because it threatens some of our most cherished assumptions. In a fundamental way, we are deluded about happiness, permanence, and the nature of who we think we are. First, let's take our ideas about happiness. We all understand how outer comforts can bring pleasure, ease, security. "Were these experiences not pleasant," says the Buddha, "we would not become entangled." And while we may well enjoy these forms of happiness, they are incomplete. A wise part of us knows that they alone do not bring fulfillment. Buddhist psychology encourages us to investigate the delusion of happiness.

Some of the richest and most privileged humans experience intractable suffering and heartbreak, while villagers who live in extremely poor conditions can be astonishingly happy. Happiness is within us. Studies of winners of state lotteries show that after receiving the money, the winners' happiness increases for about two years and then it usually returns to its original level. If we were already quite happy, we return to that state. If we were depressed, fearful, or miserable, even after winning millions in the lottery we will likely return to that state as well. Even more surprising is the research on those who become paralyzed, one of the worst fates many can imagine. After a few years paraplegics and quadriplegics also return to their normal state of happiness.

Changing our outer circumstances is not the true path to happiness. Genuine happiness arises from healthy states of mind; it is born of a wise and gracious heart. One woman came to Buddhist practice after her doctor called to say the lump in her breast was cancer and had spread to the lymph nodes. She would need surgery and chemotherapy. She worked as an administrator, her two children were grown, and her husband was supportive and offered to do whatever she needed. During and after the treatment, she questioned whether the illness and fear of death would ruin her life. Then she realized that she could be happy anyway. She was a warmhearted, loving person who enjoyed people. She was a friend to many. In fact, she already had what made her happy. It wasn't the comforts of her life that made her happy, nor could the cancer and difficult treatment destroy it. It was her good heart that made the difference.

In the misperception of reality, the second basic delusion is that of permanence. Delusion believes that we can hold on to experience. Yet nothing about life is solid, permanent. Where is our childhood? Where are the 1990s? Where are last year, last month, yesterday? Gone. "Experience comes trooping out of emptiness day and night," writes the poet Rumi. With the delusion of permanence, we grasp feelings, experiences, and people as if they were ours to keep. We struggle to hold on to the world and yet our days vanish like a mirage or a dream.

We can live wisely only when we accept the reality of change. At Ajahn Chah's monastery, impermanence and death were central to the curriculum. We deliberately contemplated change, our moods, the seasons, the passing of visitors, our aging, and the movement of our breath until we could see life as an unstoppable river. Zen master Shunryu Suzuki summed up Buddhist teaching in this simple phrase: "Not always so."

My favorite cartoon shows a Bedouin family on camels traveling across a vast desert landscape. The father is first, on the largest camel, followed next by the mother and then the three children, each on slightly smaller camels. The father has turned his head to respond to the smallest child: "Stop asking if we're almost there yet. We're nomads, for crying out loud!"

In our delusion we forget we are all nomads. We pretend our bodies will stay young, our children will not grow up, our fortunes are secure, our marriages will not change. Yet praise and blame, gain and loss, pleasure and pain, fame and disrepute weave an ever-changing fabric of our lives. "To call a thing good not a day longer than it appears to us good, and above all not a day earlier—that is the only way to keep joy pure," says Nietzsche.

To cut through delusion, in Ajahn Chah's monastery we contemplated a Buddhist text that might well make most ordinary people blanch: "Did you never see a man or woman eighty, ninety years old, frail, with tottering steps, broken teeth, wrinkled, with blotched limbs? And did the thought never come to you that this will happen to you? Did you never see a man or woman grievously ill, sick and afflicted, lifted by some and put to bed by others, and did the thought never come to you that you also are subject to disease? Did you never see the corpse of a man or woman one or two days after death, swollen, blue-black, full of decay, and did the thought never come to you that you also are subject to death, that you cannot escape?"

These are startling direct questions. They challenge our complacency; they guide us to live with wisdom in the light of death.

Tom had been involved with Buddhist practice for several years when he came again to retreat. Tom was a deluded type, with a tendency to be dull and flat, at times spaced out. When I directed him to focus his attention more carefully on his body—his feet, his arms, his chest—he began to notice how anxious he felt. Then he immediately began to obsess about his wife. She had been recently diagnosed with Parkinson's disease, and Tom didn't know how to respond. He said to me, "Since the diagnosis, I don't even know what I feel."

I suggested he write a letter to himself, trying to articulate whatever he sensed was hidden from his ordinary awareness. After a day of meditation he began to write about his fears for his wife and their future, his ongoing insecurity. Then he remembered this same insecurity from his childhood and his first marriage. He wrote about being shaky and angry and confused. When he read his letter to me, he came alive. He was able to feel his inner tumult, to know his own experience with greater clarity and honesty.

Tom was beginning to let himself trust awareness. But as he opened, his sense of suffering increased. His wife's difficulties and the suffering of so many others with illness and insecurity became visible to him too. Its intensity grew. When we sat together, I invited him to accept the totality of the suffering in his family and in the world and to allow it to intensify, to open, to change, as it did. At first it felt overwhelming. He wept for the suffering and sickness of all beings. The sense of suffering grew and became heat and pain in his body and mind, as if he were a fire or a star. He knew that everyone was part of this fire. And then he experienced the star expanding into space, what he called radiant emptiness. His face softened. Relief broke through his suffering. A voice in his mind said, *You are now ready to find the comfort of this world in suffering itself. You are free to love.*

As Tom pictured his wife, a new spaciousness and trust gave him a way to hold their struggles with a more gracious heart. From being spaced out, Tom had become spacious, a loving presence. When he went home, Tom was more direct with his wife, less afraid. This helped her to be less afraid as well. Tom regularly came back on retreat to renew his meditation, to be spacious and open to each new stage of her illness and their life together.

Our delusions about happiness and permanence are rooted in the deepest delusion of all, forgetting who we are. When we forget our true nature, we feel ourselves as separate, lost in a small perspective, moving like a horse with blinders. In the same way that we grasp our body, we grasp our fleeting feelings and thoughts, and take them to be our fundamental identity. Just as the meditation on aging and decay challenges our perception of the body, the Buddhist teachings go on to undermine any clinging to the mind: "To say that mind, or mind states, or mind consciousness constitutes the self, such an assertion is unfounded. It would be better for those who lack understanding to regard this body made of elements as self, rather than the mind. The body though changing may last for a year, or for decades, but that which is called mind, its thoughts and states of consciousness, arises continuously day and night and as quickly passes away. Therefore whatever bodily experiences, feelings, perception, thoughts, or consciousness, past, present, or future, gross or subtle, should be seen clearly according to wisdom: this does not belong to me, this I am not, this is not my self."

With delusion, we lose perspective, we cling, we forget our luminous true nature. Alan Watts called this "the taboo against knowing who you are."

REMEMBERING WHO YOU ARE

How amazing. All living beings have the Buddha nature of awakening and freedom, yet they do not realize this. Unknowingly they wander on the oceans of suffering for lifetimes. It is time to realize your own Buddha nature.
—Prajnaparamita

Our delusion can be dispelled in a moment. It is never too late for the illumination of wisdom. It does not matter how long the darkness has lasted. In one famous story, a spiritual wanderer who had been searching all across India asked the Buddha to sum up his teachings in the briefest possible way. The wanderer, named Bahia, was afraid that he had not much longer to live, and indeed he died shortly after this encounter. Hearing Bahia's urgency, the Buddha pointed to the freedom beyond the self. "In the seen, there is just the seen; in the heard, there is just the heard; in the sensed, there is just the sensed; in the thought, there is just the thought." Understanding these words was enough to dispel Bahia's delusion of a separate sense of self. As the illusion of self fell away, Bahia awakened to the suchness of life, immediate and open. He found the freedom he had been seeking was in his own wise heart.

Stepping out of the delusion of separation is a relief. Philippa, a Buddhist hospice nurse, told me a story from the county hospital where she worked. A patient she was helping to care for had been brought to the hospital under guard from the local prison. Bill was forty-four years old, serving a long sentence for armed robbery, and dying from complications of HIV and hepatitis C. He had not wanted his mother to visit, because he was so ashamed of his life. But Philippa saw beneath this shame. After a heartfelt conversation, she convinced him to make contact with his mother. Several days later his mother arrived, frail, over eighty, with a grief-stricken expression.

When Bill's mother entered the room, she saw her son, who had not spoken to her for years, in prison garb, handcuffed to the bed. Philippa was afraid that the dignified and stern mother would look at her son with judgment and disappointment. Instead, she just stood there with a deep stillness and they looked each other all over. Then their eyes locked and the circumstances and sufferings, the roles and costumes, all dropped away. Philippa said that Bill's mother gazed at her son like a newborn child, like a saint witnessing a miracle, with the heart of all mothers. Bill and his mother each saw their original goodness, forgiving, eternal. They sat together for an hour and held hands. There was not much that needed to be said. When his mother left, Bill said now he could die in peace.

When the delusion of separation is dispelled, we see beneath our roles and dramas to the level of spirit. We recognize the universal dance of life, where the roles and dramas, even the very players themselves, are tentative and dream-like, being nothing and everything.

THE SPACIOUS AND CLEAR HEART

The forest master Ajahn Maha Bua explains that the state of delusion is like a village terrorized by bandits. When ignorance is dispelled, the bandits no longer hold sway and the whole village is free to go about its business, undisturbed.

A Buddhist practitioner, Charles, came to a meditation retreat, frustrated about his marriage. He had been telling himself that everything was OK, but underneath he knew it wasn't going well. For some days he sat, beginning to sense his breath, body, and mind. As his mind grew quieter and his heart more open, he told me he was able to step back and see the whole situation with the eyes of wisdom. "I've not been a very caring partner. My wife is really hurt and angry and probably wants to leave me. I have to tend to this." This same clarity arose when another practitioner, a business-woman, realized, "My backers do not have my best interest in mind; they want to take over the business for themselves." A mother saw that her newly married son who had moved to London was leading his own life now, and that her old dependent relation-ship would have to change. And a man with a serious recurrence of cancer who had been dismissing its impact realized, "Oh, I might really die soon. I had better prepare myself."

In spaciousness and clarity, we can understand that every one of us participates in the loss and suffering of life, as well as its mar-vels and beauty. This awakens our compassion instead of judgment or denial. Compassion and spaciousness arise together. When delu-sion goes, we are no longer so frightened or worried about our-self. As the illusion of separate self dissolves, the play of life becomes less personal, part of the timeless dance called "the rise and fall of the four seasons." Traditional societies throughout the world understand how important it is to dissolve the illusion of separateness. They use meditation and trance, vision quests, psy-choactive drugs, sleeplessness, music, and dance. Buddhist practice shows us how to do so regularly, in skillful and systematic ways. Whenever our delusion is dispelled, there comes a tremendous sense of freedom.

In this timeless openness, our hearts open as well. Thomas Merton tells how this struck him on an ordinary afternoon. "In Louisville, at the corner of Fourth and Walnut, in the center of the shopping district, I was suddenly overwhelmed with the realization that I loved all those people, that they were mine and I theirs, that we could not be alien to one another even though we were total strangers. It was like waking from a dream of separateness, of spurious self-isolation in a special world, the world of renunciation and supposed holiness. . . . This sense of liberation from an illusory difference was such a relief and such a joy to me that I almost laughed out loud."

When we discover spacious clarity, we become citizens of love.

IV

FINDING
FREEDOM

16

SUFFERING AND LETTING GO

There is Suffering. There is the Cause of Suffering. There is the End of Suffering. There is the Path to the End of Suffering. These Four Noble Truths teach suffering and the end of suffering.
—Buddha

In a world of tension and breakdown it is necessary for there to be those who seek to integrate their inner lives not by avoiding anguish and running away from problems, but by facing them in their naked reality and in their ordinariness.
—Thomas Merton

Anyone who has had even the briefest introduction to Buddhist teaching is familiar with its starting point: the inescapable truth that existence entails suffering. This is called the First Noble Truth. But how difficult it is to fully embrace this truth. When I first became a monk in the forest monastery, Ajahn Chah welcomed me and then said, "I hope you're not afraid to suffer." Taken aback by this greeting, I asked him what he meant. He continued, "There are two kinds of suffering. There is the suffering you run away from, which follows you everywhere. And there is the suffering you face directly, and in doing so become free." Of all the maps of Buddhist psychology, the Noble Truths, which teach the understanding of suffering and its end, are the most central. The whole purpose of Buddhist psychology, its ethics, philosophy, practices, and community life, is the discovery that freedom and joy are possible in the face of the sufferings of human life. The Four Noble Truths are laid out like a psychological diagnosis: the symptoms, the causes, the possibility of healing, and the medicinal path.

Whether we are healers, therapists, or friends, when people come to us for help, we are first a witness to their suffering. Whatever form that suffering takes—conflict, fear, depression, stress, obsession, confusion, mental illness, divorce, trouble with work or family or the law, unfulfilled creativity, or unrequited love—we must willingly acknowledge its truth.

We are also witness to their pain. Buddhist psychology makes a clear distinction between pain and suffering. Pain is an unavoidable aspect of the natural world. It is physical, biological, and social, woven into our existence as night is with day, as inevitable as hard and soft, as hot and cold. Inhabiting a human body, we experience a continuous ebb and flow of pleasure and pain, gain and loss. Inhabiting our human society is the same: we encounter praise and blame, fame and disrepute, success and failure, arising and passing endlessly.

Suffering is different from pain. Suffering is our reaction to the inevitable pain of life. Our personal suffering can include anxiety, depression, fear, confusion, grief, anger, hurt, addiction, jealousy, and frustration. But suffering is not only personal. Our collective suffering includes the sorrows of warfare and racism; the isolation and torture of prisoners everywhere; the unnecessary hunger, sickness, and abandonment of human beings on every continent. This individual and collective suffering, the First Noble Truth, is what we are called upon to understand and transform.

The Second Noble Truth describes the cause of suffering: grasping. Grasping, it explains, gives birth to aversion and delusion, and from these three roots arise all the other unhealthy states, such as jealousy, anxiety, hatred, addiction, possessiveness, and shamelessness. These are the causes of individual and global suffering.

The Third Noble Truth offers us the way out, the end of suffering. Unlike pain, suffering is not inevitable. Freedom from suffering is possible when we let go of our reactions, our fear and grasping. This freedom is called nirvana. This is the Third Noble Truth.

The Fourth Noble Truth is the path to the end of suffering. This path is called the middle way. The middle way invites us to find peace wherever we are, here and now. By neither grasping nor resisting life, we can find wakefulness and freedom in the midst of our joys and sorrows. Following the middle path, we establish integrity, we learn to quiet the mind, we learn to see with wisdom.

Here is a sixteenth principle of Buddhist psychology:

---

16   Pain is inevitable. Suffering is not. Suffering arises from grasping. Release grasping and be free of suffering.

The Four Noble Truths insist that we face our pain, the pain in our body and mind and the pain of the world. They teach us to stop running away. Only by courageously opening to the sorrow of the world as it is can we find our freedom. This is the demand placed on all who would awaken. As Joseph Campbell reminds us, "The first step to the knowledge of the wonder and mystery of life is in the recognition of the monstrous nature of the earthly human realm as well as its glory."

Of course Western psychology also thoroughly acknowledges suffering. But in certain ways it leads us to simply accept our suffering, what Freud called our ordinary level of neurosis. As Freud said in his famously resigned terms, "The goal of psychoanalysis is to claim a little more ego from the vast sea of id." Like Freud, the great existential philosophers Sartre and Camus also focused on the inevitability of our suffering. But a philosophical or psychological acceptance of normal unhappiness is a poor place to end the story.

The Four Noble Truths promise much more. They are a complete and systematic set of psychological principles and teachings that we can use to end the causes of suffering. Through their understanding we can realize freedom.

THE FIRST NOBLE TRUTH

Here is how the practices of the Four Noble Truths unfold. Acknowledging suffering is the beginning. In the monastery, Ajahn Chah would peer at his students as if taking stock of their suffering. Sometimes he would inquire out loud, "What is your kind of suffering?" When students responded, whether the answer was bodily pain or fear of ghosts, he would gaze at them with compassion and ask, "Can you bear it?" Later he might offer practices, from mindfulness to repentance, from compassion to solitude, to help them transform their suffering. But first he wanted them to learn to hold their suffering with dignity.

We are all subject to aging and illness, to losses that nothing will change. Loneliness, betrayal, insecurity have no outer cure. Of this basic suffering, the Buddha unfailingly reminded his followers, "It seems that although we thought ourselves permanent, we are not. Although we thought ourselves settled, we are not. Although we thought we would last forever, we will not." We can try to distract ourselves, but our suffering will follow us. Facing our pain and suffering honorably is the only way we can grow.

In my own life, I had to face up to the wounds I received from my father. I had to let the weight of our family's pain be felt, to experience the hurt, the betrayal, the rage, the sadness. This was an arduous process in the monastery, in therapy, and over years of practice. I had begun graduate school and teaching when my parents separated. The divorce was hard on my father. He didn't know what to do; he couldn't work. In one despondent period, a year after he moved out, my father came to stay with one of my brothers and me. He slept in the study in our big Boston apartment and crept around quietly, trying not to be too visible, trying to figure out how to create a new life for himself. Sensing his depression, my feelings went from anger to pity and finally to compassion. Eventually, he moved on to a smaller, more limited life of his own. My mother, whom I'd visit in her new Washington apartment, had created a much happier life and a whole new network of friends. Seeing this, I was astonished and frustrated at how long she had been stuck. Why did it take her so many years to leave the marriage? She honestly acknowledged how terrible those times were for all of us, which was a relief to me, but then she'd quickly want to move on, to focus on how she was living now. I couldn't do that so easily. I found it necessary to work step by step with our family's suffering. I had to be willing to grieve.

My colleague Malidoma Somé, a West African medicine man, observed that here in the West we have forgotten how to grieve. Our streets, he says, are full of the ungrieved dead. Malidoma's culture knows the value of grieving and offers rituals to honor our loss and pain. His African elders say that only by allowing our grief, outrage, longing, pain, and tears can we discover the wise heart that can contain them all. We learn to honor the First Noble Truth.

I heard about a Jungian psychologist who attended a professional workshop that included a film by one of Carl Jung's last pupils, the great dream analyst Marie-Louise von Franz. After the film, a distinguished panel of senior Jungian analysts and Carl Jung's own grandson responded to written questions from the audience that were sent up to the stage on cards.

One of these cards recounted a horrific recurring dream, in which the dreamer was subjected to Nazi torture and atrocities and stripped of all human dignity. A member of the panel read the dream out loud. As she listened, the psychologist attending the workshop began to formulate a dream interpretation in her head in anticipation of the panel's response. It really was a no-brainer, she thought, as her mind busily offered her symbolic explanations for the torture described in the dream. But this was not how the panel responded at all. When the reading of the dream was complete, Jung's grandson looked out over the large audience. "Would you all please rise?" he asked. "We will stand together in a moment of silence in response to this dream."

As the audience stood, the psychologist anticipated the discussion she was certain would follow. But when they all sat down again, the panel went on to the next question. The psychologist did not understand this at all. A few days later she asked one of her teachers, himself a Jungian analyst, about it. "Ah," he said, "there is in life a vulnerability so extreme, a suffering so unspeakable, that it goes beyond words. In the face of such suffering all we can do is stand in witness, so no one need bear it alone."

There is a sacred quality to the witnessing of our suffering that is different from suppression or repression. This witnessing is an essential part of meditation, an attentive and compassionate awareness. Sometimes witnessing is all we have to do. At other times after witnessing, a strong response is necessary. Either way, our suffering must be borne consciously. In the words of Elie Wiesel, the Nobel Prize winner who has spent a lifetime exploring the suffering caused by the Nazis, "Suffering confers neither privileges nor rights; it all depends on how one uses it. If you use it to increase the anguish of others, you are degrading, even betraying it. And yet the day will come when we shall understand that suffering can elevate human beings. . . . God help us to bear our suffering well."

THE CAUSES OF SUFFERING

Pain is physical, suffering is mental. Suffering is due entirely to clinging
or resisting. It is a sign of our unwillingness to move, to flow with life.
Although all life has pain, a wise life is free of suffering. A wise person is friendly
with the inevitable and does not suffer. Pain they know but it does not break
them. If they can, they do what is possible to restore balance.
If not, they let things take their course.
—Nisargadatta

When we learn to distinguish between pain and suffering, we discover that sometimes pain is a call to action. At other times we must simply accept our losses and tragedies. In either case, pain comes and goes. Suffering grows out of our reaction to the original pain. The Second Noble Truth tells us that when we grasp, we create suffering. When Ajahn Chah noticed that a student seemed to be having difficulty, in a bemused voice he would inquire, "Hey, are you suffering?" If the person said no, he'd laugh and say, "Well good." If they answered yes, he'd also smile and say, "Hmmm, must be holding on too tight." Suffering is like rope burn. We need to let go.

Buddhist psychology directs us to examine how grasping operates. The more we grasp, the more we experience suffering. If we try to possess and control the people around us, we will suffer. If we struggle to control our body and feelings, it is the same. If a nation acts from grasping and greed, the world around it will suffer. Meditation teaches us that we can release our clinging.

Loni, a thirty-eight-year-old woman, came to a weeklong retreat the year after her diagnosis with AIDS. In the months since her diagnosis, she had become lost in confusion and fear. On the retreat, she began to see how much suffering she was creating for herself. As she relaxed and became more mindful she discovered the fear was worse than her bodily pains. Loni began to work on releasing the fear each time the thoughts and feelings arose. At first they were tenacious, sticky, and she would soften and let go each time. After several days of this, her body relaxed, her mind eased, and she was filled with a healing love and grace she wouldn't have thought possible. Letting go was the key. Another practitioner, Steve, came on retreat in the middle of a conflict with his grown children. When he sat in meditation he saw that he was full of blame, fear, and confusion, that he was grasping at everything they did. Then he noticed that there were moments when his fear would subside and his heart would open. Instead of holding tightly to "how it should be," he could look from the perspective of "What's best for everyone at this point?" When he let go even a little, his caring started to return.

Like Steve, Pilar was full of blame and anger. She had recently lost her job in a company restructuring. She believed this was because her patriarchal boss did not like to promote women. She was so angry she thought about revenge. She wanted to file a lawsuit against her unjust dismissal. In her meditation, she could feel how much pain she was in. She was encouraged to study the causes of her suffering. She realized that if she acted primarily from grasping and anger she would suffer. She still thought the lawsuit was necessary, but she realized she could do it differently. If she acted from compassion and care for herself and those who might follow her, she could choose the same action with much less suffering.

Letting go of the causes of suffering is a process. Sometimes it simply means letting be—not trying to get rid of experience, but softening into a state of allowing. This softening brings a felt sense of release in the body and mind. Ajahn Chah encouraged us to feel the pain of grasping and then relax, to set the burden down. He told us, "These days we are caught in hurrying and forcing. Mangoes are never sweet now. Before they're ripe they are picked and artificially ripened. It's done because people want to get them in a hurry. But when you eat them, you find they are sour. This is trying to match the desires of people to get things in a hurry. To get something good, something sweet, you have to let it be sour first, according to its own natural way. But we pick them early and complain that they're sour."

When Cynthia came to Buddhist practice she described herself as a hungry ghost. She was obsessed with the feeling of intolerable emptiness and how worthless and ugly she felt inside. She had spent several years in therapy uncovering the pain and lack of love in her adoptive family, but she still suffered from binge eating. Time and again she reached for food "looking for the magic," only to have it fail and instead bring her "untold shame and suffering." She called her bingeing a memory disorder, a confusion, a loss of her humanity. "Of course," she said later, "I knew that food was neither the answer nor the problem." What slowly made the difference for Cynthia was mindfulness and kindness. "At first," she told me, "it was a victory just to accept the pain, nausea, and sleeplessness that followed a binge, rather than eating even more to numb the shame and remorse of 'having done it again.' "

It was critical that Cynthia learn how to work with the shame and remorse she carried. I asked her to bring compassion to her body when the shame was strong. She came to see me in tears, because as she let herself feel the sense of shame, it became a devouring presence. Even greater compassion and mindfulness were needed to help release her grasping. Slowly she began to heal.

This is how Cynthia later described it. "I was gradually able to see that my 'hungry ghost' tendency did not make me a failure as a human being. Because the self-hatred was so intense, I could only say, 'May this suffering body be healed, may this sad heart be free.' And recently, amazingly, when I am able to see the tendency to start on that sad old path, grasping for the illusory magic of food, a compassionate awareness will arise and say, 'Oh, I don't really want this. It will only lead to pain and sadness.' These moments are a miracle really, a release from the agony of the hungry ghost. It is as if, like the temptations of Buddha on his enlightenment night, I can feel the pain, see the grasping, and finally say, 'I see you, Mara' and let it go. This struggle has opened my heart to the suffering of others. Hungry ghosts are around us all the time. Because of my experience I see them in so many people. It's not just food, but any kind of grasping. I feel such compassion because I know how much it hurts. Only by letting go will they heal, will they free their hearts."

LETTING GO

Cynthia reminds us to be patient with the process of letting go. Sometimes it seems as though nothing is happening. This is hard for Westerners who want quick results. We need to learn to observe the tiny openings along the way. With practice we can let go and relax into any moments of stillness and compassion. We can begin to trust the moments of well-being. "If you let go a little, you will have a little peace," said Ajahn Chah. "If you let go more, you will have more peace. And if you let go completely, whatever happens, your heart will be free." Eventually, even in great pain and difficulty, we will have learned to let go.

A reporter once pressed the Dalai Lama about his oft-quoted statement that he does not hate the Chinese Communists, in spite of their systematic destruction of Tibet. In reply, the Dalai Lama explained, "They have taken over Tibet, destroyed our temples, burned our sacred texts, ruined our communities, and taken away our freedom. They have taken so much. Why should I let them also take my peace of mind?" Because he has learned to let go, the Dalai Lama can work more freely to create a better future for Tibet. He knows that clinging to suffering is not the way.

Letting go does not mean we do not care and respond. As parents, we can love, protect, instruct, and nurture our children. They want our support, but they don't want to be controlled. Parenting is a lifelong learning in letting go. We have to delicately renegotiate the balance between hands on and hands off in almost every situation. When they are young, letting them go feels like teaching them to ride a bicycle, directing and balancing them but not gripping too tightly. With each step, each new accomplishment—as our children go off on a first overnight, go to camp, learn to drive a car, go to college—we have to face new levels of letting go, yet loving and supporting them all the while.

Letting go was critical for Helen, an office manager for an insurance company. At forty-three, Helen first encountered mindfulness practice through a stress reduction program at work. Her major anxiety and loneliness focused around not having a partner or any children. She felt she was missing an important part of life and she was increasingly frightened about growing old alone. For many years Helen had not wanted children because she was too afraid that she would re-create her family. She had grown up with a tyrannical father, a depressed stepmother, and two angry half-brothers. The half-brother who had molested her had died; the other one was in jail. She had lived with anxiety for years, had worked with trauma in therapy, and was using medication to manage it. She found the stress reduction classes helpful.

Helen's mindfulness teachers suggested she follow up with a visit to Spirit Rock. She started coming regularly. Every step of her Buddhist practice involved letting go. When she paid attention to her body she saw fearful thoughts of illness, of gaining weight, of simply being in her body. Her mindfulness teacher told her to let her experience come and go moment by moment. Helen's practice became "let go, let go," with each of the thoughts and fears and judgments. Then she came to a weekend retreat. Her anxiety and loneliness got worse. She had to acknowledge that she probably never would have children. "Let go, let go," she continued gently for weeks afterward. At times she felt overwhelmed; the feelings were just "too much."

Helen was devotional in nature and became inspired by the stories of compassion she heard about Buddhist monks such as the Dalai Lama. To steady her mind when things got bad, she thought of the Dalai Lama and took a vow of kindness toward all the forces of difficulty that assailed her. After a time she could see her feelings and fears with less clinging. Still, whenever Helen saw women her age with children it would trigger her longing and memories of her family trauma. She was afraid she would never be free of their hold.

The next time Helen came on a longer retreat, I sat with her. She said she was caught up in the same old anxiety. I asked her if she could be mindful of it out loud. She described the painful state of her body, the emotions of fear and longing and despair, the repeating story. She said it was as if she were in prison. Curious, I asked, "Who has the key?" She began to wonder.

Two days later Helen recounted a vision that had come in a late-night meditation. Her brother who had died came to her, kindly now, and took her hands and said, "You are not us." Then he indicated that in her own pocket was the key. She smiled and began to say, "Free! Free! Free!" Helen felt that letting go opened her to a kind of grace. Five years after this retreat, I ran into Helen. She greeted me affectionately and seemed warmer and more lively than I remembered. She told me she had found a Tibetan teacher and was in good supportive therapy. She had a partner, an older man, and she was stepmom to two teenage kids.

When I reflect on Helen's story I also want to acknowledge that her antidepressant medication was important for her healing. In the past decade there has been a lively discussion in the Buddhist community about whether medication such as Helen's antidepressants and other psychiatric drugs are compatible with spiritual practice. Initially some teachers were afraid that medication would interfere with the necessary process of facing our fears and letting go. I liked to remind them that we'd all taken plenty of other mind-altering drugs in our day.

Critics are right that medication can be overprescribed and misused and that it can shut down some subtlety of feeling. It's especially alarming that enormous numbers of children are being put on powerful psychiatric medications to control their behavior, often without attending to the underlying causes or offering other forms of treatment. But there are also biochemical roots to anxiety and depression that can overwhelm our ability to face our experience with clarity. There are habituated chemical imbalances in our nervous system from grief, trauma, and other sources that need to be acknowledged.

Now most sensible meditation teachers I know see a place for medication, especially for an initial period of stabilization. Used properly, it can help those overwhelmed by anxiety or depression to find the capacity for mindfulness. For a time, medication becomes a support for letting go, not an impediment. In fact, in recent years a number of spiritual teachers I know have used antidepressants and similar medications themselves in difficult times. The point is not to cling to some ideal, but to respect what genuinely helps us to keep the mind balanced enough to maintain its innate wisdom and goodness.

RELEASE AND GRACE

One man who corresponds with the Insight Prison Project that is associated with Spirit Rock discovered letting go in a dramatic way:

> Today I start my twenty-eighth year in here. I laughed very hard when I read that you wrote I might as well be a monk. One of the nicknames they call me is "the monk of Trenton" or "the smiling Buddha."
>
> I wasn't always known this way. The first ten years I was mean and dangerous. In 1985 I was heavily confined for stabbing a man and my mentor appeared in the form of a hit man for the Irish mob who had become a yogi. He gave me a copy of the Anapana Breathing Sutra and convinced me that I could not live my life out of anger and rage. He put me on a hatha yoga routine with

pranayama and sitting meditation. He handed me a worn copy of
The Foundations of Mindfulness. *My journal records:*

"When I was young I wanted to be accepted. After I was accepted I wanted power. After I had power I realized that power
without wisdom leads to sorrow. After acquiring a small amount of
wisdom I no longer desired to be accepted, I desired solitude."

I closed the page of that journal with the words, "So ends this
part of my life."

For the next two years I didn't come out of my cell except to
mop the whole block and all the tiers once a day. I gave away all
my property except my law papers and my books. I gave myself up
to yoga, pranayama, and meditation. I followed the breath for a
long time and practiced mindfulness. Nothing seemed to be happening. Then I realized that the objects of my awareness began to
have texture. By texture I mean depth. This texture is deceptive because it first arises from the memory or imagination. Soon the texture reveals clarity. This is a movement to present awareness without
the distorting effects of memory or imagination. My mind settled
and I gave up all struggle. I live this way now as much as I can. I
don't know if this is what is supposed to happen. But it's what happens with me. I became still. I learned to listen, to care. It was during this time period that people started calling me "the monk of
Trenton."

There is an end to suffering, says the Buddha. Not an end to pain,
but release from its power. This is nirvana. Most Buddhist texts describe nirvana very simply because they don't want people to mis-
understand and grasp after some imagined state. "When greed,
hatred, and delusion are given up," says the Buddha, "we no longer
cause sorrow for ourselves or others. This is nirvana." Nirvana is
also called the undying and the uncreated because it is not a condition or state but the joyous natural peace and happiness when we
are not clinging to anything. Sometimes the letting go is so deep
our whole identity drops away. In these transformative moments
nirvana is experienced as the void, dark and timeless, or as the luminous emptiness of all things. Sometimes the peace and happiness
of nirvana is ordinary, a resting of the heart in awareness, undis-

turbed and steadfast as all things change. Shunryu Suzuki explains it this way: "When you realize the fact that everything changes and find your composure in it, there you find yourself in nirvana."

In Buddhist Asia, popular culture mischaracterizes nirvana, imagining it as a heavenly realm where old monks go after many lifetimes' work of purity and self-denial. Even Westerners can naively think of nirvana as far away, some transcendent state attained by yogis in the Himalayas. This is wrong. "Nirvana," says the Buddha, "is immediate, visible here and now, inviting, attractive, comprehensible to the wise heart."

Ajahn Buddhadasa, a colleague of Ajahn Chah, made a point of directing his students to look for nirvana in the simplest ways, in everyday moments. "Nirvana," he would say, "is the coolness of letting go, the inherent delight of experience when there is no grasping or resistance to life. It is always available." He explained further, "Anyone can see that if grasping and aversion were with us day and night without ceasing, who could ever stand them? Under these conditions, living things would either die or become insane. Instead we survive because there are natural periods of coolness, of wholeness and ease. In fact, they last longer than the fires of our grasping and fear. It is this that sustains us. We have periods of rest making us refreshed and well. Why don't we feel thankful for this everyday nirvana?"

We know how to do this. We love to let go of the world at night when we go to sleep. Letting go and having a good night's sleep is delicious. Letting go while we are awake is delicious too. Letting go of clinging to the changing conditions of life, we free ourselves. Ajahn Chah said, "Let go and rest in the unconditioned, in pure awareness, the One Who Knows." When we rest in the One Who Knows, time drops away, self drops away, the one who suffers is released. We are simply the awareness of it all.

Paradoxically, letting go is both the goal and the path. I see the fruits of letting go shine in all those who undertake this practice. Grace and generosity grow as we let go of the struggles of life. The Buddha describes the ease that comes as we let go: "As a bee takes the essence of a flower and pollen without destroying its beauty or perfume, so the wise wander freely in this life, carrying only blessings."

THE FRUIT OF LETTING GO

As we let go and still see others suffer, the heart fills with compassion. So much suffering is human-caused. We awaken to a poignancy and tenderness beyond our own personal injuries. One Zen master calls this caring "the tears of the way." Our personal suffering diminishes, but our awareness of the sorrow and pain in the world grows stronger. Our heart is open and we feel connected to all things.

Resting in the peaceful heart, we weep at the folly of so many who live in the suffering of greed, hatred, and delusion, who have lost their way. And, all unbidden, we act. When a child falls into the street, everyone rushes to pull him from danger. When we see suffering, we respond. Barbara Wiedner, who founded Grandmothers for Peace, describes it this way: "I began to question, what kind of a world am I leaving for my grandchildren? So I got a sign, 'A Grandmother for Peace,' and stood on a street corner. Then I joined others kneeling as a human barrier at a munitions factory. I was taken to prison, strip-searched, thrown into a cell. Something happened to me! I realized they couldn't do anything more to me. I was free." Now Barbara and her organization, Grandmothers for Peace, work in countries around the world.

The Tao Te Ching explains, "Because she has let go, she can care for the welfare of all as a mother cares for her child." When we let go of being the one who suffers, we are free to bring blessings wherever we go.

PRACTICE: LETTING GO

Letting go does not mean losing the knowledge we have gained from the past. The knowledge of the past stays with us. To let go is simply to release any images and emotions, grudges and fears, clingings and disappointments that bind our spirit. Like emptying a cup, letting go leaves us free to receive, refreshed, sensitive, and awake.

To practice letting go, let yourself sit comfortably and quietly.

Bring a kind attention to your body and breath. Relax into the ground of the present for several minutes.

Now bring into awareness any story, situation, feelings, and reactions that it is time to let go of. Name them gently (betrayal, sadness, anxiety, etc.) and allow them the space to be, to float without resistance, held in a heart of compassion. Continue to breathe. Feel the unhappiness that comes from holding on. Ask yourself, "Do I have to continue to replay this story? Do I have to hold on to these losses, these feelings? Is it time to let this go?" The heart will know. Ask yourself if it is indeed wise to release this holding. Feel the benefit, the ease that will come from this letting go.

Now begin to say to yourself, "Let go, let go," gently, over and over. Soften the body and heart and let any feelings that arise drain out of you like water draining out of a tub. Let the images go, the beliefs, the self-righteousness, the unworthiness. Let it all go. Feel the space that comes as you let go, how the heart releases and the body opens.

Now direct the mind to envision the future where this circumstance has been released. Sense the freedom, the innocence, the ease that this letting go can bring. Say to yourself "Let go" several more times. Sit quietly and notice if the feelings return. Each time they return, breathe softly as if to bow to them, and say kindly, "I've let you go."

The images and feelings may come back many times, yet as you continue to practice, they will eventually fade. Gradually the mind will come to trust the space of letting go. Gradually the heart will be easy and you will be free.

17

THE COMPASS OF THE HEART
INTENTION AND KARMA

Whatever a person does, the results will follow him to the farthest reaches.
There is nowhere, not on earth or in the sky, that the results
of our deeds will not bear fruit.
—The Dhammapada

Karma means: you don't get away with nothin'.
—Ruth Denison

I hear the word *karma* all the time. American Express advertises itself as "the official card of good karma." A *New York Times* article about Britney Spears is headlined, "Miss Bad Media Karma." When events overtake us, people say, "It's your karma." But what does karma really mean?

Karma describes the law of cause and effect: what we sow, we reap. More importantly, karma is the result of our intention. Suppose a man picks up a knife and plunges it into another man's body, causing his death. What kind of karma has he created? If the wielder of the knife is a skilled surgeon undertaking a risky procedure to relieve suffering, the karma is positive, even if the patient dies. But the same act done out of anger will produce the painful karma of murder.

Intention and motivation, the roots of karma, are absolutely central to Buddhist psychology. In leading the Tibetan people over years of exile and political struggle, the Dalai Lama says that while he may make mistakes, the one thing he can rely on is his sincere motivation. The most effective way to direct our karma is to clarify our motivation and set an intention.

When our intention is to live with nobility, respect, and compassion, and we act from these intentions, we shape a positive future. When our motivation is rooted in anger, unworthiness, grasping, self-judgment, fear, and depression, and we act from these intentions, we perpetuate these painful patterns.

This is a seventeenth principle of Buddhist psychology:

---

17   Be mindful of intention. Intention is the seed that creates our future.

KARMA AND HABIT

In the ancient texts, *karma* is written as a compound word, *karma-vipaka*. *Karma-vipaka* means "action and result," or what we call cause and effect. This is not a philosophical concept. It is a psychological description of how our experience unfolds every day.

A good way to begin to understand karma is by observing our habit patterns. When we look at habit and conditioning, we can sense how our brain and consciousness create repeated patterns. If we practice tennis enough, we will anticipate our next hit as soon as the ball leaves the other player's racquet. If we practice being angry, the slightest insult will trigger our rage. These patterns are

like a rewritable CD. When they are burned in repeatedly, the pattern becomes the regular response. Modern neuroscience has
demonstrated this quite convincingly. Our repeated patterns of
thought and action actually change our nervous system. Each time
we focus our attention and follow our intentions, our nerves fire,
synapses connect, and those neural patterns are strengthened. The
neurons literally grow along that direction.

Zen master Thich Nhat Hanh describes the karmic process of
conditioning with another metaphor: the image of planting seeds
in consciousness. The seeds we plant contain the potential to grow
when conditions support them. The seed of a magnolia or a redwood tree contains the whole life pattern of the plant, which will
respond when suitable conditions of water, earth, and sunlight
arise. A Chinese Buddhist text describes these seeds: "From intention springs the deed, from the deed springs the habits. From the
habits grow the character, from character develops destiny."

What we practice becomes habit. What may at one time be ben-
eficial can later become a form of imprisonment. Andrew Carnegie
was asked by a reporter about the gathering of riches, "You could
have stopped at any time, couldn't you, because you always had
much more than you needed." "Yes, that's right," Carnegie answered, "but I couldn't stop. I had forgotten how to." Habits have a
collective nature as well as an individual one. When King George II
heard the "Hallelujah Chorus" in the first performance of Handel's
Messiah, he was so moved that, against all form, he stood up. Of
course, when the king stands, everyone else must stand as well.
Since that day, no matter how the performance is done, the whole
audience stands. While this is a harmless convention, societies can
equally repeat destructive habits of racism, hatred, and revenge.

We can work with habits. Through the mindful process of RAIN
described in Chapter 7, we can rewire our nervous system. The
genesis of this transformation is our intention. Buddhist psychology explains that before every act there is an intention, though
often the intention is unconscious. We can use recognition, acceptance, investigation of suffering, and non-identification to create
new karma. Through mindfulness and non-identification, we can

choose a new intention. We can do this moment by moment, and we can also set long-term intentions to transform our life.

Setting a conscious intention was important for Tamara, a woman who ran a community food bank. She had come to meditation to bring balance into her life. But when she first sat quietly and tried to sense her breath, panic arose. She struggled as if she couldn't get enough air. I had her relax and shift her attention from her breath to her whole body for a time. Later when she went back to her breath, the panic arose again. Staying curious, she actually remembered the woozy feeling of ether. She flashed back to stories of her birth. Tamara had been born blue from lack of oxygen and her mother told her it took a long time before the doctor could get her to breathe. In meditation Tamara learned that she couldn't control the breath or the feelings of panic, but she could set an intention to be present with kindness and then let go. Setting a positive intention changed her meditation for the better.

Then in 2005, Tamara went down to Louisiana for two months to help with food distribution for survivors of Hurricane Katrina. She discovered that she needed the same focused intentions she had developed in meditation. She met people who were in the grip of the same kind of panic she had discovered within herself. They were frightened, angry, stressed out, trying to stay alive. Often the people in charge were in equally difficult states of overwhelm and shock. Tamara soon realized that she couldn't control the people or the situation any more than she could control her own breath. At times she became reactive, and when this happened she would breathe, set an intention to be present with goodwill, then let go. Repeatedly setting a kind intention got her through the two months without being terrified or burned out.

DEDICATION AND LONG-TERM INTENTION

Long-term intention is called dedication. In the forest monastery we would gather before dawn in the candlelit darkness and the monks would begin the sonorous morning chanting to dedicate our day. The chants reminded us that the path to awakening is possible when we dedicate ourselves to a noble way of life. We would dedicate ourselves to use the support we received for the awakening of compassion for all beings.

Setting a long-term intention is like setting the compass of our heart. No matter how rough the storms, how difficult the terrain, even if we have to backtrack around obstacles, our direction is clear. The fruits of dedication are visible in the best of human endeavors. We can see them in the political leadership of Nelson Mandela and Aung San Suu Kyi, in athletes such as Lance Armstrong and Michael Jordan, and in artists such as Yo-Yo Ma and Mary Oliver.

At times our dedications are practical: to learn to play the piano well, to build a thriving business, to plant and grow a beautiful garden. But there are overarching dedications as well. We might dedicate our life to prayer, commit ourselves to unwavering truthfulness or to work for world peace. These overarching dedications set the compass of our life, regardless of the outer conditions. They give us direction and meaning.

Rodney was a young activist who wanted to help foster peace on earth. When he learned meditation, he realized he also had to find peace within himself. He dedicated his energy to first make his own heart and family a zone of peace. From this his commitment expanded and he trained in human rights and conflict resolution at Columbia. Now he works for the UN in a mission in West Africa. In each step his dedication has carried him, and he has embodied the words of Wendell Berry: "If we are serious about peace, then we must work for it as ardently, seriously, continuously, carefully, and bravely as we now prepare for war."

When we read something like this, it is inspiring. It touches our own innate nobility and courage. But it can also bring up guilt and self-doubt: *What about me? Am I doing enough? Why isn't my life as "noble" as Rodney's?*

It is good to question our own dedication, even if it makes us uncomfortable. To what *have* we dedicated our life? How deeply do we carry this dedication? Is it time to rededicate our life? But comparing oneself to someone else is useless. Rodney's dedication is not ours. We have to be true to our own way. I heard a story about a school principal who spent part of her evenings making sandwiches for the homeless. After she finished she would travel around the poorer parts of the city and distribute them. Even though her day was already full, this late-night activity didn't overwhelm her. It actually made her happy. She didn't do it out of guilt, duty, or external pressure. She simply shared in a way that made a difference for her. Even when she was rebuffed by those to whom she offered food on the street, she didn't feel rejected or angry, because she wasn't doing it for the acceptance or appreciation.

Then the local media heard what she was doing and printed a story about her. Instantly she became a minor celebrity. The public, even her fellow teachers, started sending her money to support her work. Much to their surprise, she sent back the money to everyone with a one-line note that said: "Make your own damn sandwiches!"

Another important point about dedication: we can't just do it once and forget it. My wife, Liana, and I had a rocky courtship. We loved each other deeply but we are temperamental opposites and we each carried a history of family and relationship pain. Finally we had worked through our problems enough to commit to marriage, but I still worried about whether I could do it. How can you make a commitment in your thirties that will last "till death do us part"? So I decided to consult my favorite older married couple, David and Mary McClelland. David was chairman of the Department of Psychology and Social Relations at Harvard, Mary was a painter, and they had six children. Their large home in Cambridge was a haven for leaders in Eastern and Western psychology. The 1960s and 1970s were an exciting time, and being at David and Mary's often, I also spent time with Chögyam Trungpa, Dan Goleman, Ram Dass, Mark Epstein, and others who, like them, were the spokespeople for what was a new consciousness movement.

David and Mary were Quakers, and mutual respect was the bedrock of their relationship. Even when they argued, they addressed each other as "thee" and "thou," so the underlying tone was one of civility, caring, and intimacy. When I asked them how you can take a marriage vow that will last for the rest of your life, I was surprised by David's answer: "You don't." Then Mary explained, "You take it anew every day."

Thomas Merton once advised a young activist, "Do not depend on the hope of results. . . . you may have to face the fact that your work will be apparently worthless and even achieve no result at all, if not perhaps results opposite to what you expect. As you get used to this idea, you start more and more to concentrate not on the results but on the value, the rightness, the truth of the work itself." By aligning our dedication with our highest intention, we chart the course of our whole being. Then no matter how hard the voyage and how big the setbacks, we know where we are headed.

THE ROAD TO HELL AND DELUDED INTENTION

We've all heard the saying "The road to hell is paved with good intentions." What if our good intentions foolishly ruin a relationship or hurt someone? The explanation is quite simple. Good intentions can be mixed with delusion. Then the result will include a measure of good, but the delusion and ignorance involved will also bring suffering.

In one family I know, parents with "good Christian intentions" cut their daughter off without any support because she deliberately had a child—their grandchild—without a husband. Unfortunately, the intentions of the parents were more in line with strict Old Testament punishment than with Jesus' insistent love for the outcast, the sinner, and the poor. Their "good" intentions contained delusion about love, anger, and a self-centered grasping for control of their daughter. The suffering that resulted has gone on for years.

Several of my friends were part of the successful campaign begun in the 1970s to deinstitutionalize mental patients. As a result of their lawsuits, the courts ordered the closing of many of the terrible state hospitals of the time. The state officials promised that the same money would be made available for ongoing care of these patients in the community. But it didn't turn out that way. The compassionate intention to close the mental hospitals was not always matched by an equally powerful recognition of how long and hard would be the work needed to create alternative support structures. Often those who were released ended up in prison or simply wandering the streets, homeless, with no one to care for them.

At the worst extreme, good intentions can be mixed with profound delusion. Stalin and Mao Zedong each claimed good intentions, trying to purge the exploitations of their powerful predecessors and to enhance the welfare of the masses. Yet under their deluded intentions, millions were starved or murdered. To be wise, we have to examine our intention to ensure that it is free from delusion. The ends do not justify the means. If our actions will bring harm to others, even in the service of some "good," they are almost certainly deluded. If our actions do not come from a kind heart, from loving courage and compassion, they are deluded. If they are based on a distinction between "us" and "them," they stem from delusion. Only to the extent that we act from the wisdom of no separation, understanding how we are woven together, will our intention bring benefit.

SUPPORT FOR OUR INTENTIONS

Even our wisest intentions need support. As social beings, we are continually affected by those around us. In the monastery, the daily chanting of our vows repeatedly reinforced our intentions. Buddhist psychology helps us to make use of the power of such reinforcement. One of the ways it does so is by distinguishing two forms of response: prompted and unprompted.

Suppose we decide to sample an unfamiliar fruit in the market, perhaps a cherimoya or a rambutan. We are with a friend who says, "Ooh, rambutans. These are the most delicious tropical fruit in the world. You're going to love them." She watches us expectantly while we take our first bite. Because of her prompting, we will be strongly moved to like them. Even if our habit is to be wary of strange foods, her enthusiasm may override that conditioning. There is internal prompting as well, which works in the same way. Perhaps we have just started on a low-carb diet, with no starches or sugars, and are trying to stick to it. Then we see the rambutan sample and are drawn to taste it. But as we do, we remember that fruit undermines our commitment to a sugar-free diet. So our response is prompted by hesitancy and aversion, and we will most likely find the fruit unpleasant. Now imagine a more challenging circumstance, where someone has insulted us. Unprompted, we might simply feel hurt. But if we are prompted by others whose habits are angry reactions—"Don't let him get away with that"—we might be swayed to become angry.

Without a well-developed mindfulness, we are at the mercy of these promptings. We can easily lose our dedication. Even though benevolent states are innate to the heart, we forget. This is why Buddhist psychology emphasizes practice. We must practice wise speech, non-contentiousness, generosity, and compassion over and over again, in trivial and important situations alike.

In this I am reminded of the story of master gardener Alan Chadwick, a pioneer of biodynamic methods, who taught at the University of California, Santa Cruz. Once Chadwick took a class to a junkyard lot that was filled with rusted-out cars, broken glass, chunks of cement, sand, and abandoned trash. He asked the owner if his class could use the lot for an experiment to grow flowers and vegetables. The owner said, "Sure, but you're crazy. That soil is dead." The students put months into revitalizing the soil. This garden later became famous for its extraordinarily delicious vegetables and gorgeous flowers. In the same way, through inner practice and prompting, we plant the seeds of consciousness that can transform any difficulty.

Understanding how our states of mind are easily prompted by others, we can also see the importance of spiritual friendships. Whether in meditation communities, churches, group psychotherapy, or AA, the help we provide for one another is critical. At one time the Buddha's attendant Ananda asked if spiritual friendship was not half of the holy life. In response, the Buddha declared, "Spiritual friendship, association with wise and noble friends, and wise and noble deeds are the whole of the holy life." No matter what our intentions, we all need help from others around us as mirrors. Sometimes we need prompting in the form of fierce critical support from our AA sponsor or the honest feedback of our friends when we go astray. We also need the prompting of those who can see our goodness and who can speak with wisdom and courage to our good heart.

When negative prompting from others reinforces our sense of failure, we shrink. We see this in the ways that racism and lack of opportunity have affected young men of color in our inner cities. For twenty years I have co-led retreats for young people in trouble. My colleague and inspiration in this work is mythologist and storyteller Michael Meade. Michael deliberately goes to jails, juvenile halls, and troubled schools and asks to work with the most difficult kids. He uses myths and initiation rituals with gang members and teens. He inspires them with hard-hitting poems and ancient stories of heroes who rose out of the worst tragedy. He tells them to make their sorrows into art. Michael invites these youths to write honest, self-respecting poetry. Later, when the words are read, many of them are heartbreaking: "You expect us to fail, teach us to fail." "If you keep walking away and won't stand by us in our mistakes, who's the child here?"

These guarded young men and women are invited to read their stories out loud. Horrific survival tales of abuse and abandonment, poverty, and violence are read as works of art to their astonished teachers and probation officers. As their voices are heard and their pain is acknowledged, they start to value themselves and their experience in a more respectful way. They become more honest and closer to each other. And they start to see that they have something to say, something to contribute to the community around them. Their inherent seeds of goodness become watered and start to grow.

CLARIFYING MOMENT-TO-MOMENT INTENTION

Planting seeds for the long term is one important way to direct our lives. But we also have to understand how karma and intention operate behind the smallest of our actions. This is the moment-to-moment level of karma. In the monasteries of Thailand and Burma we were trained to analyze the microscopic steps of experience and discover how we respond to them. Developing strong concentration, we were able to cultivate extraordinarily keen powers of observation. As our minds became focused, we could sense the subtlest impression of sound or thought when they first arose, and clearly observe the rapid moment-to-moment sequence of feeling, recognition, and response. Neuroscientists from Harvard University have verified that advanced meditators can perceive events much more rapidly and subtly than has ever before been measured in humans. Using such minute observation, the ancient Buddhist psychologists discovered that each experience of perception contains seventeen microscopic mind moments. These moments were further divided into two phases, each of which takes place in a fraction of a second.

The first phase, in which we receive experience, is the result of past karma. In this phase, perception begins by waking the underlying stream of consciousness as if with a knock at the door. As a result, consciousness turns toward the sense door and begins to feel, investigate, and recognize the experience. All these receiving moments are conditioned by the past.

The second phase of perception includes the micromoments of response, which are colored by our current mental states, whether fear or mindfulness, aversion or love. Whatever response occurs is then registered in storehouse consciousness, as a pattern or a seed. In this second phase, we create new karma.

This momentary process can be translated into practical use for wise living. Here is the basic psychological law: What is past is over. It cannot be changed. We will inevitably receive the result of our past intentions and actions. Our freedom lies in how we respond to these results. Our response creates new karma, new patterns that will eventually bear fruit. By creating a healthier future we can redeem the past.

Marsha, a young meditator, came to consult me after class. She was upset and nervous and told me she thought she had created some bad karma. It seemed that she had badly upset her officemate, Judith, by flirting with Judith's boyfriend at a party and then by gossiping to him about Judith. When Marsha sat in meditation the next morning, guilt and regret arose. She knew she had damaged her relationship and that Judith would be hurt. I explained to her that she was only focusing on the first part of her karma. It was the past. There was nothing she could do about these facts. Then I explained to Marsha about how the results (vipaka) of her action (karma) would give her the chance to create new karma when she next spoke to Judith.

When she encountered the inevitable pain and anger in Judith's words, Marsha had a choice. She could be defensive, explaining that "we were all having a drink and I was only kidding." If she did so, her lack of honesty would create more distance and more painful results. Or Marsha could experience Judith's pain and her own sympathetically, and express remorse for her actions. She could pause after Judith's outburst and reflect on her own underlying intentions. "I'm really sorry for what I did. I was drinking and stupidly thought I could connect better by talking about you. I was wrong. I hope you can forgive me." In this way, she could respond caringly rather than reacting. And whether Judith could hear her or not, Marsha would be planting good seeds for the future of this relationship.

Betrayed friends, estranged family members, auto accidents, a harsh and demanding boss: these are painful results. Year-end bonus pay, loving letters from our children, a joyful holiday, creative success: these are pleasant results. Sometimes we can see how our past actions and choices have contributed to these conditions. But whether or not the causes are clear, we are receiving a result from the past. What matters now is how we respond. Karma-vipaka teaches that we can always start again. It is never too late. The Navajo believe that each day a new sun is born, and to honor the sun we must start again and make our day sacred. By responding in a sacred and compassionate way, we create a new pattern for the future.

THE SACRED PAUSE

The truth is that we are not yet free; we have merely achieved
the freedom to be free.
—Nelson Mandela

Because experience happens so quickly, habitual responses can come out of our mouth or from our hands before we know it. It helps to practice skillful responses when things are easy. That way when things are tough, our pattern is already set. It also helps to train ourselves to pause before our response. This is called the sacred pause, a moment where we stop and release our identification with problems and reactions. Without a pause our actions are automatic. In a moment of stopping, we break the spell between past result and automatic reaction. When we pause, we can notice the actual experience, the pain or pleasure, fear or excitement. In the stillness before our habits arise, we become free.

In this pause, we can examine our intention. If we have set a long-term intention or dedication for our life, we can remember our vows. Or we can simply check our motivation. Are we trying to get even, win at any cost? Or do we want to act out of respect for ourself and others to sow seeds of understanding and courage? It is in our hands.

The power of intention is most easily visible in our speech. In conversation, we get immediate feedback, and often the response we get will reflect our intention. Before we speak, we can examine our motivation. Is our motivation one of compassion and concern for everyone? Or do we want to be right? Clarifying our intention is critical in times of difficulty. When there is difference or conflict, do we genuinely want to hear about the concerns of the other? Are we open to learn, to see?

Nelson, an earnest middle school teacher, came to talk to me during a retreat. His mother had recently died and he was in a struggle with Albert, his retired stepfather, over money. Nelson had wrestled with depression and anxiety all his life, but now, with his mother gone, he trudged home from work more depressed than usual. Albert had moved into Nelson's childhood home when Nelson left for college. For eleven years Albert and Nelson had had a cordial relationship, but now Nelson was outraged because his mother had left the house and much of her money to Albert. Every time he talked to his stepfather their conflict got worse. There was a great deal of blame, recrimination, and bad feelings on both sides.

Nelson wanted help working with this conflict. As we sat together I asked him to sense what was present in his body and mind. Immediately waves of grief and feelings of loss for his mother arose. As he wept, he felt a sense of abandonment. He could see how the feelings of abandonment intensified his depression and anxiety and exacerbated his conflict with his stepfather. I suggested that Nelson practice compassion and hold the whole experience of loss and grief with kindness. After a time, I asked him to open his compassion to any others around him who might also be experiencing loss and grief. First a friend whose dog had just died came to mind, and then a neighbor whose daughter had lost a child. Gradually a flood of others arose. He thought about the images of huddled tsunami victims in Asia that were in the news that week. He remembered his cousin in Baltimore with leukemia. His pain became part of the human pain, the losses carried by the world. Finally, even Albert, his stepfather, showed up. Nelson could feel how Albert was suffering from the loss of his wife, just as Nelson was missing his mother.

Now I asked Nelson to be aware of the story he had woven about his abandonment, his failures in life, and his conflict with his stepfather. He went back to meditate. He saw how he was the star of the production, a long-suffering teacher, and how his stories were a kind of self-promotion, not precisely true nor false, just stories. Now his grief and struggles were being held in spacious awareness as well as compassion. Inwardly, he began to feel much more relaxed and free. He began to experience living in the moment and not in his stories. Several days later Nelson told me, "I feel like now I can trust life instead of money."

Finally I asked Nelson to picture meeting his stepfather again to talk about all the unresolved conflict. I asked him to get in touch with the highest intention he could hold for this meeting. This was easy for him to identify. It was an intention of well-being and compassion for both himself and Albert. Nelson felt that if he could keep this intention, he would really be able to listen to and talk to his stepfather. Later, when they did finally talk, Nelson discovered that his stepfather's anxiety, loss, and depression were not really very different from his own. He saw that Albert too was caught, afraid. Nelson's compassion grew, and in a new spirit they began to resolve their financial struggle.

Try this in your next argument or conflict: Take a pause. Hold everyone's struggle in compassion. Connect with your highest intention. Whenever things get difficult, pause before you speak and sense your wisest motivation. From there, it will all flow better. This is the secret of wise speech. As the Buddha describes it: "Speak with kindly motivation. Speak what is true and helpful, speak in due season and to the benefit of all." When we connect with our highest intention, we learn to see with eyes of compassion and everything becomes more workable.

SETTING THE HEART'S COMPASS

The poet and spiritual teacher Oriah Mountain Dreamer writes about helping a participant at a New Age meditation seminar. Here are her words:

> At the end of a very long day, a small, thin woman in an oversized parka introduced herself as Isabel. "Can I do this meditation on my own?" she asked.
>
> "Yes," I said. "I am sure you can, although many people find it easier to establish a meditation practice with the help of a group. It's just hard to keep up the discipline on your own."
>
> "But what will it give me? What will I get if I do this every day?" Her tone took on a whining quality, and I felt my irritation rise as she continued. "How fast will it work? Will I feel a difference after a week? How will I know it's working?"
>
> This was exactly the kind of thing I detested—the quest for the quick fix, the desire for guaranteed outcomes, the simple answer. Do this and you will get that. My sons were waiting for me, and I wanted to go home.
>
> I took a deep breath, looked directly at Isabel, and set my knapsack down on the floor. I tried to slow down my words, thinking that maybe if I spoke slower I would feel more patient. "Well," I said,

"meditation is more a process than a goal-oriented activity. It can help you become more aware of what is going on within and around you, and this can help reduce stress. . . . My best advice is to try it and just be patient with yourself." I picked up my bag and started to button my coat. I really did have to leave, and I wanted to get out while I was feeling virtuous for not snapping her head off.

But as I started to move away Isabel suddenly reached out and grabbed my arm with surprising strength. "But, what I want to know," she said, her voice rising in a crescendo that bordered on real panic, "is will it help me find God? If I meditate, will I have an experience of something or somebody out there listening, someone really with me?"

A wave of desperation swept out from her through me, and I was surprised to find my eyes filling with tears. This woman wasn't looking for an easy answer or a guaranteed formula because she was lazy. She didn't want a simple plan because she was unable or unwilling to think critically about what would work. She wanted something she knew would work and work quickly because she was hanging on by her fingernails. She wanted something that would work in a week because she was afraid that she simply wasn't going to make it through months or years.

I put my hand gently over Isabel's where it gripped my arm. "It's okay, Isabel, we all feel desperate at times," I said. "Nobody does it by themselves. We all need help." Her hand relaxed a little beneath mine, and she started to cry. We talked for awhile longer. There is no them. There's only us. When I left, I did not leave one of them. I said goodbye to one of us, a human being doing the best she can, searching for the home for which all our hearts long.

As Oriah Mountain Dreamer describes, we are all in it together. As we undertake this journey, first we need to set our compass on a course of compassion. When we dedicate our actions with positive intentions for all, we begin to transform the situation. Our dedication gives us the authority and freedom to act out of love no matter what. We start with the results of our past karma. But the canvas is incomplete. Now we can add to it. We can step out of unconscious habit, connect with our wise heart, and freely choose a new response.

One practitioner described this discovery with tears in her eyes. "I'm so grateful. I want you to know how freeing these teachings have been. I've been in psychotherapy forever, and I've been sober for twenty-two years. For all these years I was still caught by the pain of the past. I healed in some ways, but I never believed I could change. Meditation taught me to begin again. It gave me a window I could fly out of. I'm not that suffering person anymore." No matter what the situation, we are offered the freedom to choose our highest intention, to choose to be free. When we understand karma and intention, we are given the opportunity to set the compass of our heart and dedicate ourselves to our highest intention. This is what will transform our world.

PRACTICE: MEETING DIFFICULTY WITH WISE INTENTION

Pick a situation of difficulty or conflict with others. Reflect on your last encounters and on the motivation from which you operated. How did this work? Now imagine you can bring the highest possible intentions to your next encounter. Take a moment to reflect. What would they be? Notice if they contain the elements of compassion for others and for yourself. Notice if they are wise and courageous.

Picture reentering the difficult situation while staying true to these highest intentions. Finally, go and practice. Remember, you may lose track of these intentions. With practice they will become steady and strong.

18

SACRED VISION
IMAGINATION, RITUAL, AND REFUGE

*It will be a benefit to all who can visit the shrines and temples
dedicated to the Buddha's life of awakening.*
—Mahaparinirvana Sutra

Without ritual we are ships passing in the night.
—Malidoma Somé

Ajahn Chah's main forest monastery was in the far province
of Ubol, near Thailand's border with Laos and Cambodia. During
the Vietnam War, we often saw bombers and fighter planes over-
head. From some of Ajahn Chah's monasteries we could even see
flashes of light on the horizon. Once some Quaker friends who
were working as activists in Laos and Vietnam came to visit. They
were appalled that we forest monks were not politically active.
How could we sit by and do nothing?

They had come to the monastery tired and burned out.

Working in a war zone is fierce practice. You see tremendous acts of bravery and the worst, most panic-stricken, most depraved behavior. My friends came needing a respite. When they spoke passionately against the war, Ajahn Chah told them that stopping the war was essential. Then he pointed to his chest. "We must stop the war here. Yes, activism is good. Yet in spite of our best efforts, wars continue to come and go. We will never succeed outwardly until we also learn to stop the war inside. That is our work here."

As the days passed, my activist friends' opinions began to change. They walked among the quiet paths and silent monks and saw that the monastery functioned as a living storehouse of respect and integrity. This temple was an island of sanity, a physical symbol of peace. In the early morning the monks would chant about the wise heart. Throughout the day, they would meditate and work together in a caring manner. If you were lost or in difficulty, you would be cared for. You could drop your wallet and your money would be returned to you. Even the tiniest living beings in the temple were respected. After a week, my friends began to understand. In difficult times we humans need sanctuaries and images of the sacred to remind us of who we really are.

Most Asian Buddhist temples are filled with images of awakening. Buddhas and bodhisattvas appear in a myriad of forms, both male and female, painted, sculpted, created in bronze, butter, and clay. There is the bodhisattva of compassion, Kwan Yin, with a thousand arms to reach out to all who suffer; the goddess Tara, who offers protection and peace; and the Bodhisattva Manjusri, who carries the sword that cuts through all illusion. Enlightened ancestors are depicted as hermits and servants, as royalty and as courageous leaders. Surrounding them are stupas and mandalas, symbols of perfect harmony between birth and death, form and emptiness. To enter many Buddhist temples, we also have to pass the statues of fierce guardian demons who stand at the gates. How we walk through the demons of our own greed, aggression, and ignorance is the symbolic key to our entry into the sacred perceptions. Neither lost in denial nor enthralled by their energy, we can learn to see them clearly and walk freely in their midst.

But what has this to do with Buddhist psychology? Aren't these just trappings of religious worship? To see them as trappings is to miss a great psychological truth. Our imagination works in symbols, like the images from our dreams. We use symbols all the time: in clothing, in gestures, in advertising, in the very letters of these words. Buddhist psychology uses these human images of Buddhas and saints and enlightened ancestors as symbolic doorways, to point to and evoke the qualities of love, dedication, inner beauty, and courage. On a different level, a national flag does this, a football team logo can, even a Hermès bag or, more destructively, a swastika. Knowing the power of symbols, we can recognize them as outer forms that point to our inner world.

In Buddhist psychology, sacred images are used in specific ways. The statues and painted images of male and female Buddhas that grace temples and book covers worldwide actually represent a well-developed technology for changing consciousness.

Here is an example of how such symbols work. Imagine meditating on the most peaceful image of a Buddha you have ever seen. Imagine receiving this image from a teacher who embodies the benevolent qualities of a Buddha and reminds you that you can find these highest possibilities in yourself. Picture learning to visualize this beautiful Buddha so steadily and clearly that when you close your eyes, you can see every detail. Imagine spending some hours letting yourself actually feel the energy of calm, steadiness, and clarity depicted by this Buddha. Let these feelings touch your own heart. Now imagine a step further. Sense that you can draw this Buddha inside, to fully enter and take over your own body and mind. Now you have become a Buddha. Sense how you can actually embody the calm, clarity, and compassion. Dwell in this state for a time and allow yourself to imagine how you would act as a Buddha in your very own life and how you would see the same Buddha nature in those around you. Finally, dissolve the Buddha back into emptiness, acknowledging how the mind creates and uncreates all possibilities.

Suppose you were to repeat this practice a thousand, ten thousand times. You can feel how this visualization could affect your consciousness.

Here is an eighteenth principle of Buddhist psychology:

---

18 What we repeatedly visualize changes our body and consciousness. Visualize freedom and compassion.

THE POWER OF VISUALIZATION

Visualization is one of the most important transformational tools of Buddhist psychology. Western psychology also uses this tool, through the "active imagination" of Carl Jung, the visualization techniques of psychosynthesis, and the many applications of guided imagery. But on the whole, Buddhist visualizations are more fully developed and sophisticated. In fact, almost every possible benevolent state of consciousness is evoked through these transformative practices.

Sacred images portray the archetypal energy between the formless realm and the level of physical form. The intermediate dimension, called the *sambogakaya,* functions much like Jungian archetypes and Platonic ideals. Buddhist sacred ideals are timeless patterns through which specific worldly experiences arise. These sacred forms have a power to touch the imagination and inspire all who contact them, whether through seeing, hearing, or visualizing.

The technology of visualization is spelled out in detail. In the first stages we learn to steady the mind and create and hold a visualization. This steadying process is often supported by the repetition of chants or mantras. When the initial visualization is stabilized, further symbols, often rich and quite complex, are pictured to evoke specific qualities of the awakened heart and mind. With training, adept meditators can hold in their mind complex mandalas with hundreds of figures. And, as modern brain scans have shown, this can be done for hours at a time, demonstrating capacities for focused attention far beyond any previously believed possible by Western neuroscience. Buddhist trainings employ thousands of visualizations, each of which represents an aspect of compassion, courage, love, nobility, generosity, fierce honesty, emptiness, and a myriad of other potentials. As these are created and dissolved inside ourselves, time and again, we can learn to embody the states they represent.

In the forest monasteries of Thailand, our visualizations were basic. We used images of the Buddha and other simple images to fill our mind with devotion, dedication, wisdom, and compassion. At other Thai monasteries, we visualized awakened beings within the chakras of our own body. Buddhist visualization practices are much more extensively developed in the Tibetan and Japanese traditions. These trainings are now available in the West through the work of many skillful teachers.

While these visualizations, symbols, and rituals can be profoundly healing, we also have to understand their limitations. They should never be imposed on people. Many people come to Buddhist practice who have been injured by religion. They have had religious dogma forced upon them as a child, or suffered some kind of religious abuse. For such people, even the simplest spiritual forms appear toxic. Also, many meditation practitioners are committed to other spiritual paths. We have rabbis, Catholic nuns, and priests who come to our retreats. We have atheists and agnostics and those devoted to Allah, to Shiva, or to Wicca.

Because of this diversity, no outer religious forms are imposed on those who come to train at Spirit Rock Meditation Center. We do not bow or follow other Asian cultural practices. We simply offer the practices of compassion, mindfulness, and inner development, free of any dogma or set ritual. As Ajahn Chah used to say of Buddhism, "Call it Christianity or anything else you like. The name doesn't matter, it's the practice that counts." We start with meditations of awareness and compassion; then we add visualization, ritual, or refuge if we sense they will be helpful.

Olivia found them so. For six years, Olivia had managed a shelter for homeless women, after healing from her own history of abuse and addiction. She was dedicated to the twelve-step program and she initially came to Buddhist practice to work on the eleventh step, which in AA includes learning some form of meditation. She started practicing with her breath and mindfulness to steady her mind. But Olivia was especially touched by the images of Tara, the female bodhisattva of protection and peace who vowed to be enlightened only in a female body. Olivia undertook the visualization of Tara, with chants and prayers every morning before work.

At first Olivia found it difficult to steady the visualization, and even harder to bring Tara into her body. She had to let go of a great deal of unworthiness, fear, and resentment before she could visualize Tara in herself. But after many months, Olivia told me how the practice had changed her. "After becoming Tara, I feel so steadfast and wise. When I have to deal with the frustrating bureaucracy at work, I envision that I am Tara, with infinite peace and compassion, and it goes much better. Then sometimes I envision all those around me as Tara too, their speech and action providing the perfect opportunity to fulfill my patience and love. It's a miracle. I'm not run by my emotions anymore. I'm more generous and free. I feel like I could walk through walls."

The technology of visualization does not require Buddhist figures. Cultures worldwide use other sacred images, such as St. Francis, Guadalupe and Krishna, to inspire prayer. In the Buddhist approach we do more than pray for their blessing. As we visualize them we let their energy enter our own being. We remember that we are not separate from them, that the nobility of who they are and who we are springs from the same universal source. The Christian mystic St. Symeon captures this experience:

> We awaken in Christ's body
> as Christ awakens our bodies,
> and my poor hand is Christ,
> he enters my foot, and is infinitely me.
>
> I move my hand, and wonderfully
> my hand becomes Christ, becomes all of him.

Alex came to a meditation retreat at a difficult time in his life, and he now says that his destiny was changed by the image and story of King Ashoka. Alex had never heard of visualization nor of this ancient Indian king, although the story of King Ashoka is found in

most high school world history books. A ruler of the third century
B.C., he created the Mauryan Empire, the largest and wisest kingdom in Indian history. The remains of this kingdom and of Ashoka's
benevolent royal decrees are still found carved in stone pillars
across India. His edicts instruct the inhabitants of the land to respect one another, to lead a virtuous life, to dig wells, build roads,
care for the poor, and honor all forms of religion. But King Ashoka
was not always wise.

The most common account of Ashoka's transformation says
that it took place following a great battle. The king found himself
seated on a hill, looking over the carnage of the war for south India
that he had just won. As he gazed sorrowfully upon the broken
chariots, slain horses, and thousands upon thousands of dead warriors from both sides, Ashoka saw a Buddhist monk walking peacefully along the road next to the battleground. All at once the king
felt impoverished. He who commanded everything—armies,
palaces, wives, wealth, servants—was also one who could not
sleep at night, whose heart was not at peace. The serenity of the
monk was like nectar to the parched heart of the king. He became
the monk's student and followed his teachings of virtue, compassion, and respect for all life. Thenceforward he directed his army
to build roads and safeguard the populace, and he established the
compassionate decrees that are honored to this day.

Alex heard the story of Ashoka on a ten-day retreat. He had
come because, like Ashoka, he could not sleep. An enormously successful entrepreneur, Alex had built a chain of hardware stores from
a small start-up into a billion-dollar company through ambitious
battles and long years of work. But now his blood pressure was
high, and he was in the midst of a divorce. His older daughter was
in treatment for bulimia, and his younger son wouldn't talk to him.
He was being sued by a key investor. He tried to concentrate on his
breath to settle his mind, but he could hardly sit still. Even though
he had a strong will, it was a struggle just to stay in the room. For
six days he wrestled with his mind and aching body, plagued by his
own regrets and mistakes. Then he heard the story of King Ashoka,
and knew he had to find a way to peace.

During the next morning session, Alex was taught the practices of loving-kindness and compassion meditation. He focused first on himself and all he had suffered. He wept for most of the day. He grieved for his children, for himself, for his departing wife, for the pain of it all. As he allowed himself to experience the depth of his feelings, his mind became still. He was able to acknowledge the suffering and hold it in compassion. By the time he left the retreat his demeanor had transformed. Alex was more at peace. He could sleep. He was returning home to problems, but he could sense how different it would be to meet them with kind attention, just as he had held his own pain with compassion.

Alex did fairly well for the first month. But then he called his retreat teacher with further bad news. He had just learned that his closest friend had been diagnosed with inoperable pancreatic cancer. This news was too much for him. He sought out the local meditation group, to be in the presence of a teacher and community. He was strengthened by their care. Then he tried to meditate at home, but each time he did, he became overwhelmed with the suffering around him and the burdens he carried. The teacher told him to sit anyway.

During meditation a few days later, a vision came to him. He saw himself sitting like King Ashoka, overlooking the battlefield of his own life. He had fought so many battles, and now he was sitting, weary and reflective. As he did so, Alex saw a monk walking with great serenity toward him. To his astonishment he realized that the monk's face was his own. He felt deeply moved. It was as if this vision showed him that he could walk through the battlefield with a peaceful heart. It was he who was called to transform his world.

This vision inspired Alex to change his life. He became dedicated to meditation. He began to actively practice generosity, compassion, mindfulness, respect. Over the next years his family gradually healed and his company grew further. He became known as an exemplar of benevolent and wise leadership in the business community. The spirit of the monk and of King Ashoka was in him.

RITUAL: LANGUAGE OF THE HEART

Just as we can be transformed by visualization, we can be transformed by the power of ritual. Ritual is one of the oldest human languages, perhaps the most universal. It speaks in elemental symbols, and these symbols, like dreams, are our original language. The word *ritual* comes from the Latin *ritus,* "to fit together." Ritual weaves us together with the larger meaning and fabric of the cosmos.

Some years ago our men's retreat group was invited to bring our work with young men to one of the poorer neighborhoods of the Bay Area. There had been an escalation of gang crime, and our group included dozens of inner-city youth who were trying to leave the gang life. They first came with their mentors to the redwood forest of Mendocino for a week filled with mythic storytelling, artistic creation, meditation and martial arts, and heartbreakingly honest talk. On the last nights, Michael Meade, Malidoma Somé, poet and activist Luis Rodriguez, and I offered rituals of initiation that lasted until dawn. Without meaningful initiation, young people try to initiate themselves on the streets with drugs, guns, and fast cars. On retreat we carried offerings for dead friends to altars in the redwoods, we made prayers while passing through two roaring bonfires, we renewed ourselves plunging into moonless pools in the dark river lit only by candles. Even the hard shells of the tattooed homeboys were pierced.

At the week's end, our group left camp en masse to bring our newfound understanding back to the community. We began a procession down the main street toward the neighborhood park, led by dozens of young men playing a dance rhythm on drums, some in colorful homemade masks, some carrying long wooden staffs they had created to symbolize their intention to become protectors of the community. As we drummed and danced our way down the street, shades went up and windows and doors of run-down apartments began to crack open. We could see the curious faces of immigrants from Haiti and Mexico, Laos and Pakistan, Nicaragua and Palestine. We beckoned to them to come out and join our group. Surprisingly enough, hundreds did. They didn't know us, but they joined in our energy and laughed and danced. Many didn't speak English, but they all knew what a procession was. Whether they were Haitian, Ethiopian, Salvadoran, or Vietnamese, the universal language of ritual, drums, and procession spoke to them.

After a mile, we entered the park through a bamboo archway that had been decorated with ribbons and flowers. Here stood two young men. They bowed to each of the community members who entered, and placed in their hand a small candle. Without being told, everyone entering knew what to do. We had created an altar with flowers and symbols of peace in the center of the park. Now each person placed on it a lighted candle and made prayers for themselves, the community, the world.

Then we sang and shared food at a community feast. Youths spoke and read poetry, elders told stories, and the people connected in ways only the language of ritual can provide. Our procession did not end all gang violence, but it brought the people together in a way that hadn't happened before. You could see neighbors who had lived in fear or isolation talking to one another about the problems in the community. You could see an appreciation and admiration for the youths who stood up, spoke their experience, and read their poems. The ritual created a bridge between disparate community members that they could build on.

For the most part, ritual is absent in Western psychology. Our psychotherapists and healers meet with patients in sterile, fluorescent-lit clinics and offices, on uncomfortable chairs, unsupported by the language of ritual. Or we follow really strange rituals such as no touching, no hugs, no questions to the therapist about how she is doing, the rigid "time's up" rule. All this is designed to make the work of the heart respectable, to fit it into a medical, scientific mode of analyzing life.

This is not surprising. Our whole society has largely forgotten the necessity of ritual, especially in seasons of change or difficulty. We have a few rituals left to mark the most important changes in our life, such as weddings, graduations, and funerals, but even these often become elaborate tributes to wealth and status, rather than weaving true spiritual connection. Without ritual, as Malidoma Somé tells us, we pass one another like ships in the night.

Of course, ritual can be misused. We can absently turn a prayer wheel or finger a rosary, repeat a fossilized, rote performance out of custom or habit. Ritual can be superstitious or even corrupt. For many of us in the West rituals can also feel superstitious, silly, or awkward, like a first date (which is, of course, a particularly difficult ritual). We have a cultural discomfort with spirituality and the sacred even though we long to come together in a meaningful way.

Yet used wisely, ritual serves us in ways that we may not even understand at the time. David, an internist, told my good friend and teacher of physicians, Dr. Rachel Remen, about his experience as a doctor on a large inner-city AIDS ward. It was some years ago, before protease inhibitors and other drug therapies had become available, and almost all the patients who were admitted to his service died. Many of them were young men quite close to his own age, people whose lives mattered deeply to him. He was haunted by a sense of futility.

David had trained as a Buddhist, and to this day, when a patient dies, he lights a candle on his altar at home and, following Tibetan tradition, keeps it burning for forty-nine days. For the whole time he was at San Francisco General, he prayed for each dying young man and lit a candle on his altar. Many years afterward he speaks of this with a smile. It has made him wonder. Perhaps the reason he was there was not what he had thought. He had expected to serve by curing his patients. When their problems proved resistant to his medical expertise, he felt useless. But maybe he was not meant to be there to cure people. Perhaps he was there so that no one would die without someone to pray for them. Perhaps he had served every one of his patients flawlessly.

Buddhist psychology employs the power of ritual to transform consciousness. Rituals are constructed of elemental materials, as if to return our sensibility to the ground in which we live. The physical elements of ritual are the most ancient of languages: fire—candles, bonfires, offering fires; water—poured, blessed, sprinkled, baptized, floated, drunk; earth—buried, scattered, sacred stones, sacred ground, sanctuary; air—chants, songs, prayers, bells, drums.

These elements, combined with an altar, a gesture, a bow, the ringing of a gong, the pouring of wine, the making of a prayer, the planting of a seed, the sacred pause for a moment or a day, all help us to step out of time, out of business, out of success and failure. Even the deliberately low doors in certain temples require an entrant to ritually bow in order to enter.

The simplest gesture may become a ritual. Making a sitting circle to talk is a ritual. It was a powerful ritual gesture when Nelson Mandela invited his former prison guards to a seat of respect at his presidential inauguration. In Buddhist communities, there is a ritual of forgiveness where the abbot and elders regularly bow to the community and ask forgiveness for any errors they have made in their teaching and leadership. Every year at the end of our two-month spring retreat we do this. We invite our students' written suggestions and feedback. Then the six teachers move off their cushions and chairs and sit on the bare floor facing all the retreatants. We bow to them and their sincere practice. And then we ask their forgiveness for any way we may have harmed or misguided them. We tell them we did the best we could. Usually a lot of tears fall before the end of this ceremony.

CREATING RITUAL

As a Buddhist psychologist, I find that incorporating appropriate ritual is important for many of those I see. Sometimes before our session we bow to each other to acknowledge our Buddha nature. Often I include an initial period of meditative reflection and silence. At other times, when it feels called for, I light a candle or create a simple altar to help us hold life in a sacred perspective.

Not long ago, a psychologist named Alyssa came to a retreat. Alyssa works with the UN caring for newly arrived refugees. Her specialty includes support for those who have been tortured and are seeking political asylum in the United States. Alyssa told me she found it hard to sleep, to let go of the stories and images of suffering she was hearing from refugees of Afghanistan, Uganda, Haiti, Burma, Guatemala, Rwanda, Iraq, Bosnia, and so many other countries. She is also a regular meditator, and in her meditation the stories of torture were re-arising in vivid ways. "It is sometimes too much," she said.

During the retreat, Alyssa used practices of compassion and equanimity to work with these images. The meditation got easier. Then we talked about how these profound sorrows are not meant to be borne alone. I told Alyssa she needed backup. I suggested she create a large altar on the back wall of her office and place on it whatever inspired her spiritually. Initially she included statues and images of Kwan Yin, Tara, Buddha, Jesus, Guadalupe, and Mary. Over time, she added images of Latin American, African, and Haitian gods and an Arabic passage of mercy from the Koran. Now when the refugees arrive in her room, they see behind her the sacred images of each of their gods with a few flowers or a piece of fruit beneath them as an offering. To start each day, Alyssa calls on the gods and the ancestors to support her and hold those who bring their sufferings to her. At the end of the day she symbolically places the sorrows she has heard on the altar, in their compassionate hands.

Now she feels that she does not carry her burden entirely by herself. The altar is a daily reminder of how the forces of compassion throughout the world uphold her dedication. We do not work alone for change; the power of life works with us.

Creating a simple ritual, such as inviting a person to make a prayer or light a candle, can bring a sense of reverence and new possibility to that person's inner work. Sometimes crafting a personalized ritual on the spot is the best medicine. It may be the ceremonial burning of old love letters or the burying of relics of our grief; it may be a paper listing habits and fears to be released upon the waves, the ringing of a gong to symbolize the end of an unhealthy phase of life, or the dedication and lighting of a candle to symbolize a newfound freedom. All these rituals can release our past and reawaken our true nature.

Bruce came to his first Buddhist retreat with a body that was rigid and pained, as if he were underneath a heavy load. A physical therapist, he carried the burdens of a troubled medical system, per-

sonal conflicts, and a difficult childhood. Bruce had healed many
others; now he needed to heal himself. At first, however, the retreat brought more suffering. Bruce had heard Buddhist teachings
of compassion and emptiness, but as he began to meditate, what he
felt was the opposite: solidity, hardness, and tremendous frustration. The longer he sat, the larger his fear grew. By the time he came
to talk to me and my colleague Trudy Goodman he said he felt like
a caged werewolf inside. As he said this, his eyes narrowed and his
face actually became werewolf-like. I asked him to breathe and
mindfully notice whatever was present. He told me the werewolf
had been caged for a long time. It was ravenous.

I became curious. "What does it want to eat?" I inquired. It
wanted to eat Bruce. Then he went on, trembling, "What it really
wants is my heart." I told Bruce that in the Buddhist tradition, when
demons and hungry ghosts appear, there is a ritual practice of feeding them. In this practice we transform the worst, most rabid, most
fearful energies by deliberately visualizing what we can do for
them. We picture giving them whatever they want and need, even
our own body, until they are fully satisfied. I asked if he would be
willing to feed the werewolf. Feeding his heart to this beast seemed
extreme, frightening. The next time we sat together. Bruce's suffering had become so strong he felt he needed to do something. He
decided he would feed the werewolf. He closed his eyes and opened
the cage. But the werewolf didn't spring at Bruce. It looked at him
intently and said that when it wanted his heart, it wanted his love.
And then it walked up to him, brushed against his leg, and walked
out to the wild. Bruce was stunned.

Then he told me where the werewolf had come from. Bruce
had grown up on a cattle ranch just outside a small Texas town. And
somehow when folks in town had dogs they couldn't take care of,
they would dump them on the ranch. His father insisted that Bruce
be the one to "finish off" these "useless" dogs, which meant to shoot
them. Between the ages of eight and fourteen he was forced to
shoot sixteen different dogs. He wept as he told the story.

I invited Bruce to meditate with me. After we spent some time
simply focusing on a gentle healing breath, I began to chant out

loud and teach Bruce the practice of compassion on behalf of the dogs as well as himself as an isolated and sensitive child. "May your pain be held in great compassion. May you be free from sorrow. May you be at peace." As Bruce heard these words and breathed through his own sadness, he began to feel the suffering of all the young soldiers of the world, all the boys who are forced to carry guns and shoot to kill. His heart was opening to compassion for all of humanity.

But sometimes healing needs to be physically enacted as well. When I suggested that he create a healing ritual, Bruce's eyes lit up. Over the next few days he chose a hillside site near the retreat center and carefully formed a circle of sixteen stones, one for each of the dogs that so weighed upon his conscience. Then, one evening at dusk, Bruce, Trudy, and I headed up the hill together. The stars were becoming visible. Bruce showed us that the largest stone was oriented north to Sirius, the Dog Star, in honor of the dogs' undying spirits. At the base of each stone he placed a written prayer of atonement, and in the center he placed a small stone next to one of the largest. This, he told us through his tears, was the puppy of a dying mother who had tried to shield her, even in the last moments after she was shot. These were the last dogs he had killed. We meditated in the evening stillness. He bowed, lit candles, offered prayers, and spoke to these dogs about what his heart had learned and how their spirits would teach him for the rest of his days.

But Bruce was not yet free. He felt the dogs wanted something from him. He wanted to make atonement. Bruce decided to pledge $5,000 for animal welfare, to always keep a dog, and to work half a day each month in the nearby animal shelter for ten years. This he felt would be a labor of love. I saw Bruce six months later. He told me that his healing work was as challenging as ever, but he felt better. I could see it—his whole spirit seemed to have lightened up, and his body looked relaxed. His inner werewolf had been transformed and to my eyes had become more like a collie-shepherd-Lab mix, running free.

FINDING REFUGE

Viktor Frankl, the concentration camp survivor I mentioned in Chapter 1, was also the founder of logotherapy, which focuses on the search for meaning. He discovered that most of those who survived the camps did so become they had faith in a greater purpose for themselves and the world. Like these survivors, we each need to find our sense of purpose, to orient and support ourselves amidst the fragmented pulls of our busy modern life. Buddhist psychology's response to this need is to offer the practice of taking refuge.

Since the first days of the Buddha's teaching, if someone wanted to become a follower of the path, all that person had to do was recite, "I take refuge in the Buddha, I take refuge in the dharma [the teachings], I take refuge in the sangha [the community of practitioners]." There is nothing to join, nothing to become—simply this turning of the heart.

Refuge offers support for our journey as we move through joy and sorrow, gain and loss. In refuge, we reaffirm our sacred connection with the world. Refuge is not necessarily religious. Refuge can be as simple as making conscious our trust in a lineage of teachings. Doctors take the Hippocratic oath, dating from ancient Greece. Physicists place their faith in a long lineage of scientists including Archimedes, Galileo, Newton, and Einstein. Professional musicians proudly name their teachers and their teachers' teachers. In all our universities and psychological training institutes we find shrines to the lineage of revered and beloved elders, who gaze down from portraits and photos on the wall.

We may take refuge in a higher power, as in AA. Such faith has proved so transformative, it's astonishing that refuge and faith are so often excluded from Western psychological thinking. Much of the success of twelve-step and other support groups rests on faith and in the power of their sangha, the conscious community they create. We thrive with faith. Our faith may be spiritual or unabashedly non-religious, a faith in the natural world, in the unborn generations ahead, in life itself. To live wisely, we need to find a trusting connection to the world. Health care studies have shown that caring for a pet or even a plant will prolong life and well-being.

Like setting an intention or dedicating ourself to a goal, taking refuge reorients our life. Our refuge becomes an inspiration, a touchstone, a wellspring to draw from at every challenge we face. The Buddhist refuge need be taken just once in a lifetime, although in some trainings the refuge is recited daily. In Vajrayana practice, the refuge is repeated a hundred thousand times, each recitation enhanced by a full-body bow to the past generations of awakened beings. Whichever tradition we follow, when we take refuge we join in the stream of awakening.

Traditionally, there are three levels of Buddhist refuge: outer, inner, and innermost. On the outer level, we take refuge in the historical Buddha, a remarkably wise human being who pointed the way to inner freedom. We take refuge in the dharma, the teachings of generosity, compassion, and wisdom that bring freedom. And we take refuge in the sangha, in the Buddhist community of awakened beings. This outer refuge connects us to a tradition and to millions of followers of the Buddha's path. Taking the inner refuge in the Buddha, we shift from the historical Buddha to the Buddha nature of all beings. We take refuge in the potential for awakening in everyone we meet. The inner refuge in dharma shifts from the outer teachings to inner truth, to seeing the way things are. We entrust ourself to follow the truth and live in accord with it. The inner refuge in sangha shifts from the Buddhist community to all beings dedicated to awakening. We take refuge in this stream.

Last, we come to the innermost refuge. Here we take refuge in timeless consciousness and freedom. As Ajahn Chah explains, "We take refuge in the Buddha, but what is this Buddha? When we see with the eye of wisdom, we know that the Buddha is timeless, unborn, unrelated to any body, any history, any place. Buddha is the ground of all being, the realization of the truth of the unmoving mind. So the Buddha was not enlightened in India. In fact he was never enlightened, was never born, and never died. This timeless Buddha is our true home, our abiding place."

When we take refuge in the innermost dharma, we rest in the

eternal freedom. Zen ancestor Huang Po's words proclaim, "Your true nature is something never lost to you, even in moments of delusion, nor is it gained at the moment of enlightenment. It is the nature of your own mind, the source of all things, your original luminous brilliance. You, the richest person in the world, have been going around laboring and begging, when all the while the treasure you seek is within you. It is who you are."

When we take refuge in the innermost sangha, we acknowledge the inseparable connections of all our lives. The innermost sangha is the ultimate provenance of trust. It is voiced by the poet John Donne as "No man is an island" and echoed by Martin Luther King Jr. as "We are caught in an inescapable network of mutuality, tied in a single garment of destiny." Out of this interconnection we cannot fall or be separated. When we take refuge in the Buddha, dharma, and sangha, all things in the world become our teacher, proclaiming the one true nature of life.

The ritual of taking refuge can transform our consciousness. Ted, a long-term prisoner, began to practice from books and tapes provided through one of our Buddhist prison projects. As Viktor Frankl found in the concentration camp, Ted needed a meaningful purpose to get him through the horrors of prison. Taking refuge was a turning point for Ted. "After my teacher visited and I took refuge, I took the way I was living my life more seriously. I had taken vows not to harm, not to abuse, I had to see the Buddha even in the guards. I kept to myself more and meditated and did my refuges early in the morning. I said them over and over and I felt like I was rock solid. Then I was moved to another block. There was a lot of trouble there and I had to keep taking my refuges to stay clean. I was tempted to pay back a couple of men who did me some wrong. But then I would look them in the eye and take refuge in my heart. It helped me a lot. Everybody's got to have refuge in something to get through here."

PRACTICE: VISUALIZATION

To work with a sacred image, choose a figure from any period of history or spiritual tradition who particularly speaks to your heart. It can help to have a clear, beautiful picture that you can place in front of you while meditating. Rest your gaze softly on it, drinking in the image and feelings it embodies. Open and close your eyes gently and try repeatedly to see the vision inside. Start with whatever you can see easily, and when your attention drifts away, simply return your focus to this initial image. You may spend weeks learning to see this image. As you continue you can learn to visualize more steadily and accurately, with greater detail. Once you begin to see the sacred image steadily, visualize this figure as filled with radiant light, and let all the light, love, and illumination pour from the figure into you. Already you will feel better.

Now take the next step. Imagine that whoever you visualize can come inside your own body and mind. Release your personality and let this being enter into your heart and fill you completely with its compassion, courage, purity, and luminous radiance. Feel what it is like to inwardly become this being.

Dwell in this state for a period of time. Recognize that you can embody this energy, that you can allow it to fill every cell of your being, every corner of your consciousness. See the world with the eyes of this wise and gracious being; sense that you are holy. Practice this repeatedly until it becomes more natural to your heart than your "ordinary" identity.

And then, at the end of each period of visualization, release the image from your body, see it in front of you again, and then dissolve it into emptiness. Notice how consciousness itself creates and erases all appearances. Return and rest in pure awareness, allowing the natural world of your own body and mind to reappear, still secretly infused with the sacred consciousness of this vision.

19

BEHAVIORISM WITH HEART
BUDDHIST COGNITIVE TRAINING

*Whatever a person frequently thinks and reflects on, that will become
the inclination of their mind.*
—Buddha

*Speak and act from unwise thoughts, and sorrow will follow you as surely as the
wheel follows the ox who draws the cart. Speak and act from wise thoughts and
happiness will follow you as closely as your shadow, unshakable.*
—The Dhammapada

Ajahn Chah came from a farming village, and he reserved his
most plainspoken words for well-educated Westerners, who lived
mostly in their thoughts. One of Ajahn Chah's Western monks was
an Australian named Jim who repeatedly came and went from the
monastery, ordaining and disrobing several times. He was a likable
fellow, but he was also obsessed with petty problems and doubts.
He decided his hut was too close to the gate, and visitors disturbed
him. So he moved to a remote forest monastery, but there the food
was bad. Then he tried a monastery near Bangkok that had good

food, but he found there were too many distractions. Returning to Ajahn Chah's monastery, he would pay his respects and recite his latest doubts and dissatisfaction. Nothing was ever quite right.

Ajahn Chah watched Jim come and go with some amusement. Then one afternoon Jim told Ajahn Chah he was planning to move to yet another temple. Surrounded by several other monks, Ajahn Chah pointed to Jim and explained, "This fellow has put his monk's bag down in shit but he doesn't know it. Now wherever he goes, he says the new place smells bad!"

Whatever we regularly think colors our experience—all day, every day. Once we start to watch these thoughts, we discover that most of them are reruns. Others are about problems: "I need to call John about the roof again. I hope he can finally fix it." Some are about our preferences: "I like the way this person talks." "I really hate this traffic." Many are self-evaluation: "Oops, I'm messing up again. How do I get through this?" "Wow, I pulled that off well. I hope they notice!"

"What is thought?" ask the Buddhist texts. "Thought is your friend. Thought is your enemy. No one can harm you as much as unwise thought. No one can help you more than wise thought. Not even the most loving parent." Our life is shaped and determined by our thoughts.

Usually we are only half conscious of the way thoughts direct our life; we are lost in thoughts as if they are reality. We take our own mental creations quite seriously, endorsing them without reservation.

During the three days I thought I was a leper, my thoughts made a lifetime of leprosy seem likely. There I was, full of fear. I could sense the fear coursing in my body, the contraction in the solar plexus, the quivering of breath, the tightness of my muscles, and the sweaty palms. Added to this were the feelings of anxiety, a mood of insecurity, a shaky state of alarm. And then three days later I discovered that all these symptoms were generated by my own thoughts.

Often our fears don't turn out to be accurate predictions of anything. As Mark Twain put it, "My life has been filled with terrible misfortunes—most of which never happened!" When we become mindful of fearful thoughts, we see that fear is just a story accompanied by dramatic feelings. We don't have to take the story as truth.

As we see the productions of our mind, we discover radical freedom. The Tibetan lama Khyentse Rinpoche explains, "Mind creates both samsara and nirvana. Yet there is not much to it, it is just thoughts. Once we recognize that thoughts are empty, the mind will no longer have the power to deceive us."

Yet however much we try, sometimes we're caught in our repetitive thoughts, and knowing about their emptiness doesn't help. We can obsess for months about a past relationship or about our fear of failure at work. These difficult patterns of thought can repeat and persist, coloring our consciousness so deeply that we can be tormented by them, unable to see without their distortion. This is when we need, quite deliberately, to create positive thoughts in order to replace these unskillful patterns of mind. The understanding of these as simply unskillful states means that we can do something about them, as opposed to saying we're neurotic and there's no hope.

Buddhists were actually the first cognitive-behavioral therapists. In its current Western form, cognitive-behavioral therapy originates from the work of such figures as Albert Ellis, founder of rational emotive therapy, and psychiatrist Aaron Beck. Modern cognitive therapy grew from behavioral therapy, which rejected the psychoanalytic focus on family history and the unconscious. Instead it looked at what was happening in the here and now. The behaviorists believed that when we change behaviors, all else follows. Adding the cognitive element—the contents of our ongoing inner dialogue—provided another powerful tool for change.

We can see how this works in a standard cognitive-behavioral approach to panic attacks or phobias. We may be taught to count how many times the thought "I'm afraid" arises and touch a wristband inscribed with the words "I am strong" to replace our anxious thoughts. Then we can choose to act out of the strength. Sometimes this behavioral approach is coupled with systematic desensitization. If you are afraid of heights, you practice step by step, going to higher places until you can tolerate them. The same strategy is used to change depressive and fearful thoughts. In cognitive therapy, you see how unskillful behaviors and painful mind states originate from irrational thought patterns. You challenge these panicky, depressive thoughts, telling yourself not to believe them. Then you act positively and do what you are afraid of anyway.

Though there is considerable overlap between Eastern psychology and cognitive therapy, Buddhist training does more than offer purely rational replacement of inaccurate thought patterns. We could call the Buddhist approach "behaviorism with heart." It enlists the power of a larger, benevolent intention. We begin by using mindfulness to identify the patterns of thought that lead to our suffering. These include thoughts of unworthiness, jealousy and hatred, revenge, anxiety, clinging, and greed. Then out of compassion we change what is in our minds. We transform our thoughts as a loving protection of ourselves and of others.

This is a nineteenth principle of Buddhist psychology:

19   What we repeatedly think shapes our world. Out of compassion, substitute healthy thoughts for unhealthy ones.

THE DALAI LAMA'S FAVORITE PRACTICES

The Dalai Lama has said that transforming thought is one of his favorite practices. He instructs, "Let yourself visualize the effects of unskillful thought patterns such as annoyance, anger, self-judgment, and so forth. Inwardly see how such thoughts affect you: the tension, the raising of your pulse rate, the discomfort. Outwardly see how such thoughts affect others who hold them, making them upset, rigid, even ugly. Then make the compassionate determination, 'I will never allow such states to make me lose my peace of mind.' "

Barry became a Buddhist practitioner following a long history of anxiety and depression. From two years of therapy, he recognized some of the historical causes: his sick and absent mother, his father's early death. But such insight did not provide the relief he longed for. He needed ways to work with his mind in the present. After several classes and retreats, he learned to calm his mind by paying attention to his breathing. Still, whenever frustrations occurred, even small ones—if he accidentally got up late, or was stuck in traffic because of road construction, or his friends went somewhere without him—his anxiety and depressive thoughts would roll back in and knock him for a loop.

For Barry, mindfulness of breathing was only a start. The next step was recognizing the anxious and depressive patterns his thoughts created as they emerged. He was urged to scan back and try to locate the trigger each time he was caught. Gradually, he began to catch the first stirring of the depressive and anxious thoughts as they arose. When there was a problem at work or a rude driver cut him off in traffic, Barry observed the painful onset of this pattern. As the Dalai Lama suggests, he watched for the signals of tension and discomfort. The first time Barry consciously observed the start of his depressive thoughts, he could actually feel his body contract and go numb. He could see his mind gearing up to tell its tales of unworthiness and dread. Now he was instructed to bring compassion to these painful thoughts and feelings. He began to be kind to himself in these anxious, dark moments. And little by little, space opened up. He was able to choose another thought. As Barry said, "I used to think life was the problem. Then I paid attention and I saw that the problem was in the thinking."

Painful thoughts can take us over quite automatically. On silent retreat, the obsessive mind becomes exquisitely obvious. On a three-month retreat, one woman obsessed nearly the entire time about having brought the wrong clothes. Another man endlessly repeated a story of his father's favoritism to his younger brother thirty-five years before. We can obsess about a boyfriend, a new car, a song, how we're going to redo our living quarters, or why someone has slighted us. Even though these are "only thoughts," they can be tenacious. They sprout up like weeds in the garden. As the poet Rumi puts it, "This is the time of short crops, where what we sow comes back up quickly." Painful thought patterns can appear so quickly that we don't see them; they are the atmosphere though which we move.

Sometimes a sudden shock can show us how lost in thought we have been, literally "changing our minds" in an instant. Buddhist teacher Pema Chödrön tells of a student, a young woman, who wrote about her visit to the Middle East. One day she found herself surrounded by people jeering, yelling, and threatening to throw stones at her and her friends because they were Americans. Of course, she was terrified, and what happened next surprised her. Suddenly she identified with every person throughout history who had ever been scorned and hated. She understood what it was like to be despised, whether for one's race, ethnicity, sexual preference, or gender. Something cracked wide open and she felt herself standing in the shoes of millions of oppressed people—including those who hated her. Somehow, by staying calm, and through simple, heartfelt gestures, the young woman and her friends managed to go their way unharmed. But her realization that day changed her entire way of thinking; her deep-seated sense of separation opened up. She felt such a sense of connection, of belonging to the same family, that as she encountered others her thoughts were ones of concern, not fear. She had awakened true compassion for all life.

We can hope for sudden transformation, but in most cases radically retraining our minds requires steady, patient effort. The power to transform our mental conditioning is now scientifically documented by modern neuroscience's discovery of neuroplasticity, which shows how our brains can be retrained and reshaped at any age. This supports the profound hope and understanding built into Buddhist practice. Like its Western cognitive counterparts, Buddhist training teaches us to look at the thought distortions that create suffering. For example, we can notice when we generalize from one problem to our whole life. If we have a loss in business or a setback in our career, we may think, "I'm a loser. I'll never succeed." In cognitive therapy we would recognize the deluded nature of such thought patterns as "false generalizations" and try to notice every time they arise. Immediately we might substitute a wise thought: "I have a good life and a loving family. My life has had many successes."

The Buddhist perspective takes the process further. We can learn to see that distorted thoughts based on self-hatred, aggression, revenge, and greed are not in our genuine interest. We can actually see that these thoughts do not have our well-being in mind. They are like a bad friend or an approaching mugger, and we can recognize their harmful potential and immediately turn in another direction. Ajahn Chah described this as recognizing bad mangoes. We'd call them bad apples. "When we choose a fruit to eat, do we pick up the good mangoes or the rotten ones? It is the same in the mind. Learn to know which are the rotten thoughts and immediately turn from them to fill your basket with ripe beautiful mind states instead."

When we are depressed, frightened, or angry, cascades of unskillful thoughts will tempt us with their stories: "I can't possibly get through this." "It will always be this way." "I'll never have a good relationship." These thoughts create a painfully limited and false sense of self. Yet through practice, we can feel the pain that these thoughts produce, release them, and substitute a wiser perspective. Ajahn Chah says, "Whatever the mind tells you, don't fall for it. It's only a deception. Whatever negative comments and views it offers, just say 'That's not my business,' every time, and let it go." More specifically, the Dalai Lama suggests, "With worry and anxiety, repeatedly cultivate the following thought. 'If the problem can be remedied then there is no need to worry about it. And if there is no solution, there is no point in being worried, because nothing can be done about it anyway.' Remind yourself of these facts repeatedly." With the responsibility for the Tibetan people on his shoulders, it would be understandable for the Dalai Lama to succumb to fear and worry. Yet, while he is genuinely concerned, he also remains optimistic and joyful about life and rigorously good-hearted about what he hopes for the future.

Learning to transform thought was helpful to Margaret, who came to Buddhist practice depressed and afraid. Margaret's only brother, with whom she was very close, had recently died. She was forty-seven, worked as a paralegal, and lived alone after the end of a first marriage, which had been childless. Her mother had Alzheimer's and was in an assisted-living facility. Margaret had used antidepressants—several of them. But the side effects included peripheral numbness, loss of sexual interest, and a cotton-wool-like damping of her emotions, so she decided to stop taking them. Now, in her meditation, Margaret could see how often the thoughts of worry and hopelessness would arise. Any small setback—a critical word from her boss, a parking ticket—would set off a stream of thoughts telling her that life was worthless and that things would never get any better.

With mindfulness, Margaret could see the ephemeral nature of her thoughts, how quickly they would appear and vanish. Still, whenever circumstances were difficult, the unhealthy thoughts would overwhelm her. Gradually she learned to feel the pain of those thoughts and reject them as soon as she noticed them—like rotten mangoes or false friends giving bad advice. She was instructed to replace them with messages derived from the Buddhist teachings. She used four phrases: "I am a good and compassionate person. I have loved my family well. Life is precious. I will use my difficulties to grow stronger spiritually."

At first Margaret recited these messages sporadically and without much conviction. She doubted that such a "mechanical technique" would work. But the alternative was pain, so she kept at it. Margaret was also encouraged to practice loving-kindness meditation to strengthen this positive perspective. She initially focused on loving-kindness toward herself, the traditional ground from which all loving-kindness is developed.

Then, to extend her loving-kindness practice, Margaret decided to help others around her. She began to volunteer at a literacy program for immigrants, and she came to care deeply about her students. Together, the practices of inner and outer kindness lifted the pall of her worry and depression. Very steadily, the new messages of compassion shifted who she believed she was. Margaret's well-being grew as her positive thoughts grew stronger.

RETRAINING THE MIND

In Buddhist psychology, the instructions for thought transformation are very explicit. The Buddha instructs his followers, "Like a
skilled carpenter who removes a coarse peg by knocking it out with
a fine one, so a person removes a pain-producing thought by substituting a beautiful one." The carpenter's peg is a practical description of how we can remove unhealthy thoughts by substitution.
What is required is the selection of a helpful substitute and repeated practice. Repetition is key. Repetition, compassion, and the
belief that the painful cycles of thought can be transformed all have
a part in developing new patterns of thought.

Even so, some patterns of unhealthy thought—jealousy, anger,
fear, unworthiness, and anxiety—are so stubborn they are hard
to tame by simple substitution. For these thoughts, the Buddha
offers more forceful methods. His instructions continue, "And
when there still arise patterns of unskillful thought, the danger that
thoughts will cause pain and suffering should be clearly visualized.
Then, naturally, like the abandonment of rotting garbage, the mind
will turn from these thoughts and become steady, quiet, clear." We
can actually feel the danger when we are possessed by thoughts of
jealousy or anger, or we are in the grip of anxiety. These tighten and
stress our whole body. They keep us from rest. And when we consider acting on them, we know the results will be shameful and re-
grettable. It is important that we don't judge or recriminate with
ourselves when we see these thoughts; the practice is simply to set
a powerful new intention. We can see that our thoughts are unbidden, impersonal, painful. Out of compassion for ourselves we can
feel their danger. "Like rotten garbage," says the Buddha, "we can
put them down."

Still, some patterns of destructive thought are so strong that
even more forceful measures are needed. The Buddha tells us to
"deliberately and directly ignore these thoughts, turn away, giving
no attention, as if shutting our eyes or quickly looking away from
a disturbing and harmful sight." And if such patterns continue, "the
wildly unskillful thought stream should be gradually slowed and

stilled by slowing the breath step by step as if gradually slowing one's pace from a run to a walk to a standing."

Now we are talking about thought patterns that are as sticky as Brer Rabbit's Tar Baby. We all know them from experience, when a fear or doubt or obsession just won't go away. The thoughts may be unpleasant, but our mind gets in a groove and we don't know what to do but stay there. Like the Tar Baby, the thought of letting go of our ex-lover becomes a form of thinking about him or her. Ignoring the thoughts or walking mindfully and breathing slowly may reduce them. If not, the Buddha recommends a final and rarely used last resort: "Such thoughts should be met with force, teeth clenched, tongue pressed against the roof of the mouth, determined to constrain, crush, and subdue these thoughts as if constraining a violent criminal. In this way does one become a master of thought and its courses. In this way one becomes free."

As we can hear, these are not sweet "self-esteem" practices, looking in the mirror every morning and saying, "I am a loving person and the world will give me what I want." The destructive habits of mind can be tenacious. There is an element of fierce determination and self-discipline needed to take on the realities of the suffering world.

This fierceness became critical for a young man from the tough East St. Louis streets who was introduced to Buddhist practice at one of our multicultural men's retreats. He had recently joined a mentoring group for those who were leaving gangs. He worked on neighborhood cleanups and helped younger kids, projects paid for by the city. Over the past years of his gang affiliation, many of his friends had died. Now that he had left the gang, he expected that the chapter of violence in his life was ending. But then, in the course of four months, first a close buddy in his mentoring group and then his ex-girlfriend were shot and killed. All his gang instincts flooded his mind. His old friends pressured him to take revenge. It was a matter of honor. He had to get a gun. These dangerous thoughts would have led him to kill, and then be killed, on the streets or in a prison. He knew that he had to stop thinking this way. At the camp I gave him a necklace with beads carved like skulls, used by Tibetan monks to remind themselves to live wisely in the light of death. We talked about the fierce initiation of one who faces death and chooses life. At first he wasn't sure he could go on. In the gangs most young people cannot picture living past the age of twenty. Working together, we struggled toward a new vision. "I will live" became one of his thoughts. "I will save the lives of young kids," was another. He knew he had to face the fire of his suffering in another way. By changing his thoughts, he learned to walk step by step into a new life, a life of compassion. Now, five years later, he has become a father and a leader for youth in his community.

The transformation of thought can reorient an entire life, as it did for this former gang member. Or it can be an initial step in the process of healing. One psychiatrist used Buddhist loving-kindness meditation as a form of thought substitution for an angry and compulsive patient. Described by his doctor as a borderline psychotic with an obsessive nature, Larry was periodically enraged at his boss and his wife. The overly demanding boss was provoking murderous thoughts and revenge fantasies. He and his wife were clashing over the way to raise their child. Luckily, Larry was intrigued by the Buddhist teachings, and he soon recognized that his angry thoughts were weapons with which he was hurting himself. He became determined to replace them. First, he named them each time they arose: "Painful thought, painful thought." Then he cut them off and replaced them with a prayer of compassion. Soon he became obsessed with the notion that he should feel love for the people who were disturbing him, as well as for himself. He vigorously replaced the thoughts as often as they arose. Within a few days he reported a great relief and reduction of angry thoughts. A year later, he was still obsessive, but now he was continually repeating phrases of loving-kindness, which gave a new flavor to his traumatized mind. His doctor believed it was an important step toward a healthier life.

While a healthy obsession is better than an unhealthy one, it is hardly the goal of thought substitution. Still, severely disturbed thought can be reduced by these practices. The same psychiatrist tells of a paranoid patient who believed his neighbors were plotting against him. Anxious and agitated, he constantly thought of ways to get back at them. His doctor got him to see the pain these thoughts produced in his own body and mind and suggested substituting phrases of loving-kindness. Despite his paranoia, the man began to work with this practice. In the past, when the large dog next door barked loudly, the patient felt he was being attacked. But one day he told his doctor, "The dog is barking because I am sending out angry and negative thoughts. I need to change them." With this mixture of magical thinking and truth, the patient dedicated himself to sending out loving-kindness. And things got better. He said the dog barked less, although perhaps it was just that the barking stopped bothering him. Whatever it was, within months he became less fearful and more serene.

FREEING OURSELVES

Unhealthy thoughts can chain us to the past. They arise as vipaka, the result of past karma that we cannot change. We can, however, change our destructive thoughts in the present. Through mindfulness trainings we can recognize them as bad habits learned long ago. Then we can take the critical next step. We can discover how these obsessive thoughts cover over grief, insecurity, and loneliness. This underlying suffering needs to be held with compassion. As we gradually learn to tolerate these underlying energies, we can reduce their pull.

But even knowing their source and feeling them with compassion is not enough to transform the most difficult patterns. We have to replace them. This is the movement of creating healthier karma. Such thought replacement can be challenging, for we are loyal to our stories. They become our identity. There's an uneasy moment when the destructive stories we have been telling ourselves collapse. We can feel worried, doubtful, spacy, or frightened of the unknown.

Sometimes we have to pry ourselves loose from their power and bad advice. But underneath destructive thoughts is a part of us that knows such thoughts are not true, not valid, not alive. And with a release of these old stories, a whole new perspective dawns. Fear can be transformed into presence and excitement. Confusion can open up into interest. Uncertainty can become a gateway to surprise. And unworthiness can lead us to dignity.

TRUSTING OUR TRUE NATURE

Unskillful patterns of thought are not innate to our human condition. The Dalai Lama emphasizes this point: "Greed, anger, hatred, worry are not an integral part of our mind which cannot be changed. As children we are born ignorant; this is natural. But this ignorance can be dispelled by education and learning. In the same way, we can mentally isolate unskillful states and reduce them. Then, when happiness arises, the unskillful states have no valid foundation."

In *High Tide in Tucson,* novelist Barbara Kingsolver talks about how this transformation is possible, even when our old life is in ruins:

> Every one of us is called upon, probably many times, to start a new life. A frightening diagnosis, a marriage, a move, loss of a job or a limb or a loved one, a graduation, bringing a new baby home: it's impossible to think at first how this all will be possible. Eventually, what moves it all forward is the subterranean ebb and flow of being alive among the living.
>
> In my own worst seasons I've come back from the colorless world of despair by forcing myself to look hard, for a long time, at a single glorious thing: a flame of red geranium outside my bedroom window. And then another: my daughter in a yellow dress. And another: the perfect outline of a full, dark sphere behind the crescent moon. Until I learned to be in love with my life again. Like a stroke victim retraining new parts of the brain to grasp lost skills, I have taught myself joy, over and over again.

This is a liberating discovery, that we can shift from our unhealthy stories to well-being. Today, in our work and driving, in talking and shopping, in moving our body and taking care, we can choose which sound track to play. Will it be a broken record from the past, bringing bitterness or sorrow? Or will we release those thoughts and allow life's wonder and possibility? By transforming the landscape of our thoughts, we can revolutionize our entire world.

PRACTICE: THE COMPASSIONATE REPLACEMENT OF PAINFUL THOUGHTS

If you are a person who has regular, repeated destructive thoughts, thoughts of self-judgment, criticism, shame, or unworthiness, work with this training for a week or, even better, for a month.

First, become more carefully aware of the content and rhythm of the voices inside. What are their regular, unhealthy remarks and devastating comments? What do they sound like? What do they feel like? Begin to study how much pain they cause you. Feel how they take you over and how they hurt. When do they come out most strongly, day or night? What situations provoke them? Social occasions, family time, partners, competitive situations, work or leisure? Do they criticize your body, your mind, your actions, your whole being?

Notice the particular phrases and destructive, unhealthy perspective, the judgment, the shame, the self-denigration they engender.

Now, create a true antidote, a phrase or two or three, that completely transforms the falsehood of these unhealthy thoughts. Let the phrases be the healthiest words you can find, even if you don't believe them at first. They can be as simple as "Life is precious" or "I will use this day well." Or they can express the healthy opposite of thoughts of shame: "I will live with nobility and dignity." Or the opposite of anxiety: "I will live my life with trust." If helpful, they can be based on the phrases from loving-kindness practice:

May I love myself just as I am.
May I sense my worthiness and well-being.
May I trust this world.
May I hold myself in compassion.

*May I meet the suffering and ignorance of others with
  compassion.*

Now begin to work for a week with the phrases you have chosen.
Particularly pay attention to those situations that trigger painful
patterns. Every time you notice the destructive, unhealthy thoughts,
even if they have been playing for a while, pause and feel the pain
in them. Take a breath; hold your pain with kindness. Then inwardly
recite your phrases, firmly, deliberately. Do this over and over. It
does not matter if they sound false, if you don't quite believe them.
Say them anyway, out of compassion, as an antidote to your suffering. You may need to say them a thousand times before you realize
they are working. And they will.

20

CONCENTRATION AND THE
MYSTICAL DIMENSIONS OF MIND

*It is through the cultivation of inner concentration that luminous purity of mind
arises. It is through luminous purity that access to expanded states arises. It is
from the profound concentration of samadhi that liberating insight is revealed.*
—Majjhima Nikaya

*Concentration is like a pure empty bowl. Wisdom and understanding are the food
that fills the bowl and nourishes the heart.*
—Ajahn Chah

In the course of inner exploration I have sought mystical experiences with Indian gurus and Christian mystics. Shamans have taught me to visit the upper and lower worlds. I attended a series of all-night peyote ceremonies with Don José Rios, a 103-year-old Huichol Indian shaman. For eighty years, Don José had walked his tribe's two-hundred-mile, prayer-filled pilgrimage from the Huichol Mountains down to Wirikuta, the sacred desert wilderness, to collect buttons from the peyote cactus. The Huichols celebrate with this peyote, and its sacred spirit is woven into every thread of life. The energy of peyote expresses itself through their deer dances, visionary yarn paintings, extravagant garments, and feasts.

One night around a big fire along the edge of the Pacific Ocean, after hours of Don José's prayers and drumming, the whole world came alive. I had taken peyote and thrown up, a not uncommon reaction. And then the boundaries between "I" and "other" began to dissolve. Spirits from the trees came and danced, the fire became visions, the human and animal worlds joined, and I listened to and spoke to deer, salmon, owl, and worm. They were brothers and sisters. By the morning in the shining gleam of daylight I felt the holiness of earth open up, like seeing the divine.

Such states of openness and revelation were familiar to me from my previous training in Burmese monasteries. In one temple our daily practice included many hours of concentration on rapid yogic breathing and then exploring the expanded states that followed. Like the peyote ceremony, these powerful concentration practices in Burma opened my consciousness to luminous visions, mystical emptiness, and a sense of grace: the world was illuminated and all things were bathed in light. But instead of using the sacred medicines of peyote, mushrooms, or ayuhuasca, Buddhist psychology uses the power of the concentrated mind as a systematic gateway to expanded consciousness and mystical openings.

The most important gift of expanded consciousness is a startling shift of identity. Mystical experiences can melt our boundaries and open our hearts to a reality beyond our limited sense of self. Through them we reconnect to our place in the holiness of all creation.

Buddhism describes a vast cosmos that can be experienced by the mind. There are yogic states of luminosity and bliss, visionary states of deities and demons, descents into darkness such as those traversed by St. John of the Cross, and mystic states of emptiness and grace. Ajahn Chah's teacher Ajahn Mun described how he could see into the minds and past births of beings, how he subdued troublesome demons, and how he taught dharma in the many spirit worlds as well as the human one.

Buddhist texts offer a systematic cartography of these possibilities. One of my Indian teachers, Anagarika Munindra, taught us about dozens of kinds of silence: the silence of the mind and the silence of the heart, the silence of deep absorption, the silence of vast equanimity, the silence of non-perception, and the silence of the void. Entering into deep silence, a well-trained mind can become so unshakable that even the loudest shock will not cause the slightest reaction. Recently, neuroscience researchers Richard Davidson and Paul Ekman fired a loud gunshot next to an adept meditator practicing concentration. This meditator showed no startle response or disturbance, a stability of mind previously unimagined by Western science.

Growing up in the 1960s, the seekers of my generation had an intense curiosity about mystical and extraordinary states. We used psychedelics, music, dancing, drumming, and all-night gatherings to try to alter and expand our consciousness. There were genuinely revelatory qualities to hallucinogens such as LSD—and we benefited from our early forays into expanded realms. But after a few years, through misunderstandings and misuse, psychedelics were included in the war on drugs, and the backlash against them reinforced the broader culture's fear of non-ordinary states. One study showed that most Americans have had mystical or transcendent experiences but that the majority would not want to have them again. As a society, we have neither the training nor the understanding to deal with the power of these states.

Many of our religious traditions have colluded in this neglect. Father Thomas Keating, one of America's preeminent Christian mystics, explained that after the Protestant Reformation, the Catholic Church hid its ecstatic and mystical practices, lest people get direct revelations from God and perhaps put the Church's priests out of business. The Church has only recently revived many of these mystical practices.

Even now, the transcendent domain of human experience is virtually absent from the maps of Western psychology except for a small number of philosophers and religious specialists. In part this is the legacy of the European Enlightenment, with its elevation of reason, its long effort to separate science from religion. While this separation has brought enormous benefit, it has also left science, and much of Western learning, at sea regarding the inner life. Science developed computers and put us on the moon, it gave us antibiotics and antidepressants, but it cannot guide us in matters of virtue, love, inner meaning, or spiritual understanding.

In the last century, a handful of visionary psychologists from Carl Jung to Abraham Maslow and Stanislav Grof reintroduced these realms to Western science. But it is time to go further. When my wife, Liana, a Jungian, was studying for her psychology exams, she was disturbed by the limitations of the *DSM-IV*, the standard psychiatric reference text. She was inspired to consider a vision of an alternative manual of positive mental health. With Buddhist psychology as our guide, we could do so. We could take the hundreds of pages of psychological problems listed in the *DSM-IV* and create a positive counterpart called the DMHP—the Diagnostic Manual of Human Potential. In counterpoint to the thirty-five forms of depressive and bipolar disorders, there would be thirty-five positive forms of emotional and mental happiness—states of contentment, joy, rapture, gratitude, and extreme well-being. In place of aggression and paranoia would be highly developed capacities of trust, love, generosity, and selflessness. In place of hallucinations and psychosis would be the many forms of benevolent visions and sounds. These inner awakenings would be catalogued, from the still small voice of the divine to angelic choirs, from inspiring visions of gods and bodhisattvas to access to creative imagination and illuminated inner realms of understanding and light. In place of sleep disorders and amnesia, there would be extensive descriptions of wakefulness and lucid dreaming. Instead of anxiety disorders, there would be multiple categories of fearlessness, equanimity, dignity, and inner strength. Our psychologies don't speak of these possibilities, and we don't have an understanding of how they can be developed.

Today in the West, we access transcendental states largely by accident. Our minds may open when we're hiking in the high mountains, in a near-death experience, through transcendent art, during sexual orgasm, using psychedelic drugs, or attending the birth of a child. As we have noted, most traditional cultures deliberately summon these stories with shamanic drumming, vision quests, breath practices, chanting, and sacred medicines. In Buddhism, the main vehicle for opening to transcendent consciousness is the development of inner concentration.

Like a powerful telescope, the concentrated mind can open us to vast mystical states including realms of light, visions, rapture, and illumination. Like polishing a lens on a microscope, concentration can also allow us to see more deeply into the body and mind. Microscopic concentration initially brings a subtle awareness of body, a sensitivity to fleeting feelings, a refined perception of thoughts and memory. Going even deeper, we can open to an atomic level of perception. Our experience breaks down into numberless flashing particles, transient, selfless, and ungraspable. We become a silent witness to the flow of creation. The concentrated mind can see in entirely new ways.

Here is a twentieth principle of Buddhist psychology:

20   The power of concentration can be developed through inner training. Concentration opens consciousness to profound dimensions of healing and understanding.

Optimal mental health requires concentration. The role of concentration is explained in the Seven Factors of Enlightenment, a Buddhist description of wise human development. The clarity of mindfulness is supported by three arousing qualities and three stabilizing qualities. Concentration, calm, and equanimity are given equal weight to the arousing qualities we value so much in the West.

OPTIMAL MENTAL HEALTH:
THE FACTORS OF ENLIGHTENMENT
Mindfulness
(the central quality)

THE AROUSING QUALITIES	*THE STABILIZING QUALITIES*
Energy	*Calm*
Investigation	*Concentration*
Interest	*Equanimity*
Used in the psychology of the East and West	Used in the psychology of the East

In Western therapy, when a person presents his or her problems, we usually employ some forms of mindfulness and the arousing qualities of energy, investigation, and interest. We undertake a careful inquiry where stories are told, feelings uncovered, beliefs abandoned, and somatic and cognitive structures reorganized.

Buddhist psychology goes further. Adding the stabilizing qualities of calm, concentration, and equanimity, we can plumb the depths of our mind and heart. We can stabilize consciousness so that we can tolerate the most powerful energies, release past trauma, experience visionary revelations, and deliberately dissolve the limited sense of self.

Imagine this scenario: instead of arriving and beginning an hour of therapeutic work right from the highway or their job, clients would be asked to spend a period of time before therapy deliberately meditating, concentrating on their body and mind. The sensitivity of their consciousness would be entirely different. I have often worked this way with individuals. We would schedule their session to begin after fifteen minutes of meditation. If needed, I would offer instruction in mindfulness, concentration, and compassion practices. Our sessions seemed to start on a deeper and wiser note when preceded by meditation in this way. And if someone found coming early to meditate impossible, we would meditate together for five or ten minutes at the start of a session. It never seemed wasted.

I remember when Dolores, a meditation student, came to see me. Initially she felt overwhelmed, panicked, almost hysterical. She had just returned from San Diego, where she put her mother in a locked assisted-living facility because in the past month her mother had begun to wander and was twice picked up by the police. This was the same week Dolores and her husband had dropped their son off to begin college. We sat together and Dolores meditated. She calmed her racing mind using her breath. Then she practiced holding her mother, herself, and her family in compassion. By the time we began to speak, Dolores had already begun to use the stabilizing qualities of concentration and equanimity to regulate herself. She could feel her agitation and grief more fully. She could allow the welter of emotion with a more spacious attention. Her problems became more workable and less like emergencies. She opened to them as the inevitable changes demanded by new life cycles. Her practices of meditation and compassion supported this wiser and freer perspective.

As we have seen, Buddhist psychology is not as focused on interaction as is Western therapy, but primarily develops through extended inner training. Time spent with a teacher assists this ongoing daily practice and meditation. But most importantly it is our training that brings transformation.

The power of this inner training becomes visible at retreats. At retreats we work with people in states of particularly heightened sensitivity. After ten hours of meditation daily for a week, students' ability to concentrate and track experience in the body is increased. Their capacity to feel emotions and inner states becomes more subtle and their ability to witness thoughts without identifying with them grows.

A young man named Gabe offers an example of this process. Gabe learned meditation during a college semester abroad in India. Now, after one year of graduate school, he came to a two-month retreat. Initially, Gabe was hurt and sad. His girlfriend had just left him.

As he began to meditate, the first layer he encountered was the loss of his girlfriend. He felt fear, unworthiness, and anger. All the past rejections of his life flooded back. With mindfulness and compassion he became present for his pain and disappointment. Because his childhood experience of unworthiness went deep, he struggled with his tendency to identify with these unhealthy states. With continuing mindfulness and concentration, the identities of unworthy adult and abandoned child, winner and loser, all began to deconstruct. His feelings became impersonal states of mind: "the pain," "the anger," "the love."

Then Gabe's concentration grew stronger. As the days passed, his body changed. He sat upright and walked with a new graciousness. He experienced periods of very little thinking. Spontaneous joy and lightness arose. I directed Gabe to focus on the lightness and joy and to allow the bodily happiness to deepen and suffuse his being. Over the next weeks, several levels of concentration, called *jhana,* or absorption, became available to him. He sat with intense rapture and equanimity for hours at a time.

Then I asked Gabe to shift his focus to his body and mental states. He discovered that everything was dissolving. He experienced body and mind as the play of elements. One day the whole sense of himself as separate, as existing at all, dropped away. There was laughter, space, equanimity, peace. Gabe felt he had discovered the still point, the deathless in the midst of all things. Deep gratitude arose in him. He wanted everyone in the world to do this, to step beyond their fears, to discover the liberated heart. He wanted to dedicate his life to relieving suffering.

Each time Gabe came to speak with me, it felt like he was radiating a stream of blessings. He said his whole retreat had become a prayer. After two months Gabe began to prepare to return to the everyday world. He stopped his intensive sitting. He began to practice mindful conversation with others. His patterns of personality came back. But now he was relaxed. Everything was refreshed and tender. He entered the role of Gabe again but from a new perspective. Now he felt connected to the mystery of life, both full and empty, personal and universal.

I saw Gabe a year later. It had taken him a long time to integrate and adjust after the retreat. He had started a doctoral program in clinical psychology. He sought out a like-minded community of friends. He also began a new relationship, which felt more realistic and wiser than in the past. He became respected by those around him. He told me his sense of self felt lighter, transformed. Now when I looked into the eyes of this young man, they were steady, warm, shining with a gentle confidence and ease. Gabe had carried the benefit of his deep meditation back into the world.

Concentration can release us from our limited sense of self and bring illumination and freedom. But these experiences alone are not the end of the story. Ajahn Chah taught that any state of consciousness, no matter how glorious, is not the goal. What matters is how that revelation manifests—here and now in our daily round, when we are conversing or cooking dinner. The fruit of transcending our small self is the awakening of reverence, a newfound spirit of compassion and holy interdependence. When my friend John Hobbe was dying of AIDS, he said it was his experience of luminosity and boundlessness in meditation that let him die unafraid. This is what Ajahn Chah called "making the fruit visible." I experience this fruit in many ways when I come home from a long, silent concentration retreat. I am more generous with my wife. I don't mind doing the dishes and carrying out the garbage. Once after a retreat I had to choose between teaching on a panel with the Dalai Lama or fulfilling an important promise to help at my daughter's school. Filled with joy, I let go of the honor of being with the Dalai Lama and instead focused on the sacredness of my family.

HOW CONCENTRATION WORKS

To some degree, we all concentrate. Ordinary levels of concentration steady our mind as we read a book or cook a meal. Because concentration is a neutral quality, it can be used for both skillful or unskillful, even nefarious, purposes. A thief or burglar needs concentration, as does a card shark, a sniper, and a terrorist. The power of the concentrated mind can be directed toward the creation of suffering or well-being.

Concentration develops from our wholehearted dedication to

a subject or activity. As we develop the ability to concentrate, our steadiness and focus grow. We find ourselves able to be more fully present with our whole being. Through concentration our intuition and vision open, and we experience what Western psychologists describe as "flow," being fulfilled, transported and refreshed as we act. Skilled athletes call this "being in the zone," and for an athlete to enter the zone, concentration is a key. George Mumford is a Buddhist teacher who was hired by Phil Jackson to be the meditation coach for the Chicago Bulls and the Los Angeles Lakers. He trained the players in mindfulness and concentration. But their star player didn't need this training. Mumford reported that Michael Jordan's natural power of concentration was phenomenal. The ability to concentrate brings vitality and clarity to any activity, whether basketball, computer programming, or chess. It enhances lovemaking and turning pottery; it is essential to making music, writing legal contracts, or forging complex business deals. In each of these areas, the ability to focus is crucial.

In meditation, the systematic development of concentration brings access to deep inner states and insights. Meditative concentration grows as we become fully focused on one experience to the exclusion of others. Our consciousness becomes "absorbed," united, one with the subject of our concentration. The subject of meditative concentration can be simple. We can focus on a candle flame or a light, on a visualization or the body, on the breath or a prayer, on a mantra or a feeling.

As we concentrate, our consciousness becomes flavored by the subject of our focus. If we focus on love, the consciousness will be filled with the quality of love. If we focus on a flame, on earth or on equanimity, each of these will fill the state of concentration. If we visualize the Buddha or Kwan Yin, St. Francis or Mary, the visualizations can produce inner states filled with their particular qualities of peace or compassion.

Once a subject has been selected, concentration grows through dedication and repetition, as we connect with our subject again and again. We recite a prayer or a mantra ten thousand or a hundred thousand times. We visualize an image or concentrate on the breath over and over, releasing distractions whenever they arise. For modern minds conditioned to distraction, this is not easy. Anne Lamott writes, "I have a tape of a Tibetan nun saying a mantra of compassion over and over for an hour, eight words over and over and every line feels different, feels cared about and fully experienced as she is singing. You never once have the sense that she is glancing down at her watch thinking, 'Jesus Christ, it's only been 15 minutes.' Forty-five minutes later she is still singing each line distinctly, word by word, until the last word is sung. Mostly things are not that simple and pure, with attention to each syllable as life sings itself. But that kind of attention is the prize."

In most of Western psychology, our vision of human happiness is actually quite limited. Much greater happiness is available to us. Whole realms of joy and clarity are possible, and Buddhist psychology offers sophisticated and detailed maps of this territory as part of our human potential.

PURIFICATION: THE GATEWAY TO HIGHER STATES

Learning to concentrate, though initially difficult, works. Gradually, through repeated focus on our subject over hours and days, the mind's wandering diminishes. It settles down and steadies itself on the subject of meditation. This process of developing concentration is described by Buddhist texts as "purification." The term is not a religious or moral one, but rather describes an experience of release in body and mind. One practitioner I knew said it was as if he had been "inwardly put through the wash." Because the process of purification is not understood in Western psychology, it is worth explaining more carefully.

Purification means the release of tension, conflict, distraction, sorrow, and anxiety. The easiest way to understand it is to try to hold your concentration unwavering for just ten minutes. Suppose you direct your attention to concentrate absolutely steadily on your breath or an inspiring image. Within the first minute most people will find their attention has wandered many times. By the second and third minute, more distractions and feelings will interrupt, then the body will become restless or ache, and at the end of ten minutes, they will be lucky if they stayed with their subject for 10 percent of the time.

As we try to concentrate in meditation, our thoughts, conflicts, plans, and unfinished emotional business will get in the way. Physical tension and restlessness, memories and fears, instincts and drives will repeatedly interrupt us. Purification comes from the deliberate release of each of these distractions until the mind settles down and becomes still, contented and unwavering. As we repeatedly release the succession of tensions and thoughts, the body and mind gradually feel clearer. The process of purification can go on for days and months. Success in concentration comes not through suppression but by acknowledging each distraction and each conflict mindfully—with attention but without attachment—and letting it go until it subsides or loses its sway over us.

Eventually, after thousands of repetitions, the mind and heart begin to feel purified, released from the grip of these distractions, almost unwavering on the meditation subject. With further concentration, the mind becomes so filled with the subject, so absorbed, that nothing can distract it. Once this happens, the inner experience becomes one of wholeness and steadiness, and an inner luminosity arises. Every contemplative tradition, from Christian to Taoist, describes the experience of this inner light. It is quite literal. When we have been through a process of purification and can concentrate steadily, the body, the mind, and the whole of space can appear as being filled with light. Buddhist psychology outlines twenty-five categories of inner light, from luminous clouds and fireflies, to dazzling light like the noonday sun. When this inner light arises there also comes rapture, happiness, expansion, and the ability to enter into the profound states of silence called jhana. These simple, dry, methodical practices are, paradoxically, a path to oceanic rapture and expansiveness. In this meditative way, we systematically open to the mystical dimensions of the mind.

VAST SILENCE AND ILLUMINATION

The jhana states that open the door to illumination are divided into two major groups: *absorption concentration* and *insight concentration*. These states are so central to the Buddhist world that the word *jhana* became *Chan* in China and *Zen* in Japan.

Entering states of absorption, we feel like a scuba diver going from the windblown surface of the ocean to the silent depths below. Absorption states are discrete worlds of inner experience, each more silent and refined than the one before it. They are characterized by unwavering steadiness, purity, radiance, and happiness.

The absorption jhanas are colored by the subject used to develop them. If we use love, we become absorbed in love; if we use a visualization, we become the visualization. Many other meditative subjects are used to enter absorption of jhana, from breath and body, the elements of fire or earth, to a wide range of devotional visualizations and sacred images. With each subject we learn to focus so fully that all distraction falls away. When concentration is strong enough, we slip below the waves of ordinary senses to a deep, silent realm of first jhana. Here consciousness is filled with stillness, rapture, happiness, and a steady awareness of the chosen subject. Initially we can rest in this stable state of jhana for some minutes. With practice we can sit drenched in joy for hours.

As we continue to practice our concentration, the first of eight levels of jhana deepens to the second, and here the effort to focus becomes spontaneous and easy. Deepening yet further, in the third jhana, the coarse excitement of rapture disappears, leaving a steady current of unshakable happiness. By the fourth jhana, even the emotion of happiness fades, and an exquisite, unshakable stillness and equanimity arises. Beyond these, four more subtle jhana states follow: absorption in boundless space, absorption in boundless consciousness, and absorption in the silent realms beyond perception and non-perception. Again, the old list makers have numbered these eight states for navigational and pedagogical reasons. The numbers indicate that there is a progression of increasingly silent and refined states available with deep concentration.

In addition to these absorption jhanas, there is another category of concentration states, called *insight jhanas*. Insight jhanas do not focus on a single subject, but arise when concentration is focused and absorbed in the ever-changing sense experiences of body and mind. Concentrating on the body and mind in a fully absorbed way is like putting more and more powerful lenses on a microscope. The sixteen levels of insight jhanas systematically deconstruct the solidity of our experience.

In the first insight jhana the mind becomes a silent witness to the experience of body and mind, which shows itself as almost me-chanical, arising and passing, instant by instant. In the second deeper level of jhana, these momentary experiences reveal their patterns of conditioning, one being a cause of the next. In the third level, the body becomes more transparent and the fleeting selfless-ness of experience becomes more apparent. Over the next levels of insight we begin to experience luminosity, bliss, and then fear, followed by great joy as we dissolve into the mystical evanescence of all life. Inwardly it feels as if we move from sense organs to cells, to molecules, to atoms, to subatomic particles and waves. At each successive level of insight, equanimity grows, along with a pro-found inner freedom.

Buddhist psychology acknowledges that jhana concentration is only one of many ways to cultivate inner understanding. Not every-one can concentrate in this way. Some students do not find concen-tration states accessible to them. Others need to work through traumas and difficulties before they can concentrate. But for those who can, exploring the realms of jhana opens new dimensions and capacities, from luminous rapture to the ability to sit motionless in jhana states for days.

While Buddhist teachings repeatedly write about the develop-ment of jhana, there are few detailed, personal accounts. These inner states are hard to put into words, and they can be easily mis-understood. In fact, for some Buddhist traditions, it is taboo to openly disclose your inner experiences. In Zen you speak to the master and no one else. Otherwise it can spark competition, jeal-ousy, or disappointment.

In spite of the potential for misunderstanding, I want to

describe a few of my own experiences to make it clear that this aspect of psychology is not just theoretical but quite real. Initially, my own concentration training was difficult. I have an active mind and I was often distracted and full of thoughts. In the monastery my teacher had me focus on the breath for months, over and over, to stabilize the concentration. Then, after a year of dedicated meditation, I was trained to enter both insight jhanas and absorption jhanas. For absorption jhanas, I have used a variety of subjects such as the breath, body awareness, and loving-kindness. I learned to quiet my mind, release almost all thoughts, and intentionally enter states of silent absorption for sustained periods.

In the first levels of jhana, my body becomes joyful and my mind deliciously happy. Every cell of my being becomes suffused with rapture and happiness. My body becomes transparent, then disappears into a field of bliss. My mind becomes silent, as if in interstellar space. These states bring a sense of refreshment and inner strength. When this absorption concentration is stabilized, I can rest in these first or second jhana states for an hour or two or longer. Then I can release the excitement of the rapture and dwell in more refined states of transcendent happiness and equanimity of the third and fourth jhanas. Beyond these initial jhanas, I can then open to the fifth jhana of boundless space, where the field of meditation expands out to the farthest galaxies. With yet more refined awareness, I open to the sixth jhana of boundless consciousness, beyond space and time itself.

My favorite subject for absorption jhana is loving-kindness. When I have used loving-kindness to develop concentration, my body and mind will disappear into a love-filled radiant light for hours at a time. Following traditional loving-kindness training, I systematically extend the energy of loving-kindness to all categories of beings, human and animal, seen and unseen, in each direction of the universe. With no sense of body, I become like a combination of a laser, a fountain, and a star. Sitting in meditation, I can direct the radiance of my heart like a beam. I shine it on living beings in every part of the vast universe until all are experienced as illuminated with light and love. I have sat for hours drenched in this love. And this is only the modest beginning of concentration training in comparison to my teachers.

MALLEABILITY AND INSIGHT: THE FRUITS OF CONCENTRATION

Once concentrated, the mind can be directed in specific ways. This function is called "malleability of mind" in Buddhist psychology. It means that we can shift the focus of the mind in surprisingly easy and steady fashion. Spatially, we can change the field of concentration from small to large. If we focus a concentrated mind like a microscope on the tiniest body sensation, ten thousand microsensations will come into view. Or we can shift to a wide-angle perspective and expand our focus so that all experience floats in space, vast like a galaxy. A malleable mind can also change subjects easily, so that we can flexibly switch from one state to another, deliberately moving from unspeakable joy to strength to stillness. With concentration, no matter where we place our attention, it will stay focused.

When I first developed strong concentration, I explored this delightful flexibility and pliancy of mind. I'd place my attention on an area of my body and it would stay there. I'd bring up a thought or image for contemplation and the mind would enter into it fully. I was delighted. It was as if the mind had become a well-trained dog. Sit. Stay. Pay attention. It was unmoved by pleasure or pain (in most concentration states pain drops away). For however long I chose, it did whatever it was directed to do, with steadiness, ease, and interest.

The malleability of mind can then be combined with the power of intention. Concentrated intentions are surprisingly strong. Meditation practitioners are often amazed by this almost magical property of a well-trained mind. When the mind is deeply concentrated, if we say to ourself, "May third jhana arise," it will. If we say, "May happiness arise," we are flooded in happiness.

This concentrated and malleable consciousness is particularly useful as a tool for insight and intuitive wisdom. With concentrated intention we can ask for wisdom to arise, and it does. When I asked for an understanding of emptiness, I found myself falling backward into what felt like dark interstellar space, pulled like gravity into the void and then silent for a long time. When I made the intention for the wisdom of impermanence to arise, I was surprised when my attention focused on my balding head. Then it began to spontaneously scan down through my sixty-year-old body, to the fillings in my teeth, the ear with hearing loss, sinus problems, and a stiff neck. It focused on lungs weakened by a bout of pneumonia, a past broken wrist, the scar from an appendectomy, a weak disc in the lower back, sciatica, old knees, and sore feet. "OK," I said, "I get it: this body is truly impermanent, subject to change and decay."

Concentration has a steadying effect that supports well-being and understanding. One experienced practitioner used the power of concentration to regulate herself in the midst of numerous difficulties. Joan had a natural empathy for the world around her and was gifted in caring for others. Her regular meditation practice had helped her manage a part-time nursing job, do community service work, and care for two young children. The scale began to tip, however, when her mother-in-law, who lived nearby, had a stroke. Now Joan needed to care for her as well, and she began to feel overwhelmed. She began to have difficulty sleeping and experienced bouts of anxiety, exacerbated by menopause. When she sat in meditation her body spontaneously shook and trembled and buzzed. She felt as if all the frenetic energy around her—the news on television, the patients at her clinic, her mother-in-law's struggle—was pouring through her own body without boundaries, unstoppable.

I suggested she stop formal meditation and work with practices for grounding the frenetic energy down through her body into the earth during the day. This would have been helpful for many. But Joan intuitively felt that turning away from meditation would make her anxiety worse. Because she had a gift for easy concentration, she decided to meditate more. Joan changed her practice to loving-kindness and went on retreat with one of my colleagues to work with phrases of loving-kindness and visualization quite ardently. After some days of anxiety and big energy releases, her mind became focused and concentrated. As happiness, steadiness, and purity became strong, her anxiety fell to the background. To her amazement, she discovered that mixed in with her previous agitation was wild, unintegrated rapture. As she learned to experience this rapture as an inner wind, she learned to release the energy and rest in deep stillness. As the factors of enlightenment—calm, concentration, and equanimity—came into balance, Joan was no longer overwhelmed. Now she could contain the huge levels of trembling excitement.

When her concentration developed further, Joan's teacher told her to wait until the deepest point in her sitting meditation and then deliberately invite the states of absorption jhana to arise in consciousness. Gradually she was taught to navigate through the first four jhanas. The first two levels of jhana states still contained the strong energy of rapture and her body would become initially overwhelmed by shaking and trembling. But in the third and forth jhanas, Joan found that all the trembling and rapture ceased. Instead she sat for long periods of profound stillness, bathed in ease, filled by a sense of grace and unshakable love. This concentration practice felt healing to her, as if her nervous system was rewiring itself. When she came out of the jhana states, her mind was light and easy, her body had regained a relaxed buoyancy and flexibility.

At the urging of my colleague, Joan then began to use the jhana concentration for insight. She investigated the moment-to-moment construction of her experience. She studied how the states of jhana appear and vanish. Then, because her mind was so malleable and silent, she witnessed the coming and going of a thousand states of consciousness, one after another. Turning toward awareness itself, Joan learned to rest in the emptiness that gives birth to all states.

When Joan returned home, she felt as if her body had been refurbished from the inside. She slept better, her anxiety diminished (although she still has bouts of it), and her sense of inner strength and steadiness grew. The focus of her identity had shifted from trouble to wisdom. Her sensitivity remains, but it has become less a problem and more like a gift. She is still active in a wide range of community services. Her sensitivity to suffering keeps her heart connected to all those around, yet the wisdom and concentration remain her ground.

TRAINING PSYCHIC ABILITY

Deep levels of concentration and jhana can also become a gateway to a wide range of psychic abilities. Buddhist psychology outlines how systematic training in concentration can bring the ability to read minds, to see or hear at a remote distance, to know the past of any individual, to manipulate the elements of earth, air, fire, and water. Based on highly developed concentration, these practices and powers are detailed in such texts as Buddhaghosa's thousand-page Path of Purification and the Six Yogas of Naropa. These psychic abilities were trained and practiced by a number of my teachers, but they are misunderstood in the West. Western scientific studies of psychic abilities have failed because these abilities are usually not stable at ordinary levels of consciousness. You can't invite ordinary graduate students into a lab and expect to study psychic abilities. While there are exceptions with certain gifted individuals, most people need some form of concentration training for psychic abilities to arise strongly.

Some of the most skilled Buddhist meditators still practice the powers outlined in the Buddhist texts. During her intensive practice period in the 1960s in Burma, my Indian teacher Dipama Barua was trained in all these capacities. According to her and her teachers, she could visit people at a distance (she once went psychically to the United Nations to hear a speech by the Burmese secretary-general U Thant), she could see into past lives, and she could transport herself through time and space and appear spontaneously for her interviews. By the time I studied with her, it had been years since these trainings and she was not interested in psychic powers anymore. Of course, I wished that I had seen her demonstrate these powers. But I have seen and heard from colleagues of so many other psychic phenomena—from the spontaneous appearance of rainbows in a clear sky to the sure knowledge of someone's death or difficulty at a distance—that I am open to all possibilities. Even with moderate levels of training, some of my Western colleagues have found the ability to read minds or to project specific teachings into the dreams of their students.

Because psychic powers are considered a distraction from freedom and compassion, they are left as optional trainings for advanced students. To use jhana or psychic powers wisely, we have to take into account the dangers that accompany the territory of these refined states. There are dangers of inflation and grandiosity, taking pride in "our" attainments. There are also dangers of ambition. Even if we discount the domain of psychic powers, spiritual practitioners can hear about concentration states and jhana and then struggle after them unsuccessfully for years, not realizing that the grasping itself prevents their opening. And when we do find access to states of bliss and jhana, we can also lose them. We can peak, then crash, experiencing the kind of loss and frustration described by St. John of the Cross as "the dark night of the soul."

The point of these trainings in concentration is not to increase grasping but to use concentration states in the service of inner liberation. Through the power of concentration, the solidity of the world shows itself to be dream-like and insubstantial. In meditation we may first experience fear when we open to the groundlessness of experience. But the stability and well-being created by the concentration allows for steadiness while the whole sense of self and other dissolves. With the power of concentration we can let go and return to balance, even as all things dissolve. One student, Rosina, initially worried as her meditation showed the world as empty and insubstantial. "What about my family, my children, my career?" she asked. She feared she was deserting them for a realm of emptiness. But emptiness always gives birth to new forms. "Is it OK to dissolve, to let go this much?" Her Zen master smiled and told her not to worry: "Death OK. Resurrection OK, too." After the retreat Rosina returned to her family, emptier and more openhearted than she had ever experienced. Concentration and insight show us how to be with all things as the play of consciousness. We become free in their midst. We become wise.

A wise psychology must incorporate the transcendent dimensions of the concentrated mind. But in the end, even the most luminous states of concentration pass away, as do the insights that can arise from them. Ajahn Chah reminds us, "When blissful and extraordinary states arise from your meditation, use them but do not cling to them." Concentration is a powerful step on the journey, one important way to quiet the mind, open the heart, and discover freedom. The real blessing appears when we can bring the experiences of the transcendental to illuminate the miracle of the ordinary.

V

EMBODYING
THE
WISE HEART

21

A PSYCHOLOGY OF VIRTUE, REDEMPTION, AND FORGIVENESS

The perfume of sandalwood, rosebay, or jasmine cannot travel against the wind.
But the fragrance of virtue travels to the ends of the world.
—The Dhammapada

In Ajahn Chah's forest monastery, as in all Buddhist temples, a reverence for life is the basis for all activities. The forest teems with a thousand species of bugs and beasts, from the cicadas whose loud songs joined the monks' chants at twilight to the tropical birds and snakes that moved around us every day. Our practice was to learn to live together with them all.

When I entered the monastery, I was assigned a hut in the forest. I found a major spider, the size of my palm, living there near the ceiling. At first I wanted to put him outside, but then I realized he was only using the upper part of the hut. I didn't think he was poisonous, though I still felt a bit nervous. And I had to acknowledge that he'd been there before me. So I breathed deeply and let him be. We began to live together, and gradually I learned to coexist with him and with lots of other creatures. As I watched him repeatedly weave his web, I came to appreciate the patience of the spider's life, to see that every being was worthy of respect. Now, writing this page, I think of a poem by America's master calligrapher, Lloyd Reynolds. He wrote, "A bug crawls over the paper. Leave him be. We need all the readers we can get."

In Buddhism, this reverence for all life is called virtue, and it is considered fundamental. Ajahn Chah loved to say, "It's simple. Living a virtuous life makes the heart peaceful." Those who understand virtue live with dignity, ease, nobility, and happiness. And needless to say, it's hard to meditate after a day of lying, cheating, and killing. By our virtue we protect ourselves and other beings from harm.

To our modern ears, the word *virtue* can sound old-fashioned. We might associate it with Victorian schoolgirls being taught to be modest, prudent, patient, and obedient. Yet in Buddhism, virtue is not about young girls or tepid, law-abiding weaklings. It is the foundation for radical change. It means that we carry ourself with truthfulness, integrity, passion, and purpose in all we do. This is the powerful, even fierce force that ennobles individuals and inspires social justice and equality worldwide. Just as a life of virtue brings happiness, it also packs a punch.

In Buddhism, virtue is seen as a psychological training, not a divinely inspired set of commandments. It has three levels, explained Ajahn Chah. Training in virtue begins with stopping harmful actions. This first level, called non-harming, includes five traditional practices. These are to refrain from killing, stealing, lying, misuse of sexuality, and misuse of intoxicants. Each of these practices has great power. Imagine how our world would be transformed if even one of them was followed by all humans.

The second level of virtue is the deliberate cultivation of care. More than refraining from harm, we cultivate a reverence for life.

More than refraining from stealing, we act with stewardship for the things of the earth. More than refraining from lying, we stand up for truth. More than refraining from the misuse of sexuality, we respect our intimate relations. More than refraining from the misuse of intoxicants, we cultivate wakefulness.

The third level of virtue is called natural virtue, the spontaneous integrity of the awakened heart. Natural virtue arises when we are free from self-interest, when we are free to love. Instead of relying on rules and practices, our benevolent actions come from an innate connection. We all instinctively recognize this level of virtue, when people are authentic, kind, and unshakable in their integrity. We are inspired and moved. This is the highest level of psychological development. Gandhi, who exemplified inherent virtue for modern times, stated, "Let then our first act every morning be to make the following resolve for the day: 'I shall not fear anyone on earth. I shall fear only God. I shall not bear ill will toward anyone. I shall not submit to injustice from anyone. I shall conquer untruth by truth. And in resisting untruth, I shall put up with all suffering.' "

We can feel the increasing psychological health as virtue increases from non-harming to care, and then to the highest level of integrity.

This is a twenty-first principle of Buddhist psychology:

---

21   Virtue and integrity are necessary for genuine happiness. Guard your integrity with care.

TEACHING VIRTUE IN PSYCHOTHERAPY

A few years ago, I presented the Buddhist principles of virtue at a large psychological conference. My session was called "Teaching Virtue in Psychotherapy," and the room was packed. Hundreds of psychotherapists came to hear how the explicit training of an ethical perspective could fit with the morally neutral stance of modern psychology.

I began by acknowledging that there is an important basis for this morally neutral perspective. Freudian psychoanalysis, the basis for much of modern therapy, was, as we know, born in the repressive, stratified society of late-nineteenth-century Europe. One of the most exciting discoveries of Freud and his colleagues was that when his patients lifted the socially enforced repression of their feelings and thoughts, remarkable healing occurred. Using such techniques as free association, the early analysts had to make it clear that nothing would be judged or censored. Without this protected space, it would be impossible to expect the level of honesty that healing requires.

Buddhist psychology approaches healing in the same way. Mindfulness requires a suspension of judgment. It is an open inquiry into what is painful, pleasant, joyful, or shameful, without judging anything as right or wrong. This is the first step in healing, a clear seeing and deep acceptance of what is. But this acceptance is only the first step in the transformation of human experience.

The next steps involve inner transformation, followed by the need to acknowledge the consequences of our actions and take steps to avoid harm. In Western clinical practice, licensed therapists have a legal obligation to report cases of grave danger. We must act to prevent incest, physical abuse, suicide, and other life-threatening forms of harm. But the psychotherapists at my presentation wanted to talk about whether and how to address other levels of moral integrity. I explained that Buddhist psychology teaches the principles of virtue to everyone because integrity is considered critical for happiness. We need to be reminded about the inevitable suffering that comes when we act without integrity. I gave some examples of students with whom I had worked.

Allen, a middle-aged, single man who attended a retreat, told me in a private interview that he had secretly been taking thousands of dollars from the large company where he worked. No one could ever trace it, he said. First we were both mindful of this as a fact without judgment. As we sat with the story and our feelings, I asked Allen what he felt in his body. He reported that his body was somewhat tense, and as he became aware of the contraction, agitation and fear arose. He realized he was carrying many difficult and complex feelings about his behavior: he was pleased that he had been smart enough to get away with it, yet guilty and afraid that he might eventually be discovered. I asked him what it was like to live with this inner conflict. He acknowledged that it was hard, and that the simple act of confession had brought him relief.

Then I explained to Allen that relief comes not only through inner work but also through mending our actions. Because actions create karmic results, we need to address these external consequences of acting without integrity. I told him that in Buddhist psychology ethical questions are not framed in terms of good versus evil. We simply focus on suffering and its causes. Thus, stealing is understood to produce suffering both for the one who steals and for the wider community. Clearly, Allen's own discomfort was already evidence of the suffering caused by stealing. His actions could potentially create more suffering for himself and others.

Allen left the room both shaken and relieved. I encouraged him to be mindful of all that our conversation had stirred up. We talked together several times over the next days. As Allen reflected on his actions, he discovered a sense of deprivation and anger, and strong views of entitlement that made it seem OK to steal. As he meditated, Allen also found that underneath his anger was a frightened and shaky young man. We acknowledged that his confession to me was only a start, and I emphasized that he would not be able to heal if he continued to steal. I referred him to a Buddhist psychotherapist to continue his healing. And I told him that his karma and conscience would also require him to repair his misdeeds, to atone for them in some way, even if anonymously.

Ken was another middle-aged meditator in conflict over his actions. In our work together, Ken revealed that he had had many affairs over the sixteen years of his marriage. After a few months with a new lover, he would leave her and seek another. He claimed that lying about affairs was like lying about taxes—everyone does it. So far he had kept his affairs secret from his wife and three children. Our work began with the obvious need for Ken to examine his

inner compulsion and conflict. He started to look at the desperation in his motivation, the fears and dissatisfaction in his marriage,
and his denigrating view of women. As he opened further in meditation, he felt that he was being torn apart. He sat with the inner
turmoil of his own history of trauma and addictive relationships.
Though this introspection was an important step, his conflict could
not be solved simply by uncovering his painful past. He also had to
work directly with his addiction. I suggested he join a twelve-step
group.

I also taught Ken that the Buddhist practices of non-harming
include refraining from causing harm through sexual misconduct.
Again I explained that these practices are not based on notions of
sin or good and evil but are descriptions of the causes of human suffering based on millennia of experience. Since ancient times it has
been recognized that adultery often causes great pain. The secrecy
and compulsion that surrounded Ken's adultery were causing suffering that would only get worse. Healing would not be possible
unless Ken's integrity was restored.

For all those who come for Buddhist training, the foundation
of integrity is made clear. The basic practices are presented in a
straightforward vow:

> For the protection of myself and others, I undertake the practices:
> To refrain from killing
> To refrain from stealing
> To refrain from harmful misuse of sexuality
> To refrain from false and harmful speech
> To refrain from the misuse of intoxicants

According to Buddhist teaching, we are not functioning at a human
level without basic integrity. Until then, we may appear to be
human, but we are subhuman in our hearts. We live in the realms
of the hungry ghosts, jealous gods, and frightened predators, or in
the hell of endless conflict. Developing virtue is a psychological necessity if we are to alleviate suffering.

Traditionally, the sources of integrity include two mental factors called inner and outer conscience. Early translators mistakenly

called these qualities "moral shame" and "moral dread," words with strong Victorian echoes of Christian sin and damnation. But Buddhist psychology doesn't view the world through the lens of shame. It does not speak of a God who sets moral rules and punishes wrongdoers. Instead, it describes the natural laws of the heart, based on karma, interconnectedness, and who we really are.

Inner conscience knows when our acts are harmful and recognizes that a lack of integrity will bring suffering for ourselves. Inner conscience seeks to protect ourselves. Outer conscience knows that harmful acts will look wrong to others, and sees the collective suffering they can cause. Outer conscience seeks to act in ways respected by others and to avoid painful consequences for those around us. Both aspects of conscience grow from an open heart, the ability to feel the consequences of our acts. Without this connection we can cause great harm. Even sociopaths, who are diagnosed as being without a conscience, often feel that something is missing, as if conscience is still there, behind the distant walls that have isolated their hearts. I recently read about a serial killer who described himself as "the loneliest man in the world."

Conscience recognizes the truth; it knows when we are acting with integrity and when we are not. Conscience is an aspect of the One Who Knows, our deepest innate knowing. Conscience understands that we are all in it together, and that when we harm another, we harm ourselves.

Without integrity and conscience we lose our freedom. As social commentator Michael Ventura writes, "The people you have to lie to, own you. The things you have to lie about, own you. When your children see you owned, then they are not your children anymore, they are the children of what owns you. If money owns you, they are the children of money. If your need for pretense and illusion owns you, they are the children of pretense and illusion. If your fear of loneliness owns you, they are children of the fear of loneliness. If your fear of the truth owns you, they are children of the fear of truth."

In caring for ourselves and others, integrity is essential. Years ago I read of a study that was done at a rural Illinois state mental hospital. The hospital was out in the farmlands, just off a tollway.

The exit to the hospital had an unmanned machine to collect fifty cents from each car, but not everyone paid. A psychologist who worked at the hospital began to wonder about this. He set up a hidden camera to record who paid and who didn't. Then he looked at the hospital record of healed and discharged patients. He discovered that the patients of those doctors and therapists who paid their tolls got better more quickly than the patients of those who did not pay. It is as if we who are healers somehow communicate our integrity and it gives strength to those we work with as well.

When we tell the truth, we establish the ground of awakening. Buddhist myths tell how over many lifetimes the Buddha-to-be made many mistakes and committed many errors. He gave away what was not his, he got in conflict with family members, he caused the death of others. But the one thing he did not do was lie about his actions, to himself or others. His truthfulness carried him to freedom, even through the worst of times. Within the Buddhist community, a clear conscience is prized. Monks, nuns, and lay followers are instructed to practice with a careful attention to their conscience, so as not to bring harm to themselves or others. It was outer conscience that led the Buddha to denounce the oppressive caste system of his time and to take steps to include women in a fuller way in the ordained spiritual community. And from ancient times to modern difficulties, when community members or teachers abuse their power, even if there is initially great denial, it is the conscience and virtue of the community that must eventually call them to task and right their wrongs.

Ajahn Chah said, "Look after your virtue as a gardener takes care of his plants. Do not make a difference between big or small. Don't make excuses." In the monastery we repeatedly committed ourselves to a life of virtue. We would reflect on our successes, acknowledge any lapses, and start over. The monks and nuns would recite their vows of virtue day after day. Lay people would recommit to the five practices of virtue each time they visited.

Integrity is essential to mental health. In the end, we know that the truth will out, no matter what. As the poet Linda Hogan writes, "After the Chernobyl nuclear accident, the wind told the story that was being suppressed by the people. It gave away the truth. It carried the story of danger to other countries. It was a poet, a prophet, a scientist." Though the Buddhist texts did not know about radioactive winds, they understood "the fragrance of virtue which travels farther than the wind, safeguarding our happiness even in the face of danger."

REDEMPTION AND FORGIVENESS

No one is forgotten. It is a lie, any talk of God that does not comfort you.
—Meister Eckhart

Milarepa, the most beloved saint in the Himalayas, was a Tibetan youth whose family was terribly abused by relatives after his father died. As a result, Milarepa was urged by his mother to study black magic and take revenge on those who had mistreated them. With these powers he killed many of them. But afterward, Milarepa was filled with fear and remorse and sought out a Buddhist teacher to help him release his bad karma. Through years of extreme penance and a series of harrowing trials, Milarepa atoned for his terrible past. Then Milarepa dedicated his life to awakening and spent years teaching and caring for others. The story of his redemption is the most celebrated myth in all of Tibetan Buddhism.

In the same way, redemption transformed the worst killer of the Buddha's era, Angulimala. Indian astrologers said Angulimala was born under a robber star. Through the jealousy and lies of those around him, Angulimala was convinced that his religious duty required him to kill a thousand innocent people. Living in the thick Jalini forest, he became the most feared figure of his day, a swordsman who could run as fast as a swift horse.

The Buddha deliberately went wandering there, even though others warned him not to go. When Angulimala gave chase, the Buddha's yogic powers would not let him catch up. "Stop! Stop!" shouted Angulimala. The Buddha responded, "I have stopped, I have stopped all harm to living beings." Somehow the Buddha's fearlessness was enough to break the spell of misguided destruction. Then the Buddha demanded that Angulimala cut off the limb of a tree.

When the limb was cut, the Buddha said, "Now put it back." When Angulimala acknowledged that he was helpless to do so, the Buddha explained, "Your power is so limited, it can only destroy life. What about the power to preserve life?" Angulimala then threw away his sword to become a monk and eventually a respected disciple of the Buddha. Like Milarepa, Angulimala is now widely venerated as a saint. The great popularity of these stories speaks to the universal need for redemption, to reclaim our nobility.

Twice a month, at the full and new moon, the monks and nuns of the forest monastery seek release from past misconduct through formal practices of confession. They ritually gather together under the canopy of trees to confess their mistakes, seek understanding, and ask for forgiveness. Each confession ends with a commitment to start anew. For serious difficulties, a council of ten or twenty elders is called to listen to the confession with compassion. Then the elders prescribe practices of atonement and transformation to help the monk or nun find the way again.

In this spirit, one of the common practices that Buddhist psychologists and teachers use to help students is to listen to their confessions. When we hear their misdeeds and regrets, we work with compassion, forgiveness, and letting go. We know that this unhealthy past is not who they really are. Sometimes students reveal the worst of their deeds. Whatever is weighing on our hearts is where we work.

Confession is a necessary practice in psychology. In 1974, I was on the founding faculty of Naropa Buddhist University in Boulder, Colorado. The summer's largest class, taught by Ram Dass, was focused on paths to liberation. On the full moon in July, more than a thousand students from Ram Dass' class joined together for an all-night ritual at the foot of the Rocky Mountains. The students and some of us teachers began the night with chanting, prayers, and meditation. At the center of our circle was a huge bonfire lit in honor of the Indian goddess Kali. Kali represents destruction, especially of the false sense of self, and through this process she gives birth to the indestructible spirit.

As the night went on, the students were invited to write down whatever difficulties they needed to let go of to become free and offer them to the Kali fire. Before they approached the fire, however, they had to read their paper aloud, in ritual fashion, to Ram Dass, who stood quietly off to one side. Then Ram Dass blessed them. All night, one by one, the students revealed their most difficult secrets, then placed their suffering to be transformed in the blaze. Standing nearby, we could see relief, even joy in their faces as they turned to rejoin us. The next day Ram Dass described to us, his colleagues, the burdens that were on those papers. There were a hundred forms of pain and fear. There was widespread shame around sexuality. There was unworthiness and self-judgment. There was guilt and regret for past mistakes. For each, there was a need to forgive and start over.

Here is a twenty-second principle of Buddhist psychology:

---

22   Forgiveness is both necessary and possible. It is never too late to find forgiveness and start again.

Because Maha Ghosananda was one of the few senior Buddhist monks to survive the Cambodian genocide, he was called upon to help reestablish their Buddhist traditions. Maha Ghosananda chose to respond by teaching forgiveness and reconciliation to hundreds of thousands in the Cambodian refugee camps. Then he carried the message of forgiveness on foot across Cambodia to offer a vision of love to the dispossessed, the broken, and the frightened. He also worked with communities of displaced Cambodians in the United States. When he would appear, the refugees of that area would come together to offer a huge community meal before his teaching. But around several of the Cambodian-American temples there had grown violent factions. As Maha Ghosananda explained, the warring factions in Cambodia had brought some of the war to America with them.

In each temple, Maha Ghosananda gave teachings on compassion for all who had suffered, no matter which side they had been on. He explained the Buddha's words "In war there are no victors."

He spoke to the traumatized community members one by one: older men, younger gang leaders, mothers, men who in Cambodia might have participated in terrible deeds. He listened to their stories and confessions, he chanted words of reconciliation, he spoke of innate goodness, and he prescribed healing practices. Most important, he held each person in love and esteem. He told them that no matter what had happened, it was possible to start again. He beamed so much love at each one that for a time they couldn't hold on to their limited, old sense of self. His loving heart became a touchstone for many in these communities, a ground from which their redemption could begin.

Many Americans too still live with the trauma of our wars. Lloyd Burton, a Vietnam veteran and now a Buddhist teacher, used mindfulness and loving-kindness to find healing. I have recounted his tale in *A Path with Heart,* but it is such an articulate and heartfelt narrative that I want to print it again. In his own words, Lloyd describes a meditation retreat where he found redemption from the terrible atrocities he had witnessed as a soldier.

I had served as a field medical corpsman with the Marine Corps ground forces in the early days of the war in the mountainous provinces on the border of what was then North and South Vietnam. Our casualty rates were high, as were those of the villagers we treated when circumstances permitted.

It had been eight years since my return when I attended my first meditation retreat. At least twice a week for all those years I had sustained the same recurring nightmares common to many combat veterans: dreaming that I was back there facing the same dangers, witnessing the same incalculable suffering, waking suddenly alert, sweating, scared. At the retreat, the nightmares did not occur during sleep, they filled the mind's eye during the day, at sitting, during walking meditations, at meals. Horrific wartime flashbacks were superimposed over a quiet redwood grove at the retreat center. Sleepy students in the dormitory became body parts strewn about a makeshift morgue on the DMZ. What I gradually came to see was that as I relived these memories as a thirty-year-old spiritual seeker, I was also enduring for the first time the full emotional impact of experiences that as a twenty-year-old medic I was simply unprepared to withstand.

I began to realize that my mind was gradually yielding up memories so terrifying, so life-denying, and so spiritually eroding that I had ceased to be consciously aware that I was still carrying them around. I was, in short, beginning to undergo a profound catharsis by openly facing that which I had most feared and therefore most strongly suppressed.

At the retreat I was also plagued by a more current fear, that having released the inner demons of war I would be unable to control them, that they would now rule my days as well as my nights. But what I experienced instead was just the opposite. The visions of slain friends and dismembered children gradually gave way to other half-remembered scenes from that time and place: the entrancing, intense beauty of a jungle forest, a thousand different shades of green, a fragrant breeze blowing over beaches so white and dazzling they seemed carpeted by diamonds.

What also arose at the retreat for the first time was a deep sense of compassion for my past and present self: compassion for the idealistic, young would-be healer and physician forced to witness the unspeakable obscenities of what humankind is capable, and for the haunted veteran who could not let go of memories he could not acknowledge he carried.

Since the first retreat the compassion has stayed with me. Through practice and continued inner relaxation, it has grown to sometimes encompass those around me as well, when I'm not too self-conscious to let it do so. While the memories have also stayed with me, the nightmares have not. The last of the sweating screams happened in silence, fully awake, somewhere in Northern California many years ago.

We each need to find ways to redeem our past and return to our own nobility. No one experiences this need more actively than those who have committed serious crimes. In recent years, I have worked with several prison meditation projects that seek to change our enormous and destructive prison system. In 2003, we brought the Dalai Lama to meet with a number of former prisoners who had been helped by prison meditation projects, many of whom had served sentences of over twenty years. We wanted his support for the growing movement of prison rehabilitation and for the people whose years of inner struggle and courage had allowed them to transform their lives. One of them, Anita, was a thirty-nine-year-old woman whose warmth and understanding were immediately apparent. Two years before, she had been released after serving fourteen years as a reluctant accomplice to a botched armed robbery. Anita described how hardened and territorial people become in the degrading conditions of prisons. To stay sane, the women in her maximum-security prison established simple routines and strict boundaries in sharing their tiny cells. Periodically these routines would be disrupted by the intrusion of short-timers, women who were serving less than a year, who, because of overcrowding, were forced to double up in long-term cells. These short-term women were usually pushed away and ignored.

When Noni, a quiet young woman, came into Anita's cell for four months, Anita was wary and closed. "This is where you can put your things; here's the part of the cell you use, and don't go beyond it." For many days Anita observed as her new cellmate sat sick and depressed on her bed and would hardly take food. Then she began to throw up, especially in the morning. Finally it dawned on Anita that her cellmate was pregnant. Anita thought about this young woman and about the baby. It didn't seem right for this depressed young mother to starve herself. She was hurting her baby. Soon Anita found herself comforting Noni and listening to the whole story of her life. Slowly, she became her confidante, her protector, her supporter, making her more comfortable and making sure she was eating. Word about the pregnant girl got out, and women up and down the maximum-security cellblock began to help with special food and comfort. The impulse of compassion for Noni and her baby became communal; it brought the prisoners together.

Some months after Noni was released, news came back that her child, named Julia, had been safely delivered. Anita recalled the amazing cheer that went up among the prisoners, who felt themselves to be Julia's aunties and grandmothers. New life had touched the sorrow of their cells. And more than anyone, Anita was changed. She told our conference group that the new life in Noni had opened her barricaded heart and started her on a six-year path of healing and redemption. Now on the outside, Anita works at a project to assist other incarcerated women.

Anita, who had felt so hard, discovered new life in herself. I have seen this new life in the faces of certain men to whom I have taught meditation in prisons such as San Quentin who say, "I did something really terrible and stupid when I was eighteen and messed up on drugs. Now I'm forty-three, a quarter of a century later, and I am not that person anymore." Of course, there are also men in San Quentin who are still violent, even psychopathic. But psychopaths are not found just in prison; they also head governments in many parts of the world. The good news is that many prisoners do change, even in the harsh environment of prison.

Transformation is not just an abstract or idealistic promise; it is an actual physical possibility. For years scientists erroneously believed that the development of the brain and nervous system was complete at the age of twenty or twenty-five. Now modern neuroscience has recognized "neuroplasticity," confirming what was known by Buddhist psychology for millennia: even adults can change. The adult brain and nervous system grow and change throughout our lives. Until the very end, we are neurologically transformed by whatever we practice. We are not limited by the past.

THE PRACTICE OF FORGIVENESS

Buddhist psychology offers specific teachings and practices for redemption and the development of forgiveness. Like the practice of compassion, forgiveness does not ignore the truth of our suffering. Forgiveness is not weak. It demands courage and integrity. Yet only forgiveness and love can bring about the peace we long for. As the Indian sage Meher Baba explains, "True love is not for the faint-hearted."

We have all betrayed and hurt others, just as we have knowingly or unknowingly been harmed by them. It is inevitable in this human realm. Sometimes our betrayals are small, sometimes terrible. Extending and receiving forgiveness are essential to free us from our past. To forgive does not mean we condone the misdeeds of another. We can dedicate ourselves to making sure they never happen again. But without forgiveness the world can never be released from the sorrows of the past. Someone quipped, "Forgiveness means giving up all hope for a better past." Forgiveness is a way to move on.

In Buddhist psychology, forgiveness is not presented as a moral commandment—"Thou shalt forgive." It is understood as a way to end suffering, to bring dignity and harmony to our life. Forgiveness is fundamentally for our own sake, for our own mental health. It is a way to let go of the pain we carry. This is illustrated by the story of two former prisoners of war who meet after many years. When the first one asks, "Have you forgiven your captors yet?" the second man answers, "No, never." "Well, then," the first man replies, "they still have you in prison."

For most people, the work of forgiveness is a process. Practicing forgiveness, we may go through stages of grief, rage, sorrow, hurt, and confusion. As we let ourself feel the pain we still hold, forgiveness comes as a relief, a release for our heart in the end. Forgiveness acknowledges that no matter how much we may have suffered, we will not put another human being out of our heart.

The practice of forgiveness grows through patient repetition. One of my teachers instructed me to practice five minutes of forgiveness for myself and others, twice a day for six months, which meant 360 times. Practicing with small misdeeds, such as my uncaring treatment of a friend, over and over I inwardly asked for forgiveness and vowed to act in more caring ways.

That experience encouraged me, but when I turned to my father, the process was much more difficult. Forgiveness took many years. It was only when he lay dying that I could look back and reflect on what had released me from our family suffering. When, at age seventy-five, ten years after his first heart attack, my father was near death from congestive heart failure, frightened and in pain, I sat with him over long days and late nights. He kept asking me to stay. Because I had sat with my own pain and fear in meditation, I was not afraid. Because I had sat in the charnel grounds and with others as they died, I was able to offer the steady presence he needed. By now I also knew enough not to blurt out that I loved him, but I also knew that he could feel that I did.

Years of meditation, therapy, and forgiveness practices had come with me into that room. I'd worked with my rage at my father and my sorrow and frustration as a frightened, impotent child. One day I pictured the yellow linoleum floor in the back room where my father was beating my mother. I wanted to beat him up and to rescue her. I felt sorry for my mother at the same time as I was angry at her for her weakness and for her collusion with his brutal arrogance. I struggled to release my father and all his rigid, paranoid violence. I relived the nighttime scenes where his eyes would become glassy and crazed-looking and the old bastard would curse and hit and hurt us, his family.

As I meditated and wept, I felt the pain of my own closed heart and wondered how I could forgive him. I breathed and practiced forgiveness and got inside his own wretched history and my mother's paralyzing fear. I saw him as a young teen when his father died. Both my father and his father were caught between two women who hated each other: his coldly polished and controlling mother and his tight-fisted and iron-willed grandmother. I saw my father's paranoia and fear and how hard his uncontrollable rage must have been for him. I saw his inexcusable acts and his unmanageable pain. It helped when I discovered that my own rage was not so different from his. I learned to respect the anger, depression, cynicism, and humor that my brothers and I had used to survive. I saw that we were not alone. I felt connected to a million fathers and estranged sons, to generations of family wounds, many greater than my own. Then I gradually saw too his creative and loving side, along with his capacity to hurt those he loved, and finally his humanity, all our humanity. And in the last days in the hospital, I could sit with him in all his complexity and forgive.

Now as a Buddhist teacher, I guide others on a path of forgiveness. Josh's half-brothers had legally cheated him out of part of his inheritance. He knew that through his own inattention he was complicit as well. Over five years he had tried to straighten things out with them, with only a little success. Still he carried the suffering and betrayal like a weight in his body. He had not been a regular meditator, but to release his suffering, he undertook a systematic forgiveness practice. He knew that finding compassion and forgiveness were crucial for his well-being. At first he struggled, and whenever his bitterness arose, I suggested he pay attention to his body. He could feel a familiar block of rigid tension in his shoulders and upper arms and a constricted pain in his chest. The clenched hurt and anger were a painful sign. He didn't want to live this way. Even though he didn't get the money, he did not want to live hating his brothers. Josh knew he had to release them. Over several months of repeated practice, the spirit of forgiveness came in, and little by little he learned to let go.

Forgiveness was also important for Meryl, a college biosciences professor who worked on ecological sustainability projects in Central America. On retreat she told me how she had recently seduced a graduate student and two other young assistants in the field. She had mixed her love needs with the good work she was doing, and her activism had become a kind of self-justification for these relationships. It all came up in her meditation. Meryl was not sorry for her attempts at love and connection, but she deeply regretted the pain and betrayal she had caused.

I suggested that Meryl write the whole set of stories down. They poured out of her. Then I asked her permission to read them. She gave them to me, and when I had done so we met again. I asked her what she felt we should do next. Her eyes watered and she said she wanted to ask forgiveness. I offered her my own, and told her that she had to consciously understand and feel the impact of her actions in order to commit to not harming. She thought she would write to these women. Then she had to find a way to forgive herself so she could be released from the past and let it go.

Even in extreme cases, the Buddhist teachings counsel forgiveness. In the Dhammapada, the Buddha gives an instruction that is both fierce and compassionate. "If someone has abused you, beat you, robbed you, abandon your thoughts of anger. Soon you will die. Life is too short to live with hatred." Whenever we forgive, in small ways at home or in great ways between nations, we free ourselves from the past.

Lissa grew up with a lot of shame about being poor. Outwardly she tried to overcome this by hard work. Lissa was the first in her extended family to go to college, struggling with feeling insecure, like an outcast. After she graduated, she worked in the city for the Department of Public Safety. Sixteen years later she transferred to a farming community just in from the coast near Oxnard. She told me, "Now that I've lived in the city, when I go into the coffee shop and see the old clothes, the uneducated farmers, it's so easy to judge them and feel myself as different. We may be different in education and politics, but these are false ways we separate ourselves. Then when I really look, I just want to drop my judgments and be with them, with us.

"My father was like them. He drank too much. He berated us, his daughters. He was terrible to his sons. I was desperate to get free of him, of our family. But my shame, anger, and resentment stayed with me. When I began Buddhist practice, it was hard to sit still. After a while I realized how sad I was, how much hurt was in my body. I was just trying to cope. I was grateful to be taught the loving-kindness and forgiveness practices. I did them twice a day for two years. I needed to forgive myself for being so angry and ashamed, as much as to forgive my father. Practicing forgiveness was like learning to stand and walk and feel good about myself. Then I was able to go home, to see my family, even my father, without hurting so much. Seven years later when my father got sick, it wasn't hard to go back. I saw his slow decline until finally he was a weak old man on his bed. I knew that I loved him. I had forgiven us all." With virtue and forgiveness we repair the world.

PRACTICE: FORGIVENESS MEDITATION

To practice forgiveness meditation, let yourself sit comfortably. Allow your eyes to close and your breath to be natural and easy. Let your body and mind relax. Breathing gently into the area of your heart, let yourself feel all the barriers you have erected and the emotions that you have carried because you have not for-given—not forgiven yourself, not forgiven others. Let yourself feel the pain of keeping your heart closed. Then, breathing softly, begin asking and extending forgiveness, reciting the following words, letting the images and feelings that come up grow deeper as you repeat them.

ASKING FORGIVENESS OF OTHERS

Recite: *There are many ways that I have hurt and harmed others, betrayed or abandoned them, caused them suffering, knowingly or unknowingly, out of my pain, fear, anger, and confusion.* Let yourself remember and visualize the ways you have hurt others. See and feel the pain you have caused them out of your own fear and confusion. Feel your own sorrow and regret. Sense that finally you can release this burden and ask for forgiveness. Picture each memory that still burdens your heart. And then to each person in your mind repeat: *I ask for your forgiveness, I ask for your forgiveness.*

OFFERING FORGIVENESS TO YOURSELF

Recite: *There are many ways that I have hurt and harmed myself. I have betrayed and abandoned myself many times through thought, word, or deed, knowingly and unknowingly.* Feel your own precious body and life. Let yourself see the ways you have hurt or harmed yourself. Picture them, remember them. Feel the sorrow you have carried from this and sense that you can release these burdens. Extend forgiveness for each of them, one by one. Repeat to yourself: *For the ways I have hurt myself through action or inaction, out of fear, pain, and confusion, I now extend a full and heartfelt forgiveness. I forgive myself, I forgive myself.*

OFFERING FORGIVENESS TO THOSE WHO HAVE HURT
OR HARMED YOU

Recite: *There are many ways that I have been harmed by others, abused or abandoned, knowingly or unknowingly, in thought, word, or deed.* Let yourself picture and remember these many ways. Feel the sorrow you have carried from this past and sense that you can release this burden of pain by extending forgiveness whenever your heart is ready. Now say to yourself: *I now remember the many ways others have hurt or harmed me, wounded me, out of fear, pain, confusion, and anger. I have carried this pain in my heart too long. To the extent that I am ready, I offer you forgiveness. To those who have caused me harm, I offer my forgiveness, I forgive you.*

Let yourself gently repeat these three directions for forgiveness until you feel a release in your heart. For some great pains you may not feel a release but only the burden and the anguish or anger you have held. Touch this softly. Be forgiving of yourself for not being ready to let go and move on. Forgiveness cannot be forced; it cannot be artificial. Simply continue the practice and let the words and images work gradually in their own way. In time you can make the forgiveness meditation a regular part of your life, letting go of the past and opening your heart to each new moment with a wise loving-kindness.

22

THE BODHISATTVA
TENDING THE WORLD

*The Buddha's teaching arose in India as a spiritual force against social injustice,
against degrading superstitious rites, ceremonies and sacrifices; it denounced the
tyranny of the caste system and advocated the equality of all men;
it emancipated women and gave them spiritual freedom.*
—Walpola Rahula, *What the Buddha Taught*

*Those who say that spirituality has nothing to do with politics
do not know what spirituality really means.*
—Mahatma Gandhi

Lauren came to Buddhist meditation to relieve the overwhelm
and stress of her eight years of intense work in international
women's rights. But she also wanted a child, and she knew she
needed more balance in her life. She struggled with whether to go
back to Indonesia, where she'd been working, or to make a home
in San Francisco. The outer needs of the world seemed so pressing.
Lauren was concerned about the safety of her young feminist
Muslim partners. But her commitment to them conflicted with her
increased longing to become a mother.

During a ten-day retreat, the power of these two polarities became like a pressing koan for Lauren. A genuine koan cannot be
solved by the thinking mind. In the words of one Zen saying, it's
like having a hot iron ball caught in your throat, too hot to swallow, too hot to spit up. What do you do? Lauren sat and walked with
her dilemma for days, sometimes frustrated, sometimes in tears.
Gradually her mind quieted, her boundaries began to loosen, her
drivenness melted. Then early one evening she came to see me, quietly excited. "I've been caught-up thinking about this all wrong. I'm
not separate from the world I want to help. We're the same thing!"

Lauren had a tender smile on her face. She explained how at
first, having a child felt selfish. She always felt she was a failure, that
she hadn't done enough. Waves of pain and family shame and unworthiness flooded her. Then she realized she was trying to save the
world primarily as a way to feel better about herself. This was an
embarrassing insight, but her loving-kindness practice softened the
self-condemnation. Gradually her body and senses opened to the
Spanish moss on the trees, the rain-drenched mulch, the spring
frogs, the oak forest, the newborn fawns, the generations of children born of all mothers. She knew she could have a family and also
contribute to the world. This was a radical, true, unshakable knowing—she experienced her interconnection with life and the koan
fell away. Caring for her own life, she could care for the world; caring for the world, she could care for herself.

Like Lauren, many of us wrestle with our response to the sufferings of the world. What can we do in the face of poverty, disease, war, injustice, and environmental devastation? With the
torrent of world news, it is easy to despair, to become cynical or
numb. Our psychologies tend to treat this as a personal problem,
but it is not. We are all affected by the suffering of the world and
need to find a way to work with it. This is a pressing problem for
psychology. The Buddhist approach to this collective suffering is to
turn toward it. We understand that genuine happiness and meaning will come through tending to suffering. We overcome our own
despair by helping others to overcome theirs.

We might hear this and become afraid of being overwhelmed.
Or, like Lauren, our response might be confused with guilt,

unworthiness, and our need for personal healing. Still, even though our motivation is mixed, we have to respond. And we can. It is simple. Each of us can contribute to the sanity of the world. We can tend to ourself and we can tend to others. In doing so we discover the role of the bodhisattva.

THE BODHISATTVA

The problem with the world is that we draw our family circle too small.
—Mother Teresa

Bodhisattva is the Sanskrit word for a being who is devoted to awakening and to acting for the benefit of all that lives. The way of the bodhisattva is one of the most radical and powerful of all Buddhist forms of practice. It is radical because it states that the fulfillment of our happiness comes only from serving the welfare of others as well as ourself. Our highest happiness is connected with the well-being of others.

The bodhisattva's path is a striking contrast with the common Western modes of therapy that so often reflect the excessive individualism of our culture. Everything can get focused around me: my fears, my neurosis, my happiness, my needs, my boundaries. We can get so caught in our own drama that we stop our own growth. Reflective self-absorption can be valuable for a time, but we don't want to stop there. Therapists talk about how clients eventually become sick of listening to themselves, which is actually a good sign. It means we are moving beyond the identification with our personal suffering. We are ready to care for a world larger than our own.

Every wisdom tradition tells us that human meaning and happiness cannot be found in isolation but comes about through generosity, love, and understanding. The bodhisattva, knowing this, appears in a thousand forms, from a caring grandmother to the global citizen. Meditators often recite the bodhisattva vows when they sit, offering any benefit of their practice for the sake of others: "Sentient beings are numberless; I vow to bring liberation to us all." Like the ancient Hippocratic oath, the vow to serve the sick

taken by every physician, the bodhisattva vows to serve the welfare
of all. In a more poetic fashion, the Dalai Lama takes bodhisattva
vows based on the words of the beloved sixth-century sage
Shantideva:

May I be a guard for those who need protection
A guide for those on the path
A boat, a raft, a bridge for those who wish to cross the flood
May I be a lamp in the darkness
A resting place for the weary
A healing medicine for all who are sick
A vase of plenty, a tree of miracles
And for the boundless multitudes of living beings
May I bring sustenance and awakening
Enduring like the earth and sky
Until all beings are freed from sorrow
And all are awakened.

Psychologically this is an astonishing thing to say. Does this mean
that I am going to run around and save six billion humans and tril-
lions of other beings? How can I do so? When we think about it
from our limited sense of self, it is impossible. But when we make
it an intention of the heart, we understand. To take such a vow is a
direction, a sacred purpose, a statement of wisdom, an offering, a
blessing. When the world is seen with the eyes of a bodhisattva,
there is no I and other, there is just us.

The Dalai Lama serves as a source of love and strength to millions of oppressed Tibetans. His picture is secretly carried and hidden among sacred altars and he blesses and encourages them from
afar. But it is not just the Dalai Lama who supports others with his
bodhisattva vows. Those who care about us sustain us in ways that
transcend time and space. James Hillman, the Jungian analyst, has
described the plight of the Chinese dissident Liu Qing, who was
arrested as an activist for democracy and held in prison for eleven
years, forced by the guards to remain in silence all that time. If he
moved or talked, he was beaten. To be released he did not have to
implicate others; he only had to sign a statement saying that he had

made "errors in his thinking," to offer a simple admission of wrong ideas. Remarkably, Liu would not sign. He later explained that over the eleven years, whenever he wavered, he could see the faces of his family and friends before him and he knew he could not betray their trust. He was sustained by his visions of those who cared for him.

"We are not separate, we are interdependent," declares the Buddha. Even the most independent human being was once a helpless infant cared for by others. Ajahn Buddhadasa instructed all those in his forest temple to do a daily contemplation of interdependence. With each breath we interbreathe carbon dioxide and oxygen with the maple and oak, the dogwood and redwood trees of our biosphere. Our daily nourishment joins us with the rhythms of bees, caterpillars, and rhizomes; it connects our body with the collaborative dance of myriad species of plants and animals. Nothing is separate. Biologist Lewis Thomas explains, "The driving force in nature, on this kind of planet with this sort of biosphere, is cooperation. . . . The most inventive and novel of all schemes in nature, and perhaps the most significant in determining the great landmark events in evolution, is symbiosis, which is simply cooperative behavior carried to its extreme."

Unless we understand this, we are split between caring for ourselves or caring for the troubles of the world. "I arise in the morning," wrote essayist E. B. White, "torn between a desire to save the world and an inclination to savor it." A psychology of interdependence helps to solve this dilemma. Through meditation we discover that the duality of inner and outer is false. Thus when Gandhi was lauded for all his work for India, he demurred, "I do not do this for India, I do this for myself."

This is a twenty-third principle of Buddhist psychology:

---

23   There is no separation between inner and outer, self and other. Tending ourselves, we tend the world. Tending the world, we tend ourselves.

A LIFE OF BALANCE: TURN OFF THE NEWS

In some form, the vision of the bodhisattva is celebrated in every culture. We revere the figures of St. Francis and Kwan Yin and we take public inspiration from the medical mission of Albert Schweitzer in Africa and Dorothy Day, the founder of the Catholic Worker movement. But following the bodhisattva way does not require us to become a monk like St. Francis or to work in Central Africa like Albert Schweitzer. It is based on the truth that we can transform our own circumstances into a life of inner and outer service. To do this without being overwhelmed, the bodhisattva creates a life of balance.

This is eminently practical. If we want to act wisely in the world, the first step is to learn to quiet the mind. If our actions are born from anger, grasping, fear, and aggression, they will perpetuate the problems. How many revolutions have overthrown oppressive regimes, to then turn around and become the new oppressors? Only when our own minds and hearts are peaceful can we expect peace to come through the actions we take.

To understand this integration of inner and outer, we can again look at the life of Gandhi. Even during the most turbulent years, when he was dismantling the British Empire's control of India, Gandhi spent one day a week in silence. He meditated so that he could act from the principles of interdependence, not bringing harm to himself nor another. No matter how pressing and urgent the political situation, the day he spent in silence allowed him to quiet his mind and listen to the purest intentions of his heart.

If you want to live a life of balance, start now. Turn off the news, meditate, turn on Mozart, walk through the trees or the mountains, and begin to make yourself a zone of peace. When I return from a long retreat or from traveling for months, I'm amazed that the news is pretty much the same as when I left. We already know the plot, we know the problems. Let go of the latest current story. Listen more deeply.

Zen master Thich Nhat Hanh explains how this inner quiet serves our political lives: "When the crowded refugee boats full of families fleeing Vietnam met with storms or pirates, if everyone panicked, all would be lost. But if even one person on the boat stayed calm, it was enough. It showed the way for everyone to survive." When we react to insecurity and terrorism with fear we worsen the problem, we create a frightened, barricaded society— a fortress America. Instead we can use courage and compassion to respond calmly, with both prudent action and a fearless heart.

The quieting of our mind is a political act. The world does not need more oil or energy or food. It needs less greed, less hatred, less ignorance. Even if we have inwardly taken on the political bitterness or cynicism that exists externally, we can stop and begin to heal our own suffering, our own fear, with compassion. Through meditation and inner transformation, we can learn to make our own hearts a place of peace and integrity. Each of us knows how to do this. As Gandhi acknowledged, "I have nothing new to teach the world. Truth and non-violence are as old as the hills." It is our inner nobility and steadiness that we must call on in our personal and collective difficulties.

FACING THE TRUTH

Once we learn to quiet our mind, the second step for the bodhisattva is seeing the truth. We deliberately turn toward the difficulties of the world and shine the light of understanding. "The enemy," said Ajahn Chah, "is delusion." Delusion blames others, creates enemies, and fosters separation. The truth is that we are not separate. War, economic injustice, racism, and environmental destruction stem from the illusion of separateness. It is delusion that separates us from other human tribes and from the trees and the oceans on this increasingly small planet. When we look truthfully, we can also see that no amount of material and scientific advancement will solve our problems alone. New computer networks, innovative fuels, and biological advances can just as easily be diverted to create new weapons, exacerbate conflicts, and speed environmental degradation. Economic and political change will fail unless we also find a way to transform our consciousness. It is a delusion

that endless greed and profit, hatred and war will somehow protect us and bring us happiness.

More than half a century ago, President Dwight Eisenhower,
who had been the supreme Allied commander during World War
II, gave a remarkable address just before he left office. Eisenhower,
the world's most respected military man, spoke out against the
madness and unchecked growth of the defense industry worldwide. "Every gun that is made, every warship launched, every
rocket fired signifies, in the final sense, a theft from those who
hunger and are not fed, those who are cold and are not clothed.
This world in arms is not spending money alone. It is spending the
sweat of its laborers, the genius of its scientists, the hopes of its children. . . . This is not a way of life at all, in any true sense. Under
the cloud of threatening war, it is humanity hanging from a cross
of iron."

President Eisenhower also spoke of the immense cost of
the military-industrial complex, which, like the prison-industrial
complex and the foreign policy–power complex, chooses power
and profit instead of compassion. We must learn that this will not
make us safe. Collective well-being arises when we govern by
wisdom and loving-kindness instead of fear. "Human beings should
refrain from causing harm to one another and not allow their actions to be based on hatred and greed," said the Buddha, in words
that speak directly to modern times. "They should refrain from
killing, from stealing. They should refrain from occupations that
bring suffering, from weapons trade, from any actions that bring
the enslavement of others." Through these words, he was not proclaiming a religious code. He was providing a social psychology for
the happiness of individuals and the collective.

In facing the truth, the bodhisattva deliberately bears witness
to our personal and collective suffering with compassion. The
power of such witness was revealed to an amazed world by the operation of the Truth and Reconciliation Commission in South
Africa, which for more than two years broadcast accounts of per-
petrators and victims alike. The truth telling and revelation of so
many destructive acts committed during the apartheid era did not

stir hatred and retaliation, but somehow brought healing and calm to the suffering of the nation. It is a testament to the power of truth to allow a community to rebuild itself after so much devastation. The Reverend Bongani Finca was one of the fifteen commissioners who conducted the South African hearings. He describes how, in spite of the past atrocities and cruelty, victims and survivors wanted to find reconciliation. "I remember hearing the testimony of the daughter of one of the four gentlemen killed in Cradock, a girl who was 16 years old. She said, 'I want to forgive. But I do not know whom to forgive. If only I could know who did what to my father, I would like to forgive.' This was such a moving testimony by a young person who, at that age, we would expect to be so bitter. But there was no bitterness. Often the attitudes and responses of the victims to the Truth Commission were just amazing. It was an indication of the fact that the people who have suffered most become so generous in spirit, for some strange reason."

In the end, the unarmed truth will come out. It will be whispered in the alleyways, canonized by our poets, held in the hearts of all those who care. Martin Luther King Jr. said, "I still believe that standing up for the unarmed truth is the greatest thing in the world. This is the end of life. The end of life is not to achieve pleasure and avoid pain. The end of life is to do the will of God, come what may." These words describe the moral and psychological power that steps out of delusion and tells us the truth.

ENVISION LIBERATION AND JUSTICE

After we quiet the mind and face what is true, the next step of the boddhisattva's way is to envision liberation from suffering for ourselves, our community, and the world. Envisioning has enormous power. With our vision and imagination we can help create the future. Envisioning sets our direction, marshals our resources, makes the unmanifest possible. A boddhisattva's vision is the necessary step toward transformation of the world. We must courageously envision a world where all children have proper care and food, where instead of an arms race our creative efforts are put into conflict resolution. We must see how individuals of all castes, tribes, races, and orientations can be treated with equal respect and opportunity.

In the Buddhist texts, the bodhisattva Vimalakirti is a wild figure who exemplifies this courage. Among the wisest of beings, he deliberately seeks out the difficulties of the world and magically transforms himself to help teach there. Vimalakirti makes himself sick to teach the healers in the hospitals how to practice the path of awakening as they work. He enters the markets as a businessman and the taverns to drink. As he tends to others, he demonstrates that happiness and freedom are possible for all he meets. He uses each circumstance as the perfect place to teach the path of awakening.

Do not confuse Buddhism with withdrawal from the world. The Buddhist teachings about wise society and wise leadership are taught from childhood onward throughout the Buddhist world. In hundreds of popular tales, the Buddha-to-be often appears as a prince or an animal. In one story, the Buddha-to-be is born as a Banyan deer king who nobly offers his life to a human king in place of a pregnant doe that has been caught. His gesture so inspires the human king that the hunting of deer and other forest animals is forbidden throughout the kingdom. In another story, the Buddha-to-be is born as a small parrot, who tries to save the animals around him from a forest fire. Repeatedly dousing his wings with river water, he flies into the great flames to find and wet his frightened friends. His bravery touches the heart of the rain god, whose tears fall, quenching the flames and rescuing all the creatures from a fiery death. For those who grow up in a Buddhist culture, these beloved tales of wise leadership are recounted a thousand times.

At a more sophisticated level, Buddhist psychology shows how training in mindfulness, integrity, generosity, and respect can create a healthy society. From village schools to community meetings, Buddhist practices of right speech, right action, and right livelihood foster moral character and the creation of harmony.

Buddhist temples model this psychology. They are among the oldest living social institutions in the world. For over two thousand years, temples have served as seats of education and service, offering help with community government, community projects, social organization, and the mediation of disputes. Villagers go to the monasteries to be reminded of this healthy way to live, and the whole society is nurtured and benefited by the example of the monks and nuns. Today the Southeast Asian environmental crisis has led Burmese and Thai monks to turn their forest monasteries into wild animal sanctuaries to help preserve the remaining tigers. In Cambodia monks and nuns run addiction treatment centers and AIDS hospitals. In Thailand monks wrap their robes around the most ancient trees to "ordain them" and save thousands of acres of disappearing forest.

Even when there is conflict in the monastery, it is dealt with as a practice. There are councils of reconciliation, vows of non-harming, trainings in mindful listening, and formal methods of confession, repentance, and release. The work of both Gandhi and Martin Luther King Jr. was founded on these principles, on *ahimsa*—or non-harming—as a path to happiness.

The Buddha applied these principles quite directly. Denouncing the caste system, he created an alternative society based on equal respect for every human being. Once a local king sent his chief minister to seek the Buddha's advice about starting a war with the Vajjians. The Buddha responded with a series of question. "Do the Vajjians come together in regular and frequent assembly?" "They do, sir." "Do they honor their elders and the wise ways they have established?" "They do, sir." "Do they care for their most vulnerable members—women and children?" "They do, sir." "Do they respect the nature shrines and holy places and listen respectfully to their citizens and neighbors?" "They do, sir." "Then the Vajjians can be expected to prosper and not decline. In fact, if any society does so," explained the Buddha, "it can be expected to prosper and not decline." The minister returned with these words and the king decided to abandon his plans for war.

There is much for us to learn from these words. If we meet together in harmony and respect, care for the vulnerable among us, tend to the environment, and respect our citizens and neighbors, we will thrive and prosper. A strong and stable society arises through mutual generosity, not gross inequity. These teachings are surprisingly modern. In the Long Discourses, the Buddha states that poverty gives rise to theft, violence, and other crimes. He states that simple punishment alone cannot suppress crime. Instead he teaches us to transform the causes. "The economic conditions of the people should be improved: seed grain and help should be available to farmers, support provided for business people, adequate wages paid to workers. When the people are thus provided for, there will be contentment, and the country will be peaceful and free from crime." This is not just an idealistic vision. It is a practical way for happiness to prevail.

TENDING THE WORLD

Somewhere I have saved an old photo from the front page of the *Manila Times* in 1967. I was in my Peace Corps training at San Lazaro Hospital in the Philippines. In the photo I stand alone in front of the U.S. embassy, holding a big peace sign in a one-man demonstration against the war in Vietnam. It was the day of a huge antiwar rally in Washington and I wanted to be part of it. I thought I knew enough about Vietnam to see that we were wrong to intervene, that we were simply perpetuating the mistakes of the French colonialists before us. My first years of traveling in Thailand, Laos, and Vietnam reinforced this view, as did many of the soldiers I talked to.

Of course, the reality turned out to be more complex than I could have known. I later met people who had suffered horribly under the North Vietnamese Communists, people who were beaten in dismal camps and tortured for ideological retaliation. Similarly, I met many who had lost family members and suffered terribly under the South Vietnamese Diem regime. Up close, everyone had a compelling story. They wanted you to understand and take their side. What is certain is that there are no smug answers. Now I approach activism with a wholly different understanding. I try to bring respect to everyone involved. I'm not so stuck on my position. Instead of creating scapegoats, instead of seeing some people as all wrong and others as all right, I see suffering growing out of the powerful energies of delusion and ignorance. When I take action I do not want to add my own arrogance or aggression to our conflicts.

When Zen master Thich Nhat Hanh took a stand for peace in the 1960s in Vietnam, he understood that true peace would grow only from building schools and hospitals, not from taking sides. His book *Lotus in a Sea of Fire* described how the Young Buddhist Service Movement, which he helped to found, chose to support everyone, regardless of their politics. Martin Luther King Jr. was so inspired by this work he nominated Thich Nhat Hanh for the Nobel Peace Prize. But back in Vietnam because the Young Buddhists refused to swear allegiance to either the Northern or Southern faction, they were considered a threat by each faction. "If you're not with us, you must be with the enemy." Many of the Young Buddhists were killed by both sides. In spite of these deaths, Thich Nhat Hanh and his colleagues continued their work. A bodhisattva commits to heal suffering undaunted by outward periods of failure and success.

One of the stories from the Buddha's own life concerns the hostilities between the neighboring countries of Magadha and Kapilavatthu, where the Buddha's own Shakya clan lived. When the Shakya people realized that the king of Magadha was planning to attack, they implored the Buddha to step forward and make peace. The Buddha agreed. But although he offered many proposals for peace, the king of Magadha could not hear them. His mind would not stop burning, and finally he decided to attack.

So the Buddha went out by himself and sat in meditation under a dead tree by the side of the road leading to Kapilavatthu. The king of Magadha passed along the road with his army and saw the Buddha sitting under the dead tree in the full blast of the sun. So the king asked, "Why do you sit under this dead tree?" The Buddha answered the king, "I feel cool, even under this dead tree, because it is growing in my beautiful native country." This answer pierced the heart of the king. Recognizing the commitment and dedication the Shakyas felt for their land, he returned to his country with his army. Later, however, this same king was again incited to war. This time, Shakyamuni Buddha could not stop the conflict, and the Magadhan army destroyed Kapilavatthu.

We cannot control the outcome of our actions. Still, we can turn toward the world, plant good seeds, and trust that they will eventually bear fruit. Whenever a few people are committed to the vision of a free and just humanity, transformation can happen, despite the greatest odds. The story of one such amazing transformation is told in *Bury the Chains,* by Adam Hochschild. Hochschild's account begins in 1787, with the meeting of just a dozen men in a London printer's shop, gathered to consider the evils of slavery. The Caribbean slave trade was the economic underpinning of the entire British Empire, but these men chose to envision an empire without slavery. The key protagonist was Thomas Clarkson, who joined together with a small group of other dedicated abolitionists, especially Quakers, to change the society's views on slavery.

These few men began a long, deliberate campaign. Clarkson himself rode on horseback thirty thousand miles around England over several decades in service of this vision. He brought a few ex-slaves who were well educated and articulate, who spoke of the horror of their experiences, into the parlors and the meeting houses of British folk. By 1833, this small group had succeeded in getting Parliament to pass a law outlawing slavery in the British Empire, which in turn catalyzed the process of ending slavery around the world.

Hochschild tells us that the Quakers of the time refused to take their hats off to King George or to any king other than God. But when Clarkson died, even the Quakers took their hats off to honor what he had done for humanity.

We are limited only by our imagination. Yes, there will always be a shadow. Yes, greed and fear and ignorance will be part of our psychology. But there are ways we can live wisely. For the bodhisattva, raising a family, running a conscious business, and righting an injustice all can contribute to the fabric of the whole. Every one of us can sense this potential. Human beings can live with more compassion, with more care for one another, with less prejudice and racism and fear. There are wise ways of solving conflict that await our hands and hearts.

PRACTICE: BODHISATTVA VOWS

Consider undertaking the vows and practice of a bodhisattva. In taking these vows you will join with the millions of Buddhists who have done so. As is traditional, you might seek out a Buddhist center or temple and take the bodhisattva vows in the presence of a teacher. Or, if you cannot do so, you can take them at home. Create a sacred space and place there the images of bodhisattvas or Buddhas who have gone before you. If you wish, invite a friend or friends to be your witness. Sit quietly for a time and reflect on the beauty and value of a life dedicated to the benefit of all. When you are ready, add any meaningful ritual, such as the lighting of candles or the taking of refuge. Then recite your vows. Here is one traditional version, but there are many others:

> *Suffering beings are numberless, I vow to liberate them all.*
> *Attachment is inexhaustible, I vow to release it all.*
> *The gates to truth are numberless, I vow to master them all.*
> *The ways of awakening are supreme, I vow to realize them all.*

You can change the wording of these vows so that they speak your deepest dedication. Then you can repeat them every time you sit in meditation, to direct and dedicate your practice.

23

THE WISDOM OF THE MIDDLE WAY

At one time I had wanted to find someplace where I could take shelter, but I never
saw any such place. There is nothing in this world that is solid at base
and not a part of it that is changeless.
—Sutta Nipata

Hence the purpose of Holy Life does not consist in acquiring merit, honor, or
fame, nor in gaining morality, concentration, or the eye of knowledge. That
unshakable deliverance, the sure heart's release, that indeed is the object
of the Holy Life, that is its essence, that is its goal.
—Majjhima Nikaya

Buddhist psychology is neither a path of denial nor of affirmation. It shows us the paradox of the universe, within and beyond the opposites. It teaches us to be *in* the world but not *of* the world. This realization is called the middle way. Ajahn Chah talked about the middle way every day. In the monastery we contemplated the middle way. At twilight, a hundred monks could be found seated in the open-air meditation pavilion, surrounded by the towering trees and dense green forest, reciting these original verses: "There is a middle way between the extremes of indulgence and self-denial, free from sorrow and suffering. This is the way to peace and liberation in this very life."

If we seek happiness purely through indulgence, we are not free. If we fight against ourselves and reject the world, we are not free. It is the middle path that brings freedom. This is a universal truth discovered by all those who awaken. "It is as if while traveling through a great forest, one should come upon an ancient path, an ancient road traversed by people of former days. . . . Even so have I, monks, seen an ancient path, an ancient road traversed by the rightly enlightened ones of former times," said the Buddha.

The middle way describes the middle ground between attachment and aversion, between being and non-being, between form and emptiness, between free will and determinism. The more we delve into the middle way the more deeply we come to rest between the play of opposites. Sometimes Ajahn Chah described it like a koan, where "there is neither going forward, nor going backward, nor standing still." To discover the middle way, he went on, "Try to be mindful, and let things take their natural course. Then your mind will become still in any surroundings, like a clear forest pool. All kinds of wonderful, rare animals will come to drink at the pool, and you will clearly see the nature of all things. You will see many strange and wonderful things come and go, but you will be still. This is the happiness of the Buddha."

Learning to rest in the middle way requires trust in life itself. It is like learning to swim. I remember first taking swimming lessons when I was seven years old. I was a skinny, shivering boy flailing around, trying to stay afloat in a cold pool. But one morning there came a magical moment lying on my back when I was held by the teacher and then released. I realized that the water would hold me, that I could float. I began to trust. Trusting in the middle way, there is an ease and grace, a cellular knowing that we too can float in the ever-changing ocean of life that has always held us.

Buddhist teaching invites us to discover this ease everywhere: in meditation, in the marketplace, wherever we are. In the middle way, we come to rest in the reality of the present, where all the opposites exist. T. S. Eliot calls this the "still point of the turning world. Neither flesh nor fleshless;/Neither from nor towards; . . . neither arrest nor movement." The sage Shantideva calls the middle way "complete non-referential ease." The Perfect Wisdom Text describes it as "realization of suchness beyond attainment of good or bad, ever present with all things, as both the path and the goal."

What do these mysterious words mean? They are attempts to describe the joyful experience of moving out of time, out of gaining or losing, out of duality. They describe the ability to live in the reality of the present. As one teacher put it, "The middle path does not go from here to there. It goes from there to here." The middle path describes the presence of eternity. In the reality of the present, life is clear, vivid, awake, empty and yet filled with possibility.

When we discover the middle path, we neither remove ourselves from the world nor get lost in it. We can be with all our experience in its complexity, with our own exact thoughts and feelings and drama. We learn to embrace tension, paradox, change. Instead of seeking resolution, waiting for the chord at the end of a song, we let ourselves open and relax in the middle. In the middle we discover that the world is workable. Ajahn Sumedo teaches us to open to the way things are: "Of course we can always imagine more perfect conditions, how it should be ideally, how everyone else should behave. But it's not our task to create an ideal. It's our task to see how it is, and to learn from the world as it is. For the awakening of the heart, conditions are always good enough."

Here is a twenty-fourth principle of Buddhist psychology:

---

24   The middle way is found between all opposites. Rest in the middle and find well-being wherever you are.

Ginger was a fifty-one-year-old social worker who had worked for years in a clinic in California's Central Valley. A committed meditator, she took a month off to come to our spring retreat. At first it was hard for her to quiet her mind. Her beloved younger brother had reentered the psych ward where he had first been hospitalized for a schizophrenic break. She told me she was awash in emotion, overwhelmed by fear, confusion, shakiness, anger, and grief. I counseled her to let it all be, to just sit and walk on the earth and let things settle in their own time. But as she sat, the feelings and stories got stronger. I recited to her Ajahn Chah's teaching of sitting like a clear forest pool. I encouraged her to acknowledge, one by one, all the inner wild animals that came to drink at the pool.

She began to name them: fear of loss of control, fear of death, fear of living fully, grief and clinging to a previous relationship, longing for a partner but wanting to be independent, fear for her brother, anxiety about money, anger at the health care system she had to battle every day at her job, gratitude for her co-workers.

I invited her to sit in the middle of it all, the paradox, the messiness, the hopes and fears. "Take your seat like a queen on the throne," I said, "and allow the play of life, the joys and sorrows, the fears and confusions, the birth and death around you. Don't think you have to fix it."

Ginger practiced, sitting and walking, allowing it all to be. As the intense feelings continued to come and go, she relaxed and gradually she became more still and present. Her meditation felt more spacious; the strong states and feelings that arose seemed like impersonal waves of energy. Her body became lighter, and joy arose. Two days later things got worse. She came down with the flu, she felt extremely weak and unsafe, and she became depressed. Because Ginger also had hepatitis C, she worried that her body would never be strong enough to meditate well or live with ease.

I reminded her about sitting in the middle of it all, and she came the next day, still and happy again. She said, "I've returned to the center. I'm not going to let my past karma and these obstacles rob me of my presence." She laughed and went on, "Like the Buddha, I realized, 'Oh, this is just Mara.' I just say, 'I see you, Mara.' Mara can be my grief or my hopes, my body pain or my fear. All of it is just life, and the middle way is so deep, it's all of them and none of them. It's always here."

I've seen Ginger now over several years since she left the

retreat. Her outer circumstances have not really improved. Her work, her brother, and her health are all difficulties she continues to face. But her heart is more at ease. She sits quietly almost every day in the messiness of her life. Ginger tells me her meditation has helped her find the middle path and the inner freedom she hoped for.

AT EASE WITH INSECURITY

Security is mostly a superstition. It does not exist in nature, nor do children as a whole experience it. Avoiding danger is not safer in the long run than outright exposure. Life is either a daring adventure or nothing.
—Helen Keller

One day Ajahn Chah held up a beautiful Chinese teacup. "To me this cup is already broken. Because I know its fate, I can enjoy it fully here and now. And when it's gone, it's gone." When we understand the truth of uncertainty and relax, we become free.

The broken cup helps us see beyond our illusion of control. When we commit ourselves to raising a child, building a business, creating a work of art, or righting an injustice, some measure of failure as well as success will be ours. This is a fierce teaching. Emilee is an aid worker whose clinic in Kosovo was burned to the ground, yet she began again. She knows that her work is helping people through success and failure. Rosa, who lost her most promising math student to a gang shooting, was brokenhearted. But she doesn't regret having tutored him, and now she is tutoring several others in his honor.

We may lose our best piece of pottery in the firing, the charter school we work so hard to create may fold, our start-up business may go under, our children may develop problems beyond our control. If we focus only on the results, we will be devastated. But if we know the cup is broken, we can give our best to the process, create what we can, and trust the larger process of life itself. We can plan, care for, tend, and respond. But we cannot control. Instead we take a breath, and open to what is unfolding, where we are. This is a profound shift, from holding on, to letting go. As Shunryu Suzuki says, "When we understand the truth of impermanence and find our composure in it, there we find ourselves in nirvana."

When people asked Ajahn Chah questions about enlightenment, or what happens at death, or whether meditation would heal their illness, or whether Buddhist teachings could be practiced equally by Westerners, he would smile and say, "It's uncertain, isn't it?" Chögyam Trungpa called this uncertainty "groundlessness." With the wisdom of uncertainty, Ajahn Chah could simply relax. Around him was an enormous sense of ease. He didn't hold his breath or try to manipulate events. He responded to the situation at hand. When a senior Western nun left the Buddhist order to become a born-again Christian missionary and then returned to the monastery to try to convert her old friends, many were upset: "How could she do this?" Confused, they asked Ajahn Chah about her. He responded with a laugh, "Maybe she's right." With these words, everyone relaxed. Yet in the midst of uncertainty Ajahn Chah could also act. He could plan the construction of a great temple or oversee the network of more than a hundred monasteries started by his monks. When disciplining misbehaving monks, he could be decisive, demanding, and stern. But there was a spaciousness around all these actions, as if he could turn to you a moment later and smile—like a wink—and say, "It's uncertain, isn't it?" He was living proof of the secret of life described in the Bhagavad Gita: "to act well without attachment to the fruits of your actions."

The trust expressed by Ajahn Chah comes whenever our consciousness rests in the eternal present. "From where I sit," he said, "no one comes and no one goes. Resting in the middle way, there is no one who is strong or weak, young or old, no one who is born and no one who dies. This is the unconditioned. The heart is free." The ancient Zen masters call this the liberation of the trusting mind. How do we achieve this wisdom? As the Zen texts explain, "To live in trusting mind is to be without anxiety about nonperfection." The world is "imperfect." Instead of struggling to perfect the world, we relax, we rest in the uncertainty. Then we can act with compassion and give our best without attachment to the outcome. We can bring fearlessness and trust to any circumstances.

When Chas began Buddhist practice, the Internet company he worked for was in trouble. His marriage felt stale. And he still suffered the effects of growing up with his father's long-term depression. He looked to meditation training to help him with his anxiety about the future, the insecurity in his marriage, and how often he felt disconnected from himself.

Chas also had a deeply mystical sense of the world. One of the most important moments in his adult life came in a dream about Katie, his youngest daughter. At age four, Katie was hospitalized for viral meningitis and went into a coma. Chas and his wife spent their days at her bedside. The doctors were cautious about her chances of recovery. After five weeks of no change and endless worrying, Katie came to Chas in a dream and told him, "Don't worry, Daddy, it's all OK." The next morning as Chas walked into Katie's room, she opened her eyes and smiled at him. Now she is a healthy teenager.

Chas had glimpsed the truth that there is a grace beyond all our plans. Learning meditation reawakened this trust in him. With mindfulness his stress lifted and he began to feel his body and his senses open. In one sitting Chas said his body felt like tall, graceful kelp floating beneath the waves. His feelings of being stuck and anxious transformed into moments of interest, curiosity, and appreciation. He became less worried, more present—more "juicy," he called it. "Letting go of my fears is like removing an overcoat of self. When thoughts and problems that I can't solve arise, they don't stick. I rest like kelp in the ocean, in the trusting mind." Periodically Chas said he forgets this and his insecurity returns. The worrying mind takes hold. Should he stay in his marriage? Should he continue in an uncertain job? Then he remembers the dream of his daughter, and Chas relaxes and trusts the not knowing. "Every marriage and every job is insecure if we are honest," he said.

Eight years later Chas is still in his marriage and still working at a now successful Internet company. His meditation has taught him a trust that is not separate from the insecurity and paradox of life itself.

Here is a twenty-fifth principle of Buddhist psychology:

---

25 Release opinions, free yourself from views. Be open to mystery.

FREE FROM VIEWS

The emergence and blossoming of understanding, love and intelligence has nothing to do with any tradition, no matter how ancient or impressive—it has nothing to do with time. It happens completely on its own when a human being questions, wonders, listens and looks without getting stuck in fear, pleasure and pain. When self-concern is quiet, in abeyance, heaven and earth are open.
—Toni Packer

The wisdom of uncertainty frees us from what Buddhist psychology calls the thicket of views and opinions. "Seeing misery in those who cling to views, a wise person should not adopt any of them. A wise person does not by opinions become arrogant. How could anyone bother those who are free, who do not grasp at any views? But those who grasp after views and opinions wander about the world annoying people." I like to think that the Buddha said this last sentence with a laugh. Ajahn Chah used to shake his head and smile, "You have so many opinions. And you suffer so much from them. Why not let them go?" I have noticed that when people come on retreat at Spirit Rock they are grateful to step out of the din of political pundits, talk radio, bumper stickers, and the good old American right to have your own opinion.

Freedom from views is like a cleaning of the glass, a breath of fresh air. Zen master Shunryu Suzuki calls this open-mindedness "beginner's mind." Listen to Rachel Carson, the great naturalist, as she evokes it: "A child's world is fresh and new and beautiful, full of wonder and excitement. It is our misfortune that for most of us that clear-eyed vision, that true instinct for what is beautiful and awe-inspiring, is dimmed and even lost before we reach adulthood.

If I had influence with the good fairy who is supposed to preside over all children, I should ask that her gift to each child in the world be a sense of wonder so indestructible that it would last throughout life."

When we are free from views, we are willing to learn. What we know for sure in this great turning universe is actually very limited. Seung Sahn, a Korean Zen master, tells us to value this "don't-know mind." He would ask his students questions such as "What is love? What is consciousness? Where did your life come from? What is going to happen tomorrow?" Each time, the students would answer, "I don't know." "Good," Seung Sahn replied. "Keep this 'don't-know mind.' It is an open mind, a clear mind."

I love this story told by the mother of a five-year-old girl. The child had taken a stethoscope out of her mother's doctor bag and was playing with it. As she put the stethoscope to her ears, her mother thought proudly, *She seems interested in medicine. Maybe she will grow up and become a doctor like me.* After a time the little girl put the listening end of the stethoscope up to her mouth and exclaimed, "Welcome to McDonald's. May I take your order, please?" At this, the mother had to laugh with her daughter, and smiled to herself about how easily we can project our ideas on one another.

In close relationships, if we rely on assumptions, we lose our freshness. Whether as parents or lovers, what we see about those close to us is only a small part of their mystery. In many ways we don't really know them at all. Through beginner's mind we learn to see one another mindfully, free from views. Without views, we listen more deeply and see more clearly. "For there are moments," says Rilke, "when something new has entered into us, something unknown; our feelings grow mute in shy perplexity, everything in us withdraws, a stillness comes, and the new, which no one knows, stands in the midst of it and is silent."

Aliveness is one of the hallmarks of a mindful psychology. Many years ago, Buddhist teacher and psychiatrist Robert Hall arranged for his mentor, Fritz Perls, to speak at the annual conference of the American Psychiatric Association. Perls had been a disciple of Freud but had broken with the focus on the past that was common in psychoanalysis. He introduced a new approach called Gestalt therapy. Influenced in part by Zen, Gestalt therapy focused on aliveness, here and now. Perls' approach was viewed with great suspicion by traditional psychiatry. But at the conference, over a thousand doctors came to see what he had to say. Perls did not present a traditional case history—instead he asked for volunteers to work with him on the stage. None of the doctors raised their hands, but one woman, a psychiatric assistant named Linda, volunteered.

Linda sat in a chair across from Perls. He began by asking how she was feeling in the moment. She talked about being anxious in front of so many people and how she wanted his help with a difficult romantic relationship. She lit a cigarette. As she talked, she held the box of matches in her lap, nervously opening and closing it. Perls noticed this small movement and asked her to exaggerate it. As she slid the box open and closed, he had her speak about what she was experiencing. First she talked about how hard it was to open (herself), and then, within a minute, the matchbox became her father's coffin. She was overcome with tears and the unfinished grief from his sudden death poured out. Perls helped her to stay present. Then she talked about her difficult relationship and once again her tears poured out. Within a few minutes, Linda realized how much of her current anxiety and struggle was fear of another loss. Her healing began as Perls helped her to listen openly to what was within.

Such listening is never more powerful than when we are face-to-face with the mystery of death. When we sit with those who are dying, the only way to be helpful is to come with no agenda. Sometimes dying people weep and grieve. Sometimes they are filled with love. Sometimes they struggle. Those around them can also be caught in anger, grief, fear, or blame. As companions to the dying, we are most helpful if we can maintain an open mind and heart, bowing to their experience, without any judgment. And often, when the person's whole experience is allowed, everyone present relaxes into the luminous mystery.

Buddhist hospice volunteers are trained to sit with the dying, to talk and listen, even when outwardly it appears that the patient is confused or unresponsive. Stephen and Ondrea Levine, pioneers in

this work, have documented that even when people are apparently
lost in a coma, they are listening. Consider this account by Arnold
Mindell, a Jungian psychiatrist. In an interview with Stephan Bodian,
he describes how he sits and breathes in unison with his patients as
a way to connect his consciousness with theirs. He tells about visiting an old man in a Veterans Administration hospital.

*John had been lying in a coma for six months, rasping and making
lots of noise and waking up all the other patients. I went to see him
and made noises with him while gently squeezing his hand. After
about ten minutes, he opened his eyes and said, "You saw that too?"
I said, "I did see it. What do you see?" "A big white ship is a-comin'
for John!" "Are you going to take it?" I asked. "Not me," he yelled.
"I'm not gettin' on that ship." "Why not?" I asked. "That ship's goin'
on vacation, it's a cruise ship. I gotta get up in the morning and go
to work."*

*John had worked hard all his life and was now in his 80's. His
cancer had reduced him to a bag of bones. He was stuck at the end
of life because he couldn't allow himself to go on vacation. So I told
him, "Well, getting up in the morning and going to work sounds
good to me. But before we do it, let's check the ship out. Take a look
inside and see who's driving that ship." So he went down into the
ship and said with great excitement, "Whew! There's angels down
there driving that ship." "Do you want to find out where it's going?"
I asked. He went inside again and turned his eyes to the right, apparently listening to something. "That ship is a-goin' to Bermuda."
"Well, what's it cost?" I said, knowing he was a practical guy. After
a minute he said, "It don't cost nothin'." "Think about it," I said.
"Ever have a vacation?" "I never had a vacation. Never. I've been
workin' and workin' and workin'." "Well, think about it. Make your
choice." Finally, he said, "I'm goin' on vacation. It don't cost
nothin', and it's goin' to Bermuda." I said, "Chances are, if you don't
like it, maybe it'll turn around and come back." "Yeah, I can always
get off that ship." "You do what you want," I said. "I'll trust your
judgment. I'm busy and have to go see somebody else now." So he
closed his eyes and that was it. When we came back 30 minutes later
he had died. He'd gone to Bermuda.*

OPEN TO MYSTERY

Marcel Proust once said, "The voyage of discovery lies not in finding new landscapes, but in having new eyes." Buddhist practice gives us new eyes. It offers an invitation to awe. Several years ago the great Hubble space telescope was turned toward the darkest square inch in the sky to collect any stray light that happened to appear. To their amazement, astronomers found in that square inch images of a billion distant, unseen galaxies. Equally amazing, when we turn our lens from the largest to the smallest, we see cells, molecules, atoms, subatomic particles, and energy—an astonishing universe unfolds, as vast as a galaxy in each grain of sand. Looking in yet another direction, microbiologists see that one tablespoon of rich soil contains a billion life-forms—insects, bacteria, fungi—all living and dying in a vast collaboration that forms the planetary web of life.

What is most amazing of all is that we can spend days, even months taking the mystery for granted. Of course, our automatic habits serve us and help us function. We might have a hard time functioning if we were in a constant state of awe. But the all too common deadening of our senses is far from the middle path. As naturalist Annie Dillard reminds us, "If the landscape reveals one certainty, it is that the extravagant gesture is the very stuff of creation. After the one extravagant gesture of creation in the first place, the universe has continued to deal exclusively in extravagances, flinging intricacies and colossi down aeons of emptiness. . . . The whole show has been on fire from the word go."

We are a part of this mystery. Our eyeballs and eardrums, our voices and emotions, our delusion and awakening are woven together with, contained within, the mystery. We not only are witness to this mystery, we *are* the mystery looking at itself.

People who come to Buddhist practice hope that it will help them with the ordinary sufferings of their life, and often it will. But a deeper current flows through Buddhist teachings. When I sit with students, I do not just want to help them solve their problems. I want to find a moment with each person where their mind stops and their eyes open. I want us to be together as if we were lying in a field on the underside of the earth on a clear summer night, held only by the magnet of gravity, looking down into a bottomless sea of stars. I want us to remember together the beauty all around us. Patricia comes in sick and frightened, but if she can let go and sense the precious and ephemeral dance of her days on this timeless earth, it is a blessing. If Jelan can step out of being the injured child and appreciate the mysterious dance that led to his adoption and current search for his birth mother, his heart becomes wise. If Marylinda can release her worries about retirement and sense the grace that has carried her and her children for twenty-four years, then our work is a success.

PLANTING SEEDS ON THE MIDDLE PATH

Though I do not believe a plant will spring up where no seed has been, I have great faith in a seed. Convince me you have a seed there, and I am prepared to expect wonders.
—Thoreau

A. T. Ariyaratne, a former schoolteacher and Buddhist elder, is considered the Gandhi of Sri Lanka. He refuses to take sides in any form of conflict; his life is an expression of the middle way. For over two decades there has been a devastating civil war in Sri Lanka. In 2002, the Norwegians brokered a peace agreement. With the peace treaty in effect, Ariyaratne called the followers of his Sarvodaya movement together to support the peace. The Sarvodaya movement has used Buddhist principles of right action to organize one-third of the nation's villages to dig wells, build schools, and work collaboratively as a form of spiritual practice. Upon Ariyaratne's invitation, a huge gathering of 650,000 Sarvodaya members came to hear his vision for the future of Sri Lanka. Speaking to his followers and the nation, Ariyaratne proposed a five-hundred-year peace plan. "Buddhist teachings tell us that to transform ourselves, we must understand causes and conditions. It has taken five hundred years to create the suffering of our civil war." Ariyaratne described the primary causes, including the painful effects of four hundred years of colonialism, five hundred years of struggle between Hindus, Muslims, and Buddhists, and several centuries of economic disparity. He went on, "Therefore, it will take us five hundred years to change these conditions." Ariyaratne then proposed his long-term plan to heal the country.

The plan begins with several years of cease-fire and ten years of rebuilding roads and schools. Then it goes on to twenty-five years of programs to learn each other's languages and cultures and fifty years of specific projects to right economic injustice and bring the islanders back together as a whole. And for five centuries, every hundred years there will be a council of elders to take stock of how the plan is going.

Ariyaratne is not worried about the next election. He is not worried that he will die before his plan is fulfilled. His is a timeless vision, a sacred intention. He is simply living freely in the middle of it all, planting seeds of goodness and wisdom. Like Ariyaratne, when we find the middle way we can act, not out of aversion or grasping but as a labor of love. Our actions are a product of our wisdom and compassion, even when the immediate result is uncertain or not visible. Remember how Thomas Merton counseled to not depend on the hope of results but to concentrate on the value, the rightness, the truth of the work itself. This does not mean that the middle way is easy. Ariyaratne has been challenged and blamed, his life threatened. When we act for the long term, there will be pressure to take sides, grasp opinions, constantly measure the results, and try to control everything. But grasping is not the way of wisdom. Praise and blame, obstacles and triumph rise and fall as we follow the middle way.

I think of Rob, a dedicated Buddhist practitioner who worked as a paralegal for a public interest law firm in San Francisco. His life had been transformed by fifteen years of devoted meditation, and even though he was sick with AIDS, he was not often afraid. Though he was loved in his community, his family had never accepted the fact that he was gay, and had shunned him for most of his adult life. When he was dying, his father and sister came to visit him. They were deeply distressed by his lifestyle and the fact that he was dying of AIDS. His sister asked him, "What good have you done with your life anyway?" Rob was too stunned to answer. I met with Rob after the visit, and it was clear that her judgment had hurt him deeply. But then he looked at me and said with the humility of one facing death,

"I may not have done much, but I can say two things. I was kind and I found the dharma. And maybe that is enough for one lifetime."

It is not given to us to know how our life will affect the world. What *is* given to us is to tend the intentions of our heart and to plant beautiful seeds with our deeds. Do not doubt that your good actions will bear fruit, and that change for the better can be born from your life.

PRACTICE: DON'T KNOW MIND

Use this practice to bring wisdom to a situation of inner or outer conflict. Initially begin while sitting in meditation. Later you can practice in social situations.

Sit quietly and easily. Focus on your breath or body. When you feel settled, bring to mind a time ten years ahead. Recognize that you don't know what will happen then. Feel the not knowing and relax with it. Think of the earth spinning through space with hundreds of thousands of people being born and dying every day. Where does each life come from? How did it start? What changes are ahead for us? There are so many things we don't know. Feel the truth of don't-know mind, relax, and become comfortable with it.

Now, bring to mind a conflict, inner or outer. Be aware of all the thoughts and opinions you have about how things should be, about how other people should be. Now recognize that you don't really know. Maybe the wrong thing will lead to something better. You don't know.

Consider how it would be to approach yourself, the situation, the other people with don't-know mind. Don't know. Not sure. No fixed opinion. Allow yourself to want to understand anew. Approach it with don't-know mind, with openness.

How does resting in don't-know mind affect the situation? Does it improve it, make it wiser, easier? More relaxed?

Practice don't-know mind until you are comfortable resting in uncertainty, until you can do your best and laugh and say, "Don't know."

24

THE AWAKENED HEART

*With wisdom let your mind full of love pervade one-quarter of the world, and so
too the second, third and fourth quarter. Fill the whole wide world, above, below,
around, pervade the world with love filled thought, free from
any ill will, love abounding, sublime, beyond measure.*
—Digha Nikaya

*If we cannot be happy in spite of our difficulties, what good
is our spiritual practice?*
—Maha Ghosananda

Who, being loved, is poor?
—Oscar Wilde

We have within us an extraordinary capacity for love, joy, and
unshakable freedom. Buddhist psychology describes this as optimal
mental health. Dipama Barua, whom I have introduced before,
demonstrated these qualities. When I studied with her, Dipama was
a grandmother and householder, and also one of the most accom-
plished meditators of the Theravada lineage. Until her mid-thirties,
Dipama had been an ordinary devout Buddhist. Then in the space
of a few years she lost two of her three young children to illness.
Devastated, her engineer husband died of a heart attack soon there-

after. After a year of lying in bed with paralyzing grief, Dipama dragged herself to a meditation temple. Desperate, she threw herself into the meditation, and through her ardent nature and innate ability, she emerged with a deep realization. Dipama was then trained and became a master of dozens of kinds of meditation. Through her intense dedication and shining spirit, she became a revered teacher for many.

In the late 1970s, I visited Calcutta to see Dipama again. I had been meditating for a month in Bodh Gaya, India. Because of difficulty with my air ticket, I had only half a day to spend with her. It was a hot day, over 100 degrees. The air in Calcutta was smoggy and dirty. After I paid my respects to her, we spent some hours in deep conversation. Although I had been teaching successfully for five years, I was having a hard time. I had been suffering severe back pain, I was upset about a failed relationship, and before coming to India I had been working sixty hours a week for months. Given all this suffering and stress, I told her that I had begun to doubt my own capacities and ability to embody the teachings. Though she could see how shaky I was, she encouraged me to be steady in spite of it all. When it was time for me to go, Dipama gave me her usual Bengali bear hug. Then she said she had a special blessing for me. Because she was so tiny, when I got down on my knees for the blessing, I was equal to her in height.

Dipama stroked her hands gently across my head and my whole body. She blew her breath on me and recited lovingkindness chants at the same time. At first it seemed like a very long prayer, but as she continued blessing me, I started to feel better and better. After ten long minutes my whole body was tingling and open. I was smiling from ear to ear. "Go and teach a good retreat for all those people," she said at last. "Go with mother's blessings." I felt as though a loving grandmother had sent me off with her good wishes, amplified with special yogic powers. I was in bliss.

I walked out into the sweltering Calcutta street and caught a taxi to Dum Dum Airport (its real name). It took two hours to get there, with the driver leaning on his horn the whole way, dodging between rickshaws and traffic and fumes and trash. At the airport

I went through the tedious Indian customs, hours of standing around while officials looked through my stuff, grilled me, and stamped my documents. Eventually I got on the airplane for the three-hour flight to Bangkok. Bangkok was also hot and busy, like Los Angeles. The airport had long lines and more customs. Then I spent an hour and a half riding to my hotel through the slow, crowded Bangkok traffic.

All the while I could not stop grinning. Through the customs lines, plane rides, taxi rides, and traffic jams, I sat there with this huge smile on my face. It would not wear off. I went to sleep smiling and woke up smiling. I smiled continuously for days and felt uplifted for months following Dipama's blessing.

Dipama and other Buddhist teachers demonstrate the psychological possibilities of the awakened heart. In *Transformations of Consciousness,* Harvard psychologist Jack Engler reports a study of Dipama and other advanced meditators. He found a degree of mental health and well-being that was the most remarkable ever seen by any scientists. He took their histories and gave them an extensive battery of tests, including the Rorschach and Thematic Apperception Tests, which measure both personality and perception. Dipama's test protocols confirmed her description of a luminous, loving mind, peaceful and completely untroubled with anger, fear, greed, or conflict of any kind. She was totally open about her inner life. Engler reports, "The tests show a cognitive-emotional transformation and integration that reflected the deepest levels of inner liberation. Dipama spontaneously wove her test responses into an ongoing spiritual story, a narrative that revealed the whole teaching of the dharma and at the same time showed clear comprehension of the tests—a remarkable achievement none of the researchers had ever witnessed."

Dipama shows what is possible when we return to our Buddha nature. But let us remember that the shining of the heart is not unique to meditation masters and advanced practitioners. It is here in us all. My colleague Sharon Salzberg tells this story from a daylong loving-kindness retreat in Oakland, California.

"Whenever I teach loving-kindness retreats in an urban set-

ting," Sharon explains, "I ask students to do their walking meditation out on the streets. I suggest they choose individuals they see
and, with care and awareness, wish them well by silently repeating
the traditional phrases of the loving-kindness practice, 'May you be
happy, may you be peaceful.' I tell them that even if they don't *feel*
loving, the power of their intention to offer love is not diminished.
On this day our retreat took place a few blocks from downtown
Oakland. Since we were directly across the street from the Amtrak
station, several people chose to do their practice on the train plat-
form.

"When a train pulled in, one woman from the class noticed a
man disembark and decided to make him the recipient of her
loving-kindness meditation. Silently she began reciting the phrases
for him. Almost immediately she began judging herself: *I must not
be doing it right because I feel so distant. I don't have a great wash of warm
feeling coming over me.* Nonetheless, reaffirming her intention to
look on all beings with kindness instead of estrangement, she continued, reciting, 'May you be happy, may you be peaceful.' Taking
another look at the man, who was dressed in a suit and tie and
seemed nervous, she began judging him: *He looks so rigid and up-
tight.* Judging herself, she thought, *Here I am trying to send loving-
kindness to someone and instead I'm disparaging him.* Still, she
continued repeating the phrases, aligning her energy with her deep
intention: to be a force of love in the world. At that moment the
man walked over to her and said, 'I've never done anything like this
before in my life, but I'd like to ask you to pray for me. I am about
to face a very difficult situation in my life. You somehow seem to
have a really loving heart, and I'd just like to know that you're pray-
ing for me.' "

THE FOUR RADIANT ABODES

The old Buddhist list makers had a joyous time mapping the highest possibilities of human development. They enumerate the four
degrees of noble hearts, five spiritual powers, five ranks, eight

satoris, ten ox-herding pictures, ten stages of a bodhisattva, and thirty-seven factors of enlightenment. But the most treasured description of human awakening, what we in the West might call optimal mental health, is the Four Radiant Abodes.

These Four Radiant Abodes are loving-kindness, compassion, joy, and equanimity or peace. These abodes are treasured because of the natural human happiness they express. They are immediate and simple, the universal description of an open heart. Even when we hear their names—love, compassion, joy, peace—they touch us directly. When we meet another who is filled with these qualities, our heart lights up. When we touch peace, love, joy, and compassion in ourselves, we are transformed.

Love is our true nature, but as we have seen, it is covered over by a protective layer of fear. We have learned how Buddhist practices unearth the gold beneath the clay and return us to our natural goodness. Even though this love is innate, the Buddhist path also uses systematic trainings to cultivate this love. They strengthen our capacity for love, compassion, joy, and peace. The practices that develop these qualities combine repeated thoughts, visualization, and feelings. These trainings have been employed by millions of practitioners to transform their own hearts.

When the Radiant Abodes are developed, their complementary qualities help to balance one another. This balance is considered essential in Buddhist psychology. Because love, compassion, and joy can lead to excessive attachment, their warmth needs to be balanced with equanimity. Because equanimity can lead to excessive detachment, its coolness needs to be balanced with love, compassion, and joy. Established together, these radiant qualities express optimal mental harmony.

The natural flow of these awakened qualities comes from inner peace. When consciousness is peaceful and open, we rest in equanimity. As our peaceful heart meets other beings, it fills with love. When this love meets pain, it transforms itself naturally into compassion. And when this same openhearted love meets happiness, it becomes joy. In this way, the radiant abodes spontaneously reflect and connect the whole of the world.

Here is a twenty-sixth principle of Buddhist psychology:

---

26 A peaceful heart gives birth to love. When love meets suffering, it turns to compassion. When love meets happiness, it turns to joy.

AWAKENING LOVE

Loving-kindness is the first training of the Radiant Abodes. In the initial stages of this loving-kindness practice, students are asked to visualize themselves and repeat four or five traditional phrases of well-wishing, such as "May I be safe and healthy. May I be happy." Along with the recitation, students are encouraged to sense how the quality of loving-kindness can be reflected in the body and heart.

The quality of loving-kindness develops as we repeat these phrases thousands of times, over days and months. Initially it can feel difficult to offer love to ourself: for many it can trigger feelings of shame and unworthiness. Yet it is a particularly powerful practice, because whatever we do not love in our own self, we will not accept in another. Buddhist teachings explain, "You can search the whole universe and not find any being more worthy of love than yourself."

After many repetitions, strong love for oneself can be established. Then the loving-kindness practice is systematically extended to others by categories. First we visualize and offer love to our benefactors, then loved ones, friends, neutral people, and eventually difficult people, even our enemies. Next, we extend the well-wishing of loving-kindness further—to all humans, animals, and insects, to beings of the earth, water, and air, to beings large and small, young and old, visible and not visible—until beings in every direction are included. At each step of the process, we deliberately extend our field of loving consciousness. If we find difficulty opening to the next area of loving-kindness, we try to gradually let go and forgive, repeatedly offering loving intentions until the obstacles dissolve.

Ruby has been a Buddhist practitioner for fifteen years. Today Ruby exudes happiness and joy, but this is not because her life has been so easy. Several years ago, Ruby asked me what might be helpful next steps in her training and development. In addition to her work as a university administrator, she was caring for her mother and helping with two grandchildren, so she could not go on long retreats.

To balance Ruby's caring for others, I suggested that she undertake a year of loving-kindness practice just for herself. At first she resisted. "You mean a year of wishing that I be happy? It feels so self-centered. I don't know if I could do it." But she decided to try it. In her morning meditation, and throughout the day, Ruby wished herself well, with loving intention, at work, driving, shopping. At times the meditation felt tedious and difficult, but she stuck to it. Over the year Ruby became happier and more radiant. Then, I suggested she attend a weeklong retreat of loving-kindness meditation.

After two days of resistance, Ruby dropped into a silent and concentrated stillness. Through her practice, Ruby had learned not to resist her resistance, to allow all her experience to be held in love. As she did, the loving-kindness grew. Over the next days Ruby experienced a stream of luminous energy filling up the core of her body, expanding to a boundaryless ocean of love. She was incredibly happy. "I have opened," she exclaimed one morning. "I am nothing and I am the whole world. I am the crab apple tree and the frog by the stream and the tired cooks in the evening kitchen and the mud on my shoes and the stars. When my mind thinks about past and future, it is only telling stories. In loving-kindness, there is no past or future, only silence and love."

Ruby had graduated. Love was no longer a training or a practice, it was her life. It was love that Ruby brought to her mother's bedside through her long illness. Now Ruby tells me she doesn't practice loving-kindness meditation formally for herself or others much anymore, because "it just comes. We're not separate, and love is just what we are."

The experience of practicing loving-kindness in this way illuminates new possibilities. For example, when we shift our attention from benefactors and friends to neutral people, a whole new category of love opens. In this practice, neutral people are defined as people we see regularly but don't pay much attention to. We might choose our regular bank teller or a waitress at a local restaurant as our first neutral person. On one long retreat, I chose an old local gardener. I spent several days and nights picturing him and wishing him well in my meditation. Later I unexpectedly ran into him. Even though I didn't know his name, I was so happy to see him, I swooned: *Oh, my beloved neutral person!* Then I realized how many other neutral people I had ignored. As I included them in the practice of loving-kindness, my love grew deeper around me.

From neutral people, the practice of loving-kindness extends to difficult people and enemies. But this is not where we start. Only when our heart is open and our loving-kindness is strong do we bring in someone for whom we have strong aversion, someone by whom we've felt wronged, someone we've come to think of as an enemy. As we do, at first the heart shrivels and closes: "After what you did to me, I'm never going to love and forgive you, ever." But as this hatred arises, we lose the joy of our own open heart. Seeing this, we understand the cost of hatred. We realize, for our own sake, that the cost is too high. Finally we think, "OK, I'll forgive. I'll let even you into my loving-kindness—a little at first—so that I can keep my heart open." Through this repeated practice we learn to keep our heart open even in difficulty. As we cultivate this training in kindness, eventually we can end up like Dipama, radiating love to all we meet.

My colleague Sylvia Boorstein tells of Phil, a Buddhist practitioner in New York who had worked with loving-kindness practice for years. One evening on a small side street in SoHo, a disheveled man with a scraggly beard and dirty blond hair accosted Phil, pointed a gun at him, and demanded his money. Phil was carrying more than six hundred dollars in his wallet and he handed it all over. The mugger shook his gun and demanded more. Stalling for time, Phil gave him his credit cards and then the whole wallet. Looking dazed and high on some drug, the mugger said, "I'm gonna shoot you." Phil responded, "No, wait, here's my watch—it's an expensive one." Disoriented, the mugger took the watch, waved the gun, and said again, "I'm gonna shoot you." Somehow Phil managed to look at him with loving-kindness and said, "You don't have to shoot me. You did good. Look, you got nearly seven hundred dollars; you got credit cards and an expensive watch. You don't have to shoot me. You did really good." The mugger, confused, lowered the gun slowly. "I did good?" he asked. "You did really good. Go and tell your friends, you did good." Dazed, the mugger wandered off, saying softly to himself, "I did good."

Whenever our goodness is seen, it is a blessing. Every culture and tradition understands the importance of seeing one another with love. An old Hasidic rabbi asked his pupils how they could tell when the night had ended and day begun, for daybreak is the time for certain holy prayers. "Is it," proposed one student, "when you can see an animal in the distance and tell whether it is a sheep or a dog?" "No," answered the rabbi. "Is it when you can clearly see the lines on your own palm?" "Is it when you can look at a tree in the distance and tell if it is a fig or a pear tree?" "No," answered the rabbi each time. "Then what is it?" the pupils demanded. "It is when you can look on the face of any man or woman and see that they are your sister or brother. Until then it is still night."

NATURAL JOY

When Harvard psychologist Jack Engler was doing his research with Dipama, he asked her about one of the common misunderstandings of Buddhist teachings. "This can all sound very gray," he said, "getting rid of greed, getting rid of hate, getting rid of ignorance. Where's the juice?" Dipama burst out laughing. "Oh, you don't understand! There is so much sameness in ordinary life. We are always experiencing everything through the same set of lenses. Once greed, hatred, and delusion are gone, you see everything fresh and new all the time. Every moment is new. Life was dull before. Now, every day, every moment, is full of taste and zest."

When love meets pain it becomes compassion, as we have already seen. When love meets happiness, it becomes joy. Joy is an expression of the liberated and awakened heart. Recently, the Dalai Lama was co-host of a large scientific meeting in Washington, D.C. He met with physicians, neuroscientists, and several Buddhist teachers (including myself) to explore the latest clinical research on meditation and neurobiology. One morning a network television reporter interviewed him and asked about meditation and happiness. "You had the New York Times bestselling book entitled *The Art of Happiness,* and you frequently teach about happiness. Could you tell our viewers about the happiest moment in your life?" The Dalai Lama considered for a moment, smiled, and said, "I think now."

When we live in the present, joy arises for no reason. This is the happiness of consciousness that is not dependent on particular conditions. Children know this joy. Maurice Sendak, author of *Where the Wild Things Are,* tells the story of a boy who wrote to him. "He sent me a charming card with a drawing. I loved it. I answer all my children's letters—sometimes very hastily—but this one I lingered over. I sent him a postcard and I drew a picture of a Wild Thing on it. I wrote, 'Dear Jim, I loved your card.' Then I got a letter back from his mother and she said, 'Jim loved your card so much he ate it.' That to me was one of the highest compliments I've ever received. He didn't care that it was an original drawing or anything. He saw it, he loved it, he ate it."

We have seen how joy can come spontaneously in deep meditation. Students describe trembling, tears of laughter, cool waves, ripples of ecstasy, floating joy, joy like turquoise water, bodily thrilling, grateful joy, playful and delighting joy, and ecstasy of stillness. They describe joy in the body, heart, and mind, joy in the beauty of the world, and joy in the happiness of others.

Nonetheless, sometimes people mistake Buddhism for a pessimistic view of life. Certainly the Noble Truths teach about suffering and its causes and in Buddhist countries there are a few very serious, grim-duty-style meditation masters. I myself, like many other Westerners, sought them out. I was so determined to transform myself and attain some special realization that I went to the strictest monasteries and retreats, where we practiced eighteen hours a day and sat unmoving in the face of enormous pain. And at these monasteries I learned many important things.

But somehow in the seriousness of my quest, I failed to notice the extraordinary buoyancy of the Buddhist cultures around me. Thai, Lao, Tibetan, Burmese, and Nepali cultures are lighthearted; the people are filled with laughter. The children enchant you with their happy smiles. The grown-ups work, play, and pray with a light spirit. Seeking austerity, we serious Westerners failed to notice that most Buddhist temples are a riot of colors, filled with paintings and statues and images of fantastic stories of angels, devas, bodhisattvas, and Buddhas. We ignored the community life that centered around the temples, the cycles of rituals, dances, celebrations, feasts, and festivals. In our ardor, we did not appreciate how many of our greatest teachers—Ajahn Chah, Maha Ghosananda, Ananda Maitreya, the sixteenth Karmapa Lama, Anagarika Munindra—had marvelous, easy laughs and an infectious sense of joy.

When I returned to the United States and began to teach, my colleagues and I tended to emphasize the Buddha's teaching on suffering and the need to awaken. We were young and the focus on human suffering gave our retreats a seriousness and gravitas. But suffering is not the goal, it is the beginning of the path. Now in the retreats I teach, I also encourage participants to awaken to their innate joy. From the very beginning I encourage them to allow the moments of joy and well-being to deepen, to spread throughout their body and mind. Many of us are conditioned to fear joy and happiness, yet joy is necessary for awakening. As the Persian mystic Rumi instructs us, "When you go to a garden, do you look at thorns or flowers? Spend more time with roses and jasmine." André Gide, the French novelist and philosopher, enjoins us: "Know that joy is rarer, more difficult, and more beautiful than sadness. Once you make this all-important discovery, you must embrace joy as a moral obligation."

Psychologists working with the Tibetan community in exile have noted the remarkable resiliency and joyfulness among the people, even though many are survivors of great trauma and loss. Most surprising are the responses of nuns and monks who have been imprisoned and tortured. According to a study by Harvard psychologists, they show few or none of the ordinary signs of trauma, but instead have deepened in compassion and joyful appreciation of life. Their trainings in loving-kindness, compassion, and wisdom led them to pray for their enemies. One old lama recounted that over the twenty years of prison and torture, his only true fear was that he would lose his compassion and close his heart. If we want to understand optimal mental health, these monks and nuns are a striking example.

Debra Chamberlin-Taylor, a Buddhist teacher and colleague, tells the story of a community activist who participated in her yearlong training group for people of color. This woman had experienced a childhood of poverty, trauma, and abuse. She had faced the death of a parent, illness, divorce from a painful marriage, racism, and the single parenting of two children. She talked about her years of struggle to educate herself, to stand up for what she believed. She described how she had become a radical to fight for justice in local and national politics. Finally, at the last meeting this woman announced, "After all the struggles and troubles I've lived through, I've decided to do something really radical! I am going to be happy."

Just as we can reawaken to loving-kindness and compassion, we can reawaken to joy. It is innate to consciousness. As we find it in ourselves, we can see it in others. On one long spring retreat, Lorna, a young woman, came to me to talk about her reaction to one of the retreatants. She was having trouble with a big man seated nearby. He moved too often. Bud was an old ex-marine whose T-shirts revealed lots of tattoos. He smelled of tobacco smoke. His energy frightened her. Lorna tried to understand. She used loving-kindness practice and discovered how Bud triggered her painful history with men. Gradually, Lorna realized that most of what bothered her was her own imagination. Still, it seemed like a scary thing to talk to someone like Bud. Then, in the last week of retreat, Lorna came in to see me, grinning. "I'm not afraid of him anymore." She explained that after breakfast she had walked down to the stream below the dining hall. She came upon the marine there among the banks of flowers, cupping each one deliberately in his hands to smell its fragrance. On the last day of the retreat I saw Lorna in a joyful and animated conversation with Bud, standing near the flowers.

Like loving-kindness and compassion, there is a practice for joy. We begin by picturing someone we love as they experience a happy moment. We feel their well-being. Then we recite the intention "May your happiness and joy increase. May the causes for your happiness increase," repeating these intentions again and again, through any resistance, through tiredness, comparing, or jealousy, over and over until our sense of joy becomes strong. Next, we systematically extend this practice to others we love, one after another, until the quality of joy in their happiness grows even more available. Then we turn the practice of joy to ourselves, including our own joy and happiness in the well-wishing. From this we systematically and gradually open our practice of joy to all categories of beings. As we train ourselves to celebrate the joy and success of others, we awaken the Radiant Abode of joy. With joy whatever we do becomes holy. Martin Luther King Jr. understood this when he said, "If a person sweeps streets for a living, he should sweep them as Michelangelo painted, as Beethoven composed music, as Shakespeare wrote his plays."

As a support for the cultivation of joy, we can also include the practice of gratitude. Buddhist monks begin each day with a chant of gratitude for the blessings of their life. In the same way, Native American elders begin each ceremony with grateful prayers to Mother Earth and Father Sky, to the four directions, to the animal, plant, and mineral brothers and sisters who share our earth and support our life.

Gratitude is a gracious acknowledgment of all that sustains us, a bow to our blessings, great and small. Gratitude is the confidence in life itself. In it, we feel how the same force that pushes grass through cracks in the sidewalk invigorates our own life. In Tibet, the monks and nuns even offer prayers of gratitude for the suffering they have been given: "Grant that I might have enough suffering to awaken in me the deepest possible compassion and wisdom." Gratitude does not envy or compare. Gratitude receives in wonder the myriad offerings of rain and sunlight, the care that supports every single life.

As gratitude grows it gives rise to joy. We experience the courage to rejoice in our own good fortune and in the good for-

tune of others. In joy, we are not afraid of pleasure. We do not mistakenly believe it is disloyal to the suffering of the world to honor
the happiness we have been given. Joy gladdens the heart. We can
be joyful for people we love, for moments of goodness, for sunlight
and trees, and for the very breath within our lungs. Like an innocent child, we can rejoice in life itself, in being alive.

The world we live in is a temple, and the miraculous light of
the first stars is shining through it all the time. In place of original
sin, we celebrate original goodness. St. Teresa of Avila explains,
"God does not desire the soul to undertake any labor, but only to
take delight in the first fragrance of the flowers . . . the soul can
obtain sufficient nourishment from its own garden." In every meeting of the eyes and every leafing tree, in every taste of tangerine
and avocado, a blessing occurs. This is true mental health.

FREEDOM HERE AND NOW

The Four Radiant Abodes express the fruit of mental development.
When they are in balance, joy, compassion, and loving-kindness
rest in an unshakable peace. True peace is not indifference or emotional resignation; it is the still point, the living reality of the present. This dynamic stillness is what Dipama calls the crowning stage
of Buddhist training, "where consciousness becomes a symphony of
loving-kindness, playing in a silent ocean of equanimity."

We have now come full circle, arriving here where we started,
and, as T. S. Eliot writes, "knowing the place for the first time."
Coming to rest in the present, wherever we are, becomes the seat
of awakening. We are now truly alive, able to care, to work, to love,
to enter life fully, with an open heart. We see the lawfulness of life
unfolding, the causes of sorrow, and the choice for freedom. We do
whatever we can to reduce suffering, and all along we are free. This
is the final message Buddhist psychology communicates to its followers: you are free. This freedom is the very nature of our own
heart and mind.

Each of us will reflect our inner freedom in a unique way,
through our temperament, body, and culture. There are those who

express their freedom primarily through silence, others through joy. There are those who express freedom through peacefulness and others through service and love. A free and awakened consciousness is experienced as a many-faceted crystal. One facet is peace, another is love, one is strength, another is clarity, one is gratitude; others include integrity, compassion, courage, creativity, joyfulness, and abundance. Each of these qualities can fill consciousness and shine through our body, heart, and mind. This is not simply a metaphor. It becomes our actual experience. We are illuminated by these qualities, one or several at a time.

When we find freedom, even pain and illness become part of the grace of life, and they are our teachers. The Dalai Lama said, "When, at some point in our lives, we meet a real tragedy—which could happen to any one of us—we can react in two ways. Obviously, we can lose hope, let ourselves slip into discouragement, into alcohol, drugs, and unending sadness. Or else we can wake ourselves up, discover in ourselves an energy that was hidden there, and act with genuine clarity and compassion." Imperfections are part of the display of life. Joy and sorrow, birth and death are the dance of existence throughout which our awakened consciousness can shine.

This perspective is called finding the goodness in everything. As proof of the human capacity to do so, here is a prayer written by an unknown prisoner in the Ravensbruck concentration camp and left by the body of a dead child: "O Lord, remember not only the men and women of good will, but also those of ill will. But do not remember only the suffering they have inflicted on us; remember too the fruits we brought forth thanks to this suffering—our comradeship, our loyalty, our humility, our courage, our generosity, the greatness of heart which has grown out of all this. And when they come to judgment, let all the fruits which we have borne be their forgiveness."

Ajahn Buddhadasa says that finding goodness everywhere allows us to be servants of peace. *Buddhadasa* means "servant of awakening," "servant of peace." He called his monastery the garden of peace. Amidst the ancient forests, beautiful pools, bamboo, and stone sculptures, Ajahn Buddhadasa offered the teachings of lovingkindness, compassion, and peace. For fifty years, through cycles of truce, insurgency, simplicity, and modernization, tens of thousands came to hear his teachings of peace. As we awaken, we too become servants of peace, taking our place in the garden.

This is the culmination of the psychology of the wise heart. We are the beauty we have been seeking all our lives. We are consciousness knowing itself. Empty and spacious, compassionate and joyful, our very peace and equanimity begin to transform the world around us. Buddhist psychology helps us rediscover that freedom and joy are our original nature. "O Nobly Born, do not forget the luminous nature of your own mind. Trust it. It is home."

※   ※   ※

PRACTICES

A MEDITATION ON LOVING-KINDNESS

I am larger than I thought!
I did not know I held so much goodness!
—Walt Whitman

With a loving heart as the background, all that we attempt, all that we encounter will open and flow more easily. You can begin the practice of loving-kindness by meditating for fifteen or twenty minutes in a quiet place. Let yourself sit in a comfortable fashion. Let your body rest and be relaxed. Let your heart be soft. Let go of any plans or preoccupations.

Begin with yourself. Breathe gently, and recite inwardly the following traditional phrases directed toward your own well-being. You begin with yourself because without loving yourself it is almost impossible to love others.

May I be filled with loving-kindness.
May I be safe from inner and outer dangers.
May I be well in body and mind.
May I be at ease and happy.

As you repeat these phrases, picture yourself as you are now, and hold yourself in a heart of loving-kindness. Or perhaps you will find it easier to picture yourself as a young and beloved child. Adjust the words and images in any way you wish. Create the exact phrases that best open your heart of kindness. Repeat these phrases over and over again, letting the feelings permeate your body and mind. Practice this meditation for a number of weeks, until the sense of loving-kindness for yourself grows.

Be aware that this meditation may at times feel mechanical or awkward. It can also bring up feelings contrary to loving-kindness, feelings of irritation and anger. If this happens, it is especially important to be patient and kind toward yourself, allowing whatever arises to be received in a spirit of friendliness and kind affection.

When you feel you have established some stronger sense of loving-kindness for yourself, you can then expand your meditation to include others. After focusing on yourself for five or ten minutes, choose a benefactor, someone in your life who has loved and truly cared for you. Picture this person and carefully recite the same phrases:

> May you be filled with loving-kindness.
> May you be safe from inner and outer dangers.
> May you be well in body and mind.
> May you be at ease and happy.

Let the image and feelings you have for your benefactor support the meditation. Whether the image or feelings are clear or not does not matter. In meditation they will be subject to change. Simply continue to plant the seeds of loving wishes, repeating the phrases gently no matter what arises. Expressing gratitude to our benefactors is a natural form of love. In fact, some people find loving-kindness for themselves so hard, they begin their practice with a benefactor. This too is fine. The rule in loving-kindness practice is to follow the way that most easily opens your heart.

When loving-kindness for your benefactor has developed, you can gradually begin to include other people in your meditation.

Picture each beloved person; recite inwardly the same phrases, evoking a sense of loving-kindness for each person in turn.

After this you can include others. Spend some time wishing well to a wider circle of friends. Then gradually extend your meditation to include community members, neighbors, people everywhere, animals, all beings, the whole earth.

Finally, include the difficult people in your life, even your enemies, wishing that they too may be filled with loving-kindness and peace. This will take practice. But as your heart opens, first to loved ones and friends, you will find that in the end you won't want to close it anymore.

Loving-kindness can be practiced anywhere. You can use this meditation in traffic jams, in buses, and on airplanes. As you silently practice this meditation among people, you will come to feel a wonderful connection with them—the power of loving-kindness. It will calm your mind and keep you connected to your heart.

A MEDITATION ON COMPASSION

For this practice, please see Chapter 2.

A MEDITATION ON GRATITUDE AND JOY

Let yourself sit quietly and at ease. Allow your body to be relaxed and open, your breath natural, your heart easy. Begin the practice of gratitude by feeling how year after year you have cared for your own life. Now let yourself begin to acknowledge all that has supported you in this care:

With gratitude I remember the people, animals, plants, insects,
creatures of the sky and sea, air and water, fire and earth, all
whose joyful exertion blesses my life every day.
With gratitude I remember the care and labor of a thousand gen-
erations of elders and ancestors who came before me.
I offer my gratitude for the safety and well-being I have been given.

I offer my gratitude for the blessings of this earth I have been given.
I offer my gratitude for the measure of health I have been given.
I offer my gratitude for the family and friends I have been given.
I offer my gratitude for the community I have been given.
I offer my gratitude for the teachings and lessons I have been given.
I offer my gratitude for the life I have been given.

Just as we are grateful for our blessings, so we can be grateful for the blessings of others.

Now shift your practice to the cultivation of joy. Continue to breathe gently. Bring to mind someone you care about, someone it is easy to rejoice for. Picture them and feel the natural joy you have for their well-being, happiness, and success. With each breath, offer them your grateful, heartfelt wishes:

May you be joyful.
May your happiness increase.
May you not be separated from great happiness.
May your good fortune and the causes of your joy and happiness increase.

Sense the sympathetic joy and caring in each phrase. When you feel some degree of natural gratitude for the joy and well-being of this loved one, extend this practice to another person you care about. Recite the same simple phrases that express your heart's intention.

Then gradually open the meditation to other loved ones and benefactors. After the joy for them grows strong, turn back to include yourself. Let the feelings of joy more fully fill your body and mind. Continue repeating the intentions of joy over and over, through whatever resistances and difficulties arise, until you feel stabilized in joy. Next begin to systematically include the categories of neutral people, then difficult people and even enemies until you extend sympathetic joy to all beings everywhere, young and old, near and far.

Practice dwelling in joy until the deliberate effort of practice drops away and the intentions of joy blend into the natural joy of your own wise heart.

A MEDITATION ON EQUANIMITY AND PEACE

To cultivate the qualities of peace and equanimity, sit in a comfortable posture with your eyes closed. Bring a soft attention to your breath until your body and mind are calm. Reflect for a moment on the benefit of a mind that has balance and equanimity. Sense what a gift it can be to bring a peaceful heart to the world around you. Let yourself feel an inner sense of balance and ease. Then with each breath begin gently repeating such phrases as:

Breathing in, I calm my body.
Breathing out, I calm my mind.
May I be balanced.
May I be at peace.

Stay with these phrases until you feel quiet in your body and mind.

Then broaden the sense of calm into a spacious equanimity. Acknowledge that all created things arise and pass away: joys, sorrows, pleasant and painful events, people, buildings, animals, nations, even whole civilizations. Let yourself rest in the midst of them.

May I learn to see the arising and passing of all things with
equanimity and balance.
May I be open and balanced and peaceful.

When you have established a sense of equanimity and peace, begin to picture, one at a time, your loved ones. Carefully recite the same simple phrases:

May you learn to see the arising and passing of all things with
equanimity and balance.
May you be open and balanced and peaceful.

Let the image of each loved one be surrounded with peace. Continue as best you can, breathing gently, patiently wishing peace, repeating the phrases no matter what arises.

As the quality of equanimity and peace grows you can gradu-

ally expand the meditation to include others. Start with your benefactors, those who have cared for you. Picture each person in turn,
reciting inwardly the same phrases, offering a blessing of peace as
you continue. Then gradually expand the circle of the meditation
to systematically include friends, neighbors, neutral people, animals, all beings, the earth.

> *May you learn to see the arising and passing of all things with
> equanimity and balance.*
> *May you be open and balanced and peaceful.*

Finally, you can include the difficult people in your life, even those
that you might consider your enemies, wishing that they too find
equanimity and peace.

As you reflect on each person, it is traditional to acknowledge
that all beings are heirs to their own karma. All beings receive the
fruits of their actions. Their lives arise and pass away according to
the deeds created by them. We can deeply care for them, but in the
end we cannot act for them nor let go for them nor love for them.
If it is helpful in freeing the heart, you can recite:

> *Your happiness and suffering depend on your actions and not on
> my wishes for you.*

Reflecting with wisdom on beings and their deeds, you can now
picture each one and return to these simple phrases:

> *May you learn to see the arising and passing of all things with
> equanimity and balance.*
> *May you be open and balanced and peaceful.*

Continue this practice as long and as often as you wish, breathing
and resting the heart in natural great peace.

RELATED READINGS

Aronson, Harvey. *Buddhist Practice on Western Ground: Reconciling Eastern Ideals and Western Psychology*. Boston: Shambhala Publications, 2004.

Baer, Ruth A., ed. *Mindfulness-Based Treatment Approaches: Clinician's Guide to Evidence Base and Applications*. Burlington, MA: Academic Press, 2006.

Begley, Sharon. *Train Your Mind, Change Your Brain: How a New Science Reveals Our Extraordinary Potential to Transform Ourselves*. New York: Random House, 2007.

Bennett-Goleman, Tara. *Emotional Alchemy*. New York: Harmony Books, 2001.

Bien, Thomas, and Bien, Beverly. *Mindful Recovery: A Spiritual Path to Healing from Addiction*. New York: John Wiley, 2002.

Brach, Tara. *Radical Acceptance: Embracing Your Life with the Heart of a Buddha*. New York: Bantam Dell, 2003.

Brazier, David. *Zen Therapy*. New York: John Wiley, 1995.

Csikszentmihalyi, Mihaly. *Flow*. New York: HarperCollins, 1990/2002.

Davidson, Richard J., and Harrington, Anne. *Visions of Compassion: Western Scientists and Tibetan Buddhists Examine Human Nature*. Oxford: Oxford University Press, 2002.

Epstein, Mark. *Thoughts Without a Thinker: Psychotherapy from a Buddhist Perspective*. New York: Basic Books: 1995.

Epstein, Mark. *Psychotherapy Without the Self*. New Haven: Yale University, 2007.

Fishman, Barbara Miller. *Emotional Healing Through Mindfulness Meditation*. Rochester, VT: Inner Traditions, 2002.

Germer, Christopher; Siegel, Ronald D.; Fulton, Paul R., eds. *Mindfulness and Psychotherapy*. New York: Guilford Press, 2005.

Gilbert, Paul. *Compassion: Conceptualisations, Research and Use in Psychotherapy*. London: Routledge, 2005.

Glaser, Aura. *A Call to Compassion: Bringing Buddhist Practices of the Heart into the Soul of Psychology*. Berwick, ME: Nicolas-Hays, 2005.

Goleman, Daniel. *Destructive Emotions: A Scientific Dialogue with the Dalai Lama*. New York: Bantam Dell, 2003.

Goleman, Daniel. *The Meditative Mind*. New York: Tarcher/Putnam, 1988.

Kabat-Zinn, Jon. *Full Catastrophe Living*. New York: Dell, 1990.

Kornfield, Jack. *A Path with Heart: A Guide Through the Perils and Promises of Spiritual Life*. New York: Bantam, 1993.

Kumar, Sameet M. *Grieving Mindfully: A Compassionate and Spiritual Guide to Coping with Loss*. Oakland, CA: New Harbinger, 2005.

Ladner, Lorne. *The Lost Art of Compassion: Discovering the Practice of Happiness in the Meeting of Buddhism and Psychology*. New York: HarperCollins, 2004.

Langan, Robert. *Minding What Matters: Psychotherapy and the Buddha Within*. Boston: Wisdom Publications, 2006.

Linehan, Marsha M. *Skills Training Manual for Treating Borderline Personality Disorder*. New York: Guilford Press, 1993.

Linley, P. Alex, and Joseph, Stephen, eds. *Positive Psychology in Practice*. Hoboken: John Wiley, 2004.

Magid, Barry. *Ordinary Mind: Exploring the Common Ground of Zen and Psychotherapy*. Somerville, MA: Wisdom Publications, 2002.

Marlatt, G. Alan. *Mindfulness for Addiction Problems*. In Carlson, J. (Ed.) Series VI: Spirituality. Compact disc. Washington, D.C.: American Psychological Association, 2005.

Martin, Philip. *The Zen Path Through Depression*. New York: HarperCollins, 1999.

McQuaid, John R., and Carmona, Paula E. *Peaceful Mind: Using Mindfulness and Cognitive Behavioral Psychology to Overcome Depression*. Oakland, CA: New Harbinger Publications, 2004.

Miller, Alec L.; Rathus, Jill H.; Linehan, Marsha M. *Dialectical Behavior Therapy with Suicidal Adolescents*. New York: The Guilford Press, 2007.

Molino, Anthony, ed. *The Couch and the Tree*. New York: North Point Press, 1998.

Mruk, Christopher J., with Hartzell, Joan. *Zen and Psychotherapy: Integrating Traditional and Nontraditional Approaches*. New York: Springer Publishing Company, 2003.

Nauriyal, D.K.; Drummond, Michael S.; Lal, Y.B.; eds. *Buddhist Thought and Applied Psychological Research: Transcending the Boundaries*. New York: Routledge, 2006.

Rosenbaum, Robert. *Zen and the Heart of Psychotherapy*. New York: Plenum Press, 1999.

Rubin, Jeffrey B. *Psychotherapy and Buddhism*. New York: Plenum Press, 1996.

Safran, Jeremy. *Psychoanalysis & Buddhism: An Unfolding Dialogue.* Somerville, MA: Wisdom Publications, 2003.

Salzberg, Sharon. *Lovingkindness: The Revolutionary Art of Happiness.* Boston: Shambhala Publications, 1995.

Schwartz, Jeffrey M., and Begley, Sharon. *The Mind and the Brain: Neuroplasticity and the Power of Mental Force.* New York: HarperCollins, 2002.

Segal, Zindel V.; Williams, J. Mark G.; Teasdale, John D. *Mindfulness-Based Cognitive Therapy for Depression: A New Approach to Preventing Relapse.* New York: The Guilford Press, 2002.

Segall, Seth Robert, ed. *Encountering Buddhism: Western Psychology and Buddhist Teachings.* Albany, NY: State University of New York Press, 2003.

Siegel, Daniel. *The Mindful Brain: Reflection and Attunement in the Cultivation of Well-Being.* New York: Norton and Company, 2007.

Suler, John R. *Contemporary Psychoanalysis and Eastern Thought.* Albany, NY: State University of New York Press, 1993.

Suzuki, D.T.; Fromm, Erich; De Martino, Richard. *Zen Buddhism and Psychoanalysis.* New York: Harper & Row, 1960.

Thera, Nyanaponika. *Abhidhamma Studies.* Somerville, MA: Wisdom Publications, 1998.

Thondup, Tulku. *The Healing Power of Mind.* Boston: Shambhala Publications, 1998.

Tsering, Geshe Tashi. *Buddhist Psychology: The Foundation of Buddhist Thought.* Somerville, MA: Wisdom Publications, 2006.

Unno, Mark, ed. *Buddhism and Psychotherapy Across Cultures.* Boston: Wisdom Publications, 2006.

Wallin, David J. *Attachment in Psychotherapy.* New York: The Guilford Press, 2007.

Welwood, John. *Toward a Psychology of Awakening: Buddhism, Psychotherapy, and the Path of Personal and Spiritual Transformation.* Boston: Shambhala Publications, 2000.

Wilber, Ken; Engler, Jack; Brown, Daniel P. *Transformations of Consciousness*. Boston: Shambhala Publications, 1986/2008.

Young-Eisendrath, Polly, and Muramoto, Shoji, eds. *Awakening and Insight: Zen Buddhism and Psychotherapy*. New York: Taylor & Francis, 2002.

PERMISSIONS

ACKNOWLEDGMENTS

I am blessed to work with two remarkable editors. Noelle Oxenhandler has lovingly brought the bones of structure, the refined skill of her writer's craft, and her hard-won dharma clarity to patiently steward and edit this book from its very genesis. Toni Burbank at Bantam, whom many of us regard as one of the publishing world's great treasures, has followed Noelle's work and unstintingly shepherded and masterfully pruned this project with a fierce eye for truth and a wise and knowing heart. I am indebted to both for their work, vision, and kindness.

In addition, my good-hearted and invincible assistant on this project, Sara Sparling, has brought her care and dedication to countless rewrites and changes, and I thank her for her shining steadiness.

This was a very long project of cultural translation. Many heart companions in this same work, including Tara Brach, Mark Epstein, Roger Walsh, Trudy Goodman, Richard Heckler, Shauna Shapiro, Sylvia Boorstein, Dan Siegel, and Ajahn Amaro, have read through drafts and offered suggestions and encouragement.

Wes "Scoop" Nisker and Bokara Legendre, true friends, fellow authors, and honest critics, shared with me the world's best writer's retreat in Bali. They were enormously helpful—what a way to write!

As always, I want to honor my beloved teaching colleagues, the twenty-one members of the Spirit Rock Teacher's Council and the collective of Insight Meditation Society teachers who have joined me in this adventure of bringing the wisdom of the East into accessible Western forms. And to the many sincere students whose stories appear here, some recorded, some sent to me on request, too many to name, from whom I have learned so much—I bow in gratitude.

I feel enormous blessings to have received these transformative teachings from a living lineage of great masters, including Ajahn Chah, Mahasi Sayadaw, Maha Ghosananda, Ajahn Buddhadasa, Ajahn Jumnian, Asabha Sayadaw, Dipama Barua, Anagarika Munindra, Sri Nisargadatta, Kalu Rinpoche, and His Holiness the Dalai Lama.

I also want to acknowledge the privilege of being part of and learning from a whole generation of Western visionary explorers, most especially Hameed Ali, Stan and Christina Grof, Michael Meade, Ram Dass, Dora Kalff, Jon Kabat-Zinn, Myron Sharaf, Michael and Sandra Harner, Angeles Arrien, Malidoma and Sobonfu Somé, Luis Rodriguez, Daniel Goleman, Peter Levine, and others.

Michael Katz agented this book like the knowing old Zen monk that he is, sometimes with a shout, more often with a whisper. I thank him for both.

Finally, I offer my heart's gratitude for the ongoing blessings I receive from my wife, Liana, an extraodinary wellspring of inspiration and depth; my beloved daughter, Caroline, a compassionate young visionary; and my wildly creative brothers and their families.

INDEX

A

abandonment, 90, 119–20, 191, 242, 266, 270

Abdul Kassem Ismael, 51

Abhidhamma (Abhidharma), 3, 50

abundance, 157, 180, 184, 185, 188, 223, 396; fulfillment and, 198–200; from grasping to abundance, 196–98

acceptance, 158, 178, 186, 244, 334; balanced, 90; RAIN and, 101, 102, 107, 129, 132, 259, 334; self, 5, 168, 175–79

addictions, 242; desire and, 189; grasping and, 55, 175–76; as hungry ghost, 248–49, 287; practicing non-intoxication, 191

African proverb, 201

aggression, 14, 15, 24, 31, 148, 151, 163, 210, 220, 275, 299, 315, 357, 364; aversive temperament, 174; non-contentiousness as opposite, 218–19; recognition of, 213; releasing unhealthy, 168–69; roots of, 206; transforming with compassion, 208–9; universal energy, 208

alcoholism, 169–70, 174

Alzheimer's disease, 181–82

ambition, 31, 102, 115, 139, 142, 187, 195, 196, 327

Anapana Breathing Sutra, 252

anger, 5, 13, 42, 49, 57, 59, 104, 126, 128, 130, 131, 132, 144, 205, 206–8, 223, 248, 249, 252, 258, 263, 266, 296, 301, 305, 315, 335, 347, 350, 351, 357, 370, 376, 384, 398; blaming and, 207; delusion and, 227, 229; denial, confronting, 229; facing, 206–8; habit of, 258; Kornfield's, 211–12; letting go of, therapeutic approaches, 114, 120, 125, 133–34, 135, 162, 168, 211–13, 214–15, 219, 220, 247–48, 314–16, 348; as motivation, 258; non-contentiousness to oppose, 220; practice: discovering pain and fear behind, 220–21; recognizing, 60, 64, 102, 128, 163, 208, 211, 213, 216–17, 219, 230; root of unhealthy mental states, 162, 174, 205, 206, 207, 209–10; suffering and, 205, 301; transforming, 22, 23, 132, 180, 208–9, 245; as universal energy, 208, 209

Angulimala, 339–40

anxiety, 3, 24, 55, 67, 95, 105, 111, 132, 148, 158, 179, 220, 242, 256, 269, 270, 294, 299, 306, 311, 318, 370, 372, 373, 376; deluded temperament and, 174; desire and, 189; facing, 14;

anxiety (cont'd)
fostering, 228; healing, 200;
mindfulness practice for, 127,
250–51; past-life unconscious and,
159–60; prescription drugs for,
251–52; self-image and, 15; as state
of mind, 53; suffering and, 296, 301;
therapeutic work in, 324–25;
transforming thoughts to release, 297
Ardrey, Robert, 209
Ariyaratne, A.T., 379–80
Armstrong, Lance, 261
Art of Happiness, The (Dalai Lama), 391
Ashoka, Indian king, 279–80, 281
Aung San Suu Kyi, 14–15, 261
Autry, James, 180–81
aversion, 53, 102, 104, 114, 119, 133, 173,
206, 207, 208, 210, 213, 223, 265,
267, 368, 380, 389; arising from
painful feelings, 129; to desire,
191–92; hatred from, 55; healing,
therapeutic approaches to, 213–16;
mindfulness of, 133; personality type,
171–74, 176–80; as root of unhealthy
mental states, 54, 55, 162, 170, 207,
208, 209, 210, 242, 254;
transforming, 170
awakening, 4, 5, 6, 7, 234, 260, 261, 290,
311, 316, 339, 354, 355, 366, 369,
378, 386, 392, 395, 396; acceptance
of one's nature, 178; awakened heart,
382–402; Buddha's, 274; core
principles, 275; dedication to noble
life and, 260–61; from delusion,
222–24, 234; Four Radiant Abodes,
386; goal of Buddhist practices, 16;
integrity and, 338; to love, 387–90;
mindfulness as means to, 7; non-
identification as abode of, 106; optimal
mental health and, 382; to pure
consciousness, 40–43; sacred images
of, 275; terms, 5–6; understanding of
both personal and universal nature
and, 80, 81. See also bodhisattva
awareness, 105–6, 216; bringing
unconscious patterns into, 153; "clear
open sky of awareness," 38, 44–47; as
consciousness, 37, 38, 39, 44, 49, 64;
as flow state, 45, 317; of mind, 148;

mindfulness as, 96; release from
delusion and, 224; resting in, 44,
45–46, 64, 78; self and, 70, 73, 75; of
the unconscious, 156, 163

B

Baba, Meher, 345
Baldwin, James, 211
Beck, Aaron, 295
beginner's mind, 98–99, 374, 375
Be Here Now (Ram Dass), 73
Bergantino, Len, 147
Berry, Wendell, 261
Bhagavad Gita, 372
Blake, William, 187, 212
blaming, 49, 62, 81, 98, 155, 158, 205,
207, 209, 210, 211, 215, 216, 217,
219, 220, 221, 232, 242, 269, 358,
376, 380; letting go of, 247–48;
recognition of, 213
bodhisattva, 352–66; envisioning liberation
and justice, 360–63; facing the truth
and, 358–60; life of balance and,
357–58; path of, vs. the West, 354;
practice: vows, 366; sacred images of,
275; tending the world, 363–65;
vows of, 354, 355
Bodhisattva Manjusri, 275
body, 110–23; being mindful of, 110–14;
death of, 118–22; elements, primary
and secondary, 119–22; emotions in,
115–17; gardening to ground the body,
116; guiding the heart back to, 115–17;
identified as self, 73; mindfulness of,
103–4, 115–17, 142; mortification of,
111; release of clinging to, 73; sankharas
and, 152; self and, 234; suffering and,
112; trainings in movement and, 116;
universal dimension of, 118–20;
valuing and caring for, 117; walking
meditation for, 122–23; well-being
arising from, 112; Western culture's
outer appearance, 118
Bohm, David, 154
Boorstein, Sylvia, 126, 389
Buddha: alternative society of, 362–63;
Ananda and, 265; on anger, 217; on

beauty, 203; on the body, 110; on cognitive strategies, 293; compassion for his own painful life, 64; conscience and, 338; on consciousness, 48; describing temperaments, 167; dream of his birth, 160; enlightenment of, 105, 207, 223, 249; entanglement in comforts, 230; on experience and consciousness, 49–50; facing his fears, 101, 105, 207; freeing oneself from unhealthy states, 16; on human creativity, 52; inquiries about the self, 64–65; on interdependence, 356; on the legacy of hatred, 208; letting go of anger, 214; light a lamp in the darkness, 102; lists of, 50; Long Discourses, 363; material abundance and, 202; on mind, 137; on mindfulness, 95, 97; on nirvana, 254; no victors in war, 341–42, 364; on past life, 157; on replacing unhealthy thought, 301–2; sacred images of, 275, 286, 317; seeing through the blindness of self, 71–72; on suffering, 244; taking refuge in, 289, 290; on thoughts and opinions, 75, 374; two arrows, 214; on wise speech, 271

Buddhadasa, Ajahn, 4, 101, 137, 142, 254, 356; mindfulness of feelings work, 127–29; monastery of, garden of peace, 396–97

Buddhaghosa, 326

Buddha nature, 12, 384, 397; acknowledging with ritual, 285; first principle, Buddhist psychology, 12–20; greeting: *namaste,* 17; healthy mental states and, 57; hostage's experience, 18; love as, 386; Michael Meade's work and, 266; practice: seeing the secret goodness, 21; sacred perception and, 17–20; seeing in all people, 13, 17–20; seeing in ourselves, 18; as self, 234–35; teacher's class exercise, 19–20; trusting, 305–6

Buddhayama, 4

Buddhism: disciplines of virtue, 191; joy of, 391–92; many planes of existence,

156; mystic and visionary states, 309–10; as religion, 7; reverence for life (virtue), 331–33; as science of the mind, xi, 7; as a way to understand/ release suffering, 7; wise society/leadership teaching, 361

Burton, Lloyd, 342–43

Bury the Chains (Hochschild), 365

C

Campbell, Joseph, 243

Camus, Albert, 134, 243–44

Carnegie, Andrew, 259

Carson, Rachel, 374

Carver, George Washington, 96

Casteneda, Carlos, 139

Chadwick, Alan, 265

Chah, Ajahn, 2, 3, 4, 6, 41, 42, 254, 309, 392; on acceptance of personality, 168; acknowledging suffering, 244; anecdote of the disturbed woman, 83–84; "be the Knowing," 43; on the body and death, 118; brain hemorrhage of, 126; changing consciousness, 50; choosing experience and, 59; on concentration, 308, 328; on concepts, 87–88; confronting denial, 229–30; on delusion, 222, 223–24, 230, 358; on experience of non-self, 72; on goal of revelation, 316; on hand opened, hand closed and, 83; on holding thoughts lightly, 146; inevitable pains of life vs. suffering, 114; on judging, 140; on the middle way, 367–68, 372; on mind states, 48–49; mindfulness of anger and, 206; on money, 89; on non-contentiousness, 217; the One Who Knows, 143; personality type and, 178; on pleasure and pain, 81; questioning one's social identity, 74; on recognizing bad thoughts, 299; on refuge in the Buddha, 290; on self, 77; on the state of the world, 190; on stilling the mind, 142; on student claiming enlightenment, 85–86; on suffering,

Chah, Ajahn (*cont'd*)
241–42, 247, 248; teaching of sitting like a clear forest pool, 368, 370; on thought, 293–94; on uncertainty, 371, 372; on the universal and the personal, 79; using the sword of wisdom, 219–20; on views, 146; on virtue, 332, 338
Chamberlin-Taylor, Debra, 97–98, 393
Chödrön, Pema, 4, 70–71, 82, 129, 298
Chuang Tzu, 167
Clarkson, Thomas, 365
cognitive strategies, 7, 293–307; Dalai Lama's favorite practices, 296–300; freeing ourselves, 304–5; practice: compassionate replacement of painful thoughts, 306–7; retraining the mind, 301–4; trusting our true nature, 305–6
compassion, 5, 7; acting from, 258; as courage, 30–31; creating new karma and, 269–71; dealing with addictions and, 248–49; forgiveness, reconciliation, and, 341–42; grief and, 135; holding the world in kindness, 22–33; inattention and, 227; innate, 17; interconnection of all things and, 23, 43, 155, 315, 356; love meeting suffering, 386, 390; meditation on, 33–34, 280–81; as our nature, 24–27; practice of, 57–58, 265, 288; the problem of self-hatred, 27–30; as a Radiant Abode, 386; as reason for existence, 81; recognizing, 14–15; second principle, Buddhist psychology, 22–33; spacious and clear heart awakening of, 235; storehouse consciousness and, 155; suffering and, 255; transforming thoughts with, 296, 298, 300
concentration, 7; absorption states, 317; developing through inner training, 312; doors to illumination and, 320–23; how it works, 316–18; loving-kindness to develop, 322; luminosity/boundlessness in, 309, 316, 319, 321; malleability and insight, 323–26; mystical dimensions, 308–28; purification in, 318–19;

Seven Factors of Enlightenment, 312–13; sports application, 317; training psychic ability, 326–28
concepts, realm of, 87–91
consciousness, 7, 44; absorption states and, 320; awakening to pure consciousness, 40–43; beyond the brain and body, 36; Buddha on, 48; "clear open sky of awareness," 38–39, 40, 46; colorings of, 48–52; expanded (mystical dimensions), 308–28; experience distinguished from, 36, 42, 45; eye consciousness, 51, 52, 54; gravity metaphor and, 37–38; happiness and, 49; healthy or unhealthy mental states, 48–58; meditation and, 40–41; mind and, 37; mind as sixth sense door, 51; mindfulness to explore, 37–39, 40; "mind ground" or "mind essence," 42; nature of, 35–39; "Original Mind" or "One Who Knows," 42, 337; particle-like nature, 40, 50; personality type held in, 177–78; practice: recognizing mental states, 60; practice: the river of sound, 46–47; "prosperity consciousness," 199; releasing unhealthy conditioning, 58–60; resting in, 41–42, 45; *rigpa,* 42; secondary feelings and, 129; sense experiences, 51, 52, 54; storehouse consciousness, 150–51, 154–57; suffering and happiness dependent on, 7–8; third eye and, 44; timeless witness, 42; training with cognitive strategies, 293–307; turning toward our essence, 43–46; two dimensions of, 39–40; visualization to change, 276; Western psychology and, 38
contemplative traditions, 318
Crick, Francis, 38

D

Dalai Lama (Tenzin Gyatso), xi, 7, 249–51, 314–16, 343–44, 355, 391; favorite practices, 296–300; on intention,

258; meeting tragedy, 396; on replacing unhealthy thought, 305; sacred perception and, 18–19; vows of bodhisattva and, 355

Davidson, Richard, 310

Day, Dorothy, 357

death: Buddhist practices for, 117; as dissolution of the elements, 121–22; as illusion, 43; as inevitable, 232; living in the here and now and, 90; meditations on, 101–2, 121; mindfulness as fearless presence, 99–101; mystery of, 376–77; reality of change and, 231; reflecting on, 142; Salam's experience, 42–43; Shunryu Suzuki and, 199; sitting with corpses, 112; universal dimension of, 80–82, 156

deathless, 118–20, 220, 315

dedication, 260–63

delusion, 14, 31, 83, 132, 222–37, 255, 378; denial and, 227–30; "false generalizations" and, 298; illusion of separateness, 236; inattention as first level of, 225–27; intention and, 263–64; interdependence as truth vs., 358–60; Mara as god of, 207; mindfulness and release from, 225–26, 227; misperception of reality, 230–34; of permanence, 231; personality type, 172, 174–75, 177, 178, 232–33; psychosis and, 224; releasing, healing from, 102, 223, 224, 234–35, 236, 253, 364, 390; as root of unhealthy mental states, 54, 55, 69, 162, 170, 223, 224, 242, 291, 358–60; seductive power of, 224; of self, 233–35; Soviet propaganda and, 228–29; spacious, clear heart and release, 235–37; symptoms, 226–27; transforming, 170

denial, 102, 111, 129, 236, 275, 338, 367–68; delusion and, 227–30; recognition vs., 102; self-, 254; societal, 228–29

Denison, Ruth, 257

depression: clinging to notion of suffering, 85; cognitive-behavioral therapy, 296;

creating new karma and, 269–71; facing, 14; healing, 200; lack of desire (anhedonia), 196; mindfulness of, 128, 131–32; as motivation, 258; prescription drugs, 251–52; self-image and, 15

desire, 184–204; abundance and fulfillment, 198–200; adornment, 202–3; affect on Ladakh, India, 190–91; aversion to, 191–92; on global scale, 190; grasping temperament and, 173; from grasping to abundance, 196–98; healthy, 185, 187, 188, 195–96; holding lightly, 189; letting go of, 191; loss of touch with, 186–87; materialism, 185, 190–91; mindfulness of, 128; natural generosity, 201–2; practice: generosity, 203–4; "prosperity consciousness," 199; self vs., 192–95; unhealthy, 188, 189–92; will to do, 187

detachment: as coping mechanism, 41; pathological, 41, 45, 77; resting in consciousness as, 41; selflessness as, 77

Dhammapada, 48, 80, 205, 257, 293, 331, 348

dharma, 290–91, 309, 381; as foundation of mindfulness, 103, 104–5; meanings, 104

Diagnostic and Statistical Manual of Mental Disorders, 15, 311

Digha Nikaya, 205, 382

Dillard, Annie, 378

Dipama (Nani Bala Barua), 76–77, 326–27, 382–84, 389, 390, 395

divorce: dealing with, 15; dealing with anger, blame, and grief, 215–16; disentangling from the story, 144–45; mindfulness of feelings and, 104, 133–34; mindfulness of mental states and, 57–58; suffering and, 244–45

Dogen, 61

Donne, John, 291

Douglas, William O., 124

dreams: Buddhist dream work, 161, 162; dream yoga, 161; interpretation of,

dreams (cont'd)
160–61; lucid dreaming, 161–62;
unconscious and, 160–62

E

Eckhart, Meister, 339
Eisenhower, Dwight, 359
Ekman, Paul, 310
elements: air or vibratory element, of the
body, 119; earth element of the body,
119; fire element of the body, 119; of
three root temperaments, 173, 174;
used in ritual, 284–85; water element
of the body, 119
Eliot, T. S., 83, 368–69, 395
Ellis, Albert, 295
emotions: arising from feelings, 129; as
innately human, 129; meditation on
grief, 135–36; meditation retreats
and, 131; releasing with mindfulness,
100–101; resistance to, 133;
transitory nature of, 132, 133;
working with, 129–35. See also
feelings; specific emotions
emptiness, 3, 26, 79, 80, 83, 86, 87, 104,
113, 116, 120, 127, 134, 142, 160,
190, 191, 193–95, 216, 231, 233,
248, 275, 295; reflecting on, 142;
transformational or mystical, 253,
276, 278, 287, 292, 309, 324, 325,
327, 368, 378
Engler, Jack, 384, 390
enlightenment, 5, 13, 86, 180, 291, 372;
awakening from delusion and, 223;
Buddha's, 105, 207, 223, 249; factors
of, 50, 312, 313, 325, 386; levels, 85,
163; mindfulness of the body and, 112;
optimal mental health and the factors
of, 313; working with feelings and, 126
Epstein, Mark, 262
equanimity: arising from neutral feelings,
129; freedom in the here and now,
395–97; letting go of suffering,
249–52; making a zone of peace,
357–58; meditation on, 401–2;
optimal mental health and, 312, 313;
as Radiant Abode, 386

Erikson, Erik, 171
Esalen Institute, 5
experience: "the all" (three-part system),
51, 54; aversive temperament and,
173–74; body, 103; Buddha's two
arrows, 214; clarifying moment-to-
moment intention and, 266–68;
consciousness vs., 36, 42, 45;
delusion obscuring, 222; dharma and,
103, 104; erroneous habitual
perception of, 222–23; eye
consciousness, 51, 54; feelings and,
103; mind and, 103; misperception of
reality, 230–34; neutral, 226; non-self
and, 75; reaction vs. response to, 214;
sense experiences, 51, 54; states of
mind and, 49–52, 54; the teachings
of, 102

F

fear: arising from painful feelings, 129;
Buddha's, 100; of emotions and
feelings, 134–35; healthy response
and freedom from, 57, 65, 86,
99–101, 102, 106, 107, 130, 133–35,
142, 153, 168, 201, 206, 210,
211–16, 221, 243, 251, 255–56, 279,
286, 296, 298, 304, 305, 315, 333,
347, 358, 373; masquerading as
wisdom, 129; mindfulness of, 99,
128; mindfulness of the body and,
119–20; as motivation, 258; past-life
unconscious and, 159–60; practice:
discovering the pain and fear behind
anger, 220–21; as predecessor to
anger and hate, 209–10; roots of
unhealthy mental states and, 162,
205; temperament and, 179;
therapeutic work in, 314–16;
unconscious and, 150–51; as
unhealthy reaction and cause of
suffering, 1, 2, 12, 14, 15, 16, 18, 23,
26, 28, 31, 32, 39, 45, 57, 58, 63, 64,
69, 90, 100, 104, 115, 116, 119, 120,
128, 130, 131, 138, 139, 140, 141,
142, 144–45, 148, 150–51, 152,
155, 162, 163, 182, 186, 191,

194–95, 202, 205, 206, 218, 220, 223, 230, 232–33, 242, 247, 250, 267, 269, 287, 294–96, 301, 302, 315, 319, 321, 327, 335, 336, 337, 341, 343, 350, 351, 354, 357, 358, 365, 370, 376

feelings, 124–36; emotions distinguished from, 129; experiencing difficult, 130–31; mindfulness of, 104, 130–35; neutral, 124, 126, 129; painful, 124, 126, 129; pleasant, 124, 126, 129; primary, 125–29; reclaiming, 130; secondary (emotions), 128, 129–35; stream of, daily, 126, 128; suffering and, 133; unhealthy suppression of, 124–25, 130

Feiffer, Jules, 207

Fifty Verses on the Nature of Consciousness, 150

Finca, Rev. Bongani, 360

First Noble Truth, 126, 211, 242, 244–46

forgiveness, 339–51; atonement and, 288, 340; confession, 340–41; meditation, 349–51; practice of, 345–49; as principle of Buddhist psychology, 341; prison meditation projects and, 252–53, 343–45; redemption and, 339–45

form (particulars of life, *suchness*), 79, 83–87, 91, 234, 369; exploring, 86–87; finding freedom and enlightenment, 86; honoring, 83; personal responsibility and, 85; realm of concepts and, 87–91; resistance to, 86

Fossey, Dian, 95–96

Four Noble Truths, 13–14, 241, 242, 244, 391; First, 126, 211, 242, 244–46; Fourth, 243; Second, 242–43, 247; Third, 243

Four Radiant Abodes, 285–87, 387–90, 395

Francis of Assisi, Saint, 317, 357

Frankl, Viktor, 16, 289, 291

Freud, Sigmund, 15, 151, 161, 163, 171, 375; aggression and, 209; "ever hovering attention," 99; "ordinary level of neurosis," 243; psychoanalytic

approach, 333; stages of self's (ego) development, 65

Fromm, Erich, 171

G

Gandhi, Mahatma, 214, 219, 333, 352, 356, 357, 358, 362

generosity, 2; as Buddha nature, 57; cultivating, 201; happiness and, 354; letting go of suffering and, 254; natural generosity, 201–2; practice, 203–4, 265; as root of healthy mental states, 54, 55

George II, King of England, 259

Gestalt pyschotherapy, 99, 375–76

Gide, André, 392

Goldstein, Joseph, 4

Goleman, Dan, 262

Goodman, Trudy, 287

Gorbachev, Mikhail, 228–29

Gorillas in the Mist (film), 95–96

grace, 252–54

Grace Cathedral, San Francisco, 85

Grandmothers for Peace, 255

grasping and greed, 129; addictions arising from, 55, 189; awareness of, 60; delusion of permanence and, 231; desire and, 189–92; from grasping to abundance, 196–98; as motivation, 258; pattern of thought leading to suffering, 296; personality type, 171, 172, 173, 175–76, 177, 180, 186; as root of unhealthy mental states, 54, 55, 162, 242; as source of suffering, 14, 242–43, 247; transforming, 170. *See also* addictions; desire

gratitude, 200, 315, 398; meditation on, 399–400; practice for cultivating, 394

Great Discourse on Mindfulness, The, 124

grief, 245; facing, 14; healing, 33; meditation on, 135–36; meditation opening door to, 211–12; sleepiness as symptom, 226–27; universal dimension of death and, 81; as water element, 120–21

Grof, Stanislav, 311

Guadalupe, 286
Guy, Buddy, 211

H

habit, 258–60, 269–71
Hafiz, 130–31, 209–10
Haight, Richard, 145
Hall, Robert, 153, 375
happiness: arising from painful feelings, 129; avoiding discomfort in pursuit of, 14; Buddhist psychology and, 49; consciousness and, 7–8; delusion and, 233; from healthy states of mind, 187–88, 231; joy and, 390–95; middle way and, 368; misperception and delusion about, 230–31; past-life unconscious, 157–58; respecting both the universal and personal nature of life and, 80; as state of mind, 55; tending to suffering and, 353; virtue, integrity, and, 333, 334–39; Western culture and, 49
hatred, 205–21, 242; aversion as root of, 55, 210; aversive temperament and, 174; experience colored by, 208; facing, 207–8; fear as predecessor, 209–10; by love alone is healed, 214–15; mindfulness of, 133; nature of, 208–10; non-contentiousness to oppose, 218–19; pattern of thought leading to suffering, 296; self-hatred, 27–33, 249; as source of suffering, 14; transforming with compassion, 208–9; as universal energy, 208
healthy mental states: happiness and, 231; list of, 54, 56; mindfulness as, 59; motivations and, 258; practice: recognizing mental states, 60; resonance in others, 17; three roots of, 54, 55–56
heart: abundant, 199; awakened, 382–402; compass of: intention and karma, 257–73; Four Radiant Abodes, 385–87; happiness and gracious, 231; natural virtue and integrity of, 333; resting in the peaceful heart, 255; resting in the wise heart, 220; ritual

language of, 282–85; setting a long-term intention and the compass of, 261; spacious and clear, 235–37. *See also* inner freedom and liberation of the heart
Heart Sutra, 3–4, 79
Hesse, Herman, 115
High Tide in Tucson (Kingsolver), 305
Hillman, James, 355
Hina-Tyana Dhamma Loka, 61
Hinduism: "timeless witness," 42
Hobbe, John, 316
Hoblitzelle, Harrison, 181–82
Hochschild, Adam, 365
Hogan, Linda, 338–39
Hover, Robert, 50–51
How Can I Help? (Ram Dass), 106
Hsi Tang, 189
Huang Po, 291
hungry ghosts, 248–49, 287

I

identification and identities. *See* self
illusion, 223. *See also* delusion
Indian greeting: *namaste,* 17
inner freedom and liberation of the heart, 7, 16–17; abundance and, beyond healthy desire, 188; anger prevention, 217; awareness of the unconscious and, 156; Buddhism disciplines of virtue and, 191; Buddhist practices and trainings for, 16; from hatred (diagram), 210; in the here and now, 395–97; liberation of the trusting mind, 372; living in the here and now, 89–90, 112; mystical dimensions of the mind and, 308–28; non-contention and, 210; no-self and, 72; from pain, 114; recognizing it, 20; releasing emotions with mindfulness and, 100–102; respecting both the universal and personal nature of life and, 80
Insight Meditation Society, 168
integrity, 2, 3, 67, 86, 180, 188, 202, 275, 332; basic practices, 336; inner and outer conscience, 336–37; mental

health and, 338–39; middle path and, 243; natural virtue and, 59, 333

intention. *See* karma

interconnection of self and all things, 23, 43, 155, 315, 356, 357

investigation, 103–5. *See also* RAIN

J

Jackson, Phil, 317

jealousy, 119–20, 129, 189, 242, 296, 301

Jesus, sacred images of, 286

jhana (silence), 319, 320–23; absorption states and, 320, 322, 325; eight states of, 320; insight states, 321, 322; psychic ability and, 326, 327

John of the Cross, Saint, 309, 327

Johnson, Robert, 12

Jones, Alan, 85

Jordan, Michael, 261, 317

joy, 315, 390–95; cultivating gratitude, 394; love meeting happiness, 386, 390; meditation on, 399–400; practice for cultivating, 394; as a Radiant Abode, 386; reawakening, 393

Joyce, James, 111

Juan, Don, 139

judgment: arising from painful feelings, 129; aversive temperament and, 173–74; delusion and, 227; as inner critic, 206–7; mindfulness of, 133

Jumnian, Ajahn, 43–44, 168–70, 178, 180, 187, 198

Jung, Carl, 12, 103, 111, 151, 154, 161, 171, 245, 277, 311

K

Kabat-Zinn, Jon, 227

Kabir, 198

Kaleau, 187

Kali, 340

Kalu Rinpoche, 77, 121, 223

karma, 257–73, 337, 339; Cambodian genocide and, 158; clarifying moment-to-moment intention,

266–68; creating new karma, 267–68; dedication and long-term intention, 260–63; deluded intention and, 263–64; forgiveness and, 346; habit and, 258–60; intention and motivation as roots of, 258; power of intention, 323; practice: meeting difficulty with wise intention, 273; the sacred pause, 268–71; setting the heart's compass, 271–73; support for intention, 264–66; using RAIN to create new karma, 259–60; -vipaka, 258, 268, 304

Karmapa Lama, 126, 392

Keating, Father Thomas, 310

Keller, Helen, 371

Khan, Pir Vilayat, 22

Khyentse Rinpoche, 295

King, Martin Luther, Jr., 214, 219, 291, 360, 362, 364

Kingsolver, Barbara, 305

Kitts Peak astronomical laboratory, 90–91

Kornfield, Liana, 25, 69, 211, 213, 262, 311

Krishnamurti, 102, 178

Kwan Yin, 275, 286, 317, 357

L

LaBerge, Stephen, 161

Ladakh, India, 190–91

Lamott, Anne, 141–43, 318

latent roots, 163, 164

Lavoisier, Antoine, 179

lethargy, 129

letting go: of anger, therapeutic approaches, 114, 120, 125, 133–34, 135, 162, 168, 211–13, 214–15, 219, 220, 247–48, 314–16, 348; of blaming, 247–48; of desire, 191; fruits of, 255; practice, 255–56; of suffering, 247, 249–56

Levine, Stephen and Ondrea, 376–77

liberation. *See* inner freedom and liberation of the heart

Lindbergh, Ann Morrow, 114

Liu Qing, 355–56

logotherapy, 289

loneliness, 6, 90, 100, 104, 131, 176, 193, 211, 226, 244, 250–51, 304, 337; desire and, 193; mindfulness practice for, 250–51; sleepiness as symptom, 226–27
Longchempa, 3, 4, 22
Lorenz, Konrad, 209
Lotus in a Sea of Fire (Thich Nhat Hanh), 364
Lotus Sutra, 184
love, 96; awakening, 387–90; awareness of, 45; as Buddha nature, 57; concentration practices and, 322, 324, 325; for difficult people or enemies, 389–90, 399; dispelling the illusion of separateness and, 236–37; happiness and, 354, 386; "I am everything," 68, 69; inner freedom and liberation, 233; for neutral people, 389, 399; as our nature, 386; reflecting on, 142; as root of healthy mental states, 54, 55; for self, 388–89; as subject of meditative concentration, 317; suffering and compassion, 386; true strength and, 219. See also loving-kindness
loving-kindness, 2, 349; absorption states and, 322; collective well-being and, 359; dealing with addictions and, 248–49; meditation, 280–81, 300, 397–99; phrases from practice, 306, 387; practice in, 387–90; as a Radiant Abode, 386

M

Maha Bua, Ajahn, 235
Maha Ghosananda, 81–82, 106, 215, 341–42, 382, 392
Mahaparinirvana Sutra, 274
Maharshi, Ramana, 126
Mahasi Sayadaw, 52
Mahayan Buddhist tradition, 4
Maitreya, Ananda, 392
Majjhima Nikaya, 40, 157, 184, 205, 308, 367
Mandela, Nelson, 15, 20, 261, 268, 285

mantra, 142, 277, 317–18
Mao Zedong, 264
Mara, 207, 209, 370
Mary, 286, 317
Maslow, Abraham, 311
McClelland, David and Mary, 262–63
Meade, Michael, 266, 282
meditation: acknowledging pain, 248; advanced meditators, 267, 384, 390, 392–93; on aging and decay, 232, 234; on compassion, 33–34; concentrating on the breath, 142; consciousness and, 40–41; on death, 101–2; difficulty and mindful attention, 97–98; don't know mind, 381; emotions and, 131; on equanimity and peace, 401–2; establishing a daily meditation, 107–9; examining suffering, 248; fear and groundlessness of experience, 327; filled with thought, 143–44; forgiveness, 349–51; on gratitude and joy, 399–400; on grief, 135–36; grounding practices, 324; ignoring distractions and, 223; interplay of individual and universal unconscious, 155–56; investigation of unconscious forces, 163–64; loving-kindness, 280–81, 300, 322, 324, 384–85, 397–99; luminosity and boundlessness in, 314–16; mindfulness practice, 52; neuropsychology and, 5; opening door to emotions, 211–12; past-life unconscious and, 158–60; release from grasping and, 247; repeating a mantra, 142; to see the body as an energy field, 118; for stress reduction, 112–13; subject of, effects, 317–19; as therapeutic approach, 314–16, 373; training in mindfulness, 96; walking meditation, 116, 122–23, 142. See also concentration
mental health, 7; Four Radiant Abodes, 385–87, 395; integrity and, 338–39; neutral factor, will to do, 187; optimal, 7, 312, 382, 386, 392–93; sense of self and, 62; Seven Factors of

Enlightenment, 312–13. *See also* healthy mental states; unhealthy mental states

Merton, Thomas, 11, 17, 236–37, 241, 380

middle way, 243, 367–81; freedom from views and opinions, 374–77; open to mystery, 378–79; planting seeds on the middle path, 379–81; practice: don't know mind, 381–82; in Sri Lanka, 379–80; therapeutic work in, 370–71; truth of uncertainty, 371–74

Milarepa, 339

mind: the abyss and the heart, 147; the ancient unconscious, 150–64; blinded by beliefs, opinions, fears, 140–41; Buddha on, 137; clarity of thought and intellect, 147–48; clinging to, as delusion, 233–34; cognitive strategies and, 293–307; consciousness and, 37; disentangling from the story, 143–45; examining thoughts, 141–43; exercise, counting your thoughts, 140; experience and states of, 52; as foundation of mindfulness, 104; holding thoughts lightly, 146; judging, 140, 142; kinds of thoughts, 140; liberation of the trusting mind, 372; "malleability of the mind," 323–26; meditation to examine mental states, 53; mental states, 52, 54, 55; mystical dimensions of, 308–28; naming top ten thoughts, 142; number of thoughts per day, 139; points of view, allowing other, 146; practice: one-sided thoughts, 148–49; practices to quiet, examine, or release thoughts, 142; quiet, and the One Who Knows, 143; quieting of as political act, 358; the reality below the thoughts, 145–47; repetitive thoughts, 295; retraining, 301–4; *samsara* and, 141–42, 295; self and, 234; as sixth sense door, 51; stilling, 142–43; storytelling mind, 137–49; stream of thoughts, 138–39; thirteen universal qualities, 55. *See also* healthy mental states; unhealthy mental states

Mindell, Stephan Bodian, 377

mindfulness, 2, 7; ability to choose mental state and, 59–60; for anxiety, 250–51; as attention, 96; awareness and, 96, 110–11; of the body, 103–4, 110–14, 142; dealing with addictions and, 248–49; defined, 99; delusion, awareness of, 225–26, 227; desire, awareness of, 192–95; of dharma, 104–5; disentangling from the story, 143–45; distinguishing two dimensions of consciousness, 40; dream work, 161; examining thoughts (mind), 137–49; facing death and, 90; factors of enlightenment and, 313; as fearless presence, 99–101, 107; of feelings, 104, 127–29; four foundations of, 103–5; four principles for transformation, 101–6; fruits of non-identification, 106–7; as healthy state, 59; liberating power of, 95–99; living in the here and now, 89–90, 112; meditation and, 96, 107–9; meeting pain and fear, 210; mental states, awareness of, 56–57; of the mind, 104; painful thoughts and, 64; practice: recognizing mental states, 60; prompted and unprompted response, 265–66; releasing emotions with, 100–101; releasing states of mind with, 104; releasing unhealthy mental states and, 163; as root of healthy mental states, 56; seeing thought skillfully, 147–48; stream of thoughts ("seeing the waterfall"), 138–39; of thoughts, 137–49; transforming power, 37–39, 102–6, 129, 170; uncovering patterns in the unconscious, 152–53

Mountain Dreamer, Oriah, 271–72

Mumford, George, 317

Mun, Ajahn, 41, 110, 309

Munindra, Anagarika, 310, 392

mystery, openness to, 374

mystical dimensions of the mind, 308–28; hallucinogens and, 308–9, 310; jhana (silence), 319, 320–23; luminosity and boundlessness, 309, 316, 319,

mystical dimensions (*cont'd*)
321; malleability and insight, 323–26;
psychic ability, 326–28

N

Naropa Buddhist University, 5, 340
Navajo, 268
neuroplasticity, 298, 345
Nietzsche, Friedrich, 231
nirvana, 253–54, 295
Nisargadatta, Sri, 68, 147, 198, 246
nobility, 5, 7, 258; connecting with, 14,
128–29, 131–32; etymology, 14;
finding our innate, 12, 20, 266;
recognizing in others, 17; redeeming
the past and, 343; seeing our
profound nobility, 12–13; of shadow
self, 12
non-contentiousness, 210, 216, 217–19,
265
non-harming (*ahimsa*), 57–58, 191, 332,
336, 348, 359, 362
non-identification, 101, 105–7
Norberg-Hodge, Helena, 190

O

Oliver, Mary, 261

P

Packer, Toni, 103, 374
pain, 14, 16, 22; accepting in a gracious
way, 127; acknowledging, 28, 59, 64,
98, 102, 114, 134, 216, 243, 244;
anger, aversion, and, 114, 213,
220–21; awareness and, 105, 226–27;
born of hate, 205; Buddha's two
arrows and, 214; changing or
impermanence of, 81; childhood
deficiencies and, 30; compassion and,
23, 29, 34, 64, 114, 120, 144, 145,
227; dealing with, 114; death and,
199; denial of, 102; desire as, 195;
developing a healthy response to,

211–16; fear of, 63, 101, 206; First
Noble Truth and, 126; of grief, 135;
karma and, 158; meeting with
wisdom, 210; not recognizing, 23–24,
28, 41; numbing, unhealthy, 63;
reacting and adding to, 214; releasing,
33, 58, 60, 125, 178, 200; responding
with wisdom, 217, 219; suffering
different from, 114, 208, 242,
246–47; unhealthy states and, 127; as
universal, 28, 30, 32, 49, 90, 209
panic: cognitive-behavioral therapy for,
295, 296; conscious intention and,
260; therapeutic work for, 314
Paracelsus, 97
paranoia, worry as root of, 55
past: releasing pain of, 273; unchanging
nature of, 267; unhealthy thoughts
chaining us to, 304–5. *See also* karma
Path of Purification, 158, 326
Path with a Heart, A (Kornfield), 84, 342
peace, as long-term intention, 261
peace (of mind). *See* equanimity
Perls, Fritz, 375–76
personality and temperament: acceptance
of one's own, 168, 175–79; natural
vs. unhealthy states, 168; observing
one's own, 175–79; personality as a
temporary condition, 170; self vs.,
176; temperament as inborn,
167–70, 171; three root
temperaments, 167, 171–79;
transforming unhealthy patterns into
healthy expressions, 170, 179–82
personality types, 167; aversive, 171–72,
173–74, 176–77, 178–79, 180;
deluded, 172, 174–75, 177, 178,
232–33; finding your type exercise,
171–72; grasping, 171, 172, 173,
175–76, 177, 180, 186; practice:
acknowledging your personality type,
182–83
phobias, cognitive-behavioral therapy for,
295
pleasure, 19, 49, 53, 81, 127, 128, 134,
156, 157, 162, 173, 177, 182, 184,
186, 203, 205, 217, 230, 232, 242,
269, 323, 360, 374, 395; desire and,
189; joy and, 395 (*see also* joy)

politics and social injustice: bodhisattva path and, 354–56; delusion and, 358–60; envisioning liberation and justice, 360–63; life of balance and, 356–57; practice: bodhisattva vows, 366; quieting of the mind and, 357; tending the world, 363–65

practices: acknowledging personality type, 182–83; bodhisattva vows, 366; compassionate replacement of painful thoughts, 306–7; the creation and dissolution of self, 77–78; cultivating gratitude, 394; cultivating joy, 394; discovering pain/fear behind anger, 220–21; don't know mind, 381–82; establishing a daily meditation, 107–9; generosity, 203–4; letting go, 255–56; meditation on compassion, 33–34; meditation on equanimity and peace, 401–2; meditation on gratitude and joy, 399–400; meditation on grief, 135–36; meditation on loving-kindness, 397–99; meeting difficulty with wise intention, 273; one-sided thoughts, 148–49; recognizing mental states, 60; the river of sound, 46–47; seeing from the universal perspective, 92–93; seeing the secret goodness, 21; visualization, 292; walking meditation, 122–23

Prajnaparamita, 234

Pribram, Karl, 154

pride, 53, 162, 163, 168–69, 173, 176, 327

principles. See Buddhist psychology

prison meditation projects, 252–53, 343–45

Proust, Marcel, 378

psychic ability, 326–28

psychology, Buddhist: Abhidhamma as compedium of, 3; "the all" (three-part system), 51, 54; balance of Radiant Abodes and, 386; as behaviorism with heart, 296; body, mindfulness of and, 111–14, 117; capacity to see beyond the separate self, 66; cognitive strategies, 20, 293–307; creating a healthy society, 361–62; cultivating generosity, 201; cultivating respect, 18; desire, healthy vs. unhealthy, 185, 195; development and change in, 20; dispelling the illusion of separateness, 236; dreams and, 160–62; ego in, 67; ethical trainings, 20; examining thoughts, 141–43; exploring consciousness, 35–45; feelings as distinct from emotions, 129; forgiveness practices, 339–51; Four Noble Truths and, 13–14; goal, clarity of vision, 222; going beyond stabilization, 313–16; healing and direct perception, 88; healing aversion, 213–16; healthy development of self, 65–67; how grasping operates, 247; inner light, categories of, 319; jhana concentration used in, 321; Kornfield's practice of, 6; liberation and, 16; lists and, 50–51, 52; meditations, 20 (see also meditation); mental health, understanding of, 55; mental states, 48–60; millennia of observation and, 5; natural personality vs. unhealthy states, 168; past-life unconscious and, 158; personality systems, 171; practices for inner transformation, 20, 312 (see also practices for inner transformation); principles of, 12–20, 23, 36, 50, 63, 80, 97, 112, 127, 139, 156, 170, 187, 208, 224, 243, 258, 277, 296, 312, 333, 341, 356, 369, 374, 387; as psychology of interdependence, 356; radical change offered by, 168; retreats and inner training used in, 314–16; ritual as a transformational tool, 284–88; storehouse consciousness (universal unconscious) and, 154–56; terms used in, 5; therapeutic work in, 16–17, 264–66, 313–16; training in mindfulness and, 99; Two Truths and, 79–80; virtue in, 331–39; visualization as transformational tool, 276, 277–81; worldly and spiritual problems as same, 3

psychology, Western: body awareness and, 111; cognitive-behavioral therapy,

psychology, Western (cont'd)
295, 298–99; consciousness and, 38;
denial and, 111, 229; ego, 65, 66, 67;
focus on interaction, 314; focus on
what we think about, 55; Freudian
psychoanalysis, 333; Gestalt
pyschotherapy, 99, 375–76; healthy
development of self in, 65–67;
Kornfield and, 4–5; layman's terms
and, 5; level of delusion as "normal,"
225; medical model and pathology,
15–16, 38; mindfulness used in, 99;
pharmacology and medication, 15–16;
purification not understood in, 318;
suffering and, 243–44; theories of
personality, 171; transcendent domain
absent, 310–11; visualization as
transformational tool, 277. See also
Freud, Sigmund; Jung, Carl
purification, 318–19; Path of Purification,
158, 326

R

RAIN (recognition, acceptance,
investigation, non-identification),
102–6, 107, 129, 130–35, 259–60
Ram Dass, 73–74, 106, 262, 340–41
recognition: instinctive, 333; of mental
states and thoughts, 16, 40, 41, 44,
55, 58, 60, 98, 104, 106, 120, 130,
131, 132, 135, 141, 170, 180, 212,
213, 235, 243, 267, 292, 295, 297,
298, 299, 303; of past behavior or
karma, 177; of personality type, 177;
practice: recognizing mental states,
60; RAIN and, 101–2, 103, 107, 129,
259. See also awareness; consciousness
Reich, Wilhelm, 111, 171, 212
reincarnation, 157–60
Remen, Rachel Naomi, 35, 284
Reynolds, Lloyd, 331–33
Rilke, Rainer Maria, 375
Rios, Don José, 308–9
ritual, 266, 274, 282–85; bodhisattva vows,
366; creating, 285–88; forgotten in
Western culture, 283–84; of

initiation, 282; of refuge, 290–91; as
transformational tool, 284–88
Rodriguez, Luis, 282
Rogers, Carl, 99
Rukeyser, Muriel, 138
Rumi, 231, 297–98, 392

S

sacred images, 274–76, 357; as archetypal
energy, 277; universal use of, 279;
used in ritual, 286; for visualization,
292, 317
sacred pause, 268–71
sacred perception, 17–20
Salzberg, Sharon, 4, 99, 384
samadhi, 308
sambogakaya, 277
samsara, 141–42, 295
sanctuaries and refuge, 274–76, 289–91
sangha (conscious community), 289, 290,
291
sankharas, 151–52, 154
Sartre, Jean Paul, 243–44
Schaef, Anne Wilson, 225
Schaller, George, 95–96
Schweitzer, Albert, 357
self: awareness and ability to shift identity,
216; body and, 234; Buddha nature
as, 234–35; childhood deficiencies
and, 193–94; delusion and, 233–35;
desires and, 192–95; expanded
consciousness and shift of identity,
309; healthy release of identification,
69; identification and identities,
68–69, 105–6; identification with
role and image, 69–72; inquiries into
one's true nature, 64–65; loving-
kindness for, 387–90; mind vs.,
233–34; as moment-to-moment
process, 74; non-self, 67, 68, 72–77;
the paradox of the development,
65–67; personality vs., 176; practice:
the creation/solution of self, 77–78;
practice of non-identification, 101,
105–7; practice: recognizing mental
states, 60; roles and, 62–65; self-

image, 70–71; "self-view" and
"compared view," 62; as temporary
identification, 65; turning toward our
essence, 43–46; who am I?, 61–65
selflessness (no-self), 66, 67, 68, 72; and
birth of the tender heart, 76–77;
experience and, 75; fear of loss of
self, 75–76; identification with self
and, 72–77
Sendak, Maurice, 391
Seung Sahn, 375
Seven Factors of Enlightenment, 312–13
sex and sexuality, 111, 185, 298, 300, 341;
desire and, 193; mindfulness and,
193; misuse of, 99, 191, 332, 333,
336; sexual abuse, 63; transcendence
and, 311
Shakespeare, William, 72, 81
shame, 387; anger turned inward and, 207;
Buddhist psychology and, 337;
childhood deficiencies and, 134, 178;
compassion to heal, 30; conscience
vs., 336–37; facing, 14; illness and,
117; mindfulness about, 86; money
and, 202; roots of, 54; suffering and,
14; as unhealthy mental state, 6, 15,
27, 73, 100, 138, 206; universal
unconscious and, 155; working with
feelings, 248–49
shamelessness, 54, 55, 243
Shantideva, 355, 369
Sharaf, Myron, 212–13
Simons, Daniel, 222–23
Singh, Charon, 147
Six Yogas of Naropa, 326
sociopathy, 55
Solzhenitsyn, Alekandr, 155
Somé, Malidoma, 245, 274, 282, 284
Spirit Rock Meditation Center, 1, 2, 53,
154, 180, 278; Dalai Lama at, 19;
Insight Prison Project, 252–53; Thich
Nhat Hanh at, 143
Sri Lanka, 379–80
Stalin, Josef, 264
Stephenson, Ian, 158
storehouse consciousness, 150, 154–56
stress, 1, 5, 21, 101, 102, 111; breath
practices to reduce, 179; delusion

and, 227; meditation to reduce, 112,
115, 116–17, 217, 227, 250, 352–53;
suffering and, 242
suchness. See form (particulars of life,
suchness)
suffering: acknowledging, 244;
acknowledging other people's, 13; as
always changing, 81; arising from
aversion or hatred, 208, 209, 212;
awareness and, 233; bodhisattva's
vision and transformation of the
world, 360–63; of the body, 112,
114; Buddhism to understand and
release, 7; causes of, 246–49;
childhood deficiencies and, 244;
collective, 14, 242, 353, 359;
compassion and, 255; consciousness
and, 7–8; creating a simple ritual to
alleviate, 286–88; death and, 199;
desire and, 184, 188, 189–92; as
different from pain, 114, 242;
feelings, acting on and, 133; finding
the goodness in everything, 396; First
Noble Truth, 211; forgiveness to end,
346; Four Noble Truths and, 241,
242; freedom from, 242, 243;
grasping as cause, 14, 242–43, 247;
hatred and, 205–21; healing with
gratitude, 200; human troubles and,
3; individual, 242, 354; as inevitable,
14, 126, 209, 211, 241; letting go of,
247, 249–56; mental, and beliefs,
146; middle way as to path to end,
243; our creation of, 114; past-life
unconscious and, 157–58; practice:
discovering the pain and fear behind
anger, 220–21; practice: letting go,
255–56; release and grace, 252–54;
roots in the unconscious, 162–64;
search for protection from, 95; as
self-created, 114, 246; spacious, clear
heart awakening compassion, 235;
standing in witness to, 245–46;
tending the world and bodhisattva,
352–66; transforming, 179–82,
196–204, 244; universal dimension,
156; Western acceptance of, 243–44
Sufism, 22, 181

Sumedo, Ajahn, 369
Sutta Nipata, 367
Suzuki, Shunryu, 20, 98–99, 126, 199, 231, 254, 374
Symeon, Saint, 279

T

tai chi, 116
Taizan Maezumi Roshi, 84–85
Tao Te Ching, 255
Tara, 275, 279, 286
Taungpulu Sayadaw, 117
Teresa of Avila, Saint, 395
Teresa of Calcutta, Mother, 354
Thailand: Ajahn Chah's forest monastery, 2–3, 17–18, 42, 61–62, 101–2, 112, 113, 137–38, 186, 192–93, 202, 222, 231, 232, 274–75, 278; finding of the golden Buddha, 11–12
Theraveda Buddhist tradition, 3, 4, 382; Anguttara Nikaya, 35; Digha Nikaya, 95
Thich Nhat Hanh, 1, 4, 40, 103, 121, 142–43, 259, 357–58, 364
Thomas, Lewis, 356
Thoreau, Henry David, 379
thoughts. See mind
Tibetan Buddhism: community in exile, joy of, 392–93; Mahamudra text of Longchempa, 22; recognizing consciousness, 43; rigpa, 42; Tibetan Book of the Dead, 11; Tibetan Book of the Great Liberation, 35. See also Dalai Lama
time, 89–90
Tocqueville, Alexis de, 185
Transformations of Consciousness (Engler), 384
transformative social practices, 7
trauma, 3, 24, 26, 28, 41, 75, 82, 85, 86, 130, 151, 178, 193, 200, 217, 250, 251, 252, 303, 313, 321, 336, 342, 392, 393; bringing unconscious patterns into awareness, 153; meditation and healing of, 115
Trungpa, Chögyam, 44, 262, 372
truth: interdependence as, 358–60; points of view, allowing other, 146; story of

the holy fool Mullah Nasrudin, 146; of uncertainty, 371–74. See also integrity
Truth and Reconciliation Committee, 359–60
Twain, Mark, 294
Two Truths, 79–80

U

unconscious: dreams and, 160–62; fears and, 150–51; individual, 151–53, 155–56; in meditation, 155–56; past-life unconscious, 157–60; roots of suffering in (latent roots), 162–64; sankharas, 151–52, 154; three roots of unhealthy mental states and, 162–64; universal (storehouse), 150–51, 154–57
unhealthy mental states, 54; ability to free oneself from, 16; childhood deficiencies and, 13, 15, 23, 26–27, 28, 30, 45, 63, 87, 112–13, 120, 132, 134, 140, 142, 144–45, 155, 193–94, 205–6; contagion of to others, 17; delusion and, 224; Dhammapada on, 48, 205; fundamentalism and, 146; list of, 54; meditation and mindfulness of, 97–98, 99, 101–2; motivations and, 258; releasing unhealthy conditioning, 58–60; retraining the mind, 301–4; therapeutic work in, 314–16; three roots of, 54, 55, 162, 170; transformation of, 7, 168–70. See also anger; anxiety, aversion; delusion; grasping and greed; hatred; shame; other specific emotions
universal dimension, 79, 80–82, 91; of the body, 118–20; death and, 80–82; mistake of clinging to, 83, 84, 86–87; practice: seeing from the universal perspective, 92–93; realm of concepts and, 87–91; used as a way to avoid the world, 85
unworthiness, 15, 23, 27, 104, 148, 187, 200, 256, 279, 354; as motivation, 258; pattern leading to suffering, 296,

301; self-love and, 387; therapeutic work in, 314–16; unhealthy thoughts and, 297

V

Vajrayana Buddhist tradition, 4
Ventura, Michael, 337
Vietnam, 363–64
Vimalakirti, 361
virtue, 331–39; cultivation of care, 332–33; natural virtue, 333; non-harming, 332, 336, 348; as psychological training, 332–39; as reverence for life, 331–33
visualization, 7, 296; absorption states and, 320; changing consciousness with, 276; power of, 277–81; practice, 292; sacred images for, 292, 317; subject of meditative concentration, 317–19
Visuddhimagga, 65, 222
von Franz, Marie-Louise, 245

W

Watts, Alan, 99, 234
Weisskopf, Victor, 90–91
Wells, Junior, 211
What the Buddha Taught (Rahula), 352
White, E. B., 356
Wiedner, Barbara, 255
Wiesel, Elie, 246
Wilde, Oscar, 382

will to do, 187–88
wisdom: arising from painful feelings, 129, 134; collective well-being and, 359; fear masquerading as, 129; "I am nothing," 68, 69; innate, 17; living with, in light of death, 232; malleability of the mind and insight, 323–26; meeting pain and fear with, 210; as reason for existence, 81; as root of healthy mental states, 54; true strength and the sword of, 218–20
wise speech, 265, 271
Woolf, Virginia, 190

Y

Yeats, William Butler, 219
Yeshe, Lama, 58, 126
yoga, 116; dream yoga, 161; practices and states, 309; yogic powers, 339, 383
Yo-Yo Ma, 261

Z

Zen Buddhism: on acceptance, 103; desire and, 189; development of jhana, 321; koans, 43, 353, 368; "mind ground" or "mind essence," 42; on rain, 102; response to life is "a dream," 83; saying about human life, 211; trusting mind, 372
Zorba the Greek, 103

CONTACT INFORMATION

For more information about Buddhist psychology, tapes of
lectures and meditations, and information about meditation
training and retreats, please contact:

www.jackkornfield.org

Spirit Rock Meditation Center
P.O. Box 169
Woodacre, CA 94973
001 (415) 488-0164
www.spiritrock.org

Insight Meditation Society
1230 Pleasant Street
Barre, Massachusetts 01005
001 (978) 355-2347
www.dharma.org

Also by Jack Kornfield:

A Path With Heart

Perhaps the most important book yet written on meditation, the process of inner transformation, and the integration of spiritual practice into our Western way of life, *A Path With Heart* brings alive the possibilities of inner peace, wholeness and the achievement of happiness. Its gentle wisdom will guide you through the ups and downs of contemporary living, such as addiction, psychological and emotional healing, problems with relationships and the difficulties of achieving a balanced life of simplicity. This is a warm, inspiring and, above all, practical book.

Buy Rider Books

Order further Rider titles from your local bookshop, or have them delivered to your door by Bookpost.

Also by Jack Kornfield:

☐ After The Ecstasy, The Laundry   9780712606585   £12.99

☐ A Path With Heart   9780712657808   £12.99

☐ Buddha's Little Instruction Book   9780712674362   £6.99

FREE POSTAGE AND PACKING
Overseas customers allow £2.00 per paperback

By phone: 01624 677237

By post: Random House Books
C/o Bookpost
PO Box 29
Douglas, Isle of Man
IM99 1BQ

By fax: 01624 670923

By email: bookshop@enterprise.net

Cheques (payable to Bookpost) and credit cards accepted

Prices and availability subject to change without notice.
Allow 28 days for delivery.
When placing your order, please mention if you do not wish to receive
any additional information.

www.rbooks.co.uk